The Interior Plan

The Interior Plan

CONCEPTS AND EXERCISES, 2E

Roberto J. Rengel
University of Wisconsin—Madison

FAIRCHILD BOOKS
NEW YORK · LONDON · OXFORD · NEW DELHI · SYDNEY

FAIRCHILD BOOKS
Bloomsbury Publishing Inc
1385 Broadway, New York, NY 10018, USA
50 Bedford Square, London, WC1B 3DP, UK

BLOOMSBURY, FAIRCHILD BOOKS and the Fairchild Books logo are trademarks of
Bloomsbury Publishing Plc

First edition published in the United States of America 2012
This edition published 2016
Reprinted 2017, 2018 (four times), 2019 (twice), 2020

Library of Congress Cataloging-in-Publication Data
Names: Rengel, Roberto J., author.
Title: The interior plan : concepts and exercises / Roberto J. Rengel,
University of Wisconsin—Madison.
Description: Second edition. | New York : Fairchild Books, 2016.
Identifiers: LCCN 2015038284 | ISBN 9781501310478 (paperback)
Subjects: LCSH: Interior architecture—Textbooks. | BISAC: ARCHITECTURE /
Interior Design / General.
Classification: LCC NA2850 .R46 2016 | DDC 729—dc23 LC record available at
http://lccn.loc.gov/2015038284

ISBN: PB: 978-1-5013-1047-8
ePDF: 978-1-5013-1048-5
eBook: 978-1-5013-1049-2

Typeset by Lachina
Printed and bound in the United States of America

To find out more about our authors and books visit www.fairchildbooks.com
and sign up for our newsletter.

CONTENTS

EXTENDED CONTENTS

Preface

This is an introductory-level text about the planning of interior environments. It addresses both the contents of interior environments and the process of interior planning. The book covers topics such as laying out rooms, designing effective spatial sequences, relating project parts, arranging furniture, planning effective circulation systems, creating spaces that are accessible, and designing safe environments for people.

My goal has been to produce a user-friendly book with much useful information for the beginning design student. In presenting information, I have favored a simple and direct approach over the complex and abstract approach often used in the world of design. In terms of language, the book consciously uses the basic language of design—the drawing—as its principal language. It also consciously uses a loose drawing technique and avoids the overly rigid look of finished drawings, in part as a reminder that design problem solving is a fluid process. The looseness of the style is also a way of encouraging students to use manual sketching and diagramming during the early design stages, a practice that has been affected by the prevalence of computer drafting.

The basic unit of the text is the "example." Through the inclusion of abundant examples of what to do and what to avoid, I hope to help students become better designers. The book presents many examples, from individual rooms to entire projects, and includes both good and not-so-good design solutions to help

students understand the differences. The examples shown come from real executed projects as well as student work. Many of the projects chosen to illustrate ideas are from the past, some from the modern tradition of the twentieth century, and some even from classical architecture. These were chosen because of their straightforward approach, which results in clarity for the student. Numerous exercises throughout the book are meant to facilitate learning by encouraging students to apply ideas and concepts immediately after reading about them.

I have received much good feedback on the Interior Plan since the publication of the first edition. I am pleased that instructors and, most important, their students, are using the book and finding it helpful. It is hard to predict how different instructors will use a book like this. Some use it in their studio courses and others for other courses. One of the goals for this book has been making it useful in a variety of settings, which makes it possible for instructors to pick and choose the relevant content and the best sequence of dissemination for their specific course. That is still the intent with this second edition.

Based on feedback from some reviewers, I have reorganized the order of the chapters in this edition. This is always a tricky endeavor because any sequence chosen is sure to please some and upset others. Some instructors prefer a strict arrangement that goes well with the existing sequence of their courses. Others feel comfortable going back and forth in a custom sequence that suits their needs.

"My goal has been to produce a user-friendly book with much useful information for the beginning design student."

The main change is that the chapters dealing with design for people and the design process have been moved up front, following the introduction chapter. This places these fundamental topics early in the going, which seemed to make sense. The chapters that present interior spaces from the single unit (the room) to the totality (the project) follow. The chapters "Residential Design" and "Nonresidential Design" are still at the end.

The new structure looks like this:

1. Introduction
2. Design Is for People (formerly Chapter 6)
3. Design Process (formerly Chapter 5)
4. The Room (formerly Chapter 2)
5. Beyond the Room (formerly Chapter 3)
6. The Project (formerly Chapter 4)
7. Residential Design
8. Nonresidential design

Users seemed pleased with the contents of the book. For that reason, most of the original material is still there. However, I have added more than a dozen new spreads with new content about design process, iterative design, and so on. In order to do this without making the text longer, I had to delete a few of the original spreads.

The drawings and exercises still follow the original approach. I have avoided the use of color and finished pictures of projects as I continue to stress the premises that drawings are the language of design process, and that loose, free-hand drawings are an important tool, as they are efficient and promote a more direct contact between the brain and the paper. We noticed that some images could be improved, so we did upgrade a number of images to increase their clarity and overall quality. In keeping with current practices by Fairchild Books, a glossary containing key terms and definitions has been added at the end of the book.

Acknowledgments

Once again, the production of this edition has been a team effort. I am indebted to the entire staff at Fairchild Books for their continued support and expertise. Very special thanks go to Priscilla McGeehon and Joseph Miranda for their leadership, and Edie Weinberg for working with the artwork of this edition. My gratitude also goes to the professionals who provided valuable feedback about the direction of the new edition: William Furman, Winthrop University; Crandon Gustafson, Boston Architectural College; Jim Dawkins, Florida State University; Marciann Patton, Missouri State University; Rebecca Graaff, De Montfort University, UK; Belinda Mitchell, Portsmouth University, UK; and to the many students and educators who have used the previous editions and have approached me with useful comments and recommendations.

Finally, a very special thanks goes to Julie Foote, who continues to be my right-hand person during production and provided immeasurable help with the artwork and layout of the book pages.

1 Introduction to Interior Planning

Interiors: Content and Organization

At a general level, designing interiors entails two basic kinds of knowledge: knowing what things need to be included (partitions, rooms, furnishings, accessories) and knowing how to organize those things to achieve a functional and perceptually good solution. The main goals of this text are to increase your awareness of the things that are included in interior projects and to show you some of the ways of arranging them successfully.

Think of the things included in projects in terms of (1) **fixed architectural elements** (these are usually given and cannot be changed, e.g., a row of structural columns); (2) **interior architectural elements** (e.g., partitions, doors, and so on); and (3) **furnishings** (this category, commonly referred to as ff&e, includes fixtures, e.g., lighting and other decorative fixtures, and equipment, e.g., laboratory equipment for a hospital or exercise equipment for a health club). Your task as a designer is to arrange these three sets of elements efficiently and harmoniously. The interior architectural elements and the furnishings become your kit of parts.

There is another category of things you must also be aware of: the user things that require accommodation. These include everything from food items that need to be stored in cabinets, to neatly folded shirts that need to be placed in drawers, to piles of papers that need to be arranged in trays on a desk. Think about it this way: you provide containers and placeholders for all the things people bring to a space (e.g., cabinets, closets, desks), and then you make spaces for these containers and placeholders. In addition, you create areas that serve as a stage for people and their interactions. In a nutshell, you provide places for people and their things.

Clothes and things in closet

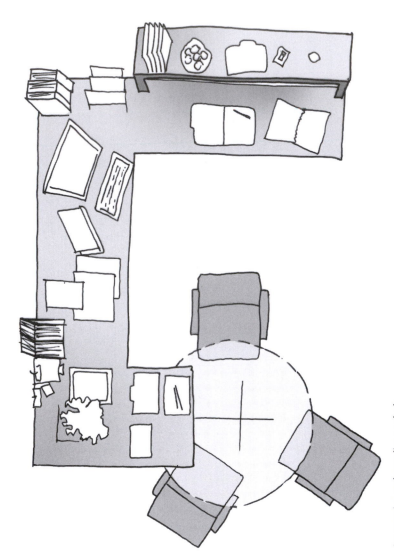

Accessories and supplies on desk

One of the most elemental tasks for novice designers is to become familiar with the basic contents of interior spaces. The product offerings in the furniture category alone are endless. For initial planning purposes, you don't need to think in terms of brands and models, but you do need to have a sense of what kinds of pieces may be adequate for a given circumstance, their size, how to combine various pieces into groups, and how to do that within a space (e.g., a room), such that people can get to the pieces, move around them, and so on.

The images on these pages show some examples of various scales of things ("stuff") and how they are contained and arranged in a closet, on a desk, and, on a larger scale, within the bounding walls of an entire project.

Many Functions within Library Project

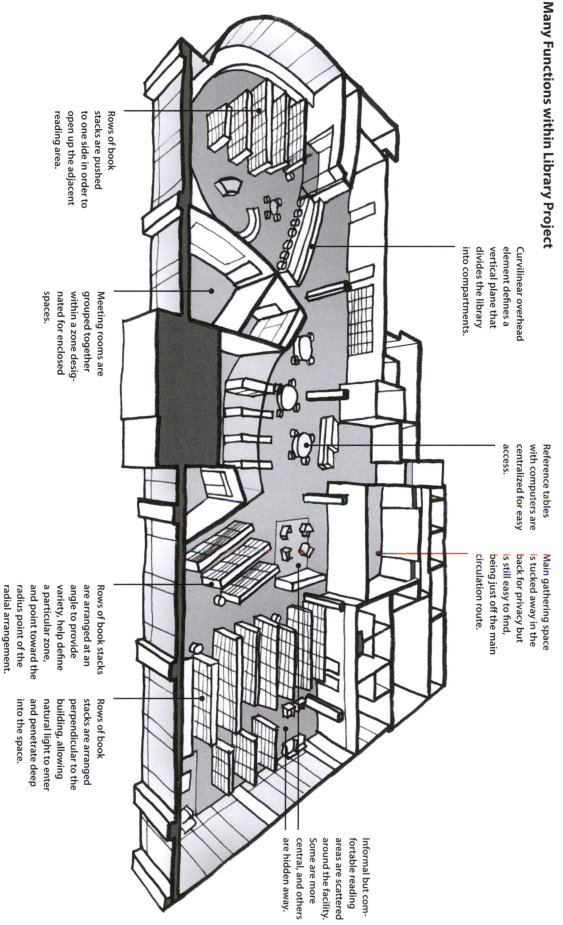

Rows of book stacks are pushed to one side in order to open up the adjacent reading area.

Curvilinear overhead element defines a vertical plane that divides the library into compartments.

Meeting rooms are grouped together within a zone designated for enclosed spaces.

Reference tables with computers are centralized for easy access.

Main gathering space is tucked away in the back for privacy but is still easy to find, being just off the main circulation route.

Rows of book stacks are arranged at an angle to provide variety, help define a particular zone, and point toward the radius point of the radial arrangement.

Rows of book stacks are arranged perpendicular to the building, allowing natural light to enter and penetrate deep into the space.

Informal but comfortable reading areas are scattered around the facility. Some are more central, and others are hidden away.

Concepts of Accommodation

Accommodating humans and all their needs is a complex task. Not only are people different from other people, but the same person is often different in different settings and roles as well. Moreover, the needs of a home are different from the needs of an office, a library, and so on. As a designer, you have to be constantly making choices among the different ways of doing things in order to address user needs.

Here, we present seven universal concepts related to the arrangement of people and their environments. As you begin to plan interiors, you will realize that these basic concepts and the choices they entail will be present in all your projects:

1. Insiders/Outsiders
2. Hierarchical arrangement
3. Individuals versus community
4. Invitation versus rejection
5. Openness versus enclosure
6. Integration versus segregation
7. Combination versus dispersion

The street as living room: from a scene of workers and their families in nineteenth-century Amsterdam (after Herman Hertzberger).

Insiders/Outsiders

Settings provide accommodations for people and their interactions. One thing all settings have in common is that they are inhabited (or controlled) by certain users. These users selectively allow access to others from the outside. Think of the home, the office, the store, the institution. In all these cases, there are people who live (or work) there and who have free access. These are the insiders (or locals). There is often a hierarchy of ownership within a group of insiders, such as the owners and employees of a store. Outsiders can be visitors who are given access at certain times, for example, to shop, or they may be unknown or undesirable people who are denied access. This duality brings up issues related to such things as the degree of enclosure/security required and access control.

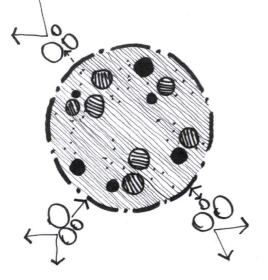

Hierarchical Arrangement

Think of settings such as villages, museums, houses, and stores. Now, think about the various places within those settings. You will note that some places are more important than others and generally demand more exclusive placement. In any complex organization there is a hierarchy of places and functions. In the example of a small village at left, the main religious structure (1) is at the culminating point of the main central axis. A ceremonial gathering ring (1) is at the center of the central/communal space. Beyond those, the end huts (2 and 3) have certain prominence based on location and exposure. The average huts (4) encompass the rest of the main linear arrangement. Finally, the village is serviced from peripheral structures housing miscellaneous functions, such as sanitation and storage (5).

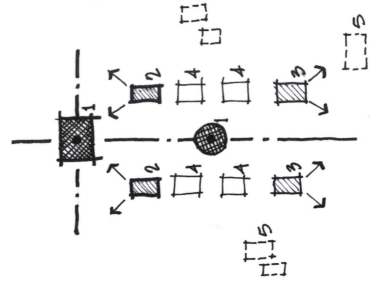

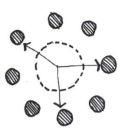

Individuals

All groups are made up of individuals. Despite their collective identity, they are people with particular needs and wants as unique human beings.

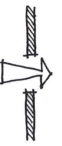

Invitation

The way a facility (or a part of it) treats its boundaries and points of access may be open and inviting, providing wide and flowing connections between "inside" and "outside."

Openness

Depending on the circumstances, you may decide that a room does not need a door or even a couple of walls. This is related to issues not only of privacy, but also of wanting a feeling of openness and connection.

Integration

Where adjacent functions exist, they may be arranged in ways that integrate them, such that, while maintaining their individual integrity, they connect and allow visual and even functional interaction.

Combination

Where multiple elements must all be present (such as rooms), depending on the circumstances, one may choose to bring them together as a cluster. This often produces economy of space (shared walls, fewer corridors) and allows for better residual space.

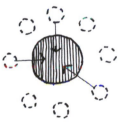

Community

Despite their singular natures, group members have shared needs and obligations at the larger community level. Group activities, such as meetings, rituals, and ceremonies have their own sets of requirements that must be accommodated.

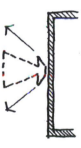

Rejection

Users usually discourage or prohibit access to the facility or parts of it. Think of a bank. You are welcomed up to the teller line but have no access to more private, back-of-the-house areas, especially the main vault.

Enclosure

Even in the most open and inviting environments, there are usually spaces that require total enclosure, whether for security or privacy issues. A meeting room that needs to provide good conditions for concentration and study, for instance, often must have four walls and a door.

Segregation

The elements separating one space from the next may intentionally discourage integration. A solid wall between the two spaces will often accomplish this. There are, however, several in-between options such as selective opening/closing of movable walls.

Dispersion

Sometimes, separating rooms and other elements is inevitable based on function and other needs, such as privacy and degree of autonomy. In this case, the elements are separated and dispersed within the overall setting.

Interiors: The Microscale

Imagine you had to design an entire house based on information from the user about a single drawer in her chest of drawers. Imagine this drawer stored the user's most valued possessions and summed up her whole approach to life and dwelling. Crazy, some may say; fascinating, others might exclaim. Planning interiors has to do with the chest of drawers, individual drawers, and even drawer compartments. It is also about the shelf, the closet, and even the hangers in the closet.

Think about the next scale up from drawers and individual shelves. It is the scale of tables, chairs, beds, desks, and cabinets. It is also the scale of small alcoves and niches and of special accessories. This is all part of the microscale of design. In the furniture category, microscale encompasses many of the objects found in interior spaces. Several of these become the final destination for users in a house or facility: the chair, the bed, the desk, the bathtub. In the architectural category, microscale encompasses some of the most meaningful and endearing components of interior environments: niches, alcoves, and cubbies.

Start becoming aware of your surroundings at the microlevel. Note the little compartments that provide holding places for our notebooks and pencils, the plants, the easels, the writing surfaces, the bookshelves, the artwork, the curtains, and the details of each. Begin incorporating these into your design repertoire.

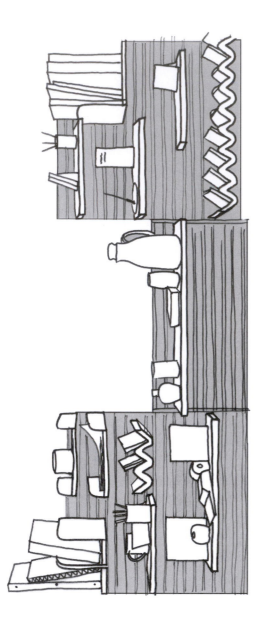

A slat wall provides convenient storage for notebooks, binders, writing objects, vases, mugs, pictures, and other personal items.

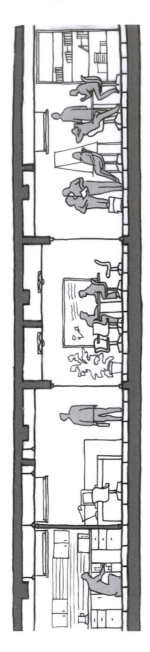

This cross-section through an office environment shows the contained objects at the microlevel. These include storage walls, cabinets, files, desks, computers, plants, whiteboards, easels, tables, and storage cabinets.

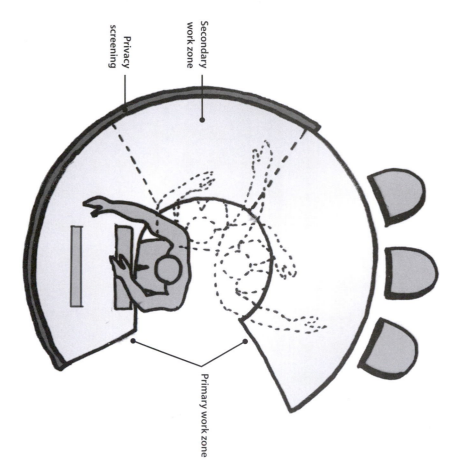

Secondary work zone

Privacy screening

Primary work zone

This study of a room divider and seating area by Josef Hoffmann (after Norman Diekman and John F. Pile) is a good example of design at the microscale. Note all the small details, some of them decorative; note that it is often this microscale of design that accomplishes the essential task of breaking down the scale of our living environments to a truly human one that relates to our bodies, our arms, our hands, and even our fingers.

Reception desk: A desk is one of the most basic units in many environments. Designing a desk forces us to think about humans and their operational dimensions as well as functional concerns, such as how to receive visitors, privacy, equipment, and so on.

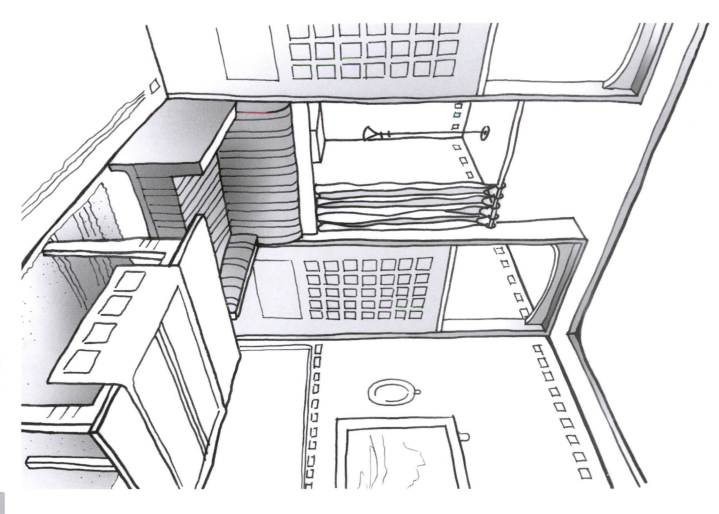

Interiors: The Macroscale

At the opposite end of the spectrum from the microscale is the macroscale of projects. This scale does not entail drawers and shelves, but rather entire floors and sometimes entire buildings and complexes. Design at this scale requires the careful planning of the many rooms and other spaces that encompass the whole project. Some projects are very large and complex (e.g., a major hospital), while most are more modest in size.

To understand the macroscale the designer has to, at first, zoom out to see the total picture. These are sometimes complex projects involving many functions and very specific requirements related to adjacencies and special relationships between the parts. Large projects can also be relatively simple, with a small set of parts that repeats many times.

Large projects begin with a master planning phase. Once decisions are made at the macrolevel, designers can concentrate on increasingly smaller units (floors, departments, zones, rooms), until they get to the microscale. An essential part of the process, however, is to work sequentially, from large to small. Even though the scales change, the basic problems at each phase are similar: accommodating parts based on given conditions, shaping them, and, ultimately, refining them.

These pages contain examples of a large hospital complex, an administrative floor of an academic building, and three floors from a stacking plan exercise for an office project. The hospital plan focuses on the main circulation system of the large facility. Along the major spine (called Main Street) are a number of cores (B, D, E, H, and K) from which users access the different hospital units, both horizontally and vertically via elevator banks at those locations.

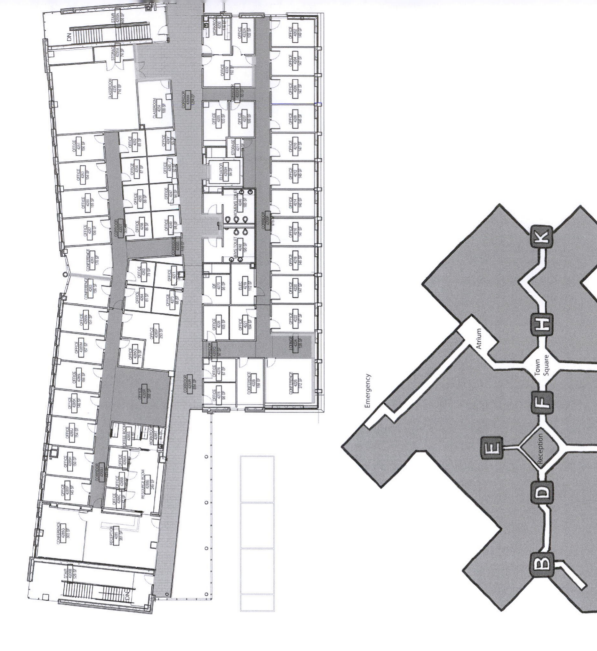

Wayfinding plan for a major hospital

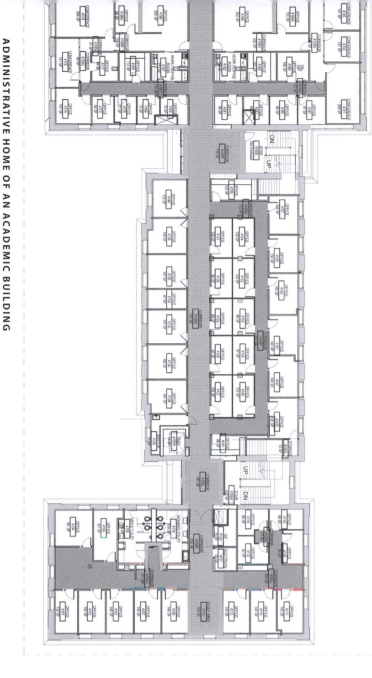

The academic building on this page is made up of two adjacent structures (the original plus an addition). The main circulation is linear and direct. The floor contains a large number of small rooms (mostly private offices). These were first determined as blocks and eventually shown as rooms on the plan. As decisions were concretized, each area was studied and developed in greater detail.

The stacking plans for a large corporate facility show three of the many floors occupied by the user. Large

corporations will often occupy several floors of a multifloor building. In these cases, designers have to figure out how to allocate units, not only horizontally, within the same floor, but also vertically, from one floor to the next. That way, adjacencies are explored both within the same floor and between floors. The example is a very early study in which the gross square feet for each unit were plugged in to determine such things as how many units would fit on each floor and how many total floors would be required for the entire company.

Stacking diagrams

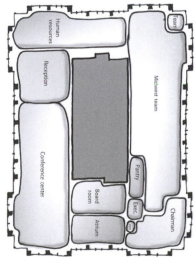

Floor 25

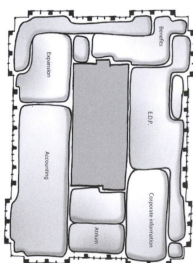

Floor 24

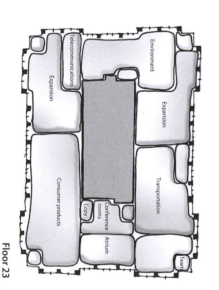

Floor 23

Nature of Interior Planning

The approach for interior planning in existing buildings is quite different from the planning process for new buildings. Whereas with new buildings the required spaces can have a push-pull effect and actually shape the building envelope, for most interior projects the envelope is existing and therefore not alterable. For this reason, planning interiors is more an exercise in subdividing a container into individual spaces than in adding spaces to shape the container. Think about it.

You are given a certain amount of space of particular dimensions and proportions within which you must arrive at a design solution. You are also given a list of rooms and other areas that need to be arranged in the given space. Your job, then, becomes to subdivide the total footprint and assign spaces. Louis I. Kahn's Richards Medical Research Building, below left, is an example of what is possible when programmatic requirements are allowed to shape the building. In this

case, the building became a series of linked square boxes extending out in linear fashion. Had the project required more spaces, the architect could have continued to add linked square boxes.

Interior projects, however, tend to be more like the one below right, a country house by Charles-Étienne Briseux, where all functions and spaces happen within a given box. The box is subdivided

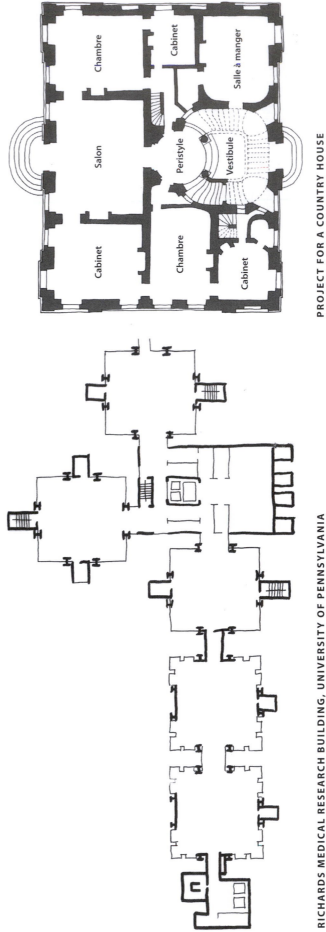

PROJECT FOR A COUNTRY HOUSE

RICHARDS MEDICAL RESEARCH BUILDING, UNIVERSITY OF PENNSYLVANIA

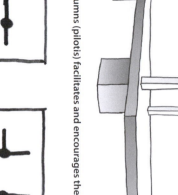

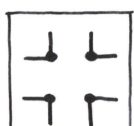

A.
Engaging columns

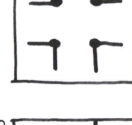

B.

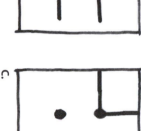

C.

Free wall around columns

The use of columns (pilotis) facilitates and encourages the free plan.

as necessary to accommodate the required functions. Not all interior sites are rectangular boxes, but the principle remains the same, regardless, and so, your task becomes to subdivide and assign space.

Another important aspect of interior planning is the structural system. Because most interior projects involve existing buildings, the structural system has already been designed by others and is in place. The implications of this are enormous. This tells you that for many, if not most, interior projects, you will be dealing with nonstructural members. Your walls will not be required to support the roof above. They are free!

The various drawings on this page are diagrams with structural columns (or pilotis, as Le Corbusier, who advocated the virtues of the free plan, called them.) If the existing columns are taking care of supporting the floors above and the roof, then you may work with or around them as you see fit. You may engage (meet) the columns, as some of the examples show, but you may also let your walls, partitions, and furnishings float free from the columns. The main thing to remember is this: most of your interior walls and other vertical elements are non-load-bearing; this means they have more freedom than you can imagine.

Note that the examples given are for reference and show a greater density of columns than you are likely to encounter. Also note that some project sites may not have columns—they may have load-bearing walls, which you have to respect, or other structural systems, such as long-span trusses.

Anatomy of a Space Plan

The space plan is the principal tool of the interior planner. Even the untrained person can look at one and get a sense of what goes where. A mother may point and tell her daughter that such-and-such space is her bedroom, and the child can see it. She sees the space, the desk, the bed. She may notice important adjacencies and exclaim, "Look, it's right next to the playroom!"

Looking at a good space plan can be very satisfying. One sees the efficiency, the flow, the correct placement of rooms. The plan may even appear easy to do. Producing a good plan is not as easy as it may seem, however; it almost always requires trial and error and many refinements before becoming a good plan.

Show people a space plan and ask them, "What do you see?" The majority will tend to speak in terms of the rooms: "Here is the kitchen, here is the dining room, and, yes, here is the living room." They may also point to the size of the rooms and complain if the bathroom seems too small or give praise if the master bedroom is "nice and spacious." What should designers see when they look at a space plan? Well, certainly more than the average, untrained person. As a designer, you should be able to identify the following:

Design elements: These include architectural elements, such as walls and doors, and nonarchitectural elements, such as furnishings and fixtures.

Spaces and rooms: These are defined by the design elements.

Relationships and locations: These describe adjacencies and geographic placement, such as the kitchen is at the center, the living and dining rooms are on the sunny side, and so on. You may also notice that a given

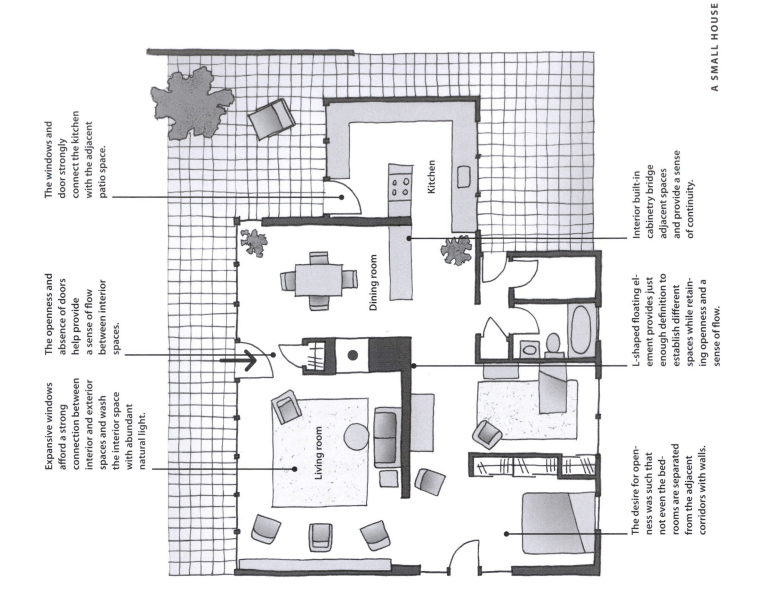

The windows and door strongly connect the kitchen with the adjacent patio space.

The openness and absence of doors help provide a sense of flow between interior spaces.

Expansive windows afford a strong connection between interior and exterior spaces and wash the interior space with abundant natural light.

Kitchen

Dining room

Living room

Interior built-in cabinetry bridge adjacent spaces and provide a sense of continuity.

L-shaped floating element provides just enough definition to establish different spaces while retaining openness and a sense of flow.

The desire for openness was such that not even the bedrooms are separated from the adjacent corridors with walls.

space is up front and that another is all the way in the back, almost hidden.

Properties: These are concrete, observable physical characteristics. They may be described as the elongated room, the angularity of the walls, the straightness of the arrangement, or the curvature of the wall around the conference rooms.

Attributes: These are subjective qualities resulting from the design. One may talk about an open and airy feeling, the coziness or spaciousness of a room, the privacy afforded by the room in the back, the openness of a plan, or the loudness of the lobby area.

Look at the two plans shown, one of a modest two-bedroom house, and the other of an office environment. Orient yourself. See what kinds of rooms and spaces are included. Once you have a sense of the total plans and their spaces, shift your attention to the elements used. Are there many or few walls? Are there many doors? A lot of enclosed rooms? Next, pay attention to relationships. How are functions placed in relation to existing windows? What's easily accessible from the main entrance? What is in the central area? Next, look for properties and attributes. What are some of the physical properties of the spaces? The attributes? Finally, see yourself walking through the spaces. What are the nice spots? Which spaces are public? Which spaces are private? Look at the annotations for some of the properties and attributes of these two spaces.

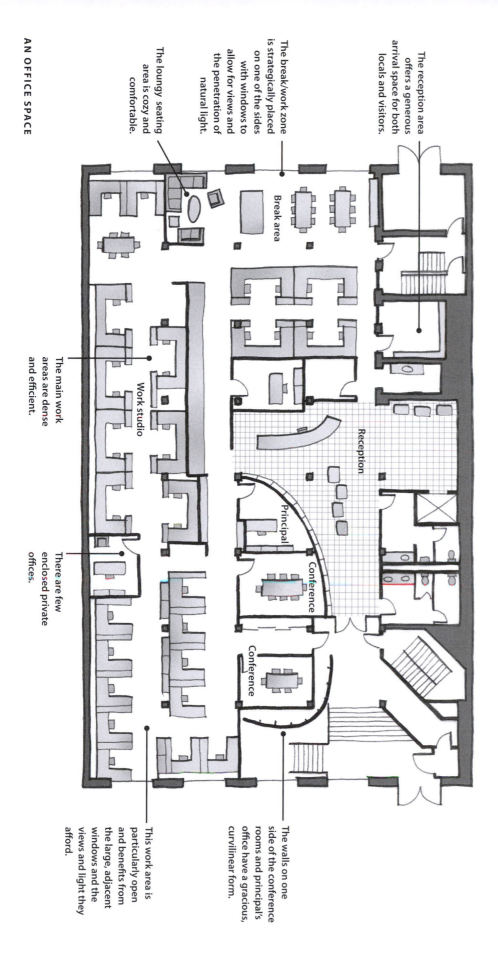

The reception area offers a generous arrival space for both locals and visitors.

The break/work zone is strategically placed on one of the sides with windows to allow for views and the penetration of natural light.

The loungy seating area is cozy and comfortable.

The main work areas are dense and efficient.

There are few enclosed private offices.

The walls on one side of the conference rooms and principal's office have a gracious, curvilinear form.

This work area is particularly open and benefits from the large, adjacent windows and the views and light they afford.

Break area

Work studio

Reception

Principal

Conference

Conference

The Space Plan in Context

In this text we will be working almost exclusively with **space plans.** That is because the space plan is the ideal drawing for making decisions about and showing where different spaces are going, how the furniture is being placed, and so on. There is no better type of drawing for accomplishing these tasks effectively. Yet, when you plan interior spaces, what you are really designing are three-dimensional environments full of elements and qualities that floor plans can't show. A plan may show a partition, but how high is it, and what is it made of? How tall, or short, are the various spaces? Are there ceiling changes? Are there things suspended from the ceiling?

The space plan is a useful and versatile kind of drawing, but it is limited. It is a two-dimensional drawing, and it only looks down, toward the floor. When you work on design projects, both in school and beyond, you will be using the space plan and other drawings to plan, envision, and communicate a full, three-dimensional totality (see "Drawing as Design Tool," this chapter).

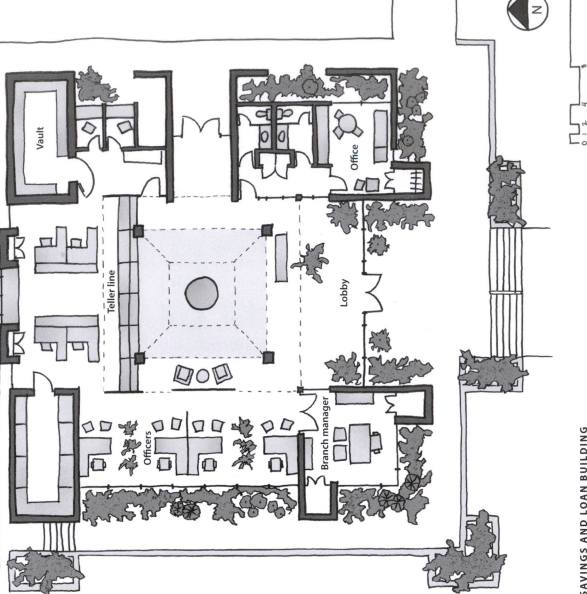

SAVINGS AND LOAN BUILDING

Presented on these pages are three drawings of the Western Savings and Loan Association, designed by Calvin C. Straub. Looking at the floor plan, one gets the basic idea of a banking lobby at the center and four solid masses at the four corners housing various required functions. One also sees the distribution of space, the placement of desks, and so on, all of it informative and helpful. The convention of showing the location of major overhead elements dashed on the plan, when used, helps to communicate that there is something of importance happening overhead. The space plan on the preceding page shows dashed lines at the center of the plan indicating the presence of architectural elements above. However, one doesn't begin to fully understand the three-dimensional presence of the space until one sees other drawings, such as the **cross-section** and the **perspective drawings** shown on this page. One would otherwise never know about the articulation of the ceiling planes, the height of the various spaces, or the configuration of the skylights above. As a designer, you need to be aware of the three-dimensional totality you are creating and to remember that it takes several types of drawings carefully coordinated to achieve this. While our emphasis is on plans and plan diagrams, you have to be thinking three-dimensionally as you design.

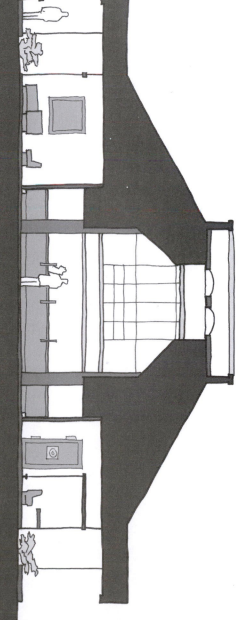

Section looking north

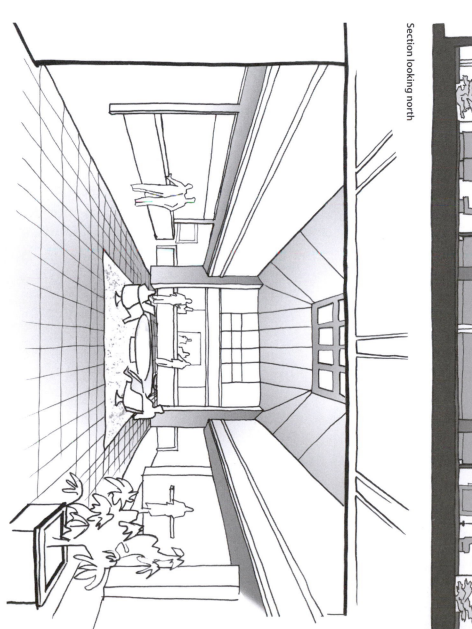

Perspective view

Drawing as Design Tool

The drawing is the language of the designer. It is through drawings that the designer forms and communicates design ideas. By now, you know that the floor plan is the principal drawing you will use to plan interior spaces. You also know that the plan, without other, complementary drawings, will not help you conceive and communicate total three-dimensional environments. Additional drawings you will need to explore and communicate design ideas are interior elevations, building sections, axonometrics, and perspectives.

In these pages I present a few common drawing types you will need to use in order to explore and communicate design ideas fully. They are the architectural floor plan, the furniture plan (or space plan), the section/elevation, and the versatile three-dimensional axonometric. Use these, as well as perspectives, to get a total sense of your design creations.

Your plans, elevations, sections, and axonometrics must be drawn to scale using an architectural scale like the one shown on the following page. Make a habit of indicating the scale of drawings under the drawings (usually below the drawing title). If the drawing will be reduced or enlarged, include a graphic scale that will shrink or grow at the same rate as the plan. Refer to the examples on the next page.

All elements, including architectural elements and furnishings, fixtures, and equipment, need to be drawn to scale. This will ensure that the various parts of the drawings have all been reduced the same way proportionally.

{Additionally, always know and indicate which way your building is oriented related to the cardinal points. To that end, make a habit of including a north arrow with your plans in order to illustrate which way your site is facing. Some examples are shown on the next page.

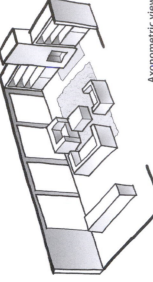

Axonometric view

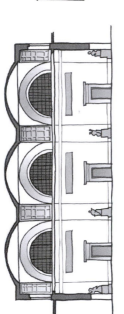

Section/Elevation

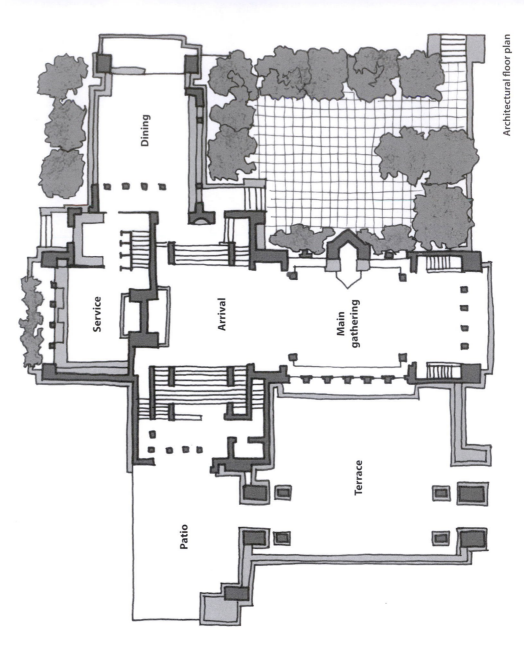

Architectural floor plan

Furniture plan

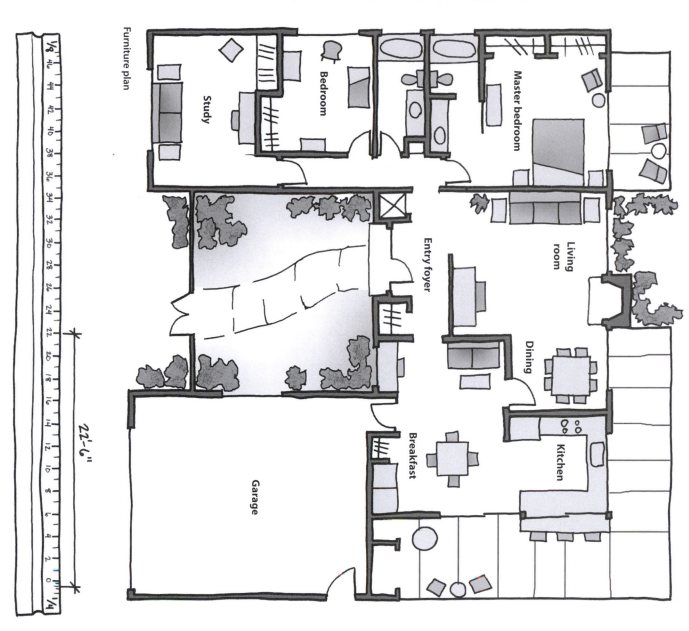

Study

Bedroom

Master bedroom

Living room

Entry foyer

Dining

Kitchen

Breakfast

Garage

Architectural scale

22'-6"

North arrows

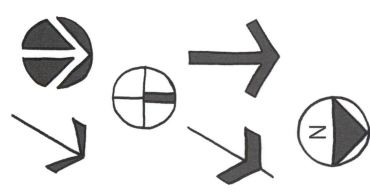

N

Graphic scale

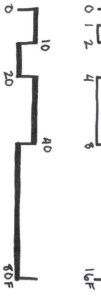

0 5 10 20 30 40 50M

0 5 10 20 30 40 50Ft

0 10 20 40 60F

0 10 20 40 60F

0 2 4 6 16F

Diagramming as Design Tool

Often dismissed by the inexperienced designer as unnecessary doodles required by instructors, diagrams are one of the best tools of the interior space planner. Diagrams allow designers to make sense of information efficiently without much time investment. They are great for showing relationships between parts and their spatial arrangements. It is possible to plan much of an interior project with the proper doodles and diagrams. Obviously, one follows the diagrams with actual plans that are more carefully drawn and that convey the solution more formally. Yet, it is possible to have most aspects of the planning worked out just through the use of diagrams.

Look at the diagrams on these pages. Diagrams 1 and 2 show relationships between parts of a project. Diagram 2 conveys a sense of hierarchy, making clear that spaces A, B, C, and D are the most important. One can also see that the relationships (and desired levels of connection) of A with B, C, and D are particularly significant. Diagram 3 begins to allocate bubble-shaped spaces and circulation routes in specific locations on the plan. It makes note of required buffer elements, screens, and desirable views. The spaces in Diagram 4 are more blocky and less like bubbles. The arrangement starts to look like a floor plan. Finally, Diagram 5 is one step short of becoming a floor plan. Although loose and schematic, it does a pretty good job of communicating the solution in plan. (Design process diagrams and diagramming will be addressed in more detail in Chapter 3.)

Relationship Diagrams

Simple diagrams can effectively convey relationships between parts, and relationships to views and traffic patterns, effectively and efficiently. Even without any explanation you can get a pretty good idea about what these various diagrams are trying to convey.

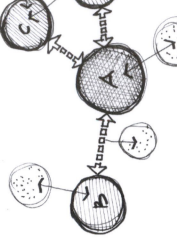

Diagram 1

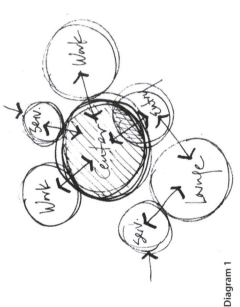

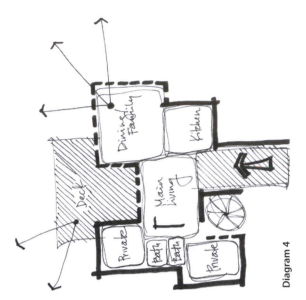

Diagram 2

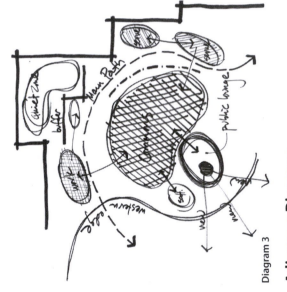

Diagram 3

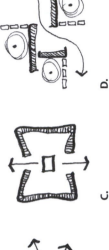

Diagram 4

Adjacency Diagrams

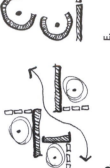

E.

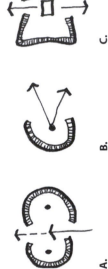

D.

C.

B.

A.

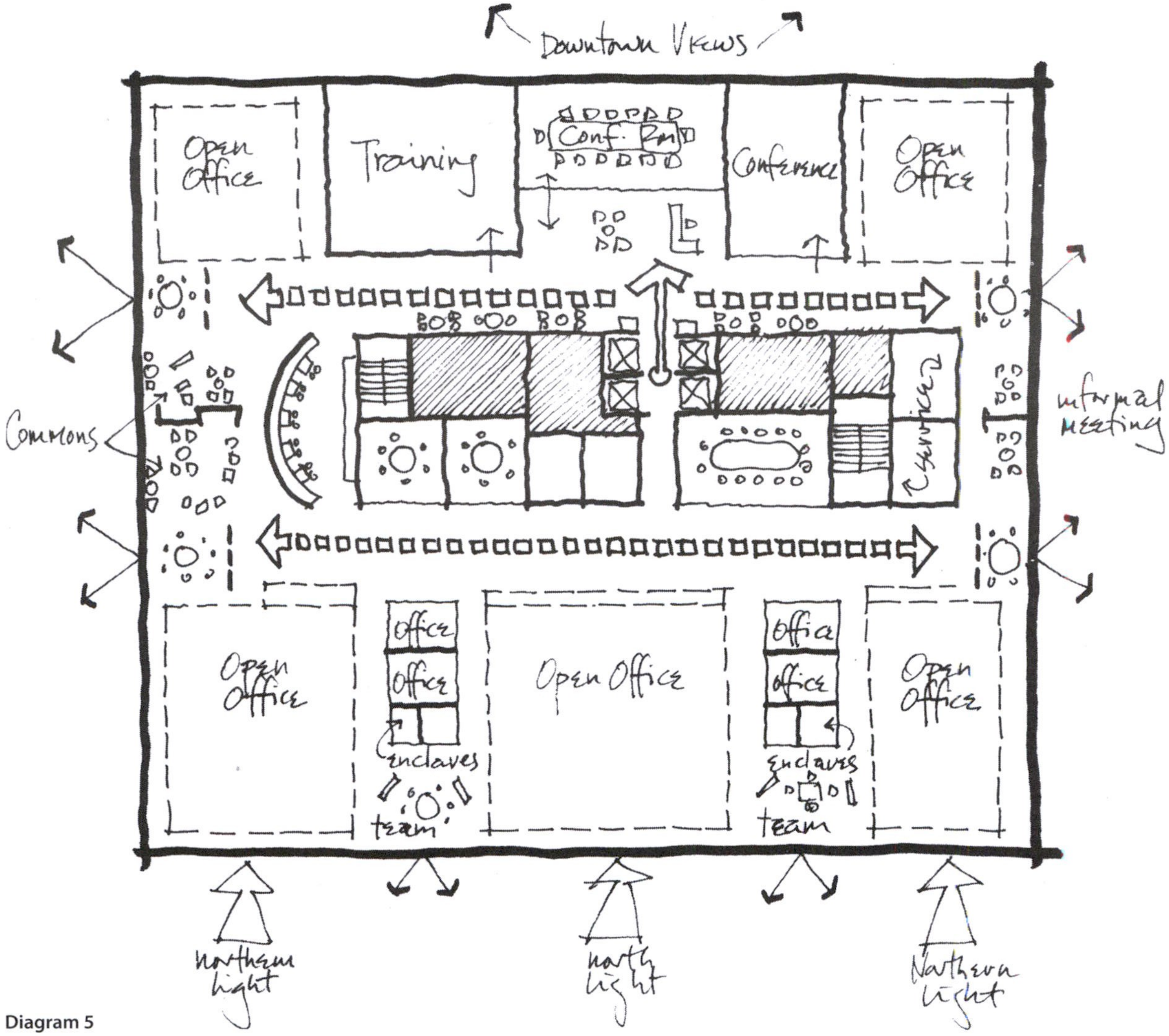

Diagram 5

F.

G.

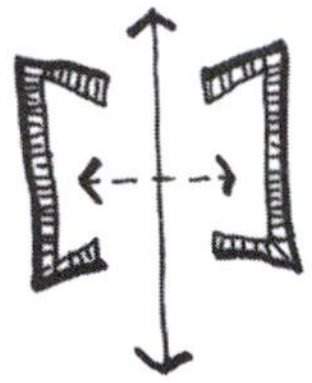

H.

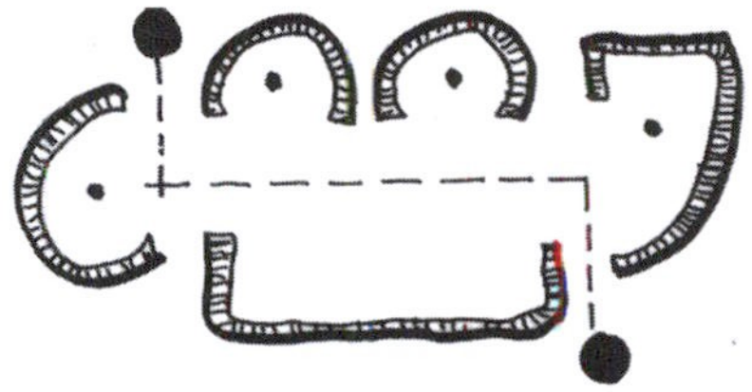

I.

Courtyards

Open Office

Open Office

Open Office

Training

Enclaves team

Office

Office

Conf. Rm

Open Office

Conference

Northern light

North light

Northern light

Open Office

Enclaves team

Office

Office

Services

Downtown Views

Informal Meeting

Section Diagrams

Section diagrams are great for exploring and communicating ideas related to levels, heights, edge conditions, relationships between adjacent spaces, and relationships between inside and outside.

1. Spatial transitions

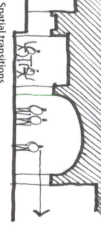

2. Inside and outside

3. Natural lighting

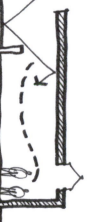

4. Air flow

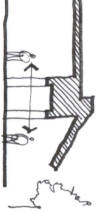

5. Views and vistas

Space Planning: Basics

The process of space planning entails a number of sequential steps that result in tangible outputs. Normally you are asked to accommodate a number of functions in a given (usually existing) space. Your job is to find a good, logical spot for every functional area in the program. The ideal location for some of the functions can be fairly straightforward. For instance, the entry foyer of a house or the reception room of a doctor's office both want to be up front, by the entrance door; the loading dock of a facility wants to be by the service alley; and so on. Not every destination is as straightforward. You'll find that some of them could occur in a number of different locations. Furthermore, once you place a certain room in a given location, it is likely that certain other rooms or zones will want to be in close proximity, so you have to make sure there is space to accommodate them accordingly.

Adjacency Matrix

NYSTROM RESIDENCE
CONDO PROJECT

	FOYER	CLOSET	KITCHEN	ZONE A: CONVERSATION / TV AREA	ZONE B: DINING SPACE	ZONE C: DEN/READING AREA	BALCONY	½ BATH
FOYER		●	◐	○	○	◐	○	○
CLOSET	●		◐	◐	◐	◐	○	○
KITCHEN	◐	◐		●	●	◐	●	◐
ZONE A: CONVERSATION / TV AREA	○	◐	●		●	●	●	◐
ZONE B: DINING SPACE	○	◐	●	●		◐	●	◐
ZONE C: DEN/READING AREA	◐	◐	◐	●	◐		◐	◐
BALCONY	○	○	●	●	●	◐		○
½ BATH	○	○	◐	◐	◐	◐	○	

LEGEND
- ● MAJOR ADJACENCY
- ◐ MINOR ADJACENCY
- ○ NOT DESIRED / NOT APPLICABLE

Bubble Diagram in Context

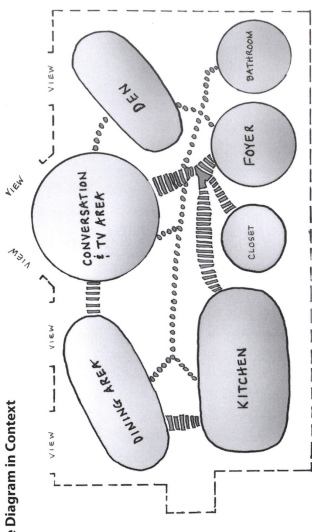

These few process drawings from a simple residential project introduce some of the steps and drawings you will be using when space planning. On this page you see a matrix diagram that is used to record the desired relationships between the spaces of the project and helps you determine what function should be next to which other function. Also on this page is a bubble diagram showing the various spaces plotted within the allocated space of the house. Normally you will do a few of these and try out different configurations.

Eventually these start evolving into actual floor plans, as shown on the next page. These are preliminary at first and eventually get refined until they are fully resolved. The refined version shows final location and configuration for each zone (including all the furniture) and starts to show more detailed features such as the floor materials.

Early Loose Plan

As you start translating bubbles to actual design elements and furnishings, you find that they take on a life of their own. What used to be a bubble for the dining area must now turn into a dining table, a china cabinet, and so on. What size and shape should the table be? Where exactly should it go? How should it be oriented? The same goes for the seating areas and all other parts. What if something doesn't work where you had it in your diagram? Maybe it doesn't fit or maybe it just doesn't feel right. The real search begins. On this first preliminary plan you notice specific attempts to furnish the dining, conversation, and den spaces in the desired locations. You also notice that the placement of the bathroom, kitchen, and storage closet have shifted, and that is fine.

Developed Plan

The developed plan shows how the designer arrived at different furniture configuration in the dining, conversation, and den spaces. You can also see greater development and refinement of the bathroom, kitchen, and foyer areas as well as floor material delineation. Things gain refinement and precision as the design is developed. No design works fully well on the first attempt.

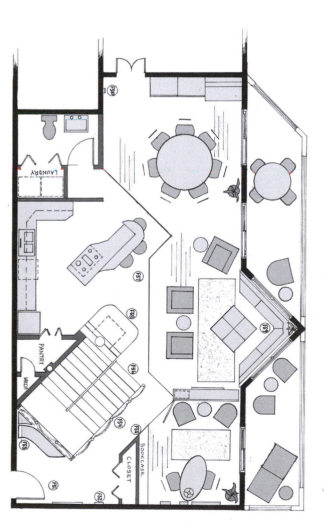

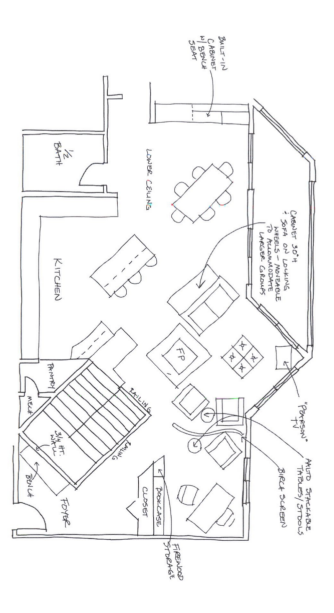

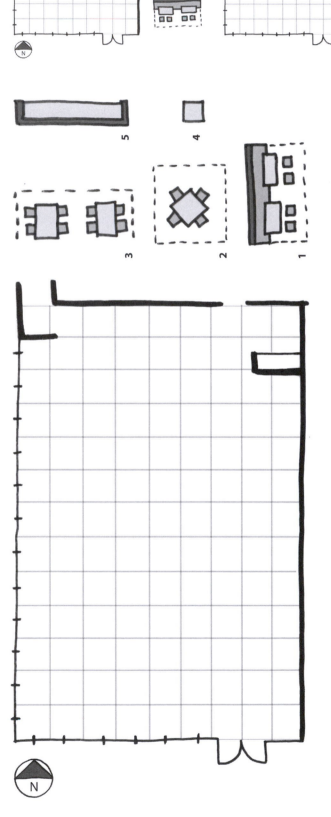

Solving Design Problems I

Let's go ahead and practice planning some spaces. These will be guided exercises, so you'll be given tips and hints to help you along the way. The templates are shown at large and small scales. The two small ones are for doodling and practice. The large one is for your final solution. They all have a 4' × 4' (122 cm × 122 cm) grid overlay to give you a general sense of scale.

Don't think too hard. Try to work quickly and have some fun. Don't try to show how creative you are. Save that for later. Strive, for now, for a straightforward and utilitarian solution. The required furnishings and other elements are included to scale on the side for your reference and use. If you draw your furnishings at that same size, you will be working at the correct scale.

EXERCISE 1: A RESTAURANT

The long dimension of the space is oriented south to north. North is to the right. A corridor on the northwest corner leads to the restrooms. An opening on the northeast side leads back to the kitchen. In that same corner there is an existing small waiter station. The entrance is through the double doors on the south wall. There are nice rows of windows going almost all the way down to the floor on the south and west sides.

You are given five elements to use in your design:

1. is banquette seating (two tables are shown, but you can make the area longer).

2. is a typical square table placed at a 458 angle and shows the required clearances around the table (you may group several of these by butting the dashed squares next to each other).

3. shows a pair of individual tables for four with required clearances for placement against a wall or in the open.

4. shows the size of the host station up front.

5. shows a waitstaff station with a partial-height wall and a counter on the back side.

Accommodate the following:

- Three or four tables for four along the south wall
- Thirteen tables for four, in any combination of straight and angled versions
- Eight banquette seating tables along one of the walls
- The waitstaff station floating toward the back of the space, close to the kitchen
- The host station and a small bench (not shown) up front by the entrance doors

EXERCISE 2: A SHOE STORE

The floor template consists of a long space oriented along the north–south axis. North is to the right. The walls along the east, west, and north sides are solid. Only the south wall, facing the exterior, has glass. The entrance is through the opening on the south wall. The rear opening goes to the warehouse area in the back.

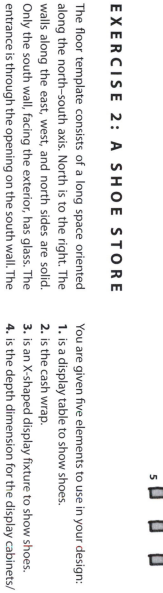

1
2
3
4
5

You are given five elements to use in your design:

1. is a display table to show shoes.

2. is the cash wrap.

3. is an X-shaped display fixture to show shoes.

4. is the depth dimension for the display cabinets/fixtures to be used along the sidewalls and also the depth dimension for the storefront displays by the front windows.

5. is a shoe bench with three shoe try-on stools.

Accommodate the following:

- Storefront zones along the front windows
- Three of the large X-shaped display units
- Four display tables
- One shoe bench with try-on stools
- One cash wrap
- As much linear footage as possible of the side display cabinets/fixtures along the two long walls

Have fun!

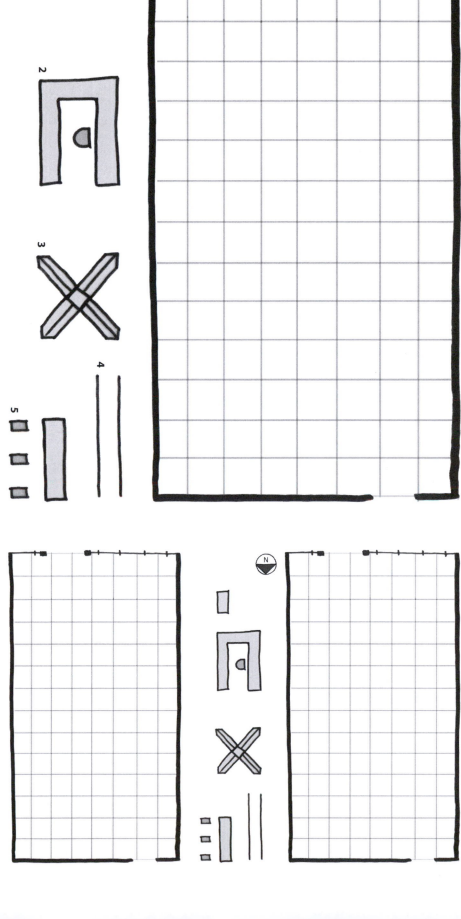

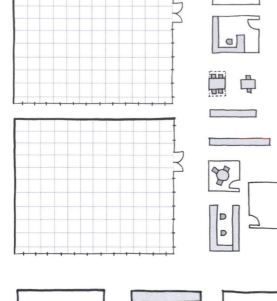

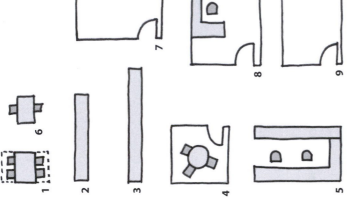

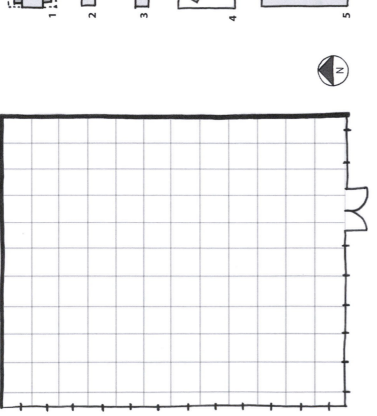

Solving Design Problems II

Now, plan two more spaces. Again, these will be guided exercises, with the templates shown at large and small scales. The two small ones are for doodling and practice. The large one is for your final solution. They all have a 4′ × 4′ (122 cm × 122 cm) grid overlay to give you a general sense of scale.

As with the previous exercises, try not to think too hard. Work quickly, and have fun. Don't get too expressive. Keep it simple. Strive for straightforward and utilitarian solutions. The required furnishings and other elements are included once again beside the template. They are to scale, so copy them at that same size, and you will be working at the correct scale.

EXERCISE 1: A LIBRARY

The floor template is a rectangular space, with the long side along the north–south axis. North is up. The entrance/exit is on the south wall. There are generous glass windows along the south and west walls with window treatments that will control any potential glare problems.

You are given nine elements to use on your design:

1. is a table for four people.

2. is a short library shelving unit (two sided).

3. is a long library shelving unit (two sided).

4. is a small meeting room.

5. is the librarian's station/counter.

6. is a two-person, back-to-back carrel.

7. is a medium-size meeting room.

8. is the librarian's office.

9. is a storage room.

7, 8, and **9** are the same size. You may change the orientation of rooms and the location of doors.

Accommodate the following:

- Three small meeting rooms
- One medium-size meeting room
- One librarian's office
- One storage room
- One librarian's station/counter (close to the entrance/exit doors)
- Four two-person carrels
- Two four-person tables
- Two to three long shelving units
- Three to four short shelving units

EXERCISE 2: AN OFFICE

The floor template is a rectangular space, with the long side along the east-west axis. North is up. There are solid walls on the east, south, and west sides. The north wall is fully glazed. The entrance/exit is through the double doors on the south wall and leads to a public corridor system. You may need a second exit to the corridor at the other end of the south wall.

You are given ten elements to use in your design:

1. is the depth of a countertop with files underneath to be used as much as possible along solid walls.

2. is a typical cluster of six workstations.

3. is a countertop (standing height) with files underneath, floating or dividing space.

4. is a partial-height wall approximately 6' (182 cm) high with files on one side.

5. is a long, narrow coffee/copy area (the access can be from either side).

6. is the reception desk.

7. is a typical cluster of four workstations.

8. is a private office.

9. is a conference room.

10a and **10b** are two options for the waiting area.

Accommodate the following:

- One reception area close to the entry doors with the reception desk and a waiting area

- Countertop with files underneath along solid bounding walls (as much as feasible)

- A second exit (swinging out) to the far west of the south wall

- One coffee/copy room convenient to the conference room

- One private office for the president (must be by a window)

- One or more space dividers (element number 4) as long as necessary to provide privacy to the work areas

- Workstations for twenty-two employees

- Floating countertops with files underneath (element number 3) to divide sections and provide storage (number and length at your discretion)

- One conference room not too far from the reception area

Enjoy!

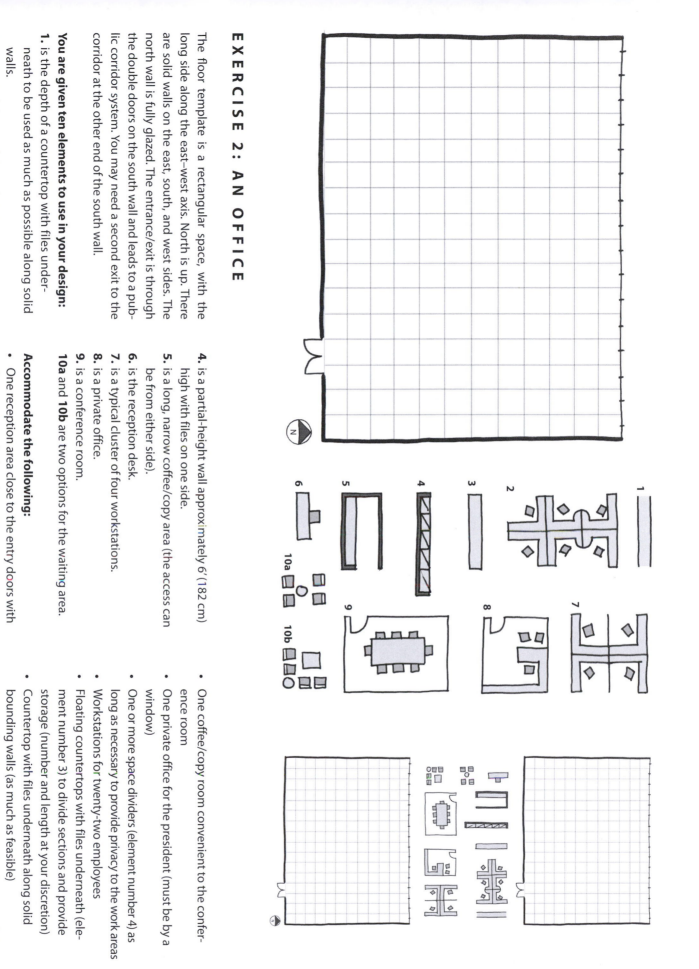

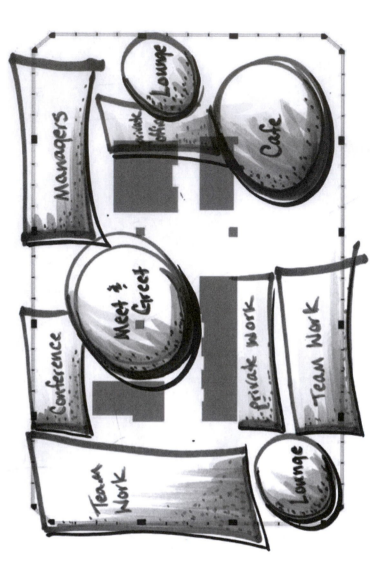

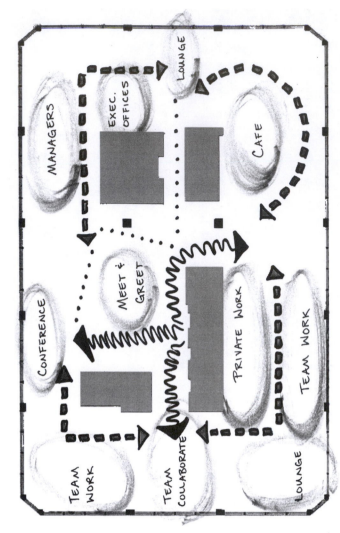

The Rest of This Book

In the pages that follow I will present useful concepts and exercises to help you become a successful planner of interior environments. We will first focus on the crucial topic of users. We examine human needs in buildings, issues of accessibility and universal design, and building codes that affect interior space planning. In Chapter 3 we dive into the nuts and bolts of planning interior spaces and the design process itself, and I will show numerous examples of how to go about planning interiors. Chapter 4 focuses on the basic unit of interior space, the single room. If you learn to design a single room successfully, you will possess much of the knowledge needed to design entire projects. After the room, we will turn our attention to groups of spaces or rooms (Chapter 5) and see how those can be combined to maximize the positive interaction between them. After this we will examine entire projects (Chapter 6) and look at how they are composed of single rooms and spatial sequences. Through this sequence of chapters, you'll recognize that the principles and concerns are similar whether you are designing single rooms or entire projects. What changes is the scale and the amount of complexity.

The book concludes with chapters devoted to residential design (Chapter 7) and nonresidential design (Chapter 8). These will address specific issues and concerns related to residential, office, retail, and hospitality environments. All along the way, there will be exercises for you to practice what you have just learned.

The journey has barely begun. Get ready.

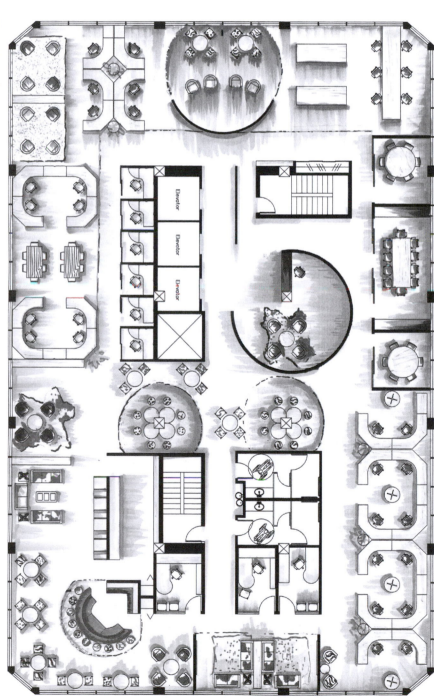

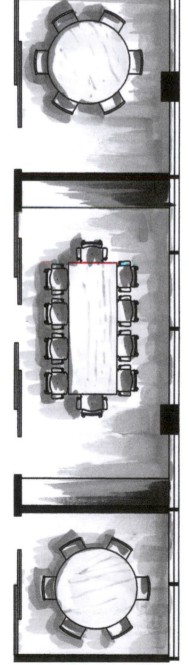

2 Projects for People: Health, Safety, and Welfare

Basic Human Needs

In this chapter we will examine some of the characteristics of space occupants and ways to protect and enhance their health, safety, and welfare.

The landscape architect Michael Laurie explains human behavior in environments in terms of three categories of human factors: physical, physiological, and psychological.[1] **Physical factors** explore the relationships between the physical characteristics of people and the form of the environment. Researchers have studied the measurements of the human body and how it moves. This information is helpful to designers for determining the appropriate dimensions of buildings, rooms, and furnishings, from door sizes to chair heights. The second group, **physiological factors**, addresses the interaction of our biological conditions with the physical environment. Of concern here are basic needs related to survival, such as food, air, water, and livable climatic conditions. Interior environments in buildings can contribute to this set of needs by providing things like adequate shelter, clean air, and sunlight. In addition, elements controlled by building codes, such as proportions of treads and risers in stairs and handrail requirements, ensure our safety and address issues related to physical security.

The third group, **psychological factors**, encompasses human aspects related to behavior patterns and social needs. Specific personal needs in this category can vary according to such factors as age, social class, cultural background, and past experience. Laurie classifies inner human needs into five general need groups: social, stabilizing, individual, self-expression, and enrichment.

Included in **social needs** are the needs for social interaction, group affiliation, companionship, and love. Environmental attributes to address those needs may include particular arrangements that draw people together and that encourage interaction. **Stabilizing needs** address our need to be free from fear, anxiety, and danger. Included here is our need for clear environments that help us feel oriented and free from the anxiety of feeling lost. Also addressed are human needs to shape the environments and to leave a mark.

Individual needs concern the specific needs of humans as single individuals. One crucial need in this category is the need for individual privacy. In addition are needs related to self-determination, the expression of personal uniqueness in the environment, and the ability to select from available options. People have an opportunity to express their unique sense of identity when there are choices in the environment, such as a selection of seating in a public area.

Self-expression needs include the needs for self-assertion, achievement, esteem, and power. In terms of the physical environment, these often translate into issues of territoriality, which is concerned with the areas allotted to (or defined by) individuals or groups and their location. The study of how much space we need and optimal distances between ourselves and others is of relevance here. One aspect of note is that territorial and separation needs have been determined to vary somewhat based on cultural background and nationality.

Enrichment needs is the last group of human needs defined by Laurie. Included here are needs for knowledge, creativity, and aesthetic experience. Environments that are aesthetically pleasing and that promote creativity can thus make important contributions to the positive manifestation of users' enrichment needs.

Some awareness of these basic human needs can help produce more responsive environments. The thing to remember is that the manifestation of these needs will vary from individual to individual and from group to group. It is therefore important to, first, understand fully the needs of the group one is designing for and, second, provide arrangements that address those needs and that will not prevent the fulfillment of the needs of the next group of users in the future.

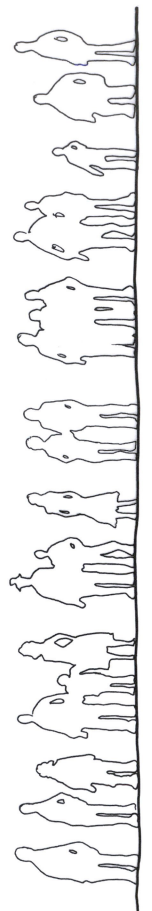

As a designer, seek to create environments that offer choices within a certain range of possibilities. The design of interiors requires you to make decisions that will result in environments that provide

- structure, while allowing for some freedom;
- opportunities for both social interaction and retreat;
- a sense of order, but with variety and intrigue;
- a sense of orientation, but not in rigid, military fashion;
- both stimulation and repose;
- both personal and collective expression;
- a sense of both stability and adaptability;
- security and control, but with some freedom; and
- spatial comfort without being wasteful.

There are not too many ways in which humans operate to carry on their activities. In fact, there are only six principal activity modes that designers need to address in order to accommodate users' needs: standing, sitting, walking, running, moving, and lying down. The chart below illustrates how these modes correlate with common human activities.

Think of users as beneficiaries of your good design intentions. Users rely on you to design for them a safe, healthy, and stimulating environment. At right is a brief list of what they may reasonably expect from an interior environment. Feel free to add a few more in the spaces provided.

1. Michael Laurie, An Introduction to Landscape Architecture, 2nd ed. (New York: Elsevier, 1986).

Activity	Standing	Sitting	Walking	Running	Moving	Lying Down/Reclining
Thinking	✓	✓				
Reading	✓	✓				
Watching	✓	✓	✓			
Eating	✓	✓				
Cooking	✓	✓			✓	
Serving	✓	✓	✓		✓	
Sleeping						✓
Bath/Shower	✓	✓				✓
Shopping	✓	✓	✓		✓	
See exhibit	✓	✓	✓		✓	
Watch show	✓	✓	✓			
Dance	✓				✓	
Office work	✓	✓	✓		✓	
Factory work	✓	✓	✓		✓	
Meeting	✓	✓			✓	
Jogging	✓	✓		✓	✓	
Workout	✓	✓	✓	✓	✓	✓

User's Bill of Rights

1. Reasonable access and accommodation for people of all abilities and backgrounds
2. Safe space sheltered from the elements
3. Arrangements that facilitate required function(s)
4. Provisions for privacy
5. Some degree of control
6. Some degree of flexibility
7. Access to natural light and views
8. Healthy ambient conditions
9. Connection to other relevant parts/spaces
10. Safety from external threats
11. Clear orientation
12. Efficient emergency egress
13. Reasonable comfort
14. Reasonable overall convenience
15. A pleasant environment
16. You add:

17. You add:

18. You add:

19. You add:

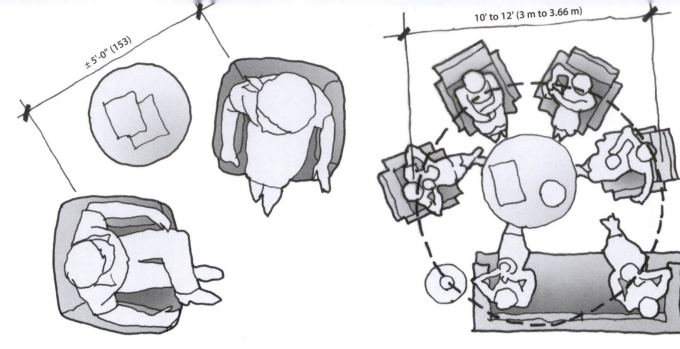

Humans in Buildings

Planning interior spaces requires the consideration of many human factors. Privacy, territoriality, and personal space are among the most important. Entire books have been written on interactions between humans and their environments. I encourage you to become familiar with this literature and also to become an avid observer of how people behave inside buildings. Here, I briefly introduce some important concepts that affect space planning decisions.

Privacy

We are all familiar with the concept of privacy. Privacy concerns one's ability to control environmental conditions so as to regulate the back-and-forth exposure to visual, auditory, and olfactory stimuli. There are times we don't want to be heard and there are times we don't want to hear others; sometimes, we need to control interruptions in order to concentrate on something. The scenarios are numerous. The social scientist Alan F. Westin identifies four types of privacy: solitude (being alone), intimacy (being alone with someone else), anonymity (blending in with a crowd), and reserve (using psychological barriers to control intrusion).[2] When designing environments, we use walls (thick, thin, solid, transparent), screens, distance, and other real (or symbolic) territorial demarcations to achieve various degrees of privacy.

Personal Space

The psychologist Robert Sommer introduced the concept of personal space in 1969. Personal space is the space (or bubble) surrounding our individual body and designating the area that is off limits to all but (perhaps) our loved ones.[3] It is the zone that, when encroached by others, causes discomfort and triggers a reaction of alert. We have all experienced the awkwardness of a long ride inside a crowded elevator. The extent of the personal space zone varies from person to person and across cultures and backgrounds.

Proxemics

Proxemics, introduced by the anthropologist Edward T. Hall in 1966, is the study of the distances between people as they interact. Proxemics answers questions about desirable distances between, say, a receptionist and a visitor sitting across the aisle, or between two people sitting across a dining table. Hall identified four distance categories:

1. Intimate distance: 6" to 18" (15 cm to 46 cm)
2. Personal distance: 18" to 48" (46 cm to 120 cm)
3. Social distance: 4' to 12' (1.2 m to 3.7 m)
4. Public distance: 12' to 25' (3.7 m to 7.6 m) and beyond[4]

Dimensions

Knowing the recommended ranges of dimensions between people for different functions helps you plan functional arrangements that will work well. You can refer to dimensions shown in this and other reference books. In some cases involving familiar scenarios, you can do a quick mockup with the help of a few friends and a tape measure and come up with a good sense of what a certain dimension should be.

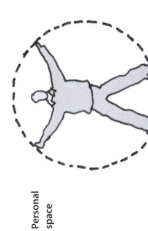

Personal space

Of these, personal and social distances are the most relevant to interior designers, as most required space-planning decisions occur within those ranges.

Territoriality

A territory is a certain extent of space to which a person or group lays claim. The boundaries may be clearly marked or somewhat ambiguous, and users belonging in the territory will defend it against intrusion. The concept is important because in most situations, people need a sense of having their own territory. Examples include one's bedroom in the house, the cubicle in the office, and the particular table at the restaurant. In the case of bedrooms, houses, and offices, users often personalize the space and make it their own, which contributes to a positive sense of identity.

Hussein M. Aly El-Sharkawy's classification of four different types of territories is useful for designers.

1. Attached territory refers to one's own personal space.
2. Central territories are highly personalized (a bedroom, a cubicle at work).
3. Supporting territories are shared but close to home so that people have a sense of ownership and may personalize them. Examples include common lounges and the sidewalk in front of one's house.

2. Alan F. Westin, *Privacy and Freedom* (New York: Atheneum, 1976).
3. Robert Sommer, *Personal Space: The Behavioral Basis of Design* (Englewood Cliffs, NJ: Prentice-Hall, 1969).
4. Edward T. Hall, *The Hidden Dimension* (Garden City, NY: Doubleday, 1966).
5. Hussein M. El-Sharkawy, Territoriality: A Model for Design, PhD diss., University of Pennsylvania, 1979.

4. Peripheral territories are clearly public and people use them but without having a particular sense of ownership over them.[5]

Defensible Space

Defensible space, a concept introduced by the architect and city planner Oscar Newman, is an arrangement (spatial or otherwise) that increases territorial definition and opportunities for surveillance and that fosters a sense of joint ownership and control of particular territories. An example of this is a residential vestibule shared by three apartment entrances in a complex. With a clear spatial demarcation and a small window facing the vestibule, all three neighbors can keep a watchful eye on their shared territory and identify approaching people who may not belong in the area.

Sociopetal/Sociofugal Space

The doctor Humphrey Osmond introduced the concept of sociopetal and sociofugal arrangements in 1957. It is an important concept for interior designers, as it refers to how the orientation of adjacent spaces or furnishings may encourage or discourage interaction. In sociopetal arrangements, the elements, say seating, face each other to promote face-to-face contact. Sociofugal arrangements, such as back-to-back seating in a waiting room, allow proximity while discouraging (without preventing) interaction. The concept is simple but powerful, and its application is straightforward and easy to implement once understood.

Orientation

In addition to knowing functional distances between people in different situations it is also necessary to understand the role of orientation. In some cases, such as a living room, sociopetal orientations will be desirable. In other cases, such as a waiting room at the doctor's office or an airport, a combination of sociopetal and sociofugal arrangements will give people options, depending on their circumstances.

Seats for waiting

What should this distance be?

Reception Desk

What do you think the distance between the receptionist and the seated visitor ought to be? Should it be within the social distance range or the public distance range?

Humans in Action

Before designers can decide the size of a room, which furniture to provide, how to arrange it, and how to relate all this to other adjacent spaces, they have to understand the nature of the activities (primary and secondary) in those spaces.

There are many ways of conceptually looking at people and their activities in interior settings. The model presented here examines people's behavior in terms of two variables: the number of people (from one to many) and the kind of activity being performed (from task-related to leisure). You can look at most conceivable scenarios (at home, at work, at a pub) in terms of these two variables. By finding out who the users of a given space are, how many there are, what activities they are performing, and how they are performing those activities, you can devise workable room and furniture scenarios to satisfy the required combinations. Similar models with different variables are also possible for addressing specific types of populations and environments.

The user/activity matrix shows possible scenarios involving one or more people performing a range of activities, from leisure to work related. Each case has specific design implications in terms of room size and characteristics, optimal level of privacy, and furniture arrangement.

Work

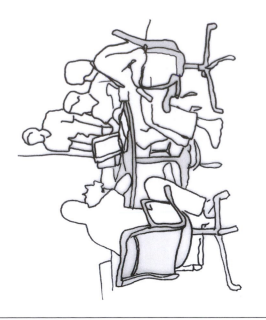

With others

Alone

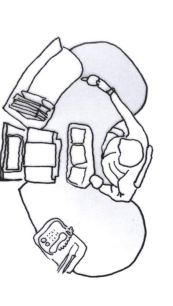

Leisure

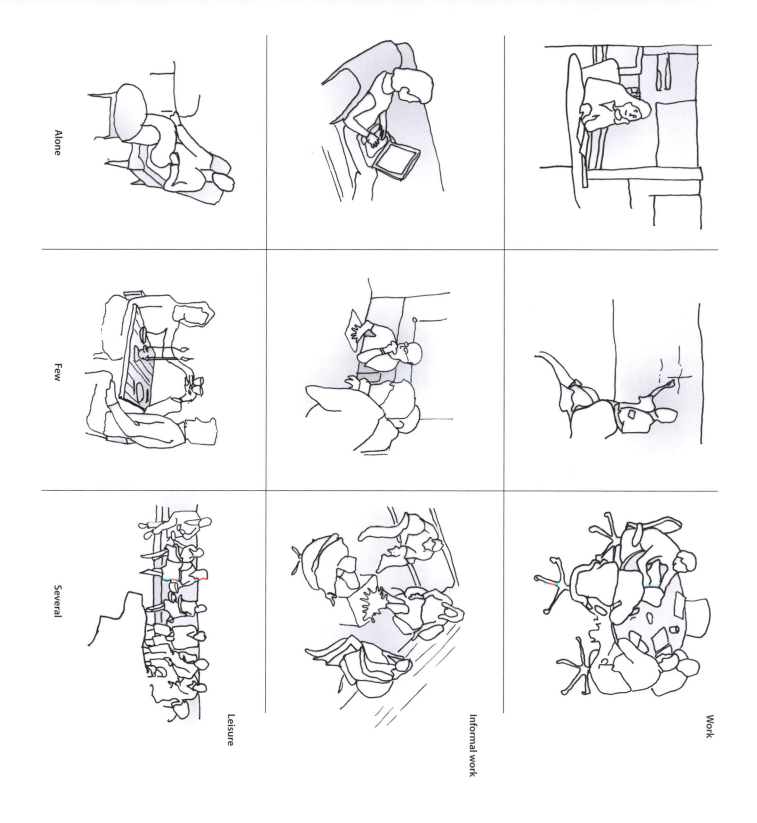

Comfort

Young designers try really hard to produce expressive designs that will amuse and delight. Delight, after all, is one of the main objectives of good design. To many, the equation for good design consists of a combination of good functionality mixed with inspired beauty. Although this is somewhat true, there is an element of goodness in design that is simpler and far more innocent than the attempts by designers to be exceptionally creative and refined. I am referring to the simple but enduring pleasures of the environment.

Look at the illustration of a girl reading at right. Note the setting—a cozy space with good lighting, a comfortable chair, a vase with flowers, and a fireplace to keep things warm; add the girl, a good book, and some time to seize the moment, and you have nearly perfect conditions for producing pleasure from comfort. It doesn't take great design gestures.

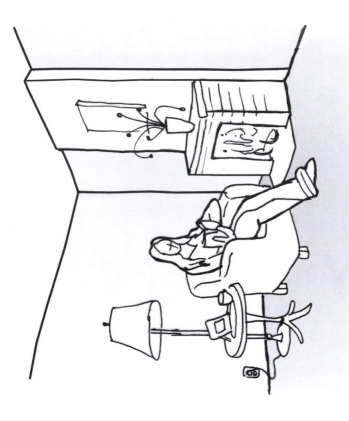

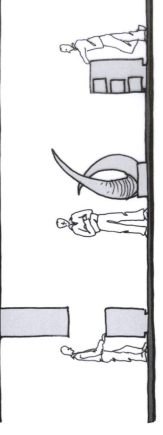

A young woman reads a book comfortably.

Consider the size and height of objects and fixtures in relation to the project's users.

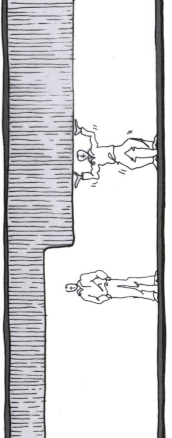

Seek to produce spaces of human scale.

Producing comfort and delight requires recognizing and responding to external forces, such as the sun, the wind, views, smells, and noises. Doing so entails careful treatment of exterior walls and openings as well as proper distribution of rooms and functions.

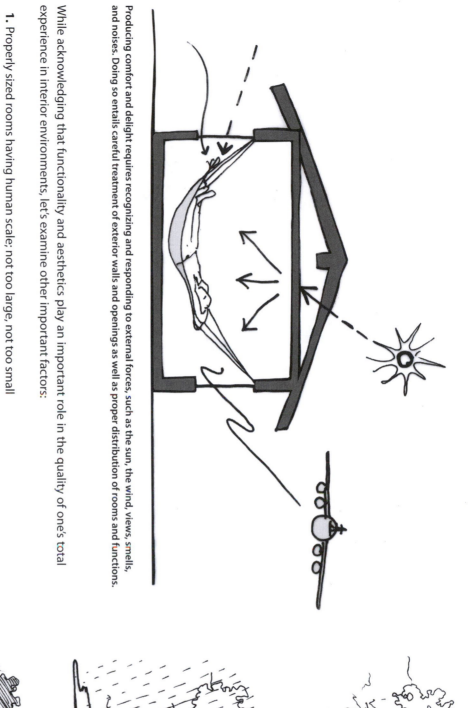

While acknowledging that functionality and aesthetics play an important role in the quality of one's total experience in interior environments, let's examine other important factors:

1. Properly sized rooms having human scale; not too large, not too small
2. Good room-to-contents (e.g., furnishings) proportion
3. Properly sized objects and fixtures at comfortable heights
4. Comfortable furniture
5. Convenient routes and travel distances
6. Control of unwanted noise
7. Good natural light
8. Good artificial light
9. Good ventilation, natural and otherwise
10. Good relation to the sun (shade or sun penetration as appropriate)
11. Good exposure to external (and internal) views

Note that there is nothing fancy (or expensive) about the factors in this list. Even low-budget jobs can have these attributes and be comfortable and delightful.

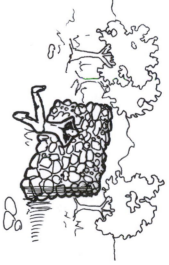

Give a man a wall, and you ground him. Give him a roof, and you protect him from the elements. Add some enclosure, warmth, and a soft pillow, and you will have given him everything he needs for a comfortable, delightful afternoon experience.

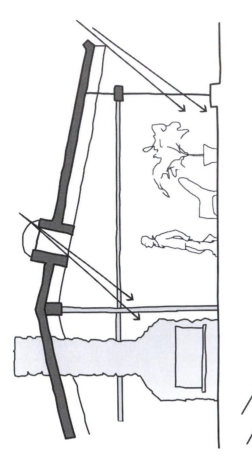

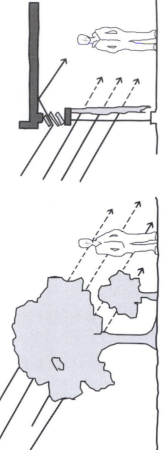

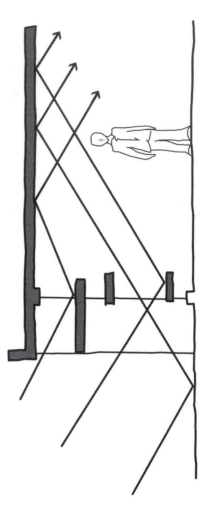

Analyze the exterior walls of your project's site in relation to the sun path, and strive to maximize the use of natural light. Place rooms needing good natural light strategically, and make sure to control glare with shading devices.

Light and Sound

Two environmental factors are so important for a positive environmental experience that they deserve special attention: sound/noise control and the utilization of natural light. Sound in interiors is produced by many sources, some internal and some external. Sound is generally something neutral, neither good nor bad; it is only when sound is unwelcome that it becomes a problem, and then we call it **noise.** Loud sounds from equipment inside or the street outside are often objectionable and cause people to complain. A not-so-loud telephone conversation by your neighbor can be just as annoying if you are trying to concentrate. (Even if your immediate task does not require concentration, you may not be interested in hearing your neighbor's business.) In some cases, there is not much you can do, and people just have to be tolerant and learn to live together. In many cases, though, you can avoid or solve acoustical problems through proper space planning. These are some specific recommendations:

- In acoustic-sensitive areas, take dividing partitions all the way to the underside of the floor or roof above to reduce sound transmission.
- Place noisy equipment in isolated rooms.
- Place very loud equipment in rooms as far away as possible.
- Plan the location of doors carefully to reduce flanking sound transmission.
- Separate quiet rooms and loud ones into different zones away from each other or with neutral rooms providing a buffer zone between them.

Although the building for a project, its windows, and the sun path are usually in place when you are hired to design an interior project, there are some decisions you can make concerning what functions and spaces to place on the various sides of your site as well as how to treat perimeter walls to provide shading, bounce light, and so on. Don't underestimate your ability to make the most of existing conditions. Strive to maximize natural light penetration, while controlling glare. Combine shading devices and reflective surfaces and planes to maximize the effects of natural light. Not only will you save energy by doing so, but you will also enhance the mood of the users of those rooms.

Plan the placement of doors carefully, balancing aesthetic needs with good acoustical practices to reduce sound transmission between spaces.

Sometimes, it is impossible to place rooms far apart. In those cases, you have to rely on partitions with a high resistance to sound transmission and, when possible, take them all the way to the underside of the floor or to the roof above.

Place offensively loud equipment in isolated rooms. Place the rooms remotely if necessary.

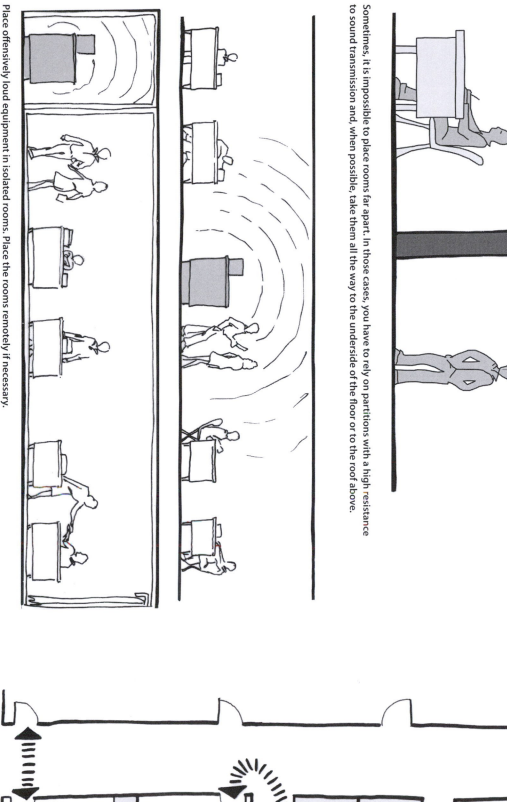

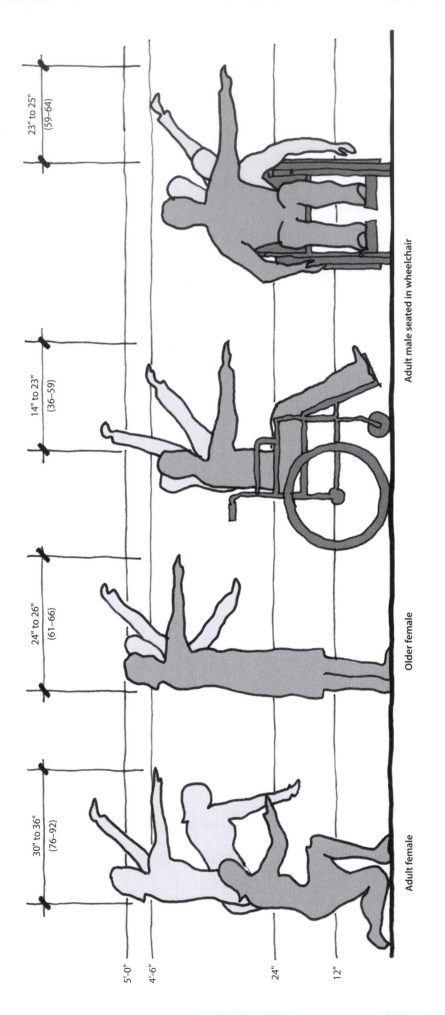

23" to 25"
(59–64)

14" to 23"
(36–59)

24" to 26"
(61–66)

30" to 36"
(76–92)

5'-0"

4'-6"

24"

12"

Adult female

Older female

Adult male seated in wheelchair

Anthropometrics

Anthropometrics are measurements of the human body used to determine design standards in relation to range of motion. Recognizing that body sizes vary widely, design standards aim at serving 90 percent of the user population, usually between the 5th percentile to the 95th percentile. Motion also affects how users perform

certain activities. The ability to bend, lean, kneel, or reach is partially a function of the hinge points of the body, such as knees and elbows. A number of factors, such as weight and sex, affect the range of joint movement. Although age by itself does not significantly reduce range of motion, many older people have difficulty bending or

kneeling because of stiff joints, arthritis, or dizziness associated with inner-ear problems. Wheelchair-bound space users perform activities from the seated position, which reduces their range of motion. Similarly, ambulatory users who need to use crutches or walkers to maintain balance have difficulty with low or high vertical reach.

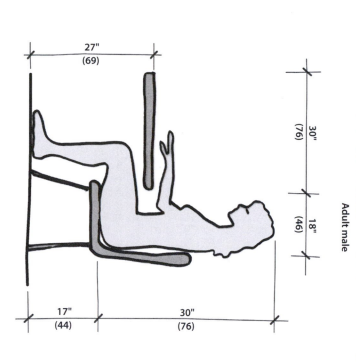

27" (69)

30" (76) 18" (46)

17" (44) 30" (76)

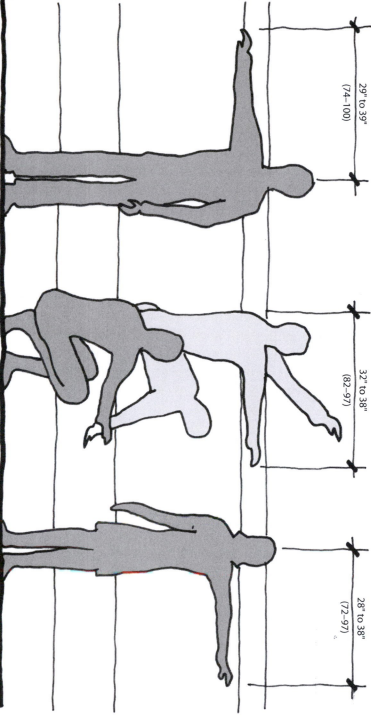

29" to 39" (74–100)

32" to 38" (82–97)

28" to 38" (72–97)

Adult male

Adult female

The range of motion of space users is determined by their anthropometric measurements and their ability to bend, kneel, lean, or stretch. A vertical zone between 27" (69 cm) and 4'-6" (137 cm) and a maximum horizontal reach of 24" (61 cm) are recommended for the comfort of most users.

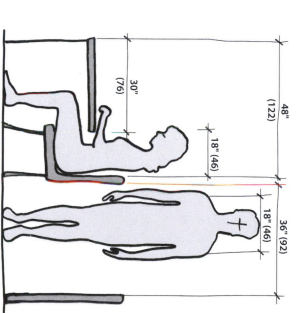

30" (76)

48" (122)

18" (46)

18" (46)

36" (92)

Basic dimensions of woman seated at work and recommended aisle behind

Cast of Users

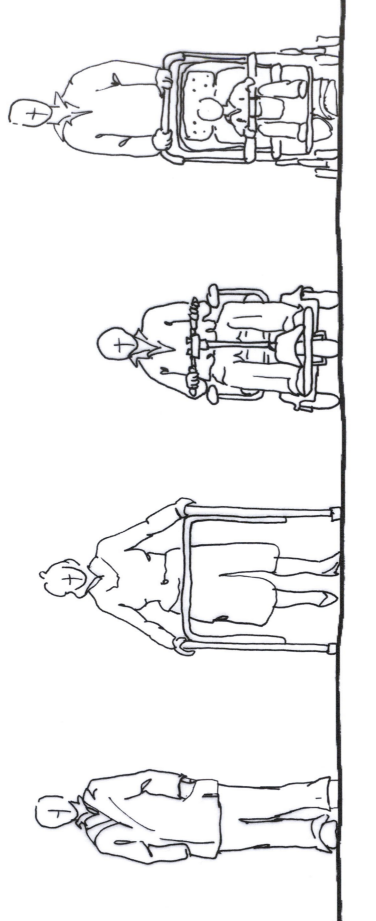

Be aware that the cast of users for your projects is likely to be broad and varied and will often include people of all ages and with a wide range of abilities, both physical and cognitive. In the United States, the Americans with Disabilities Act (ADA) requires that all places of public accommodation and commercial facilities comply with its accessibility guidelines. Similar acts exist in other countries, such as the United Kingdom (Equality Act 2010) and Australia (Disability Discrimination Act), as well as in provinces within a country, such as the Accessibility

for Ontarians with Disabilities Act in Ontario, Canada. Private homes do not have specific accessibility requirements dictated by law, although the practice of creating adaptable designs (designs that can be easily made accessible later) is becoming more prevalent.

The cast of users needing special accommodations is diverse. Some users have a limited range of motion. Limiting horizontal reaches to less than 24" (61 cm) and providing aids to balance such as grab bars and

handrails, are among the things you can do to assist them. Some users have limited strength or stamina for performing daily living activities as a result of a medical condition or advancing age. Providing elevators, automatic doors, and seating in waiting areas and minimizing distances between destinations are some of the things you can do to address this group.

Some of the users have wheelchairs or other walking aids (crutches, canes, walkers) for mobility. Wheelchairs can be manual or electric. A three-wheeled electric wheelchair with a single front wheel is also available. Canes are used to reduce stress on leg muscles and joints. Stairs pose problems for users with canes, and handrails are important for maintaining balance. Crutches also reduce the stress of weight bearing on the lower extremities. They are typically angled away from the body for stability, requiring additional width at doors and openings. Walkers reduce lower extremity stress and act as aids to balance. They can be large

and cumbersome and also necessitate wider doors and openings and greater maneuvering room in confined spaces.

Users with restricted mobility can be assisted by doors, openings, and corridors that provide proper maneuvering clearances and ramps, elevators, and lifts for vertical transportation. Other considerations include arrangements that limit travel distances; aids to balance and wheelchair transfer, such as handrails and

grab bars; and controls and switches that are within comfortable reach ranges and that do not require fine hand control or a strong grip to operate.

Some users will have impaired cognitive abilities, such as mental retardation or Alzheimer's disease. For these users, designers need to create environments that are not confusing or intimidating and that have clear circulation systems with good way-finding cues (symbols, colors, and other easily identifiable spatial cues).

Universal Design

The principles of **universal design** were compiled by the Center for Universal Design at North Carolina State University to guide a wide range of design disciplines, including environments, products, and communications. These seven principles may be applied to evaluate existing designs, guide the design process, and educate both designers and consumers about the characteristics of more usable products and environments.

The principles of universal design aim to make environments, products, and communications user-friendly to people of all abilities. The way these principles inform interior settings specifically is very similar to the ADA guidelines and other similar accessibility guidelines. On these pages are some examples of designs that are in accordance with these principles.

The Principles

Principle One: Equitable Use

The design is useful and marketable to people with diverse abilities.

Guidelines:

1a. Provide the same means of use for all users: identical whenever possible; equivalent when not.

1b. Avoid segregating or stigmatizing any users.

1c. Provisions for privacy, security, and safety should be equally available to all users.

1d. Make the design appealing to all users.

Principle Two: Flexibility in Use

The design accommodates a wide range of individual preferences and abilities.

Guidelines:

2a. Provide choice in methods of use.

2b. Accommodate right- or left-handed access and use.

2c. Facilitate the user's accuracy and precision.

2d. Provide adaptability to the user's pace.

Principle Three: Simple and Intuitive Use

Use of the design is easy to understand, regardless of the user's experience, knowledge, language skills, or current concentration level.

Guidelines:

3a. Eliminate unnecessary complexity.

3b. Be consistent with user expectations and intuition.

3c. Accommodate a wide range of literacy and language skills.

3d. Arrange information consistent with its importance.

3e. Provide effective prompting and feedback during and after task completion.

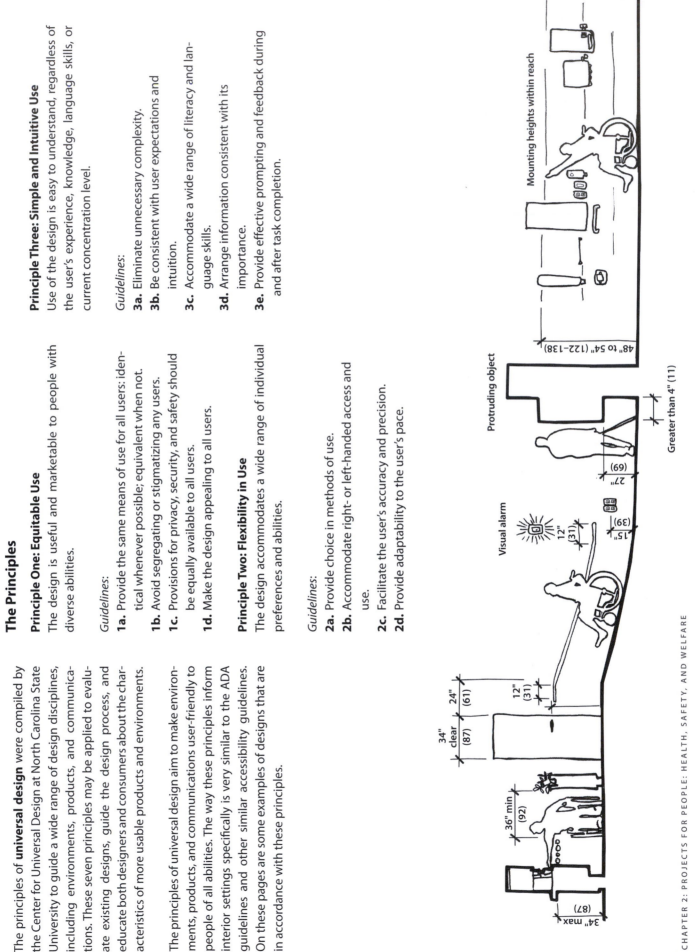

Mounting heights within reach

48" to 54" (122–138)

Protruding object

Greater than 4" (11)

Visual alarm

27" (69)

15" (39)

12" (31)

34" clear (87)

24" (61)

12" (31)

36" min (92)

34" max (87)

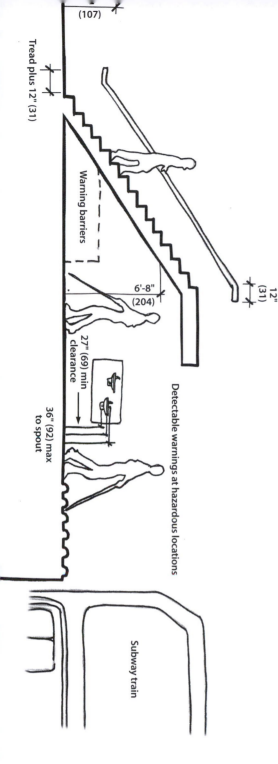

(107)

Tread plus 12" (31)

Warning barriers

6'-8"
(204)

27" (69) min
clearance

12"
(31)

36" (92) max
to spout

Detectable warnings at hazardous locations

Subway train

Principle Four: Perceptible Information

The design communicates necessary information effectively to the user, regardless of ambient conditions or the user's sensory abilities.

Guidelines:

4a. Use different modes (pictorial, verbal, tactile) for redundant presentation of essential information.

4b. Provide adequate contrast between essential information and its surroundings.

4c. Maximize "legibility" of essential information.

4d. Differentiate elements in ways that can be described (i.e., make it easy to give instructions or directions).

4e. Provide compatibility with a variety of techniques or devices used by people with sensory limitations.

Principle Five: Tolerance for Error

The design minimizes hazards and the adverse consequences of accidental or unintended actions.

Guidelines:

5a. Arrange elements to minimize hazards and errors: make the most used elements the most accessible; eliminate, isolate, or shield hazardous elements.

5b. Provide warnings of hazards and errors.

5c. Provide fail-safe features.

5d. Discourage unconscious action in tasks that require vigilance.

Principle Six: Low Physical Effort

The design can be used efficiently and comfortably and with a minimum of fatigue.

Guidelines:

6a. Allow the user to maintain a neutral body position.

6b. Use reasonable operating forces.

6c. Minimize repetitive actions.

6d. Minimize sustained physical effort.

Principle Seven: Size and Space for Approach and Use

Appropriate size and space are provided for approach, reach, manipulation, and use regardless of the user's body size, posture, or mobility.

Guidelines:

7a. Provide a clear line of sight to important elements for any seated or standing user.

7b. Make reach to all components comfortable for any seated or standing user.

7c. Accommodate variations in hand and grip size.

7d. Provide adequate space for the use of assistive devices or personal assistance.

Source: "The Principles of Universal Design." Version 2.0. The Center for Universal Design, North Carolina State University, 1997. http://www .ncsu.edu/www/ncsu/design/sod5/cud/about_ud/udprinciples.htm

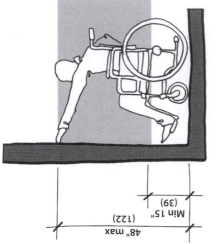

Forward reaches (high and low)

48" max (122)

Min 15" (39)

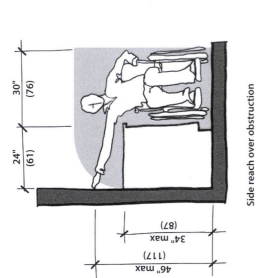

Side reach over obstruction

30" (76)

24" (61)

46" max (117)

34" max (87)

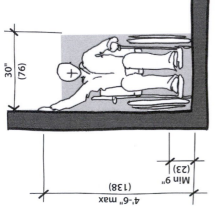

Side reaches (high and low)

30" (76)

4'-6" max (138)

Min 9" (23)

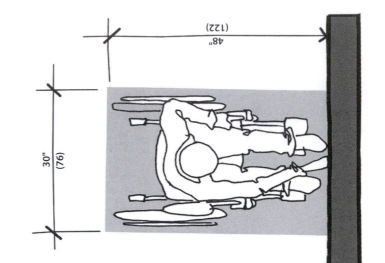

Clear floor space (forward reach)

48" (122)

30" (76)

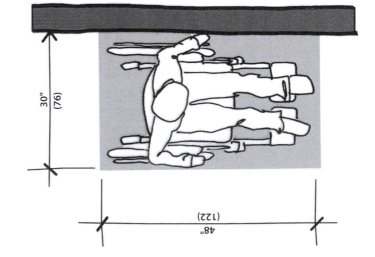

Clear floor space (parallel approach)

30" (76)

48" (122)

Wheelchairs

Users in wheelchairs have a range of movement different from that of ambulatory users. High vertical reach is restricted, because a seated position must be maintained. Low reach is more awkward, because the wheelchair must be maneuvered directly above the objective. Horizontal reach is usually easier to the side, because without a knee space, the footrests restrict forward reach. Eye level in a seated position is more than 12"(30 cm) lower than that of most standing adults.

Wheelchairs are available in many models and sizes. In the United States, the most common wheelchairs are made of aluminum tubing, with large rear drive wheels and small front caster wheels. Wheelchairs with large front drive wheels and small rear caster wheels are popular in Europe. These are more maneuverable, but the large front wheels restrict access to desks or counters and are often less suitable for outdoor use.

The frame of the wheelchair is usually collapsible in the middle for storage and transport. Footrests and armrests are generally removable or hinged to swing to the side. Most wheelchairs are propelled with hand rims on the rear wheels.

Motorized wheelchairs are also available. These are driven by electric motors powered by batteries below the seat. They are approximately the same size as manual chairs but are heavy and less maneuverable.

Basic wheelchair dimensions and related dimensions for turning and forward and side reaches are shown on these pages.

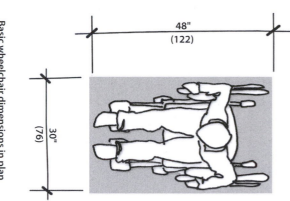

Basic wheelchair dimensions in plan

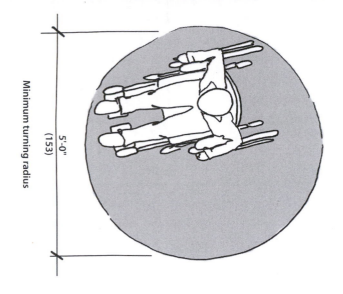

Minimum turning radius

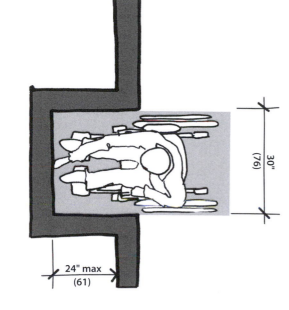

Clear floor space in alcove

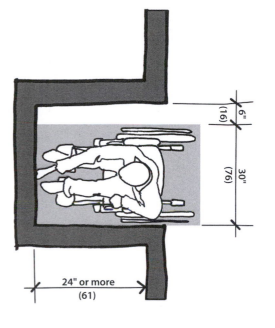

Maneuvering clearances at alcove

Accessibility: Navigating Space

Corridors and other public circulation areas should meet **ADA requirements** for accessible routes. These call for a minimum width of 36" (92 cm), except at cased openings or passage points, and greater clearances where an accessible route turns 180°. Doors on accessible routes should have a minimum clear opening of 32" (82 cm). Clear maneuvering space

should be provided for door operation appropriate to the specific door type and to the direction of approach (see pages 48–49). Vertical-level changes should be avoided whenever possible, and ramps or other alternatives should be provided where steps are necessary to transition between areas at different elevations.

Note: While the minimum width for wheelchair accessibility is 36" (92 cm), building codes usually require a minimum width dimension of 44" (112 cm) for egress corridors.

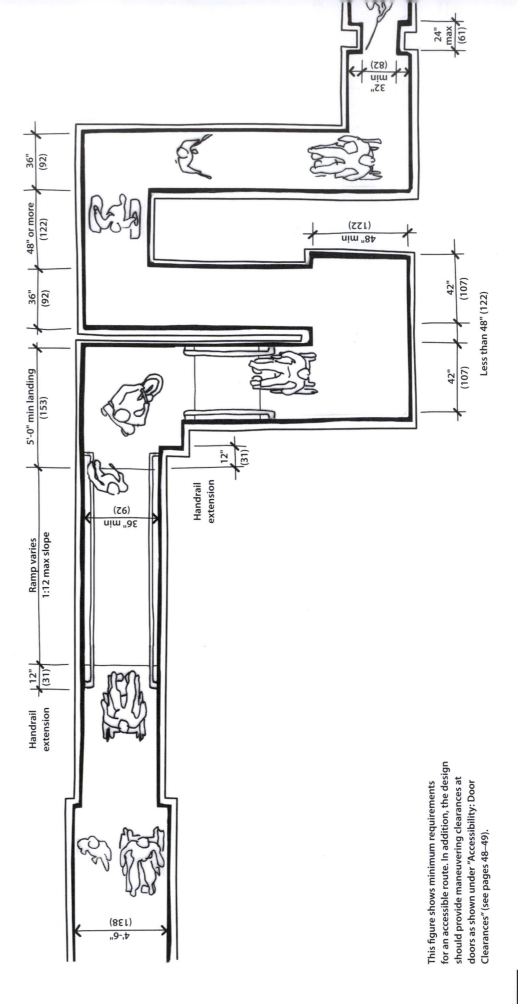

This figure shows minimum requirements for an accessible route. In addition, the design should provide maneuvering clearances at doors as shown under "Accessibility: Door Clearances" (see pages 48–49).

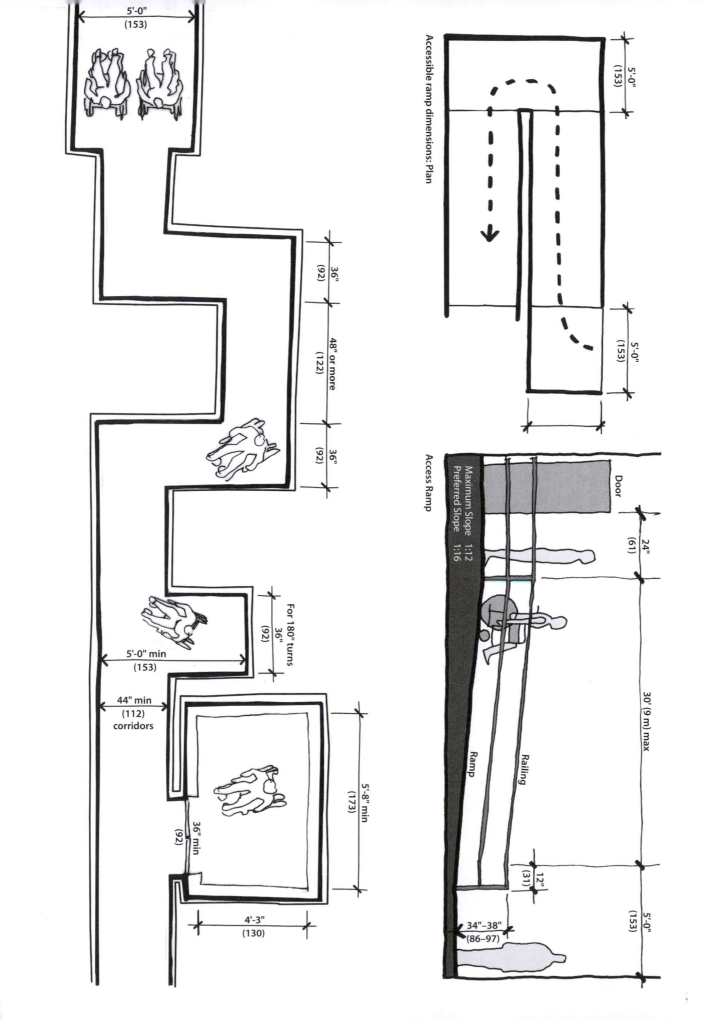

5'-0"
(153)

Accessible ramp dimensions: Plan

5'-0"
(153)

5'-0"
(153)

36"
(92)

48" or more
(122)

36"
(92)

For 180° turns
36"
(92)

5'-0" min
(153)

44" min
(112)
corridors

5'-8" min
(173)

36" min
(92)

4'-3"
(130)

Access Ramp

Door

Maximum Slope   1:12
Preferred Slope   1:16

Ramp

Railing

24"
(61)

30' (9 m) max

12"
(31)

5'-0"
(153)

34"–38"
(86–97)

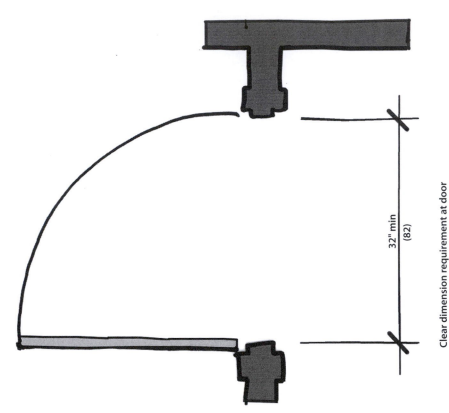

Clear dimension requirement at door

32" min (82)

Accessibility: Door Clearances

Accessible doors require a clear opening of 32" (82 cm) when the door is open 908, measured between the face of the door and the opposite stop at the frame. Doors that are not automatic or power assisted must have maneuvering clearance. This allows the wheelchair user to position the wheelchair in front of and to the side of the door in such a way as to permit pushing or pulling the door open as needed. Each door condition necessitates different maneuvering clearance, depending on the direction of the door swing and of approach.

48" min (122)

12" min (31)

Doors in series: Opposite swing

48" min (122)

Doors in series: Same-direction swing

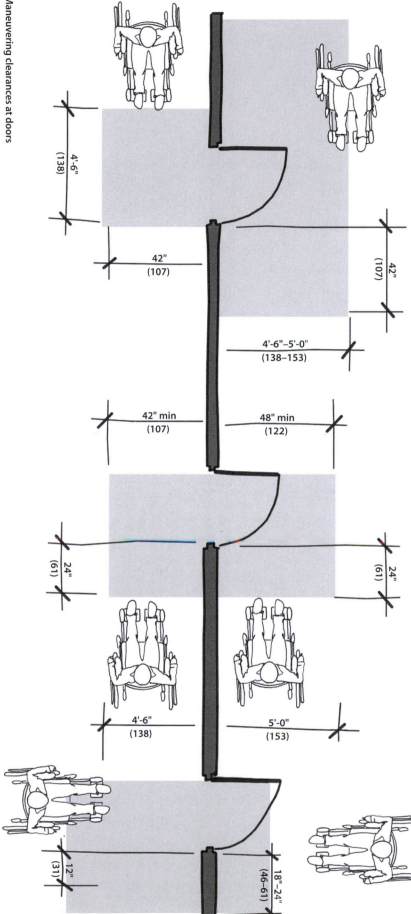

Maneuvering clearances at doors

Accessibility: Restrooms and Drinking Fountains

Accessible plumbing fixtures need appropriate clear space to allow their use by wheelchair-bound users. Required dimensions are shown. Toilets and bathtubs must have grab bars to assist users with the necessary transfer back and forth from the wheelchair. Clear floor space at toilets may be arranged for either a left-handed or right-handed approach. Standard toilet stalls with a minimum depth of 56" (142 cm) require wall-mounted toilet fixtures. If the depth is increased by a minimum of 3" (8 cm), a floor-mounted toilet fixture may be used. Alternate toilet stalls are allowed only when providing a standard stall is infeasible in instances of alteration work.

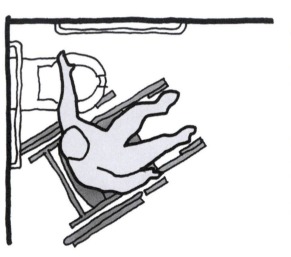

Partial illustration of wheelchair-to-toilet side transfer

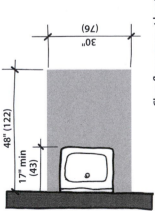

17" min (43)   48" (122)   30" (76)

Clear floor space at lavatory

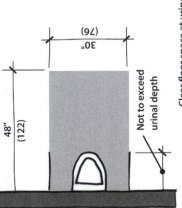

48" (122)   30" (76)   Not to exceed urinal depth

Clear floor space at urinal

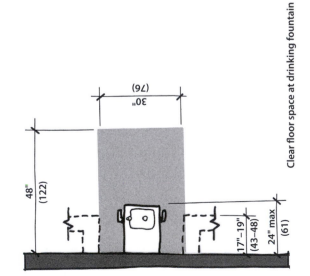

48" (122)   30" (76)   17"–19" (43–48)   24" max (61)

Clear floor space at drinking fountain

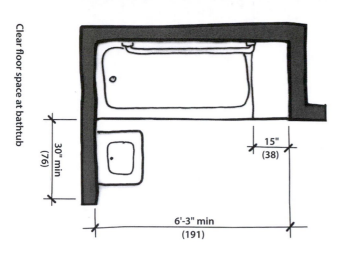

Clear floor space at bathtub

30" min (76)

15" (38)

6'-3" min (191)

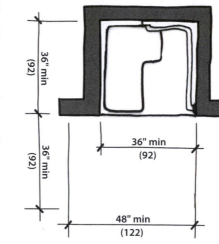

Clear floor space at shower stall

36" min (92)

36" min (92)

36" min (92)

48" min (122)

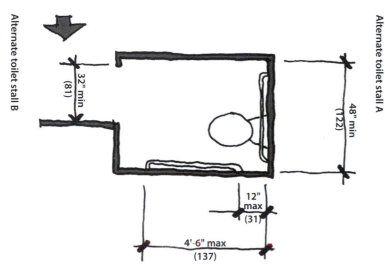

Alternate toilet stall B

32" min (81)

48" min (122)

12" max (31)

4'-6" max (137)

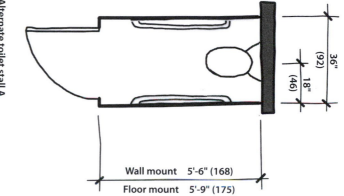

Alternate toilet stall A

36" (92)

18" (46)

Wall mount   5'-6" (168)
Floor mount   5'-9" (175)

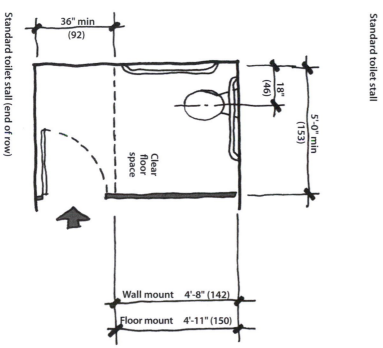

Standard toilet stall (end of row)

36" min (92)

18" (46)

5'-0" min (153)

Clear floor space

Wall mount   4'-8" (142)

Floor mount   4'-11" (150)

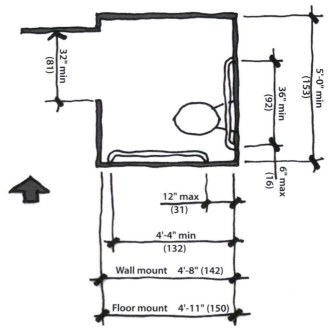

Standard toilet stall

32" min (81)

5'-0" min (153)

36" min (92)

6" max (16)

12" max (31)

4'-4" min (132)

Wall mount   4'-8" (142)

Floor mount   4'-11" (150)

Accessibility Application: Master Bedroom Suite Project

Shown here are two solutions to a fully accessible master bedroom suite project that include the bedroom space, a master bathroom, closet space, and a seating area. The scenario presents an older couple wanting a design solution employing universal design principles such that it would allow them to easily adapt the space for future wheelchair use. The clients do not want a master bedroom suite that looks like a medical facility for a disabled person.

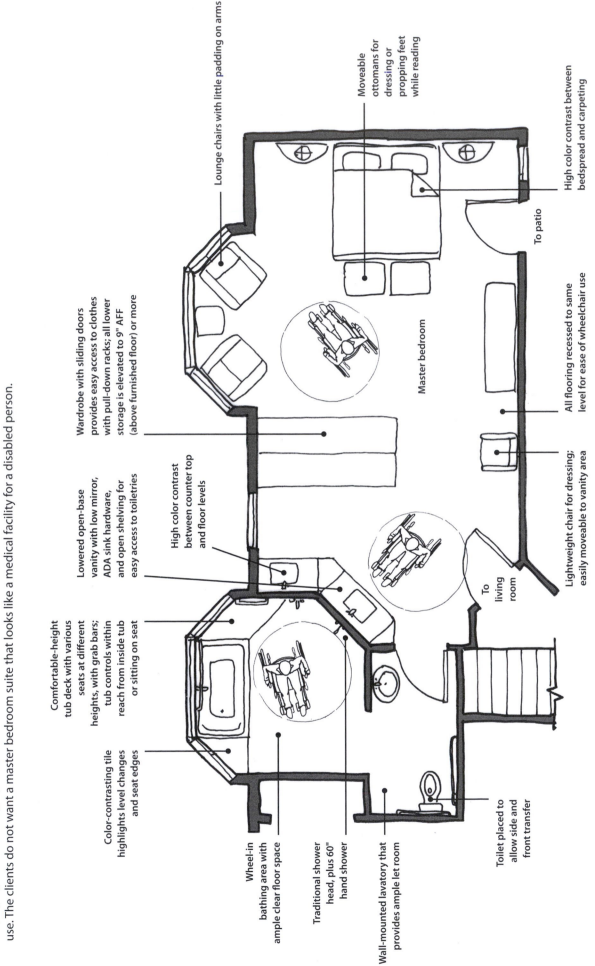

Lounge chairs with little padding on arms

Moveable ottomans for dressing or propping feet while reading

High color contrast between bedspread and carpeting

To patio

Wardrobe with sliding doors provides easy access to clothes with pull-down racks; all lower storage is elevated to 9" AFF (above furnished floor) or more

Master bedroom

All flooring recessed to same level for ease of wheelchair use

Lowered open-base vanity with low mirror, ADA sink hardware, and open shelving for easy access to toiletries

High color contrast between counter top and floor levels

Lightweight chair for dressing; easily moveable to vanity area

To living room

Comfortable-height tub deck with various seats at different heights, with grab bars; tub controls within reach from inside tub or sitting on seat

Color-contrasting tile highlights level changes and seat edges

Wheel-in bathing area with ample clear floor space

Traditional shower head, plus 60" hand shower

Wall-mounted lavatory that provides ample let room

Toilet placed to allow side and front transfer

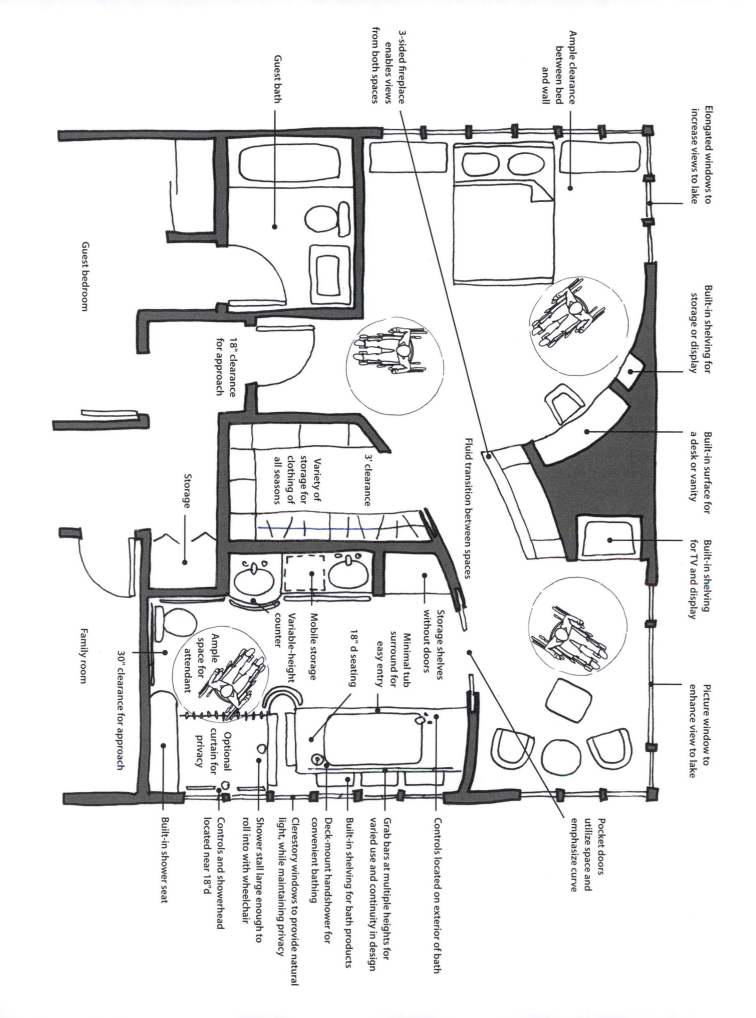

Elongated windows to increase views to lake

Ample clearance between bed and wall

Built-in shelving for storage or display

Guest bath

Built-in surface for a desk or vanity

3-sided fireplace enables views from both spaces

Built-in shelving for TV and display

Guest bedroom

18" clearance for approach

3' clearance

Fluid transition between spaces

Picture window to enhance view to lake

Variety of storage for clothing of all seasons

Storage

Storage shelves without doors

Pocket doors utilize space and emphasize curve

Minimal tub surround for easy entry

Controls located on exterior of bath

18" d seating

Family room

Mobile storage

Variable-height counter

Ample space for attendant

30" clearance for approach

Optional curtain for privacy

Built-in shelving for bath products

Grab bars at multiple heights for varied use and continuity in design

Deck-mount handshower for convenient bathing

Clerestory windows to provide natural light, while maintaining privacy

Shower stall large enough to roll into with wheelchair

Controls and showerhead located near 18"d

Built-in shower seat

Life Safety: Egress Concepts

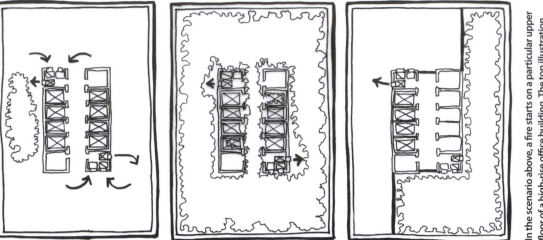

Exit discharge (open to public way)

Egress route

Direct egress route

Complex egress route

Egress blocked by smoke

Alternate egress routes

Building codes exist to protect the **health, safety, and welfare** of building occupants. They address a wide range of topics related to buildings, their materials, and their systems. Of particular concern to space planners are the codes dealing with life safety related to fires. Included are requirements pertaining to the compartmentalization of building parts to prevent the spread of fire, the use of automatic suppression systems (sprinklers), and the placement of stairways and other exits for safe egress in case of fire or other emergencies. **The International Building Code** is used throughout the United States and is the main source to refer to in matters of building code requirements. There are also good textbooks devoted exclusively to building codes. The intent here is to give a brief overview of some key concepts related to life safety that are important to know and that affect space planning decisions.

The codes classify building types based on use and hazard level. Among them are assembly occupancies, business occupancies, educational occupancies, factory or industrial occupancies, residential occupancies, mercantile occupancies, and hazardous occupancies. Requirements for such things as construction materials, fire ratings of walls, and means of egress vary among **user occupancies.** They are all important, but I would like to focus your attention on three specific occupancy types you will encounter frequently: assembly, business, and mercantile.

Assembly occupancies deal with high-density project types involving lots of people. Examples include theaters, banquet halls, restaurants, drinking establishments, and nightclubs. The common denominator is high density and therefore a lot of people to evacuate safely in case of emergency. Office projects will fall under **business occupancies,** so you will be referring to those sections of the code to find out specific requirements for those projects. Office projects are often housed in high-rise buildings, buildings that, because of their height, present their own challenges for firefighting and expedient, safe egress. Evacuating hundreds of people thirty stories high and above is more complicated than evacuating them at street level. Finally, retail projects will be classified as **mercantile occupancies,** and code sections under that type will have specific requirements for them.

In these and the next few pages I review a handful of life-safety concepts that should be helpful for space planning purposes.

In the scenario above, a fire starts on a particular upper floor of a high-rise office building. The top illustration shows the fire starting and the two exit stairways for egress. The middle illustration shows the rapid spread of fire and smoke in an undivided floor occupied by a single tenant. The bottom illustration shows how compartmentalizing the building using fire-rated partitions can help contain fire and smoke (at least for a while), thus facilitating egress efforts.

Your project may have one or more exits, based on code requirements. A particular concern with projects having only one exit (or two closely spaced ones) is the possibility that a fire may start near it, thus preventing users from escaping. For that reason, the code very often requires multiple exits located as remotely as possible from one another.

In a building housing multiple tenants (e.g., residential, medical, business), every tenant is required to have his or her own egress **doors**. Tenants are not allowed by code to exit through someone else's space.

An **egress system** consists of
(a) rooms, (b) **exit** access corridors,
(c) enclosed (**pro**tected) exit stairways,
and (d) exit discharges that exit into
(e) safe public **ways**.

Codes require providing **areas of refuge** where handicapped occupants with mobility limitations can wait safely for assistance.

Most multi**story** buildings will have two or more exits connected by exit access corridors. The **egress route** must be clearly identified, with exit signs along the way and at **exit doors**.

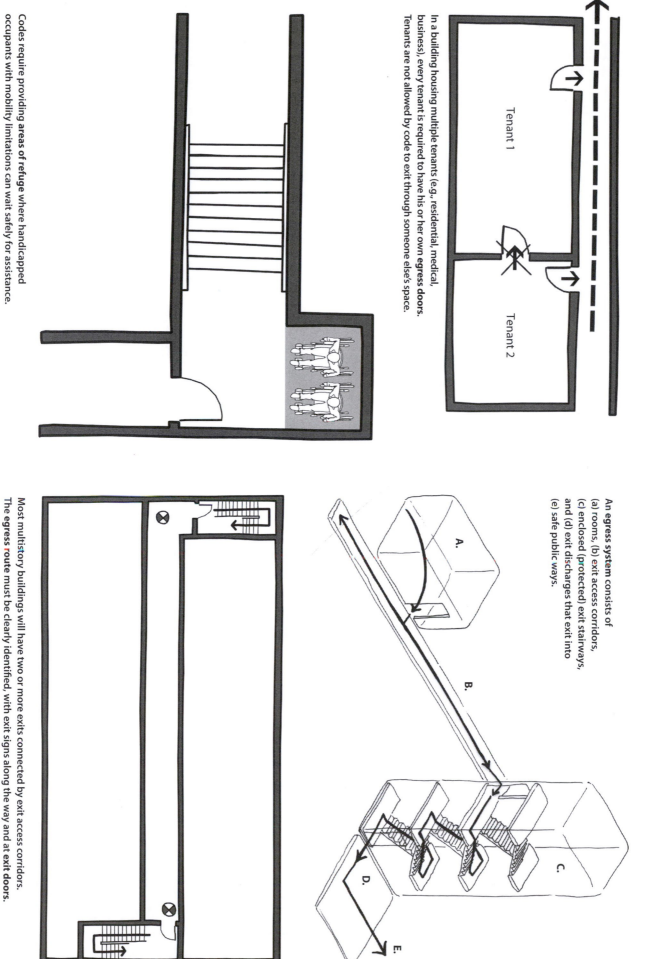

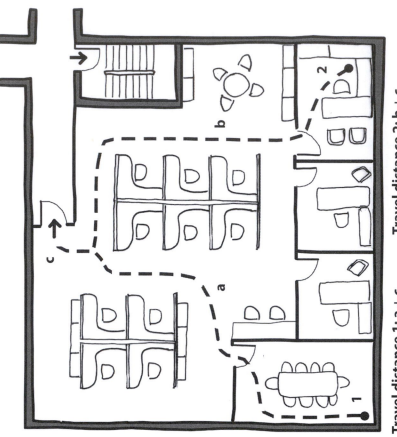

Egress: Exit and Door Requirements

Number of Exits

One-story business, mercantile, and assembly buildings (among others) not exceeding fifty occupants (determined by occupant load formulas in the codes) and 75' (22.8 m) of travel distance may have only one exit. Business and mercantile occupancy buildings that are two stories may have a single exit if the occupant load does not exceed thirty and the travel distance does not exceed 75' (22.8 m). Individual tenant spaces in all three types having an occupant load of fifty or fewer may also have a single exit. Beyond that, floors or suites with an occupant load up to five hundred require a minimum of two exits. Occupant loads between five hundred and one thousand require a minimum of three exits, and those exceeding one thousand occupants require at least four exits.

Door Width and Swing

Egress doors need to provide a minimum clear opening of 32" (82 cm). The door itself will have to be wider than that to provide the necessary clear opening. A 36" (92 cm)-door is common. Doors serving spaces with occupant loads greater than fifty need to swing in the direction of travel (usually outward, into an access corridor). Note that doors to individual offices and rooms can swing in. It is usually only the main doors of the suite that have to swing out into the public corridor.

Travel distance 1: a + c   Travel distance 2: b + c

A suite with an occupant load of fewer than 50 and a travel distance to its own exit door not exceeding 75' (22.8 m) may have only one exit. Travel distance is measured along the actual path of travel, from the most remote corner to the exit door.

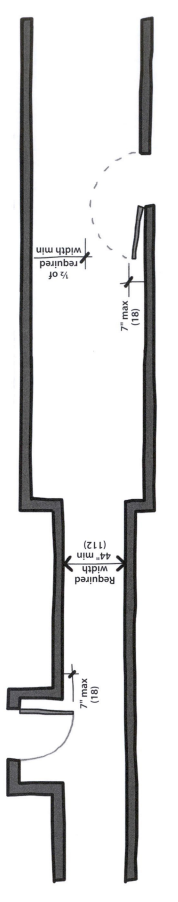

Codes require **egress corridors** to be at least 44" (112 cm) wide. For high occupant loads the requirement can be greater. A door in a vestibule may project into an access corridor no more than 7" (18 cm). A door may swing out into a corridor if the clear distance between the farthest point of its swing and the adjacent wall still leaves at least half of the required corridor width. For example, if the required corridor width is 44" (112 cm), and the distance between the swing of the door and the adjacent corridor wall leaves a clear path of 22" (56 cm) or more, then the outswinging door would be acceptable.

When two exits are needed in a suite, they should be located as far apart as possible. The code requires the separation between doors to be at least half the distance of the longest diagonal dimension of the space. The illustration above shows several examples.

* May be reduced to ⅓D in sprinklered buildings.

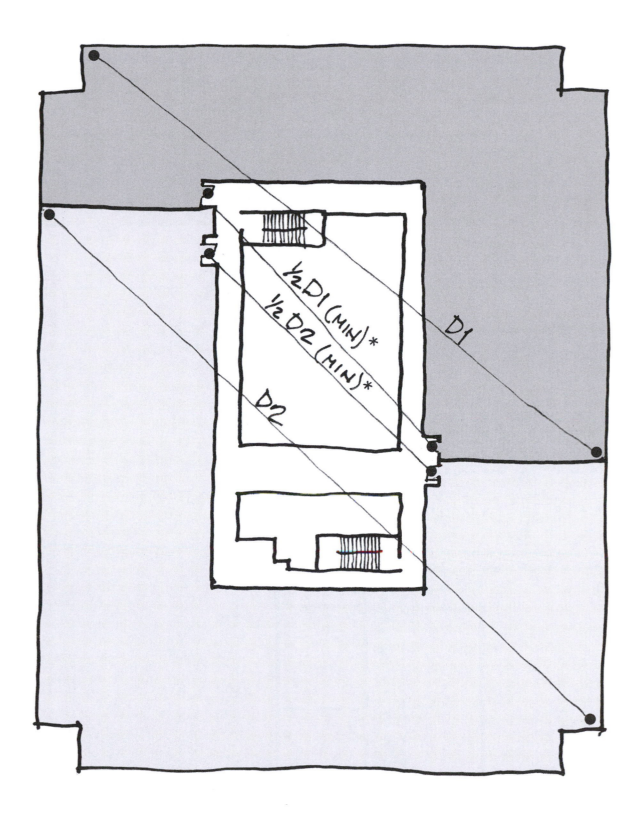

½ D1 (MIN)*
½ D2 (MIN)*
D1
D2

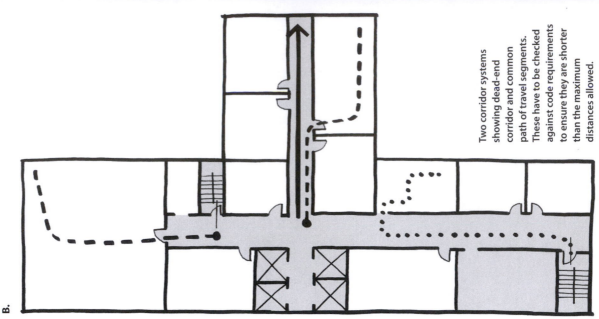

Two corridor systems showing dead-end corridor and common path of travel segments. These have to be checked against code requirements to ensure they are shorter than the maximum distances allowed.

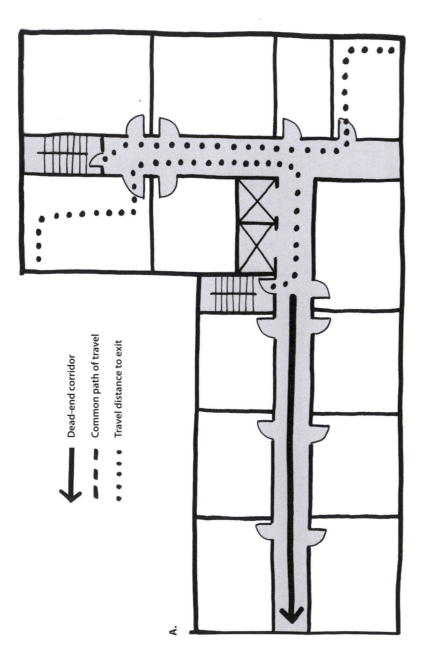

A.

→ Dead-end corridor

- - - Common path of travel

• • • Travel distance to exit

Egress: Good Practices for Egress Corridors

In general, when designing corridor systems, whether within an individual suite or for the entire floor, you want to accomplish two important objectives:

- ensuring that occupants promptly reach a point where they have a choice of two egress directions, and

- avoiding conditions in which there are long corridors that do not lead to an exit, causing occupants to have to turn back and lose valuable time during an emergency situation caused by fire.

Two concepts used in the codes address these two objectives. The first concept is the **common path of travel**. This is the distance occupants have to travel

when exiting before they reach a point where they have a choice of two ways to go. The codes set limits to keep that distance as short as possible. These limits vary from occupancy to occupancy. For business occupancies, for instance, the maximum allowed common path of travel is 75' (22.8 m) or 100' (30.5 m) if the building is sprinklered or the occupant load is fewer than thirty.

The second concept is the **dead-end corridor**. These, too, have limitations determined by the code. In most cases, dead-end corridors are limited to 20' (6.1 m). There are a few exceptions, such as allowing dead-end corridors to be up to 50' (15.25 m) for business occupancies in sprinklered buildings.

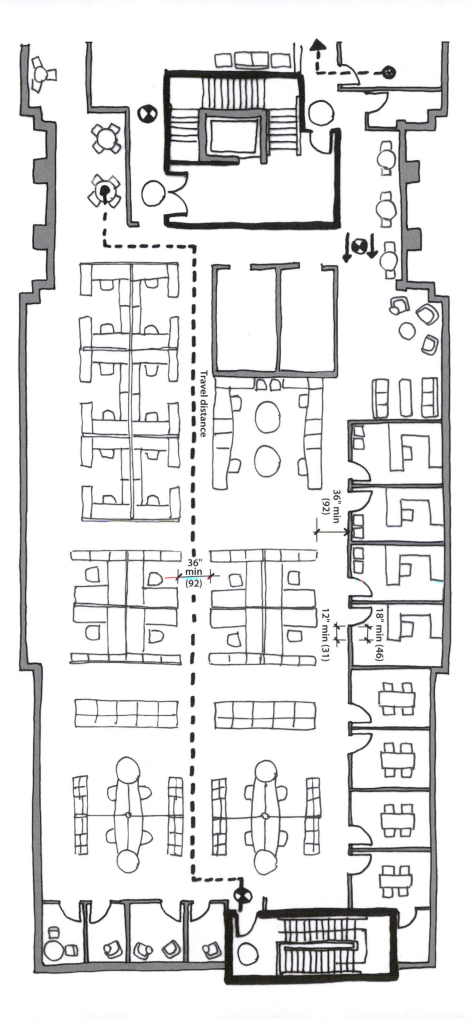

Travel distance

36" min (92)

36" min (92)

18" min (46)

12" min (31)

A code compliance plan (shown partially) for an office project. Note the identification of a representative path of travel as well as critical corridor- and door-maneuvering distances. Note also the indication of exit sign locations.

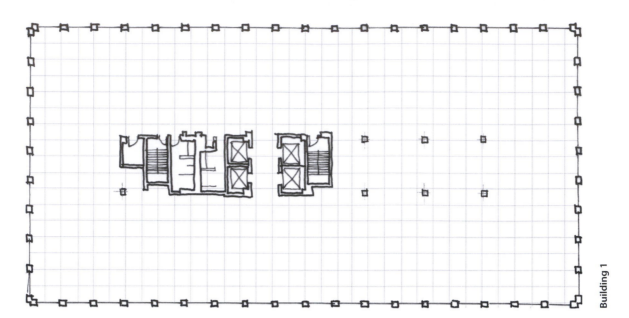

Multitenant Corridors

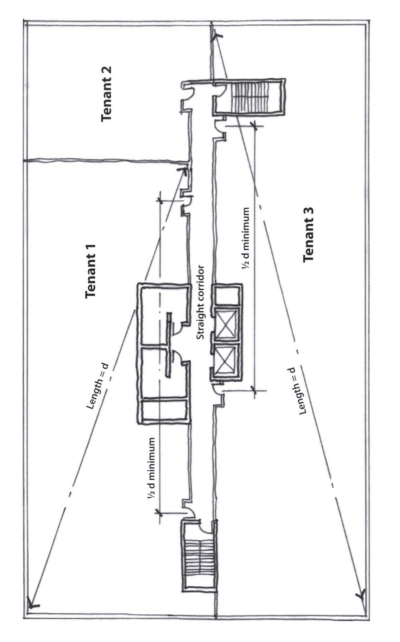

Tenant 2

Tenant 1

Length = d

½ d minimum

Straight corridor

½ d minimum

Tenant 3

Length = d

Multistory buildings for facilities such as corporate or medical offices often house various tenants on the same floor. Unlike an apartment building, in which the units are predetermined and built out from the very beginning, tenant spaces in office buildings are custom designed to cater to the needs of each tenant. Once built out entirely, one floor may consist of four midsized tenants, another may have one large and two small tenants, and the next one may have two large tenants. The actual configuration and location of the tenants are determined on a case-by-case basis. **Multi-tenant floors** on multistory buildings require careful

planning in order to provide safe egress in case of fire. Some of the concepts discussed earlier in this chapter apply here. Main issues include the number of exits required for each tenant, the location of those exits, the configuration of the public corridor system, and the avoidance of dead-end corridors. Popular corridor systems in these kinds of buildings include the straight corridor between exit stairs, the Z corridor connecting stairs at opposite ends and cutting through the elevator lobby, and the full loop around the core. Determining which is the most appropriate depends on the configuration of the building and its core elements.

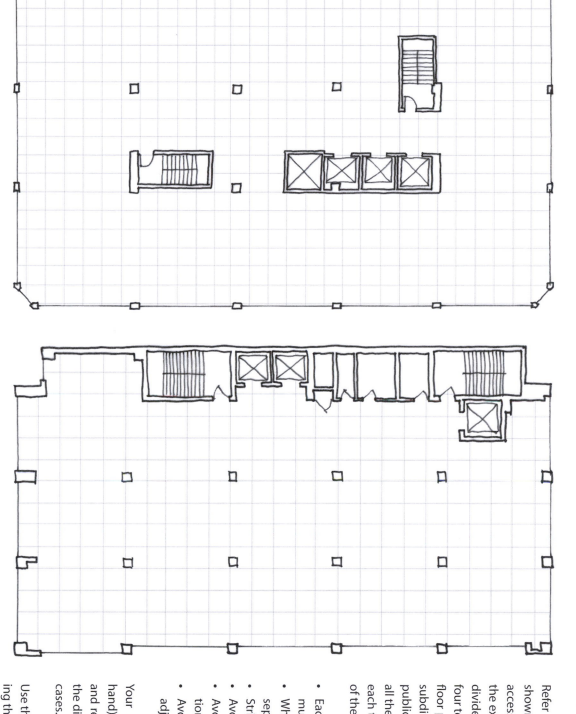

Building 2

Building 3

EXERCISE

Refer to the three blank building templates shown. Assume they are on an upper floor accessed by elevators. Emergency egress is via the existing stairs in the plan. Your task is to sub-divide the floor template into spaces for three to four tenants of various sizes. Examine each of the floor plans, and for each come up with a viable subdivision of space. You will need to create a public corridor system that will provide access to all the spaces as well as the means of egress from each to the tenant spaces. Be especially mindful of the following considerations:

- Each office suite will need to have the minimum required number of doors.

- Where multiple doors are required, their separation needs to meet code requirements.

- Strive to maximize floor efficiency.

- Avoid dead-end corridors.

- Avoid awkward public corridor configurations.

- Avoid overly grand entry lobby spaces at or adjacent to the elevator lobbies.

Your solution should be drawn loosely (free-hand) over the templates. Show door swings, and remember that exit doors need to swing in the direction of travel (i.e., outward) in almost all cases.

Use the example at far left, showing a floor housing three tenants of various sizes, as reference.

3 Design Process

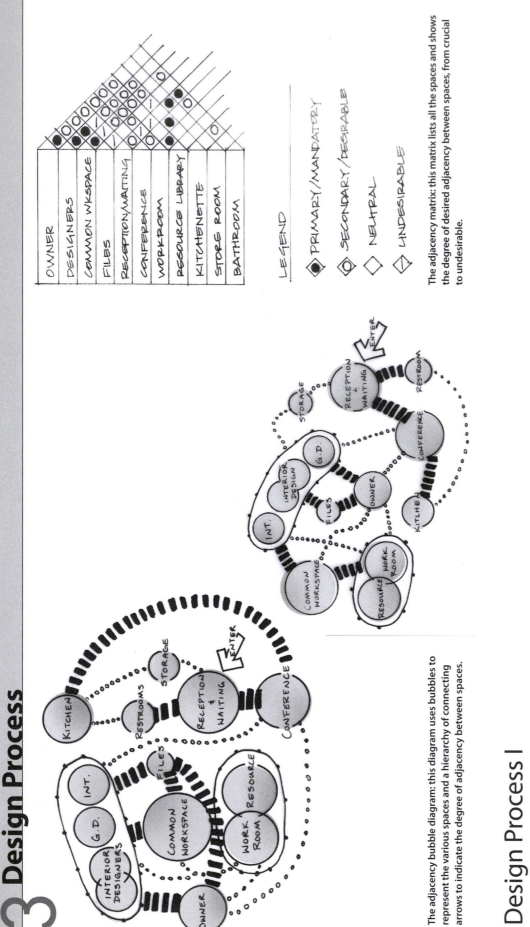

The adjacency matrix: this matrix lists all the spaces and shows the degree of desired adjacency between spaces, from crucial to undesirable.

LEGEND

- ◉ PRIMARY / MANDATORY
- ◎ SECONDARY / DESIRABLE
- ◇ NEUTRAL
- ⬦ UNDESIRABLE

The adjacency bubble diagram: this diagram uses bubbles to represent the various spaces and a hierarchy of connecting arrows to indicate the degree of adjacency between spaces.

Design Process I

Planning interior spaces can be one of the most enjoyable tasks performed by designers. It can also be one of the most frustrating for the novice designer. In some ways, it's like solving a jigsaw puzzle, except that there is no one right answer and there is no picture available of what the space is supposed to look like at the end.

The **design process** has been somewhat formalized into a series of steps that gradually and sequentially lead from all the initial fragments of information to a final space plan. There are variations, but the steps are always similar.

In very simple terms, this is what happens:

You receive a list of spaces that need to be accommodated and maybe the area (size) of the spaces. Next, you develop some idea of how the operation (e.g., the office, store, clinic, and so on) works. Between what the client tells you and your own analysis, you begin to get a sense of which spaces need to be close to one another and which ones don't. You also begin to get a sense of logical groupings based on other criteria, such as which spaces need to be easily accessible upon entering and which ones need to have the best views. After a while, you begin to understand the puzzle.

You acquire the site with the footprint of the space in which the project will take place and start looking for organizational ideas based on logic, appropriate geometries,

The adjacency bubble diagram: refined version

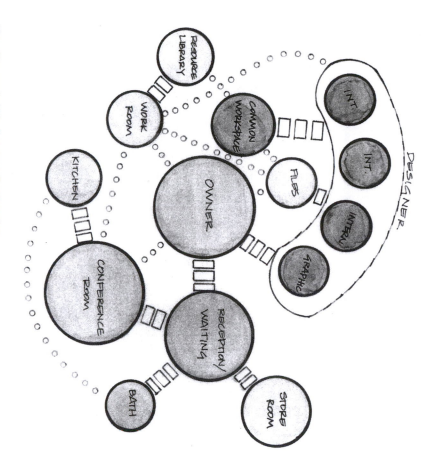

and so on. At some point, after some possible frustrations, you have your first Aha! moment. One of your organizational ideas seems promising. You are curious and try other possible arrangements. You may develop two, maybe even three ideas that might work. After getting some feedback, you may decide to zero in on one of the ideas. Or, you may decide to keep working with more than one scheme for a little longer and commit to one later.

The arrangements to this point have been based on loose diagrams. Then it is time to think more concretely, in terms of walls, rooms, and furniture. You start making decisions about their placement and the implications they have for the overall

Functional areas analysis: these loose vignettes show furniture, clearances, and circulation spaces. This information is used to determine the size of the spaces and rooms.

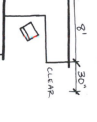

TYPICAL WORKSTATION
8' x 8' = 64' sq.

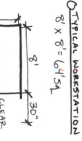

MEETING AREA
6'-6" x 6'-6" = 42'¼" sq.
TABLE 48"

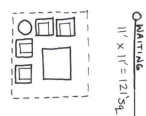

WAITING
11' x 11' = 121' sq.

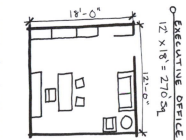

PRIVATE OFFICE
10' x 10' = 100' sq.

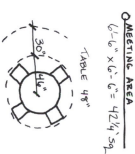

EXECUTIVE OFFICE
12' x 18' = 270' sq.

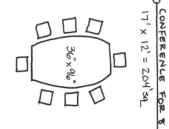

CONFERENCE FOR 8
17' x 12' = 204' sq.
36" x 96"

experience. You draw walls, doors, furniture, and other moveable pieces and explore different arrangements.

You decide on a particular scheme to continue developing and refining.

You develop and refine the chosen scheme, zooming in and solving problems at all scales. You draw the final solution nicely for the final presentation and prepare to discuss the features and benefits of your solution.

To carry out the process described above, you use process drawings, such as the ones shown here and on the next two pages. They help you understand and solve the puzzle.

Design Process II

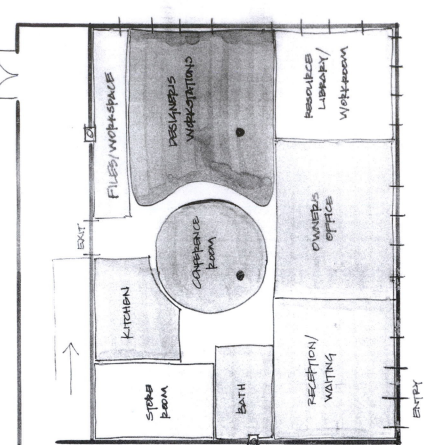

Block plans (or block diagrams): the block diagram shows blocky shapes simulating rooms and other spaces within the site footprint. It's like a blocky floor plan. The block diagram is usually the first attempt to allocate spaces within the overall space. Many of these are tried out.

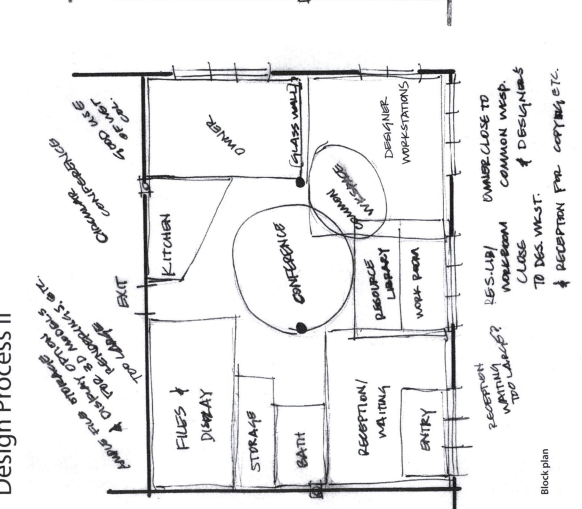

Block plan

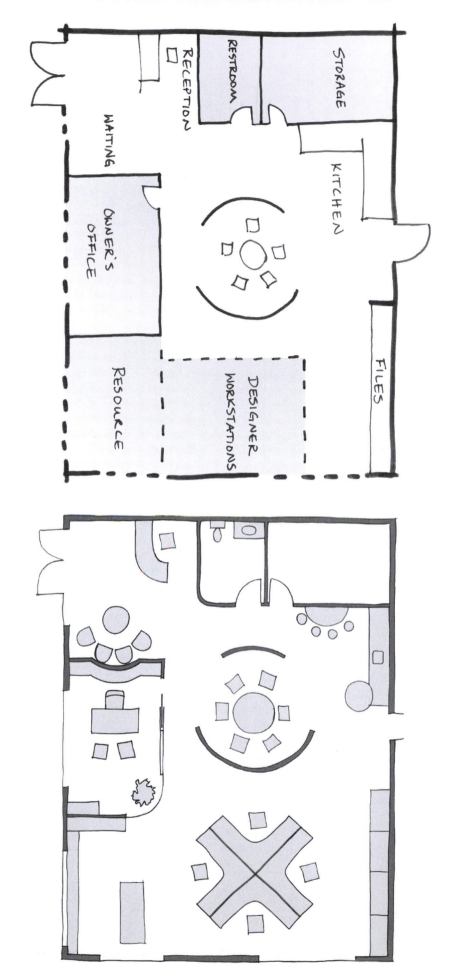

Loose plan

Loose floor plans: these take the block plans to the next level and start converting them to actual floor plans showing walls, doors, and some furniture. These plans help you and others see whether the ideas will work out.

Plan development

Refined floor plan: once the many problems (which every project has) are resolved, and after much tweaking of the various rooms and furnishings at the loose-plan level, a more detailed floor plan is drawn, showing additional refinements. There may be two or three iterations of this before arriving at the final space plan, which eventually is formalized and drawn in final form.

Programming I

The conventional name given to the document that contains the information and criteria needed to design the project is the **program** (or **brief**). For some projects, it may be a short, one-page summary. For other projects, it may be over a hundred pages. The length of the program for your school projects will vary. The specificity and level of detail will also vary. Don't expect always to get every piece of information you need conveniently laid out for you. In many cases, you will need to search for information yourself.

Shown on this page is an example of a program for an office facility that was used for a school exercise. First, it gives a brief description of the client and the circumstances. Then it lists the spaces to be provided and their sizes in square feet. It doesn't list the space dimensions to produce those square footages. You have to determine those.

Note that not much information is given to help you figure out work relationships between employees or between departments, except the statement that "they are fairly independent from each other." Someone with office-design experience might be able to make some reasonable assumptions about adjacencies based on this information. Someone inexperienced would have to ask some questions.

The **space data sheets** shown on the next page provide detailed information about individual rooms. These were produced as part of a more comprehensive program and include information such as furniture and equipment needs, materials, acoustic needs, and security needs. They also include a graphic representation (floor plans) of the spaces and furnishings.

All projects begin with some version of a program. Programming is a very detailed endeavor, and entire books are written on the subject. A full discussion about how to do programming is beyond the scope of this book. I am more concerned about explaining what to do once you have the programming information available.

AN OFFICE

Nationwide Telecommunications is a hypothetical communications company with headquarters in a prominent midwestern city in the United States. It occupies several floors in a high-rise office building downtown. The company is consolidating some external groups into this facility and needs to put them on the 20th floor, which it has just leased.

The workforce is primarily white-collar, with few layers of hierarchy. The work style is highly interactive, with the degree of work autonomy ranging from moderate to high. There will be four new groups sharing the floor. They are fairly independent from each other.

PROGRAMMATIC REQUIREMENTS

General

Reception/waiting area: 300 SF
    (waiting for 6 people)
Computer mainframe: 600–650 SF
2 Copy/Printing rooms: 150 SF each
Conference/Training room: 500–600 SF
Mailroom: 400–450 SF
Microfilm storage room (2 clerks): 320 SF
General storage room: 150 SF
As many storage closets as possible

Department A

40 employees at 68 SF
4 employees at 52 SF
2 private offices at 150 SF each
1 private office at 180 SF
16 lateral files, minimum

Department B

2 private offices at 150 SF each
4 clerks at 56 SF
1 secretary at 56 SF + 2 lateral files.
1 conference room at 150 SF
1 work area at 150 SF
4 lateral files, minimum
Department needs a strong separation from other groups but no closed doors.

Department C

28 employees at 52 SF
2 managers at 90 SF
6 employees at 72 SF
4 managers at 81 SF
4 employees at 56 SF
16 employees at 56 SF
4 private offices at 150 SF each
12 lateral files, minimum

Department D

16 employees at +/- 50 SF
2 employees at 56 SF
2 managers at 90 SF
Work area at 120 SF
Informal conference area at 150–200 SF
1 private office at 150 SF
10 lateral files, minimum

A SHORT PROGRAM FOR AN OFFICE PROJECT

Space Data Sheets

Space Data Sheets

Library

Space Type	Library
Space	
Use	Reference Area, Samples Room, & Social/Team Space
Square Footage	1200 sq ft
Materials	
Floor	Carpet
Walls	Painted Drywall
Ceiling	
Doors	Privacy Doors, though can be in open office space
Window	Access to Natural Light Preferred, can be indirect
Systems	
Acoustics	
Equipment	Reference Computer
Security	
Equipment	
Fixed	Bookcases
Moveable	Tables & Chairs
Special Requests	
Other Requirements & Notes	

Typical Space Layout

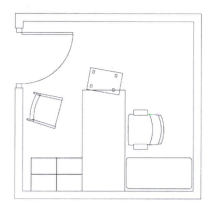

Typical Private Office

Space Type	Typical Private Office
Space	
Use	Individual Work Space
Square Footage	150 sq ft
Materials	
Floor	Carpet
Walls	Painted Drywall
Ceiling	Acoustical Tiles
Doors	Glass Doors
Window	Direct Access to Sunlight
Systems	
Acoustics	Privacy
Equipment	Personal Computer
Security	Lockable Door & Lockable Cabinets
Equipment	
Fixed	
Moveable	Desk, Bookshelves, File Cabinets, & Computer
Special Requests	
Other Requirements & Notes	Adjacency to Human Resources & Management. Needs to be customizable to each individual employee

Typical Space Layout

Programming II: User Needs

Students are often anxious to get the project's list of spaces, along with their sizes, in order to start space planning. In fact, some may think that a program is just a list of spaces to be accommodated within a given building or portion thereof. That is far from the truth. Real projects are about people who have particular needs and wants. These range from specific tangible needs, such as the need for two and a half bathrooms, to less tangible requirements, such as the desire for space that is friendly and conducive to high creativity.

Look at the five keywords on this page. These are the terms an advertising agency uses to describe itself. They were given to the designers of the agency's project to inform the design. Think about them and their implications. How does one design for a smart, inventive, and evolving group of people? Any ideas?

One of my favorite examples of a project's requirements from a client's point of view and how to go about making sense of them is from an old book by Richard Shadrin.[1] He describes a scenario in which you get called to your boss's office at a design firm. You are asked to talk to a couple interested in having a house designed for them. The scenario on the following page is paraphrased from Shadrin's description.

COLLABORATIVE

working together—learning from each other

EXPERIENCED

know what we're doing, fifty years in the business

SMART

know the right things to do

INVENTIVE

creative solutions, no matter the assignment

EVOLVING

constantly evaluating, changing, and improving always thinking of new solutions for working with clients and creating arresting and smart ideas

1. Richard Shadrin, *Design and Drawing: An Applied Approach* (Dover, MA: , 1992), 38–45.

You will need to interview the couple, take notes, and prepare a statement that lists their demands and **needs** (the hard facts) and **desires** or dreams (the soft, variable recommendations). You will have to be part good listener, part keen observer, and part clever detective. Here is what you find out.

Mr. and Mrs. David Macintosh have recently purchased one acre of oceanfront property on the south shore of Long Island, New York. He is a businessman who will soon be retiring from his work in the city. Connie, his wife, is an art school graduate who would like to start weaving fine cloth. The couple has three children; two are married, with two children of their own. Their other daughter, Patty, is a college student. The Macintoshes are selling their apartment in preparation for the house you have been asked to design for them.

After some further discussion, you find out the following:

- David wants a sailboat; it's been a lifelong dream.
- Connie has mild arthritis.
- Patty will soon graduate and move to California.
- The couple likes to have the children and grandchildren for the holidays; sometimes they sleep over.
- The land is behind the second sand dune.
- This will be their only home.
- They are both good cooks.
- Neither husband nor wife wants to spend time on household chores and fixing up.

Note the things that have special meaning. Try to uncover the impact of these elements. Some are fixed criteria, others are what Shadrin calls "desirables."

The fixed criteria are the strict facts, such as the location "behind the second sand dune." The fixed criteria shape the basic focus. Everything else is up to you to

interpret into a dynamic, exciting, fulfilling solution. First, you must list the hard facts, those bits we can't fiddle with. In this problem, they are:

- Mr. and Mrs. David Macintosh
- One acre of oceanfront property
- South shore of Long Island, New York
- His pending retirement
- The couple's three children
- Two married children, with two children of their own
- Connie's mild arthritis
- The land location behind the second sand dune
- This as their only home
- Neither husband nor wife wanting to spend time on household chores and fixing up

Next come the desirables; this is softer information but is just as important:

- Connie was an art school graduate and would like to start weaving fine cloth.
- The Macinstoshes are selling their apartment in preparation for the house.
- David wants a sailboat; it's been a lifelong dream.
- Connie has mild arthritis.
- Patty is a college student and will soon graduate and move to California.
- The couple likes to have the children and grandchildren for the holidays; sometimes they sleep over.
- This will be their only home.
- They are both good cooks.

After following a structured problem-solving method, you arrive at some conclusions and other thoughts based on your critical analysis of the situation. These include:

- The house is the central focus for the Macintoshes' extended family.

- The husband and wife want to pursue their own interests.
- They don't want to be burdened by home maintenance.
- Because they chose a beachfront location, they expect to enjoy this special environment.
- He may want access to a sailboat.
- She has arthritis, which could limit her mobility.
- There will be occasional visitors.
- They'll want maintenance-free materials.
- Some part of the house may need to be elevated to afford a view over the dunes.
- They'll want easy access to beach and boat.
- A protected outdoor space for dining, entertaining, and weaving might be nice.
- There is the possibility of having three distinct areas inside: a private space for the owners, an active living area, and an area for guests.
- You'll want to consider designing on one level (because of their age and Connie's arthritis). If the house ends up being two levels, the upper level could be for the guests.
- A well-equipped kitchen and a large central space seem appropriate.
- The house being the focus of the extended family, it might be appropriate to have some amenities such as a fireplace.
- They'll want to avoid formal landscaping requiring maintenance.
- You'll have to consider environmental factors, including sun and wind, shifting sands, and the fragile beach ecosystem.
- You'll have to remember that hurricanes sometimes batter the eastern coastline.

This brief account may give you an idea of how a project's definition and set of requirements become real and complex when you account for people (clients and other users) and their particular needs and desires. This is an example involving two principal users. Imagine designing a project for one hundred people.

Programming III: From Requirements to Diagrams

DESCRIPTION OF ZONES FOR A RESTAURANT

ENTRY AND FOYER:

Located just inside the corner front entrance

Small-scale waiting area forces customers to enter toward the bar/lounge and elimi-

nates crowded entry problems when guests arrive

Coat closet near entry

HOSTESS STAND:

Just off the entrance and foyer to greet customers on arrival

Distance between the hostess stand and the door to allow guests to enter comfort-

ably and make their own destination choice

BAR/LOUNGE:

Acts as a separate space from the main dining

Guests can enjoy drinks and conversation at multiple seating options

Bar stools, bar-height tables, booths, and comfortable lounge sofas and chairs

Possible space for hosting live music

MAIN DINING:

A more public dining experience, with booths and large-group seating

Views from the large windows out onto the street are a point of interest here

Needs to be within close proximity of the kitchen and visual prepping stations

SEMIPRIVATE DINING:

Visually and physically semiseparate from the main dining to control acoustics

Smaller tables for smaller parties create intimate seating

Close to kitchen

PRIVATE-PARTY DINING:

A small, private room away from the main dining for parties of ten to twenty people

Close to kitchen

Private wine tasting room

KITCHEN:

Clean, spacious environment allows chefs and assistants to work simultaneously

Houses variety of work spaces, including grills, ranges, ovens, sinks, washing stations,

dishwashers, and so on

FOOD STORAGE:

Freezers necessary for bulk produce to be kept over time

Refrigerators (separate ones for raw foods and produce)

Dry food shelf space

VISIBLE PREPARATION SITE:

Act as final plating area for the food

Visible to main dining, aimed at showcasing skill and offering a peek into the kitchen

RESTROOMS:

Meet accessibility codes and accommodate for the cover

STAFF OFFICE:

Meeting room and lounge, also to include single bathroom

OCCUPANCY:

The bar/lounge to accommodate about half the dining cover

Specific numbers to be determined on square footage available

SECURITY/SAFETY ISSUES:

Fire exits exist in building and will be made accessible in new design

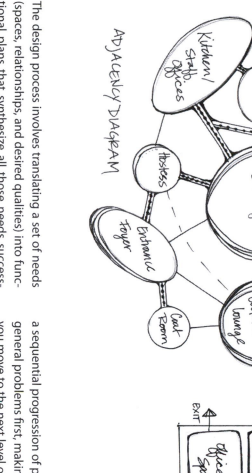

ADJACENCY DIAGRAM

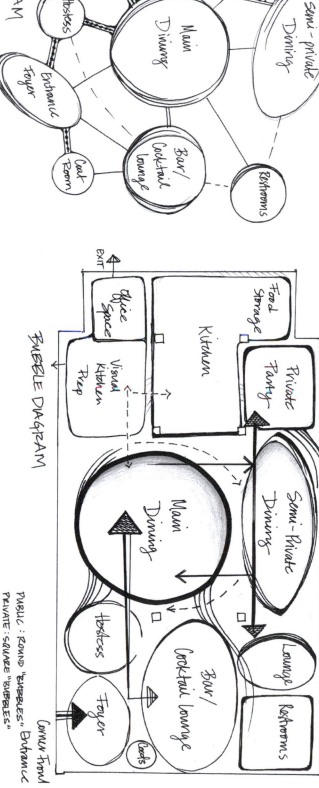

BUBBLE DIAGRAM

PUBLIC : ROUND "BUBBLES" Entrance
PRIVATE : SQUARE "BUBBLES"

Corner Front

The design process involves translating a set of needs (spaces, relationships, and desired qualities) into functional plans that synthesize all those needs successfully. Here, I show you an example of a list of required spaces for a restaurant project and how the project's designer used adjacency and **bubble diagrams** to understand the parts and their relationships and formulate the beginning of a space plan. Design follows

a sequential progression of problem solving. You solve general problems first, making specific decisions. Then you move to the next level of problem solving and try to solve the new problems based on your previous decisions. New decisions are made at this stage. You then carry those decisions forward to solve the next layer of design problems, and on and on and on until you complete the design and all its details.

Diagrams are used extensively early on. They help you solve design problems quickly and efficiently. There is no need to draw the tables and chairs initially. You need to make decisions about where to locate the various spaces first.

From Diagrams to Plan

Good space planning is informed by a good understanding of both the programmatic requirements of the project and the existing context. Performing a thoughtful analysis of the given program and the existing context will help you make good space-planning decisions.

Strive to understand the given site loosely before you start committing to specific ideas. During this early stage, try to determine the best location for open areas, the best location for enclosed spaces, and desired relationships between the programmed spaces and the various regions of the site. Move from loose, sketchy diagrams to more detailed ones until you arrive at a workable solution based on sound intentions. The example from an office suite presented here shows the path to the final plan and gives you an idea of the basis for some of the main planning decisions.

The program consists of several conference rooms, a small number of private offices, a resource library, a "community" space, and two studios. The site offers nice views and ample soft natural light to the north.

Early sketches indicate a desire to relate to the curving portion of the building through a radial arrangement in the public areas and a definite intention to keep the enclosed rooms inside and locate the open studios toward the window on the north side. The angled turning point of the building seemed like a logical zone at which to transition from one studio to the other.

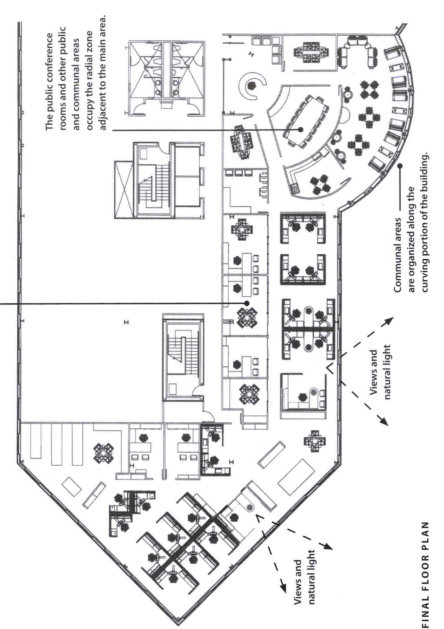

Offices and other enclosed rooms are grouped in linear fashion on the inside.

The public conference rooms and other public and communal areas occupy the radial zone adjacent to the main area.

Communal areas are organized along the curving portion of the building.

Views and natural light

Views and natural light

FINAL FLOOR PLAN

A very early concept sketch shows basic intentions.

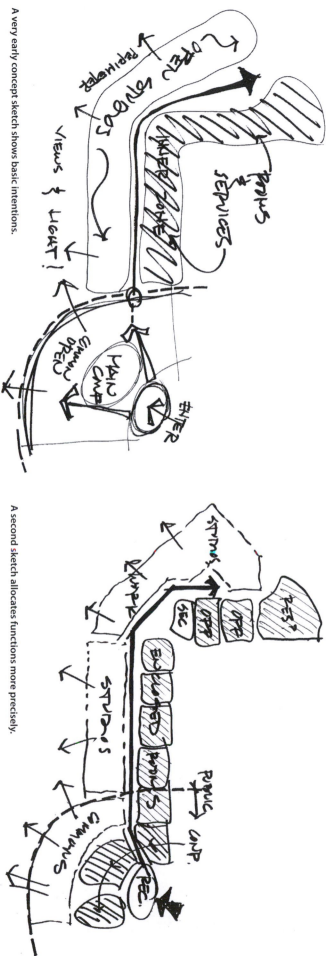

A second sketch allocates functions more precisely.

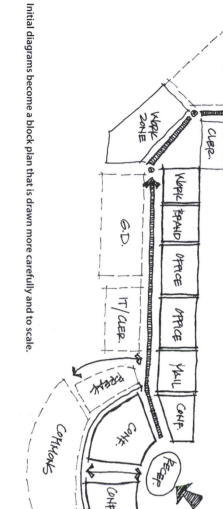

Initial diagrams become a block plan that is drawn more carefully and to scale.

The conceptual sketches on this page show the thinking process during the early design stages. These eventually lead to the final solution shown on the preceding page. The solution in this case simply became a refinement of the early diagrams.

Diagrammatic sketches enable you to think on paper and to explore ideas quickly. These sketches don't take long to draw and can help you become aware of important relationships. That way, you can solve basic planning challenges efficiently.

Allocating Spaces

After a designer has determined the size and approximate shape of rooms and spaces based on some knowledge of the activities, people, furnishings, and equipment to be housed in them, the next task is to determine where to place them within the given footprint. This entails a zoning exercise that requires a good understanding of how spaces relate to one another and the existing context. Although a lot of emphasis is placed on functional relationships between spaces, other factors come into play, too. The goal is to create logical groupings of spaces having similar needs and to find appropriate spots for them.

Every project has functions that need to be near one another. Sometimes, this means sharing the same space. Other times, it requires being in separate spaces, but next to each other. In some cases, being conveniently a few doors down the hall is good enough. Equally important is knowing that it may be important for some functions to be away from others. The need for proximity or distance will vary. These relationships can be either highly critical or merely desirable.

Based on programmatic information given to them and their experience with the type of project at hand, designers come up with ways of sorting out the functions of a project into groups that either require proximity owing to functional requirements or otherwise share certain characteristics or needs. Activities belonging together are clustered and placed in one space according to need. Rooms requiring shade will be grouped together and placed on the shady side of the building; rooms requiring peace and quiet may be grouped and placed some distance away from the loud zones. Note that in the first example, the activities are placed in relation to context (sunny versus shady side), whereas in the second they are placed in relation to project functions (loud versus quiet).

A good space adjacency analysis will provide many good clues about what should go where. There will always be choices for placing functions, but after performing a space analysis you will find that there are only a few really good and logical locations for certain functions. The analysis will help you determine the relative positions of units, appropriate levels of enclosure, and feasible groupings.

Functions may need proximity to one another for the following reasons:

- People need to go back and forth between the spaces frequently or conveniently.
- Materials need to be carried from one room to another.
- People need to talk to each other from different spaces.
- Functions in one space may need to be supervised by a person in another space.
- It may make sense to put a certain function at a specific point (beginning, middle, or end) of a sequence, such as placing the gift shop at the end of the exhibit spaces in a museum.

Functions may need separation from one another for the following reasons:

- One room needs silence and the other one is noisy.
- One rooms needs to be kept clean (or tidy), and the other one is usually dirty (or messy).
- People in one room perform tasks requiring high concentration, and the other room is often full of movement and activity.

Room Adjacencies

In addition to understanding the relative importance of the adjacency between two spaces, it is also useful to know the kind of adjacency that will work well. Illustrations A through E (at left) show various options, progressing from the most interconnected (A) to the contiguous but separated (E). Knowing the reason for expressed adjacency need between spaces is useful in this regard. Possible reasons for proximity include frequent use of meeting room, frequent need to access shared files, occasional need to use the shared copy machine, occasional need to access supplies in one room, frequent use of restrooms by clients, and so on. Note the use of the words such as *frequent* and *occasional* as clues about possible arrangements.

A. Space within another space

B. Contiguous spaces, flowing

C. Contiguous spaces with one opening

D. Contiguous spaces connected by adjacent doors outside

E. Contiguous spaces connected by remote doors outside

Room Relationships

Two adjacent rooms

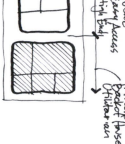

Two adjacent spaces separared by prominent barrier

Two rooms placed apart from each other

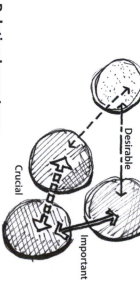
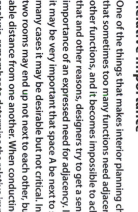
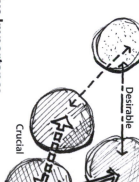

Two spaces that become one room

Public versus private

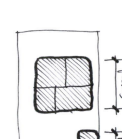

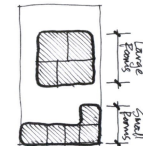

Public Easy Access High End / *Private Bedroom House Children*

Expansion Zone

Fixed versus expansion spaces

Spaces near egress point

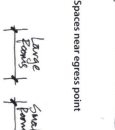
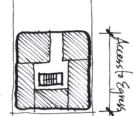
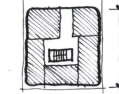

Access to Egress

Sunny versus shaded

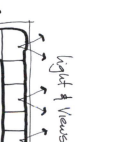

Light & Views / *Shaded Area*

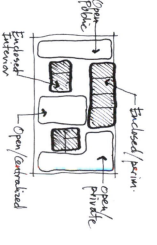
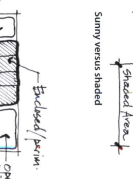

Large Rooms / *Small Rooms*

Large, public rooms versus small, private offices

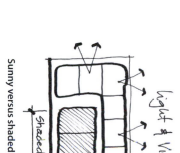

Open Public / *Enclosed Interior* / *Open/Centralized* / *Enclosed/perim.* / *open/private*

Open versus enclosed; public versus private

Relative Importance

One of the things that makes interior planning challenging is that sometimes too many functions need adjacency to certain other functions, and it becomes impossible to achieve that. For that and other reasons, designers try to get a sense of the relative importance of an expressed need for adjacency; In some cases, it may be very important that space A be next to space B, but in many cases it may be desirable but not critical. In those cases, the two rooms may end up not next to each other, but some reasonable distance from one another. When conducting an adjacency analysis, remember to determine the relative importance of each request. Possibilities include highly critical, necessary but not critical, desirable, neutral, undesirable, necessary but not critical to separate

Desirable / Crucial / Important

Sorting Qualities

The criteria to be used to form groups based on adjacency needs vary from project to project. There can be many in addition to the functional needs for adjacency. Some examples include locating parts of a department together; executives (in hierarchically conscious organizations) on the side with the best views; rooms requiring special climate control considerations together

in a zone; rooms requiring space for future growth on the side with room for growth; enclosed spaces together; open spaces together; public spaces up front, accessible to the public; service spaces used by different people and units in a centralized area; and so on. The illustrations on this page show several diagrammatic examples based on different possible sorting criteria.

Groupings and Sequences

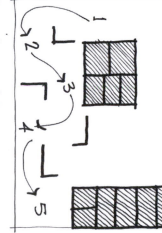
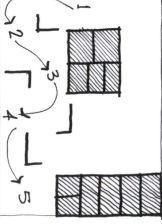
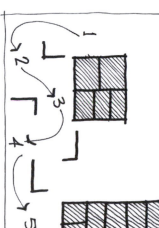

Adjacency diagrams and matrices conveniently show the relationship between any two spaces. It is important to recognize that although this information is useful, the designer's task usually requires the disposition of not just pairs of spaces, but also entire clusters that must be arranged logically. The parts of the planning puzzle need to be understood holistically, and the designer must determine their potential to form shared groupings or sequential arrangements. The example above shows a diagrammatic example illustrating two clusters of enclosed spaces, one on the perimeter and the other one floating in space, and also an intentional sequential experience from the entrance space up front (1), moving through a series of spaces, and culminating in space in the back (5).

Adjacencies: The Matrix Diagram

Two types of adjacency diagrams are widely used in the design process: the **adjacency matrix** and the **adjacency bubble diagram**. The adjacency matrix is very useful for complex projects with many spaces and intricate relationships between the parts. It serves as a reference throughout the design process for checking and double-checking proposed layouts against adjacency needs. Best of all, the matrix is a scheme-neutral diagram: it doesn't suggest layouts; it simply does its job as a reference tool and lets the designer take care of the layout. The matrix is, for the most part, very helpful. One potential misuse worth noting is the use of matrix diagrams for very simple applications, such as a modest house. In those cases, the matrix can have the counterproductive effect of making beginning designers unnecessarily rigid. Why not just draw a simple bubble diagram? Producing an adjacency matrix diagram for a simple project may be fine as an exercise, to learn and practice how to do these diagrams, but understand that they are tools meant for projects of some size and complexity.

POSITIONS

- Health Care Marketer Principal
- Human Resources Principal
- Managing Principal
- Other Principals
- Academic
- Administrative Support
- Health Care
- Engineering
- Interiors
- Landscape
- Practice Management
- Science and Technology
- Specifications
- Marketing Department
- Information Technology Specialists
- Technology Service Employees
- Human Resources
- Librarian

SPACES

- Entry/Lobby
- Public Restrooms
- Staff Restrooms
- Break Rooms
- Library
- Large Conference Rooms
- Small Conference Rooms
- Team Collaborative Meeting Areas
- Small, Private Phone Rooms
- Supplies/Mail Room
- Storage Room
- Technology Services Space
- Copy/Coffee Areas
- Information Technology Space

Adjacency Matrix

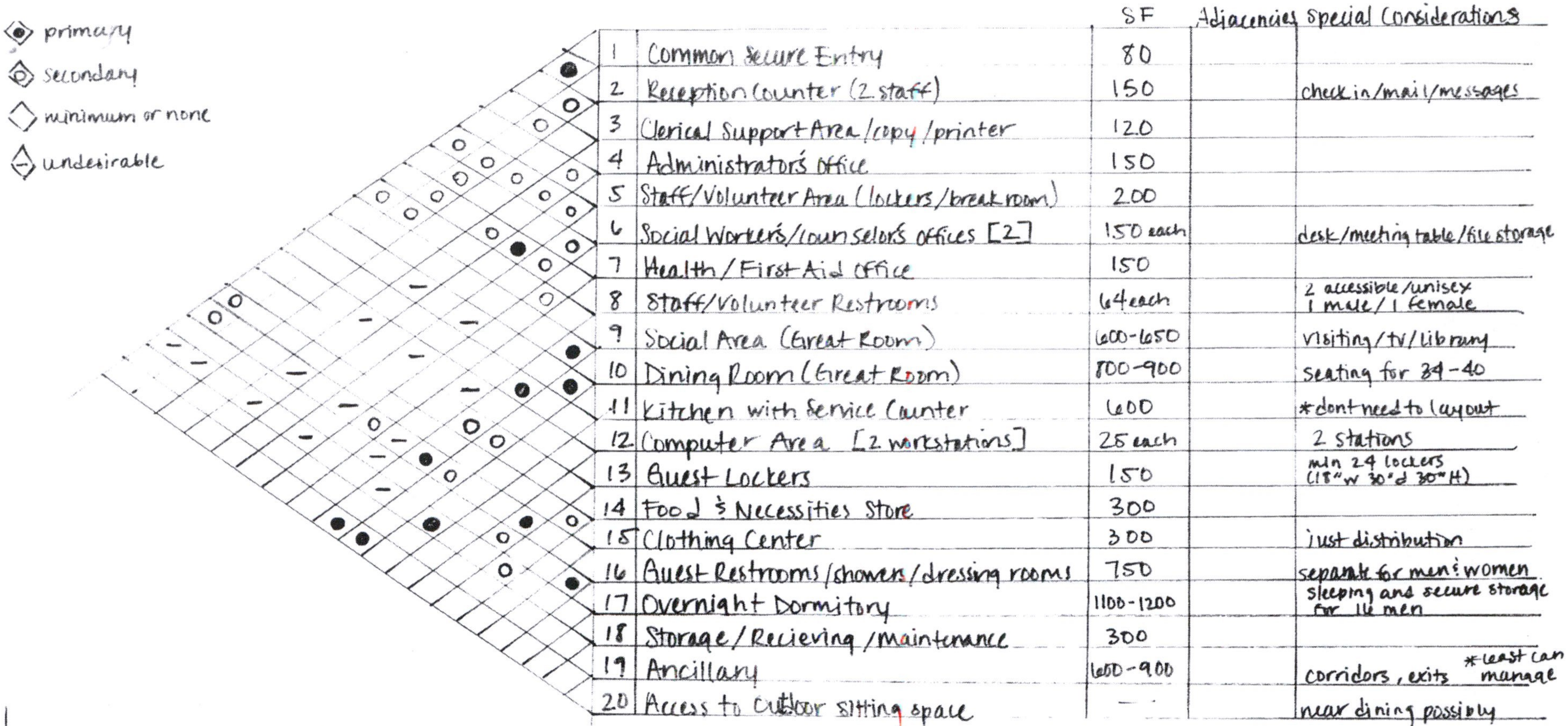

primary
secondary
minimum or none
undesirable
SF
Adjacencies
Special Considerations
1 Common Secure Entry 80
2 Reception Counter (2 staff) 150 check in/mail/messages
3 Clerical Support Area/copy/printer 120
4 Administrator's office 150
5 Staff/Volunteer Area (lockers/break room) 200
6 Social Workers/counselor's offices [2] 150 each desk/meeting table/file storage
7 Health/First Aid office 150
8 Staff/Volunteer Restrooms 64 each 2 accessible/unisex 1 male/1 female
9 Social Area (Great Room) 600-650 visiting/tv/library
10 Dining Room (Great Room) 800-900 seating for 34-40
11 Kitchen with Service Counter 600 *dont need to layout
12 Computer Area [2 workstations] 25 each 2 stations
13 Guest Lockers 150 min 24 lockers (18"w 30"d 30"H)
14 Food & Necessities Store 300
15 Clothing Center 300 just distribution
16 Guest Restrooms/showers/dressing rooms 750 separate for men & women
17 Overnight Dormitory 1100-1200 sleeping and secure storage for 16 men
18 Storage/Recieving/maintenance 300
19 Ancillary 600-900 corridors, exits *least can manage
20 Access to Outdoor sitting space near dining possibly

Expanded adjacency matrix

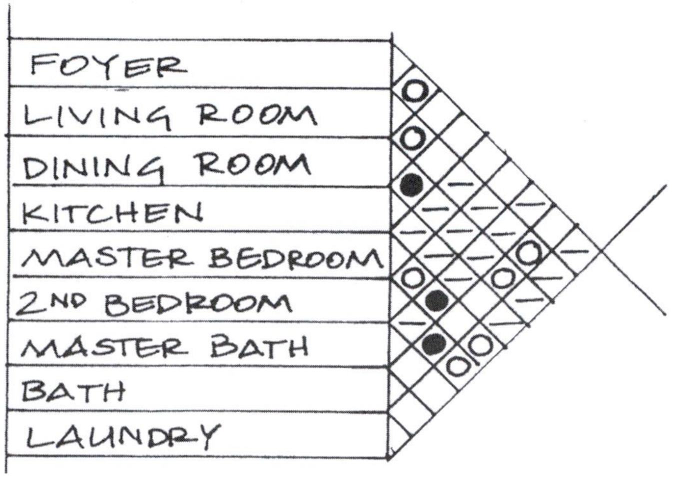

FOYER
LIVING ROOM
DINING ROOM
KITCHEN
MASTER BEDROOM
2ND BEDROOM
MASTER BATH
BATH
LAUNDRY

Adjacency matrix for a simple house

Adjacency matrix diagrams are handy references, as they present many spatial relationships at a glance. A basic matrix diagram normally addresses just the desired degree of adjacency between project spaces. Note, however, how additional information, such as square footages and other programmatic information, can be added for an even larger comprehensive view of requirements at a glance, as in the expanded matrix diagram on this page. Information you may choose to add includes the principal function of the space; the population using the space; the furnishings and equipment in the space; environmental concerns, such as strict climate controls; growth projections; and so on.

Adjacencies: The Bubble Diagram

Another type of diagram widely used for showing adjacency relationships is the bubble diagram. The **bubble diagram** can be very informative and graphically exciting when executed well. These diagrams are often done independent of the context (the project site and footprint) to show simply the adjacency relationships between spaces. Bubbles or circles are drawn and connected with arrows showing the desired degree of adjacency. These diagrams can also be very useful tools for visualizing key relationships graphically. One potential problem with bubble diagrams, when drawn independent of the project's context, is that they have the tendency to suggest layouts. Is that not part of the purpose? one may ask. The problem is that it is easy to forget that these are abstract representations of relationships between spaces and not literal depictions of arrangements. A particular adjacency bubble diagram may do a very good job of showing spatial relationships and a poor job of showing spatial arrangements. Another potential problem with adjacency bubble diagrams is that they can be just plain confusing, as is the case with the diagram for office 1, on this page.

Let's illustrate the first problem with a classic example. Most projects have high-demand spaces that need to be accessed by many people from different departments or units, such as a residential kitchen or a particular conference room in an office facility. Very often, these high-demand spaces are placed at or near the center of the diagram, with other spaces surrounding them and indicating the need to be adjacent, as in the diagram for a central conference room. What happens next is logical, but rarely optimal. Many students will insist on placing that kitchen (or conference room, mailroom, and so on) smack in the literal center of the project. Why? Well, the diagram indicated so. One important thing to remember is this: it is possible to be centrally located without being right in the middle of space. It is also possible to show high-demand spaces in places other than the center of a diagram.

A recommendation is to do adjacency bubble diagrams overlaid on the project footprint. That way, the locations shown for the various spaces can actually represent good potential locations for them. In these cases, there will be a real front and a real back, plus the shape of the footprint will give the diagram a dose of reality, thus producing a useful response. The diagram for a square-shaped footprint, for instance, will be very different from one for a long, narrow footprint. Refer to the diagrams for the Transition shelter project and Office 2 project on the following page. The out-of-context diagrams are shown on the left. On the right, the in-context bubble diagrams take the same information and place it inside the building.

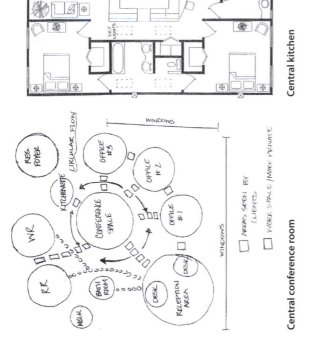

Central kitchen

Central conference room

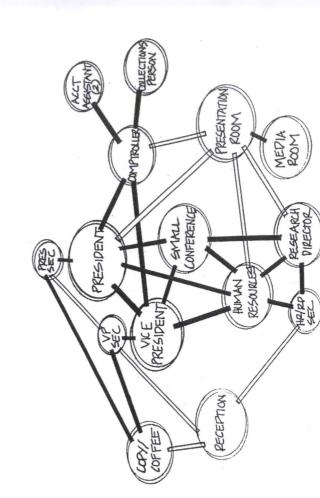

Office 1: Bubble diagram

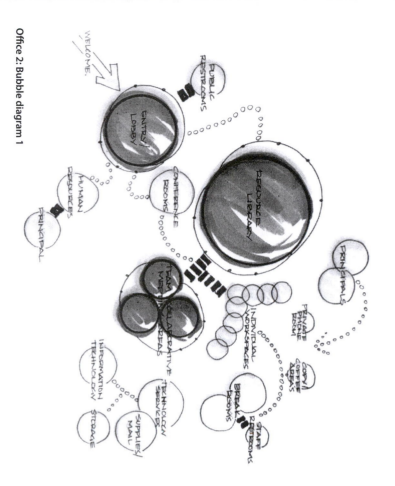

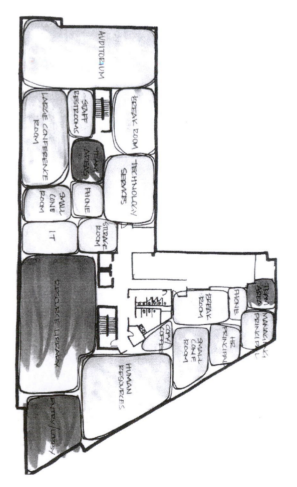

Office 2: Bubble diagram 1

Office 2: Bubble diagram 2

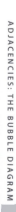

Diagram Graphics

Take pride in your diagram graphics. Pay attention to the quality of the shapes you draw. Use shading and texture. Take the proper time to draw good arrows and circulation lines. Give your graphics character. Here are some examples.

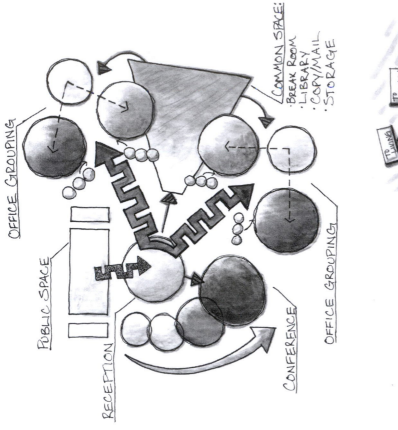

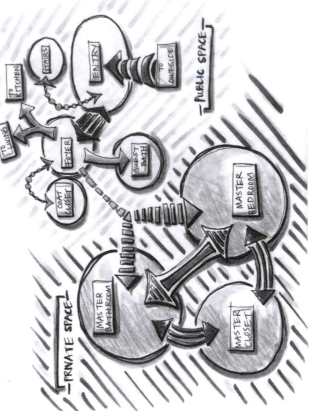

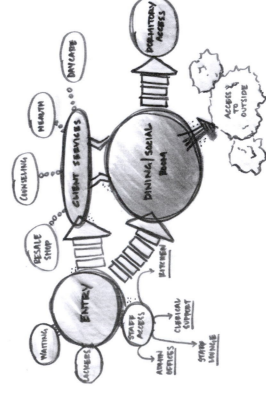

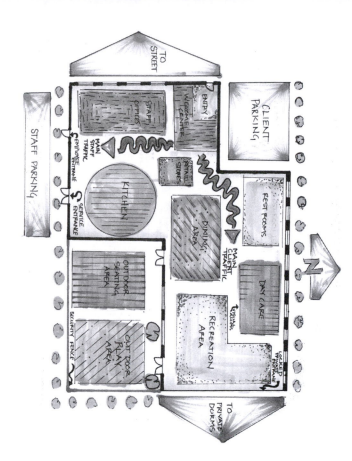

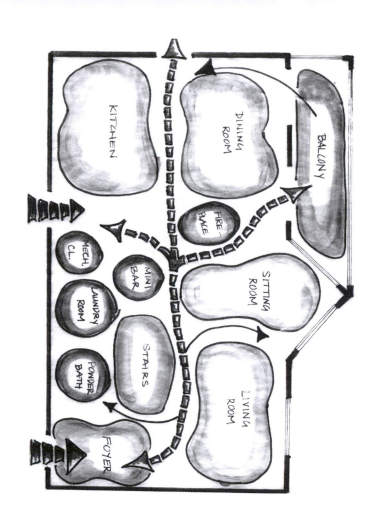

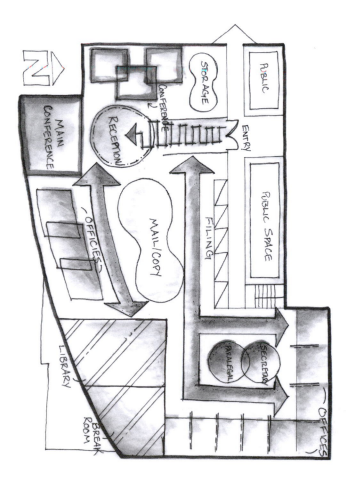

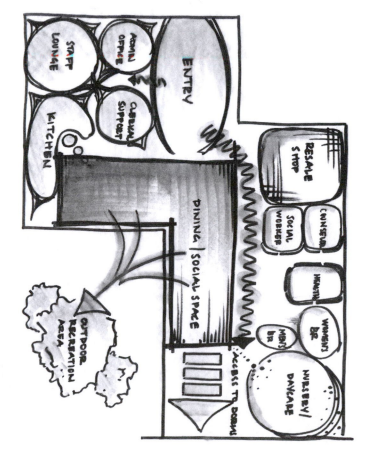

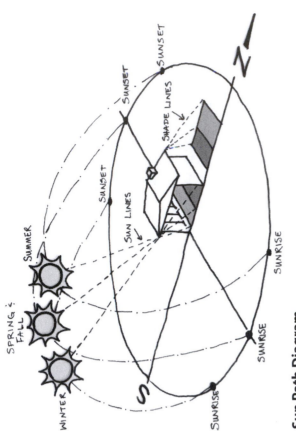

Sun Path Diagram

Contextual Factors: The Site

Even when working on interior projects, it is important to analyze contextual factors related to the site (the building and its surroundings). The sun path, winds, traffic patterns, views, and noise issues are among the variables to analyze and consider. Building exposure related to the path of the sun is a particularly significant factor to take into account, as it will inform where to place certain spaces and functions. Who will get the morning sun? Who needs soft, diffused natural light? Let's take a moment to understand where the sun is at various times of the day and the year.

In the Northern Hemisphere, the sun rises roughly in the east and sets roughly in the west. At twelve noon, the sun reaches its highest altitude and is approximately halfway between the sunrise and sunset points. The sun path, however, is not straight; it leans toward the south. In other words, at twelve noon, the sun is not perfectly straight above but rather a little toward the south, as in the sun path diagram at top. During the summer, the sun leans a little toward the south as it makes its trajectory from east to west. During the winter, it leans even more, and its maximum altitude is less. The sun-altitude diagram shows the angle of the sun in relation to a house. The angle is lower in the early morning and late afternoon and gets higher the closer it moves toward the noon hour. Once again, the angle is steeper in summer than in winter. The angles during fall and spring are between the two extremes.

Whereas buildings for interior projects are usually existing and will have a given orientation in relation to the sun path, the task of deciding where to put rooms and other spaces for an interior project will fall on the project's designer. It is up to you, then, to decide what to put in the east (early morning sun), what to put in the south (afternoon sun), what to put in the west (late afternoon sun), and what to put in the north (no direct sun). Getting exposure to the sun can be desirable or undesirable and varies from case to case. In some cases, you may get the warmth and light you want, and in others you may get unwanted heat and glare. Generally, if the building has good perimeter shading (such as overhangs and blinds), glare and excessive heat gain can be controlled and should not be big problems.

Study the diagrams on these pages to get an understanding of how the sun travels. Think about your own experience and how you might remember the sun penetrating buildings you have occupied in good and not-so-good ways. Spend some time looking at the domestic-orientations diagram. It shows potential locations for house functions in relation to the sun for the Northern Hemisphere. These are just suggestions; think about them critically. Is it really best to have the dining room toward the east, so that it gets morning light? What about dinnertime and potential sunsets? How might these placements be different for a project in a hot climate? Would northern orientation, away from the sun path, become more desirable in such a locale?

Sun Altitude

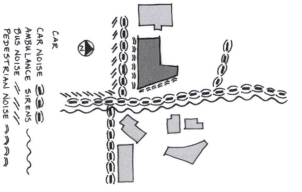

Domestic Orientations

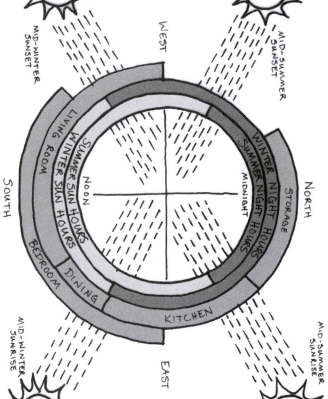

The site analysis diagrams on this page were done by a student for an office project. Students observed and recorded traffic patterns (vehicular and pedestrian), noise criteria, the sun path, and views. These resulted in the four simple but informative diagrams shown. You will find locations of bus routes for projects in which users commute by bus. Note the information about noise. Although there are mostly the ordinary sounds of cars and buses, in this case there are also ambulance sirens, as the building is around the corner from the emergency room entrance of a major hospital. This would most likely affect the placement of rooms needing quiet. The sun path and focus/views diagrams will also inform decisions about the placement of interior spaces and functions.

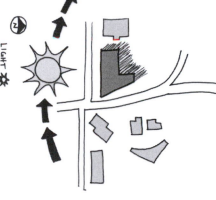

LIGHT
SHADOW

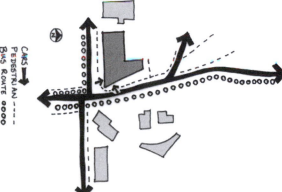

CARS
PEDESTRIAN ----
BUS ROUTE oooo

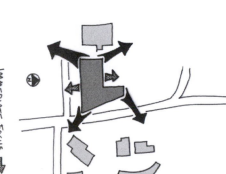

IMMEDIATE FOCUS
MAJOR VIEW

CAR
CAR NOISE
AMBULANCE SIRENS
BUS NOISE
PEDESTRIAN NOISE

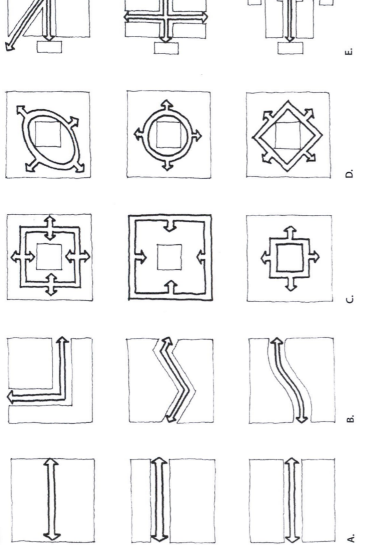

A.

B.

C.

D.

E.

F.

G.

Organization: Circulation

To do a full project of some size, it is useful to step back, move temporarily away from the functional details of all the spaces, and take a look at the project as a whole. One important design task you must ultimately achieve is to create an overall organization that is clear, cohesive, and logical. For that reason, it is a good idea to work back and forth between detailed requirements related to adjacencies, for instance, and the attempt to come up with a good overall project structure.

Interestingly, one of the most effective form shapers is a project's circulation system. For many projects, you will find that figuring out the circulation will determine the leftover space on either side and strongly suggest specific configurations. The plans on the next page show three quick studies of schemes based on circulation for an office project. The diagrams above show some basic circulation systems and how they help define space.

A. Linear (axial): these are often perfect when working with narrow footprints.

B. Inflected linear: a linear system can zigzag, undulate, and turn.

C. Loop: these work well with deep footprints

D. Loop variations: loops can be round, rotated, and even irregular.

E. Cross axial: these can be formal or informal and are suitable for many conditions.

F. Radial: these are dynamic but can be tricky to resolve.

G. Grid and organic: the formal grid and informal organic approaches can be useful for projects of various sizes and configurations.

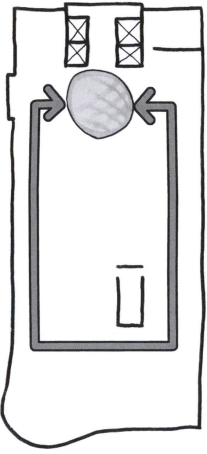

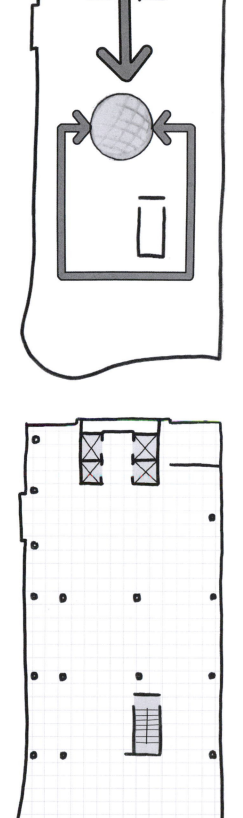

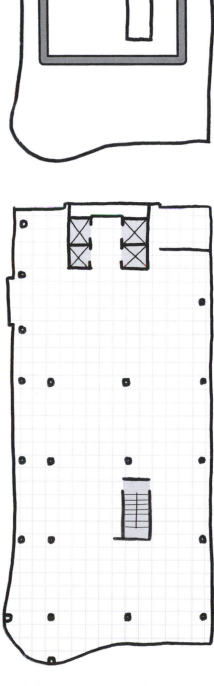

EXERCISE

On this page are three quick studies of the main circulation schemes for an office project on a relatively shallow footprint. These show the location of the main reception area (circle), the main path, and, in some cases, how the spaces feed from the main path. In the two blank spaces provided, create two more potential schemes. Feel free to refer to the diagrams on the preceding page for ideas. Could the reception area be located elsewhere? Does the path have to be straight? Could cross-axial or radial schemes work? You decide.

Organization: Solids and Voids

In addition to circulation, the handling of solids and voids (enclosed versus open spaces) plays a major role in determining the basic organization of a project. The three diagrammatic plans on this page offer alternative plan arrangement studies for an office project. Enclosed spaces are grouped and combined in masses of solids, shown shaded. The goal is to make these good shapes and also to make the leftover open spaces cohesive, well proportioned, and efficient.

Project Schemes

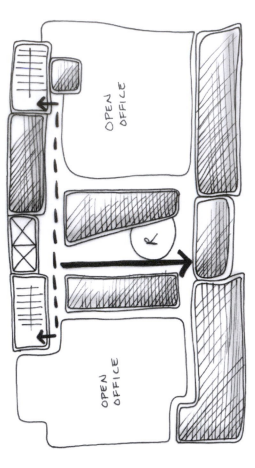

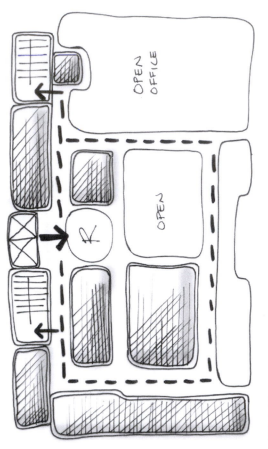

Scheme 2
Upon arrival a direct axial path leads to the reception area down the corridor, all the way in front of the main conference room. Enclosed rooms are grouped in narrow bands along each side of the main corridor and flanking the main conference room. Two large open areas are produced, one on either side.

Scheme 3
The reception area faces the elevators immediately upon arrival. Solids occur on either side of the reception area and along one of the narrow sides of the building, leaving the other side of the building mostly open.

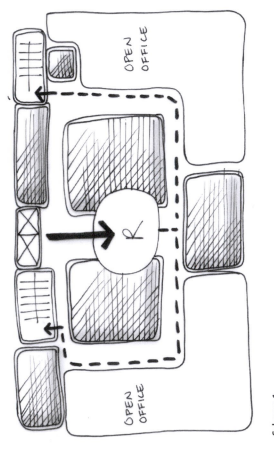

Scheme 1
Upon arrival a direct axial path leads to the reception area halfway into the space. The axial path continues straight ahead, leading to the main conference room. Solids are grouped as a mass at the center, resulting in major, L-shaped open areas on either side.

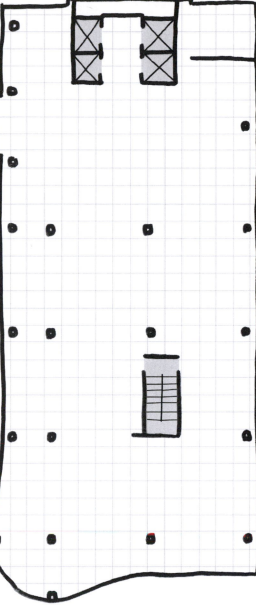
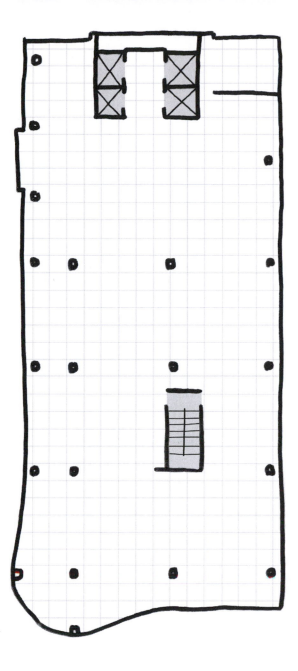

EXERCISE

Draw two different schemes showing circulation, the reception area, the main conference room, and enclosed areas (solids) amounting to roughly half of the space. Make sure the remaining open area or areas are good and substantial and have useable configurations. The floating mass is a fire egress stair. The second egress stairway is in the adjacent building, past the elevators. Use the examples on the previous page as points of reference. You may develop one of those schemes or come up with new ones. Describe in writing what your intentions are, similar to the short descriptions for schemes 1–3 on the previous page.

From Bubbles to Plan: A Transitional Home

The following six pages show examples of three projects from basic idea to developed plan. The narrative takes you through the intentions and tasks the designer was thinking about at the various stages. Analyze each example carefully.

Background: This is a facility to help former homeless persons transition into happy, productive lives through job training and a semi-independent lifestyle. In addition to the administrative offices, the facility includes dormitories (not part of the design project), a library, a day-care area, a computer area, a food store, and a clothing store, as well as living and dining areas.

Idea: Create a strong separation between the administrative areas near the entrance and the living/social areas farther into the space. Place areas needing supervision close to administration. Group enclosed spaces, such as the two stores and the kitchen, and move them to a corner, but within easy reach. Place the dining and living areas next to the adjacent garden. Strive for a very open feel in the living and dining areas, but arrange furniture such that it creates subgroups.

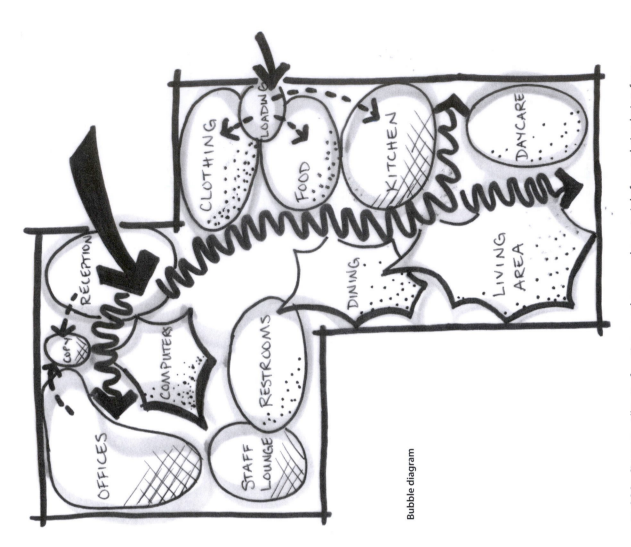

Bubble diagram

Bubble diagram: Allocate functions, and ensure clear, straightforward circulation from the entrance to administrative areas to living areas. Place stores close to the loading dock.

Block plan

Loose plan

Developed plan

Block plan: Draw areas more precisely and to scale. Explore how to create a sense of separation between administration and living areas by the configuration of the restrooms. Allocate precise areas to the living and dining functions, and double-check that access to the dormitories flows well.

Loose plan: Start articulating form to soften corners, and so on. Start placing furniture and studying possible arrangements.

Developed plan: Draw the full scheme, with developed furniture. Show furniture everywhere, and ensure there is a good sense of both subgrouping and flow.

Next steps: Check against program requirements to ensure everything is accounted for. Check the plan against code, and modify arrangements and elements as necessary to be in compliance.

From Bubbles to Plan: A Restaurant

Background: This is a full-service restaurant featuring a bar/lounge area, a main public dining area, and private dining areas.

Idea: Place the kitchen by the service alley. Try to create a connected but autonomous bar/lounge area. Place the main dining area in the heart of the space, and subdivide with furniture and soft dividers into various pockets.

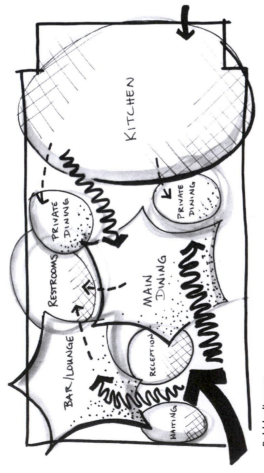

Bubble diagram

Bubble diagram: Make sure to leave adequate space for the full-service kitchen. Explore possible configurations that have the main dining in the center of the space. Study relationship between the entrance bar/lounge and dining spaces. Ensure the restrooms are within easy reach but out of the way.

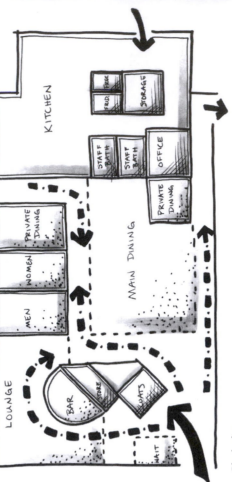

Block plan

Block plan: Refine shapes, and draw more accurately. Start exploring potential angular arrangements at bar area. Start allocating space within the kitchen area. Take a very close look at patron and service staff circulation routes. Get a feel for the size and overall configuration of the main dining space.

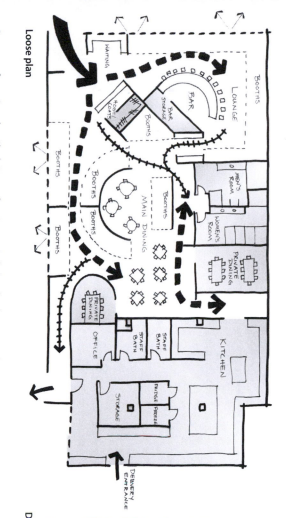

Loose plan

Loose plan: Get detailed. Draw furniture. Subdivide the main dining room into pockets. Ensure that the private dining rooms work adequately. Restudy the circulation patterns for good flows and safe egress.

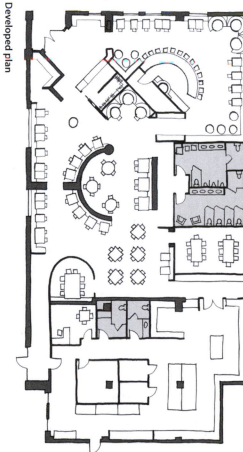

Developed plan

Developed plan: Draw carefully for the first major presentation. Space furniture carefully. Make sure there are no spaces that are either too tight or too spacious.

Next steps: Check against program requirements to ensure everything is accounted for. Check the plan against code, and modify arrangements and elements as necessary to be in compliance. See if access points to and from the kitchen can be improved.

From Bubbles to Plan: An Office

Background: This is an office facility for a business consulting firm. The work style is highly collaborative, requiring many informal and a few formal meeting spaces. There are only three private offices, so it is mostly an open-plan environment. Many of the employees travel a lot, so they utilize hoteling practices, and some of the spaces in the office are available by reservation.

Idea: Create a strong and inviting arrival hub by the elevators, with the formal meeting rooms right behind. Divide the rest of the rectangular floor into roughly four quadrants, defined by the core elements and the few enclosed rooms (offices and conference rooms) in the space. Within the open areas, use the workstation arrangement to further define subareas. Try to make workers feel as if they have the corner office. Strive for an organic feel.

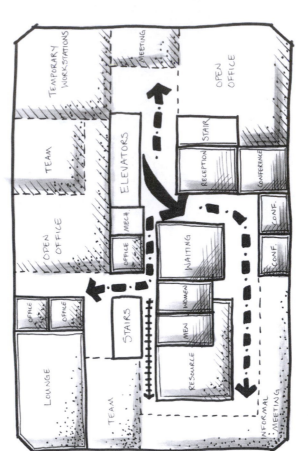

Block plan

Block plan: Draw areas more accurately, as a block/circulation plan. Ensure the dimensions of enclosed and open spaces will work and accommodate furniture effectively.

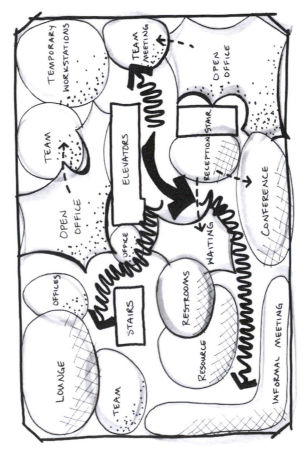

Bubble diagram

Bubble diagram: Define the terminal areas at the ends of circulation (conference rooms, corner lounge, and corner informal meeting area). Allocate all spaces (as bubbles), and try to see how everything might fit.

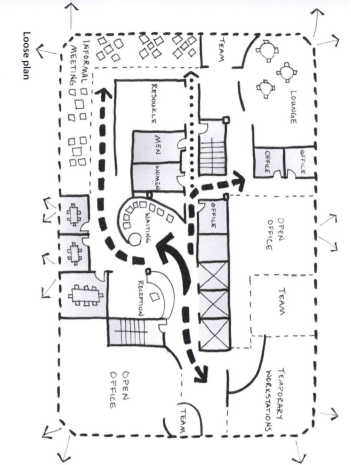

Loose plan

Loose plan: Get even more detailed. Start exploring how to inflect certain areas for a more organic feel. Check allocation of spaces against best views.

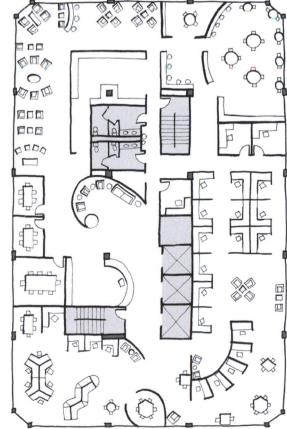

Developed plan

Developed plan: Draw furniture and push-pull spaces as needed to give them their optimal size. Spend time developing key areas, such as the reception area and the temporary "hoteling" corner. Give the permanent workers who asked for a bit more privacy a sense of enclosure while maintaining some openness.

Next steps: Check against program requirements to ensure everything is accounted for. Check the plan against code, and modify arrangements and elements as necessary to be in compliance.

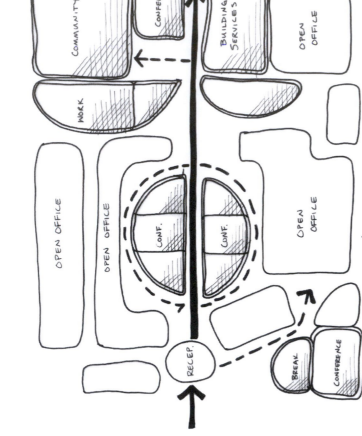

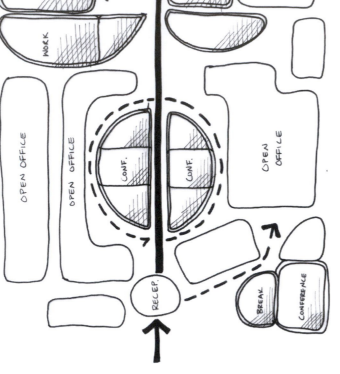

Block/Circulation Plan

This scheme accounts for all the areas in a general way. You can see some detail. The rooms at the center are conference rooms and offices. Other small meeting rooms plus the main gathering (community) room are toward the back. Open office space surrounds the floating central circular shape. The bubbles indicating open space areas roughly correspond to the groupings of the workstations.

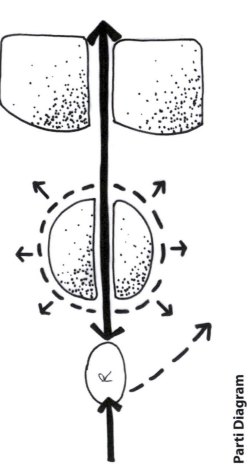

Parti Diagram

The essence of this scheme results from the decisions to have a strong axial path from front to back and to divide the bulk of the solids into a bold, round element floating at the center and a cluster of other rooms along the back.

Essence of a Scheme I

Most good schemes have a logical and straightforward organizational structure. One can follow the logic of the circulation scheme and how the handling of enclosed spaces produces a coherent distribution of space. It often starts with the diagramming early on. Sometimes, there is a back-and-forth process between the floor-plan generation

and in-progress diagrams to help understand the clarity of what is being designed, or lack of it. These pages and the next show examples of floor plans and diagrams for an office project. Two diagrams are shown for each scheme: a parti diagram showing the essence of the scheme and a block/circulation plan showing the scheme in more detail.

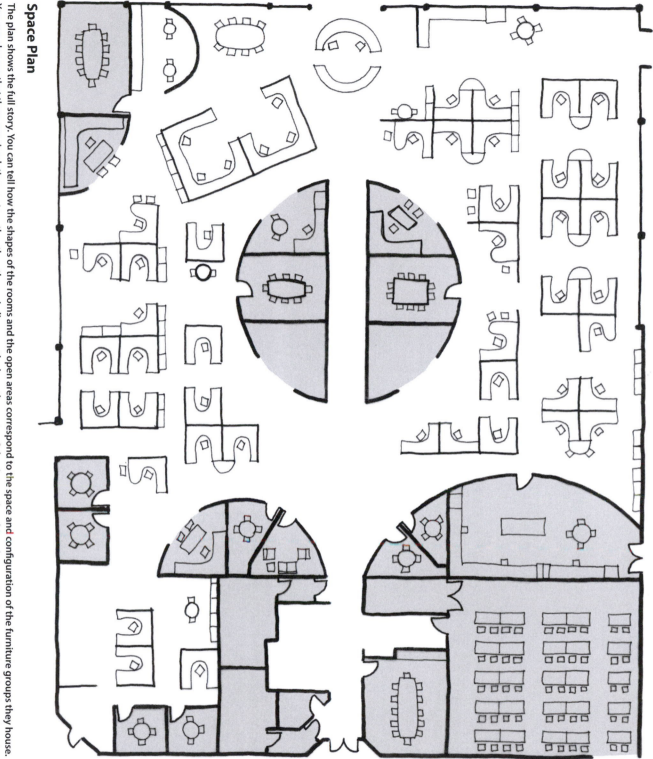

Space Plan

The plan shows the full story. You can tell how the shapes of the rooms and the open areas correspond to the space and configuration of the furniture groups they house. You can also see that there are circulation routes other than the main linear path along the center. Other interesting things happen in places at the local level, such as the rotation of a furniture group near the entrance and the use of semicircular shapes in some places. Compare the three drawings now, and try to see how they correspond.

Essence of a Scheme II

The block/circulation and parti diagrams show a clear organizational structure based on strong geometry and the strategic location of the main public destination in relation to the main circulation. The reception area faces the elevators and is immediately seen upon arrival. A rotated central mass defines the bilateral main circulation, which is at a 45° angle in each direction. The room at the point is one of the main meeting rooms. Behind it is the main open area, with open workstations. The other main conference area is at the terminal point of the main circulation route, the one leading toward the principal side of the building (with the best orientation and views). Other private offices are also placed along the main side of the building, freeing up most of the remaining area for comfortable and connected, open office space.

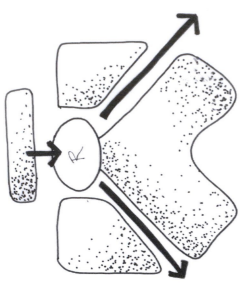

Parti diagram

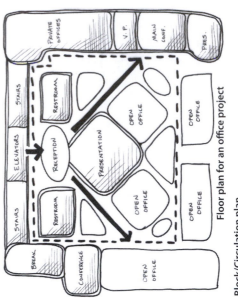

Floor plan for an office project

Block/Circulation plan

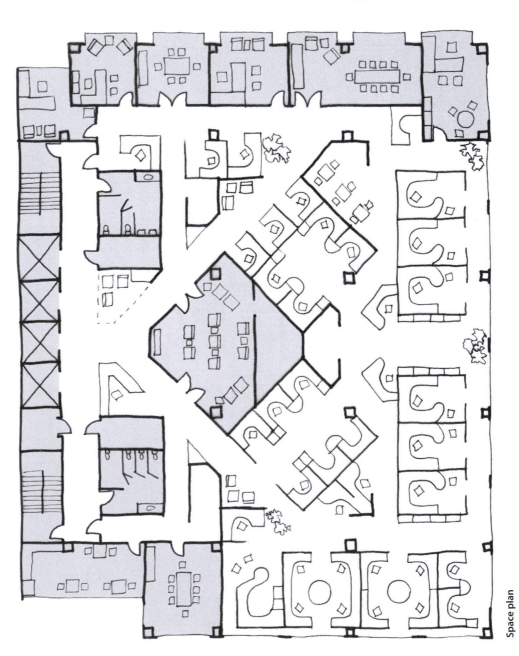

Space plan

The organizational structure of this scheme also features the reception area immediately in front of the elevators. To visit the conference rooms, one travels through a T-shaped corridor originating behind the reception area. The main conference room, once again, is placed at the culmination of one end of the T, along the front windows of the space. The rest of the solids also occur along the main side of the building but also surround the reception area, helping define the T-shaped formal circulation path. An L-shaped open area is produced toward the back of the space and the secondary side of the building.

Space plan

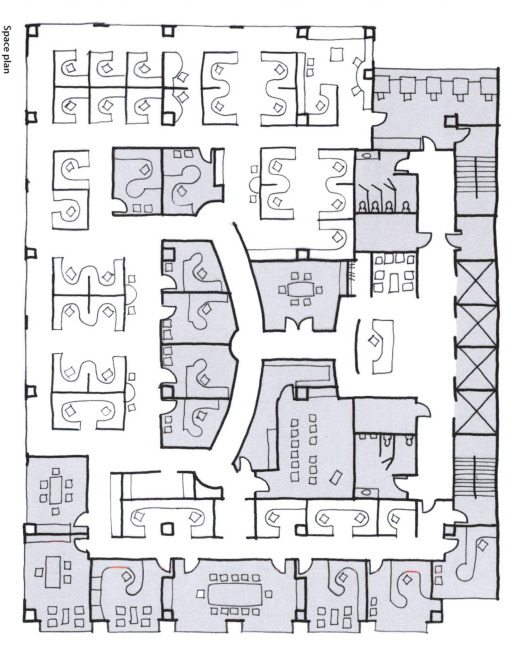

Parti diagram

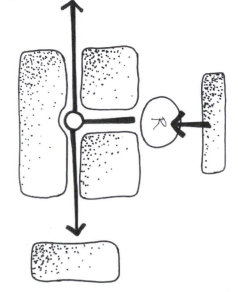

Block/Circulation plan

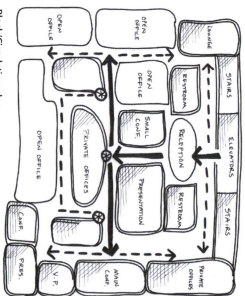

Generating Alternatives

Always develop several possible design solutions before settling on one. On pages 88–93 we looked at the early design development of a transitional home, a restaurant, and an office. We saw how the original ideas were developed, moving from a bubble diagram (within the space), to a block/circulation diagram representing the scheme, to a loose plan, to a refined plan. Students working on those projects were asked to come up with three ideas before selecting a final one to develop. Practitioners usually do the same. There is no magic number. It can be two if you are pressed for time or if the site does not allow many options; it can also be five if there are many possible approaches. However, you always want to explore more than one solution. How far you take them also varies. It's not unusual to develop approximately three at the bubble-plan stage, select two to study a little further (up to either the block-plan or the loose-plan stage), and then commit to one.

The floor plan on this page shows the scheme selected from various possibilities for an office project. Four different schemes were explored. These are shown on the next page. Each scheme was given a name. You'll notice that there are several variables at play in these—mainly the circulation scheme, the allocation of spaces, the particular geometries, and the implications of the handling of solids and voids.

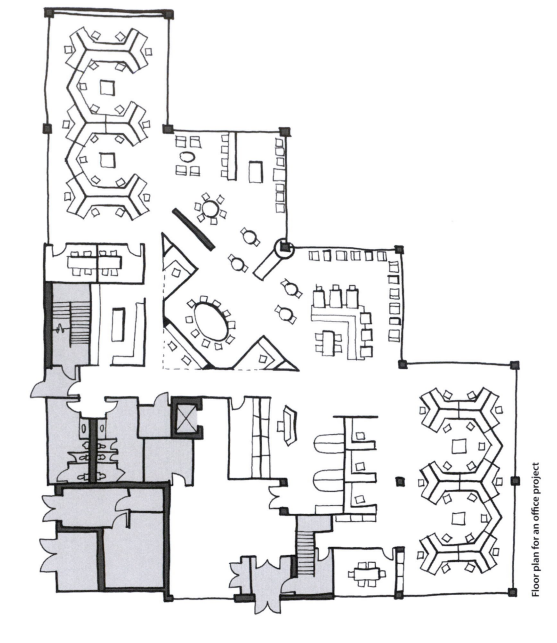

Floor plan for an office project

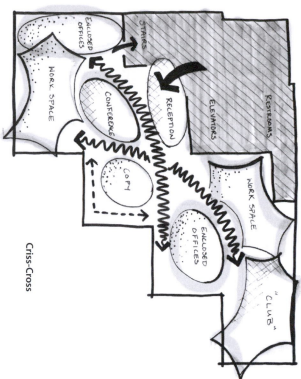

The Arrow explores a strong diagonal circulation spine. The character of the linear circulation gave the scheme its name. Open work areas are at each end of the circulation spine. This was the chosen scheme.

Arrow

The Criss-cross explores a crossing circulation system and alternative locations for some of the functions.

Criss-Cross

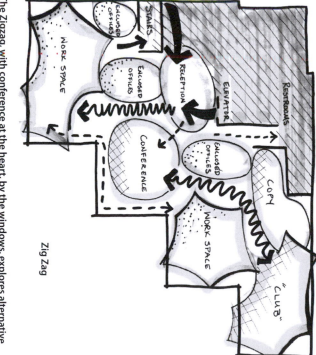

The Zigzag, with conference at the heart, by the windows, explores alternative locations for the conference room and the club.

Zig Zag

The Meanderer explores a somewhat meandering path. Like The Arrow, this scheme also places the two open work areas at the ends, with the supporting spaces in between.

Meanderer

The Patient Search

Interior planning requires a patient, ongoing search. Not only are multiple possibilities explored to test their merits, but also within each alternative there are seemingly endless variations. Furthermore, some tweaking is always needed to get an arrangement just right. As valuable as anything in the process of design are the many layers of tracing paper that never make it to presentation boards. These are the personal sketches, the false starts, the multiple nonsuccessful ideas that lead to the successful ones, the many roads explored but not taken.

My intention here is to remind you that the design process requires that kind of search. It is like that. There is nothing wrong if for every successful diagram or sketch, five end up in the trash can. You will never come up with the best solution on your first attempt. The search requires multiple iterations. There will always be refining, tweaking, improving, and problem solving that creates new problems. That is the nature of the search.

The examples shown here include diagrammatic explorations, multiple explorations at the loose-plan stage, and examples of overlay sketches for refining design solutions. Be assured that today, in this age of computer-produced drawings, the best editing is still done by hand, on trace paper over previous iterations. Avoid working on early design process on the computer; it's a stiff process that produces stiff solutions that for some reason you will want to hold onto. If you must work on the computer early in the design process, make a habit of plotting often and editing with red lines over the plot images.

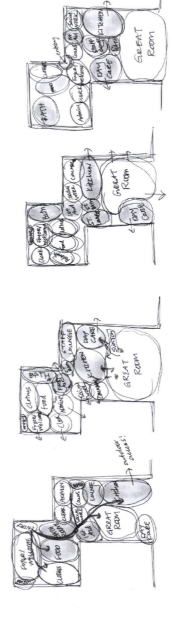

How many ways can you arrange approximately 15 bubbles for a transitional home project? Even if you rule out all the unrealistic or ridiculous possible combinations, there are probably at least ten really good schemes that would solve the problem well. Here are four early attempts by a student.

How many ways can you arrange a few pieces of furniture in a private office? Here is a collection of ideas tried by a student.

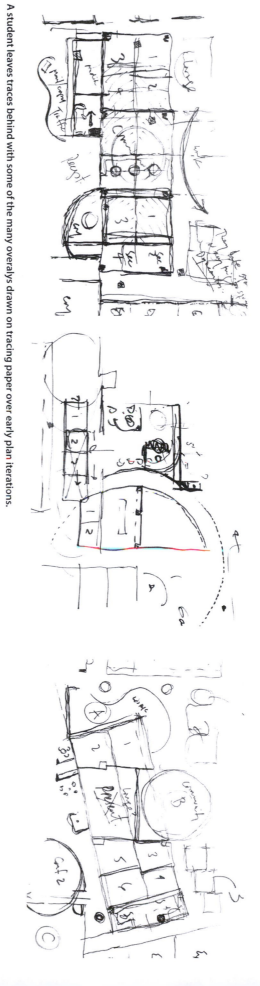

A student leaves traces behind with some of the many overalys drawn on tracing paper over early plan iterations.

A student explores several possible arrangements of domestic spaces and engages in a conversation with herself about problems and benefits.

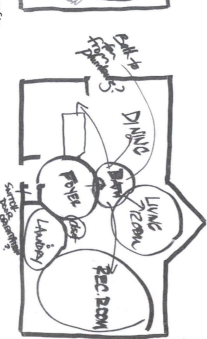

Search for Form I

Taming Form: The Search for Interest

As designers, we strive to create interesting spaces that stimulate and delight. One of the ways we can achieve this is through the use of dynamic shapes and/or dynamic compositions. These are not always easy to formulate and require a commitment to stick with the problem until you tame the form and arrive at a cohesive and balanced final arrangement. There is a burden but also a reward.

Here we see one student's search for interesting form for a small office project. At one point the student decided to explore circular and curvilinear forms for the design. Sketches 1, 2, and 3 show successive attempts to incorporate curvilinear forms into the plan. At first some of the ideas seemed erratic and disjointed, but by sketch 3, the student was onto something and we start noticing a greater sense of coherence in the scheme. Loose Plan Iteration 1 shows the further development of sketch 3. Here we begin to see that this scheme has merit and could work. The complex form has been tamed.

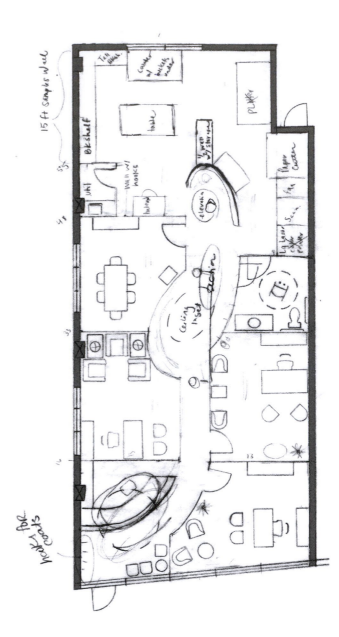

Loose Plan Iteration 1

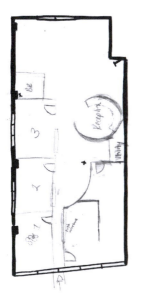

Sketch 1

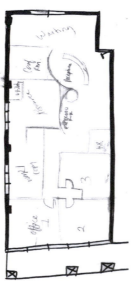

Sketch 2

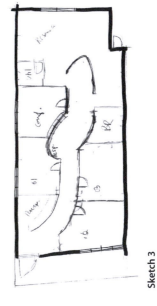

Sketch 3

In an effort to create interest, we often overdo it. We try really hard to introduce curves or angles and end up with schemes that seem to get out of hand. The scheme on this page is one such scheme. This well-intended student tried hard, but the multiple angles got out of hand and created too many twists and turns, which is uncomfortable both visually

and practically (as one walks down the corridor). Your job is to make it work, to tame the "out-of-control" angles. Work over the light plan and try to simplify. Keep using the angular scheme and see what you can come up with. Good luck!

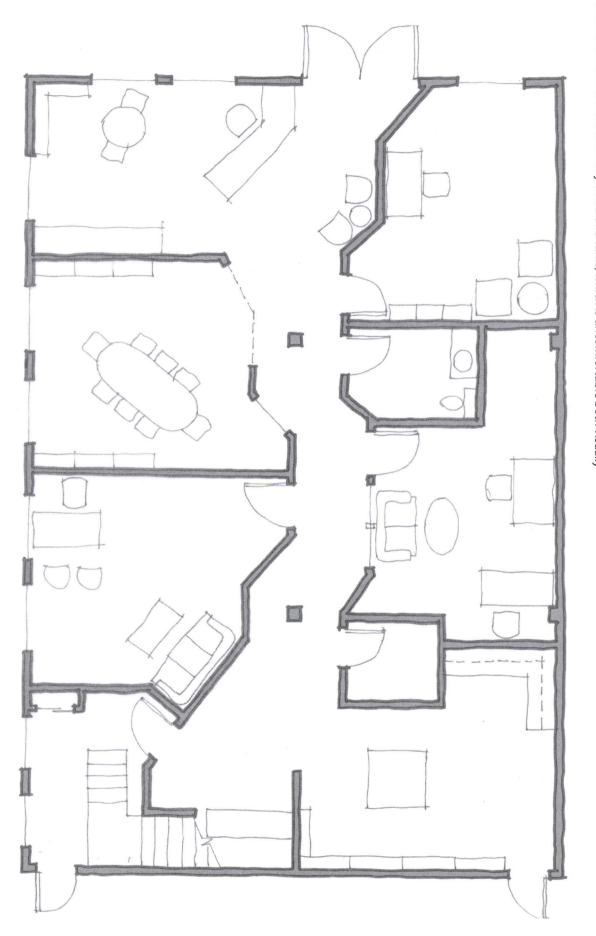

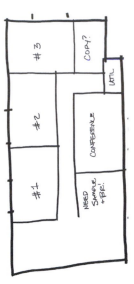
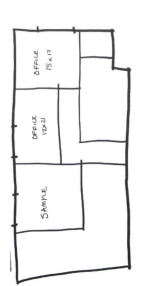
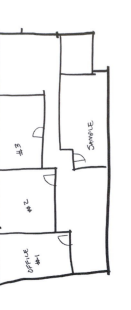

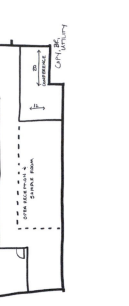
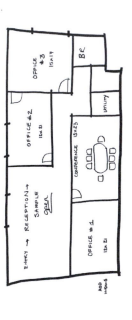
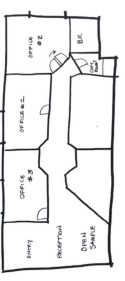
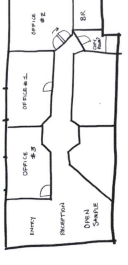
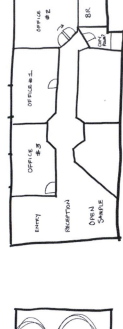

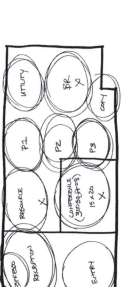
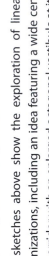

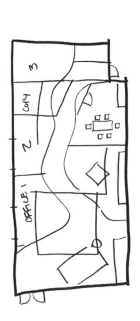

Exploring Offsets and Zigzags

These sketches start to explore offsets, and in the lower one, a zigzagging configuration with an open area in the back.

Exploring Linear Organizations

The sketches above show the exploration of linear organizations, including an idea featuring a wide central corridor with an enlarged octagonal vestibule at its core.

The Beginning

The sketches above show a couple of preliminary block plans and a bubble plan locating the various spaces in their suggested regions.

Search for Form II

These pages illustrate one student's search for form on a project for a design firm. Different configurations and geometries were explored loosely. Let's take a look. Notice how different approaches were explored initially through quick, loose plans.

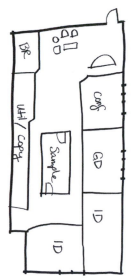

Something in the Middle

In these schemes, the designer explored the idea of floating a room near the center. In one case, the sample room was floated in the middle; in another case, the main conference room was the floating element. What do you think? Would these floating rooms in the center have a desirable effect, or are they crowding the middle?

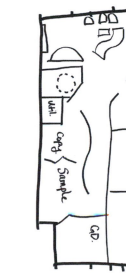

More floaters and Some Curves

The top scheme above continues the exploration of floating rooms at the center. On the lower scheme, however, the designer shifts gears and starts exploring the idea of a central open zone that features curvilinear forms, such as a free-floating partition that provides a soft separation between areas.

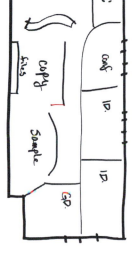

Hum! More Curves

The exploration of curvilinear forms continues on these last two schemes. Curved shapes are applied to various elements, such as the reception desk, floating partitions, and room walls. What do you think? If it were you, which of the many ideas would you pursue further?

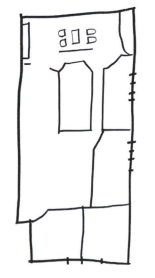

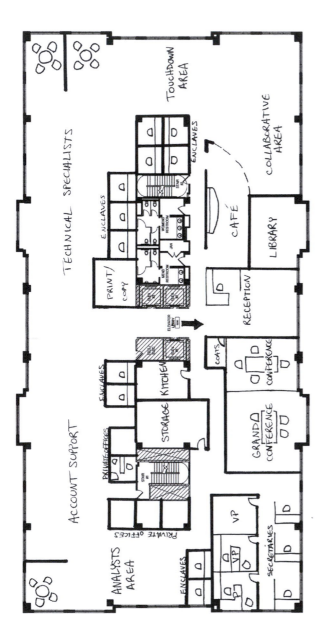

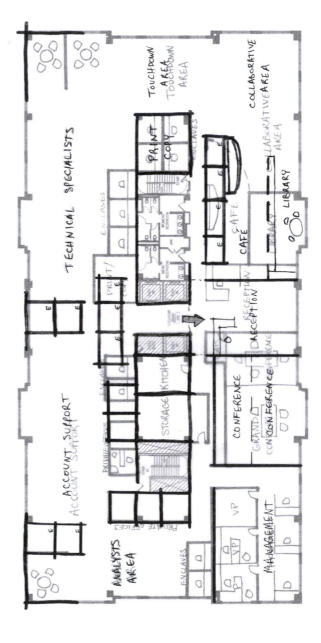

Scheme 1

For scheme 1, the designer modified the small offices in the account-support area, floated small enclave rooms, and used them to separate account support from the technical specialists. The print room was relocated, the conference room was shifted westward, and the library was opened up, and enclaves were used to separate the area from the corridor. These are all attempts to further resolve the plan.

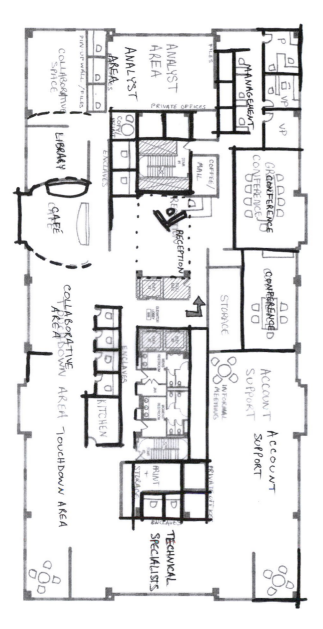

Edit Yourself

Space planning is a lot like writing. Your first attempt is seldom the best solution. Design requires not only the exploration of various possible approaches to take but also the refinement of a scheme once you commit to one. Here we look at two schemes from the same designer for an office project. In each case, the top plan shows an early plan where the designer was trying to solve the puzzle of finding the optimal place for every room and area. The lower plans show an overlay with some "edits" performed by the designer to try to improve the design. Note that when we try to improve a design, we do so at the functional level (e.g., moving a room closer to another room it needs to be close to) and also at the perceptual level. At this level, we try to clean things up, to order parts for a more cohesive and pleasant overall effect.

Scheme 2

Modifications explored for scheme 2 included achieving a greater sense of openness in the area assigned to the analysts, the library, and the café. What used to be solid walls became partially open screens. Spaces previously in front of the main conference room on the north side were moved around, resulting in a more open feel around the reception area.

Scheme 4

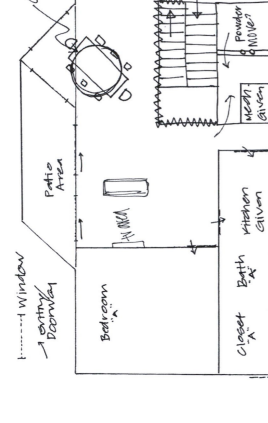

Circular Table

Formal Seat

Window

Entry Doorway

Patio Area

Bedroom

Closet "A"

Bath "A"

Kitchen Given

Mech Given

Powder Move?

Part-Area Seating can be pulled to floor area & transitioning Lowered inside

Scheme 5

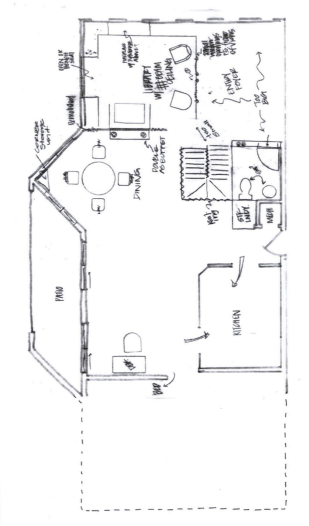

PATIO

KITCHEN

DINING

Double or Buffet

Corner Storage Unit

Remodeled

Open of Bench Seat

Mech Lndy

Mech

BBQ

Scheme 1

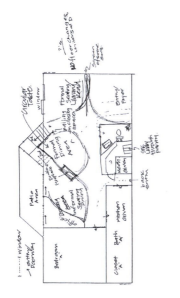

Circular Table

Window

Window

Formal Seating Area/Library Read

Formal Dining Area

Informal Seating

Patio Area

Window

Entry Doorway

Bedroom "A"

Closet "A"

Bath "A"

Kitchen Given

Mech

Entry Foyer

Scheme 2

Formal Seating Area/Library?

Entry Foyer

Screen W/arch or French Doors

TV Area and Casual Dining

Patio Area

Window

Entry Doorway

Bedroom "A"

Closet "A"

Bath "A"

Kitchen Given

Bath/Laundry

Mech Given

Scheme 3

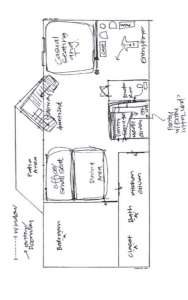

Casual Seating and TV

Coat

Entry/Sink

Office/Small Seat

Dining Area

Patio Area

Window

Entry Doorway

Bedroom

Closet "A"

Bath "A"

Kitchen Given

Powder Room

Mech Given

Pantry W/Entry W/Laund?

Social Spaces I

This spread illustrates the scheme explorations of one student for the social zones of a residence. The loose sketches on the left show five different approaches attempted by the student. One shows an angular scheme that places the stairs on the V-shaped protrusion on the top. The other three schemes feature straight (not angular) approaches with central or protruding stairs.

You can tell that resolving the stairs (size, configuration, approach, and location) was a crucial piece of the puzzle. The designer settled on a U-shaped stair with an intermediate landing below the dining table. By the time the designer got to the first CAD iteration, she had things pretty well figured out. You can see how she marked up the plan with changes to incorporate on the next iteration. The developed plan shows the entire space, fully worked out with the final furnishings and the final configurations.

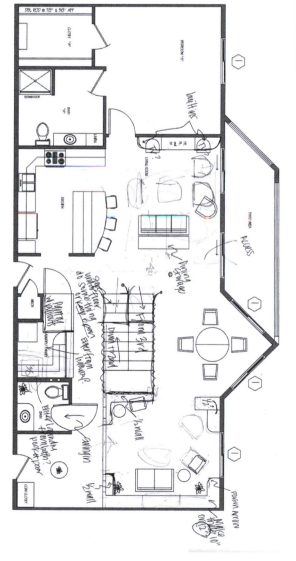

Refined CAD Iteration

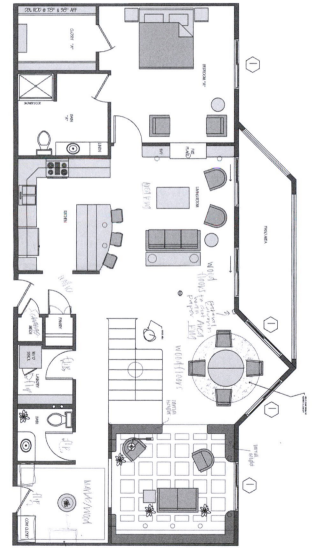

Social Spaces II

Here we see another student's approach to the previous project. The page with the notes and sketches shows a block diagram and two preliminary scheme explorations. Also displayed are some ideas for furnishings and built-ins drawn in elevation. Notice the early explorations with the dining on the left side and the stairs at the protruding V-shaped bay window.

Loose plan 1 starts to explore an alternate location for the stairs on the inside. Preliminary furniture arrangements are shown for the dining, seating, and den areas. The kitchen and the bathroom also start to take shape.

CAD iteration 1 on the next page turns the stairs, and all the furniture groupings are modified. Interestingly, the explorations continued to evolve and the designers changed the shape and approach to the stairs once again, moving the dining table to the sunny spot by the bay window and putting one of the seating areas where the dining table once was. Too many changes? Not really. It is often like this, with constant tweaks until things finally fall in place to your satisfaction (and that of the client).

Loose Plan 1

Notes and Sketches

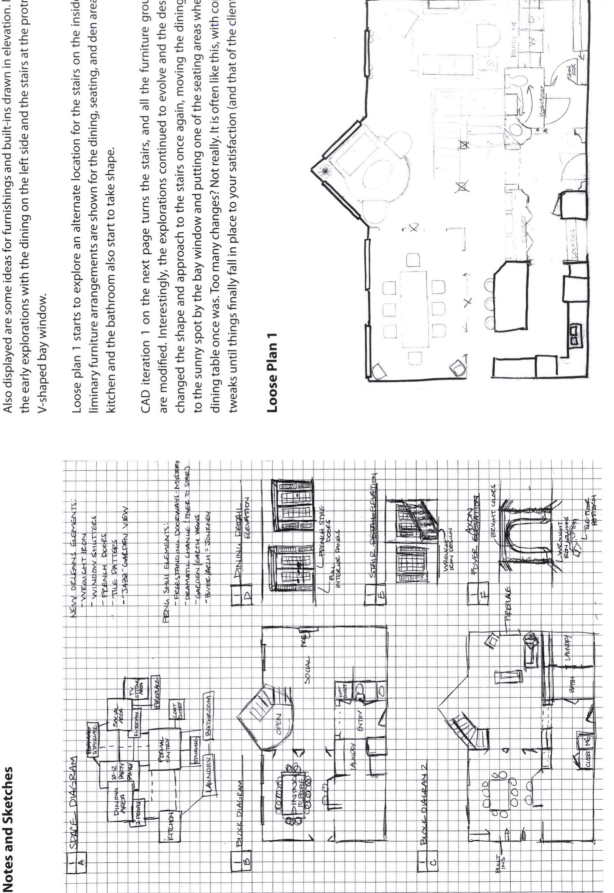

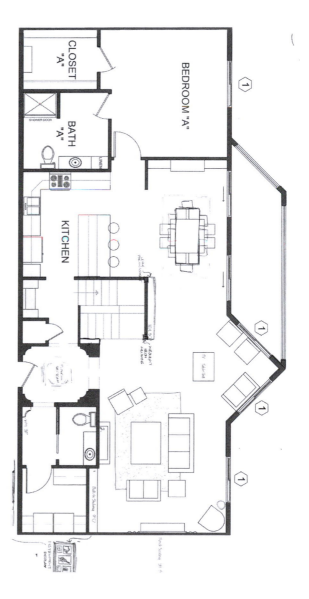

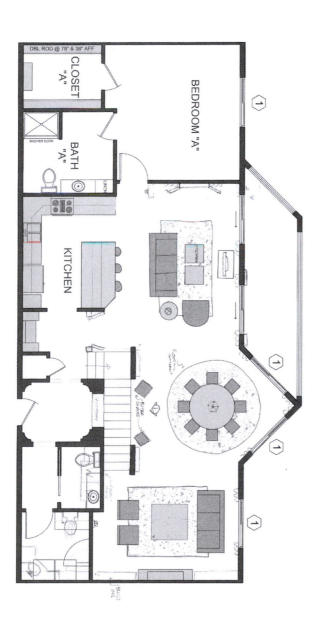

Practicing Bubble Diagramming and Block Planning

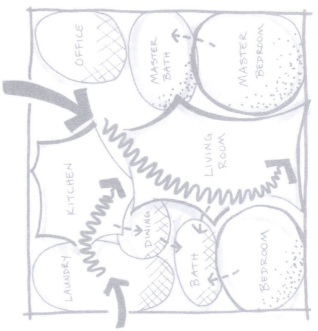

Block Plan

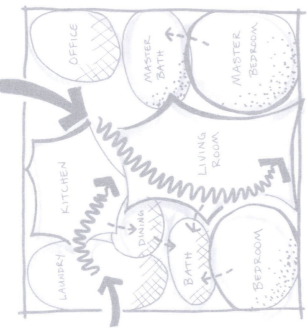

Loose plan

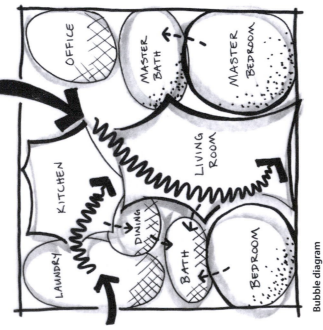

Bubble diagram

EXERCISE 1

Refer to the bubble diagram shown for an apartment on a square footprint. Develop the idea by taking the next two steps. Using the basic idea from the bubble diagram, draw a block plan on the top footprint provided at right and a loose plan on the lower footprint. Refer to the block and loose plans from this chapter. Feel free to refine and tweak as necessary to improve the scheme. Use the light footprints to develop your plan.

EXERCISE 2

Examine the loose plans shown for an office project. They are drawn lightly so that you can see the information and still draw over them. This time you are being asked to work backward. In one of the spaces, take a step back, and superimpose the block plan that might have come before the loose plan. In the other space, take still another step back, and superimpose the bubble diagram first conceived for this project. You will have to use your imagination; feel free to take some liberties. This will also give you a chance to practice your graphic skills. Make sure you produce two good-looking diagrams. Enjoy.

Practice

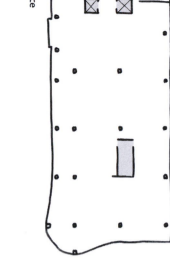

Draw block plan here

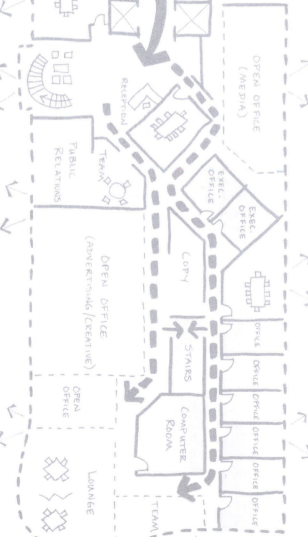

Draw bubble diagram here

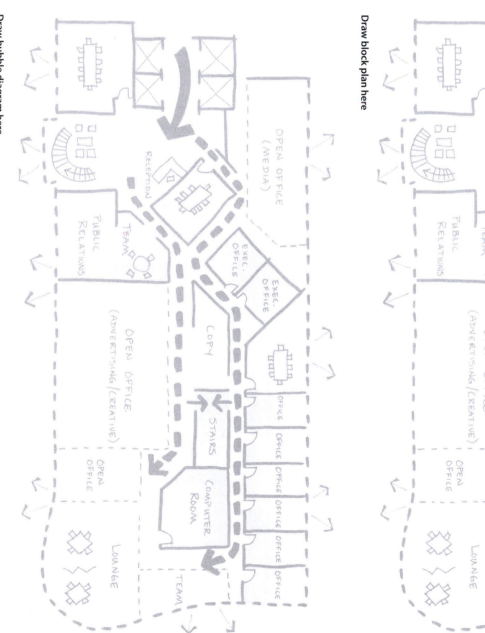

EXERCISE 3

Examine the adjacency bubble diagram shown for a condo. Translate the diagram into, first, a bubble diagram within the space, and second, a block diagram based on the bubble diagram. Use the spaces provided. A 4' × 4' (122 cm × 122 cm) grid is provided to help you keep the bubbles and blocks roughly to scale. Good luck.

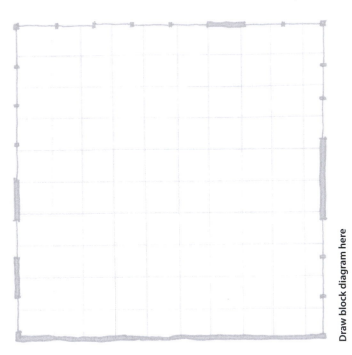

Draw bubble diagram here

Draw block diagram here

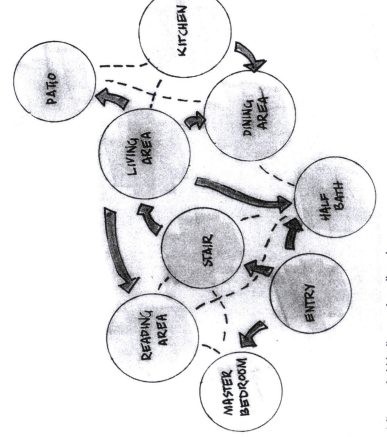

Adjacency bubble diagram: A small condo

Draw enhanced block plan I here

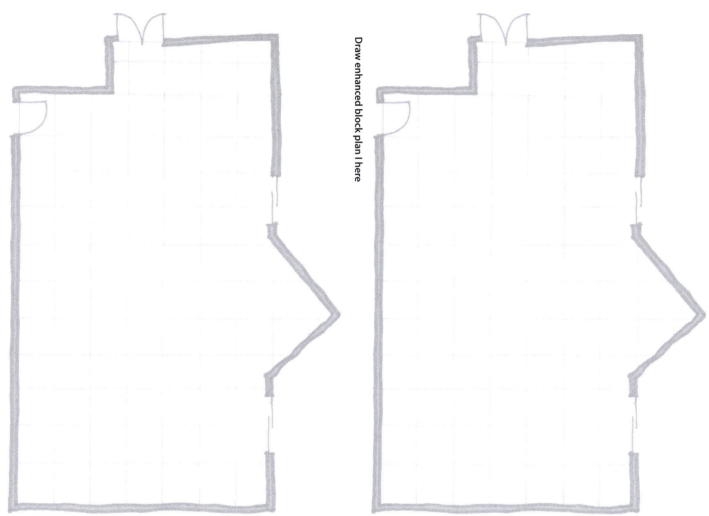

Draw enhanced block plan II here

EXERCISE 4

Refer to the two block plans shown for a residence. These reflect two different ideas. For this exercise, you will be producing enhanced block plans. If you look back at some of the block plans shown elsewhere in this chapter, you'll notice that they are more than just blocky shapes; they also indicate circulation and may even contain an asterisk or exclamation point at a crucial focal point. The block plans we are trying to promote are ones that show intentions and that have character. With that in mind, produce an enhanced version for each of these two block plans. Show circulation, and place a big asterisk at focal points, where something special might be created as the scheme is developed later. Also provide arrows pointing out toward good views (feel free to guess). As always, pay attention to the quality of your graphics. Enjoy.

Block plan II

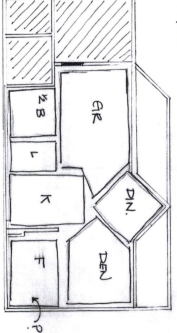

Block plan I

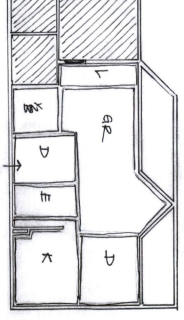

EXERCISE 5

Look at the adjacency bubble diagram shown for a small office. Develop two different bubble diagrams (in context) inside the actual space. Remember to include circulation arrows, as in the examples in this chapter. Try not to take the centrality of the conference room literally; remember that being centrally located does not mean something has to be exactly in the middle. Pay attention to your graphics. Use the 4′ × 4′ (122 cm × 122 cm) grid for scale reference. Have fun.

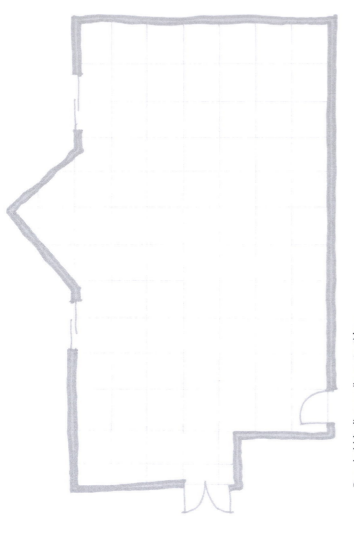

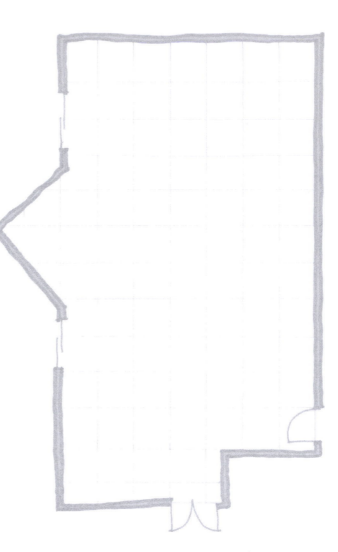

Draw bubble diagram (in context) here

Draw bubble diagram (in context) here

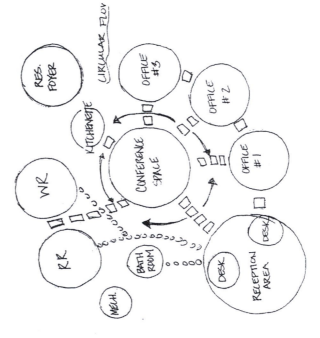

Adjacency bubble diagram: Office

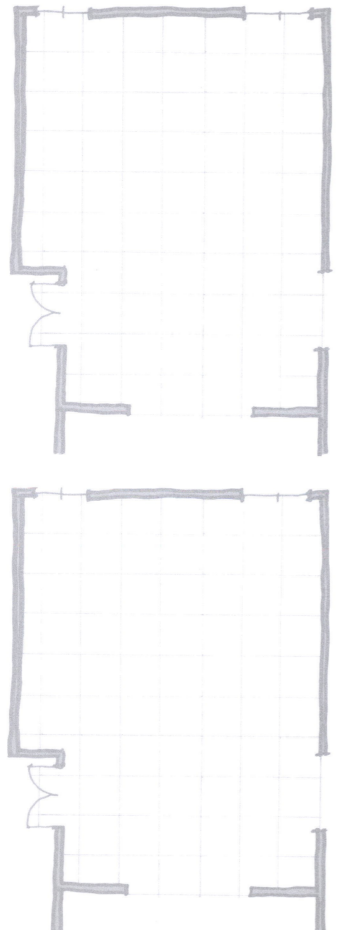

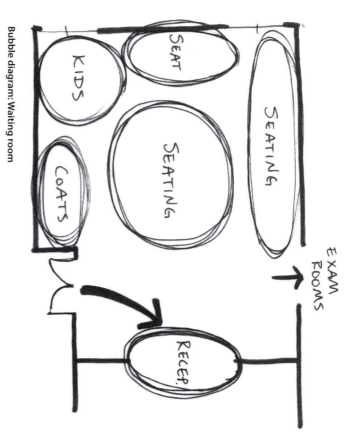

Bubble diagram: Waiting room

EXERCISE 6

Remember that bubble diagrams are useful at many scales. Here, we zero in on a single room. Refer to the in-context bubble diagram shown for the waiting area of a pediatrician's office. The bubbles indicate locations for various seating areas, including one for young kids; the location of the reception transaction counter; and a space for a coat rack or coat closet. Your task is to develop the ideas in the diagram into two loose plans. Use the 4'×4'(122 cm×122 cm) grid provided for scale reference. Draw loosely, but with care. Produce two graphically satisfying plans. Good luck.

Draw loose plan here

4 The Room

The Good Room

Most interior environments consist of rooms of various sizes that serve specific functions. In addition, there are corridors, open areas, and storage areas. Our study of interior environments starts with the room as a basic unit. For our purposes, we will use the term *room* in the common sense of the word, that is, in reference to what we normally think of as a room. Examples include fully enclosed and private rooms, such as bedrooms and private offices, as well as open rooms, such as living rooms and dining rooms.

To design a good project, you need to be able to design good individual rooms. Once you know the basics of designing a good room, you'll find that many of the principles that apply to room design also apply to the design of entire facilities. Despite the wide variation in design considerations between, say, a dentist's office and a hotel lobby, there are considerations and principles of good room design that are universal.

A good room is functional. It has adequate space for the functions it supports, is outfitted with proper furniture and equipment, is arranged in ways that support the programmed activities, and provides favorable ambient conditions for users.

Designing a good room can be challenging at first. Even after one has a pretty good idea of what the room wants to be, important questions must be addressed. For the purposes of planning, there are just a handful of crucial questions:

- What size and shape should this room be?
- What furnishings and accessories are needed?
- How should these be arranged?
- How should people enter and move through the room?
- n How should the room connect to other spaces?
- How should the room connect to the exterior?
- What will make the room multilayered and rich?

These questions boil down to five basic considerations for shaping and organizing good rooms: **envelope, contents, flow, connections,** and **scales.** Pay attention to these five basic considerations; use them to analyze existing rooms and as criteria for the rooms you design. The rest of this chapter addresses topics related to these and other aspects of basic room planning.

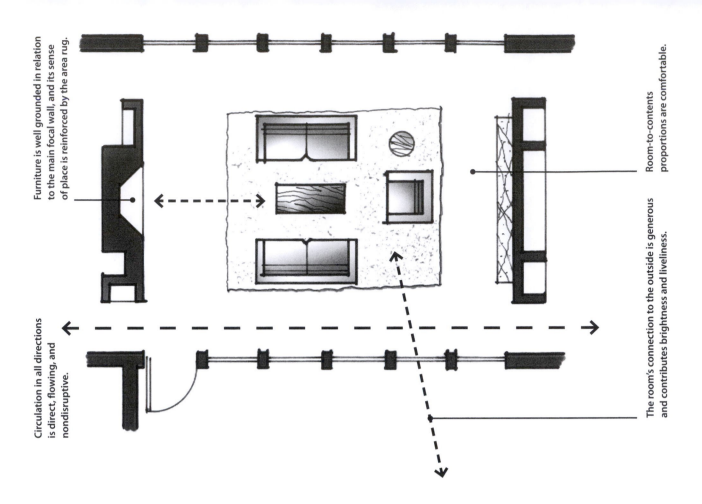

Furniture is well grounded in relation to the main focal wall, and its sense of place is reinforced by the area rug.

Circulation in all directions is direct, flowing, and nondisruptive.

Room-to-contents proportions are comfortable.

The room's connection to the outside is generous and contributes brightness and liveliness.

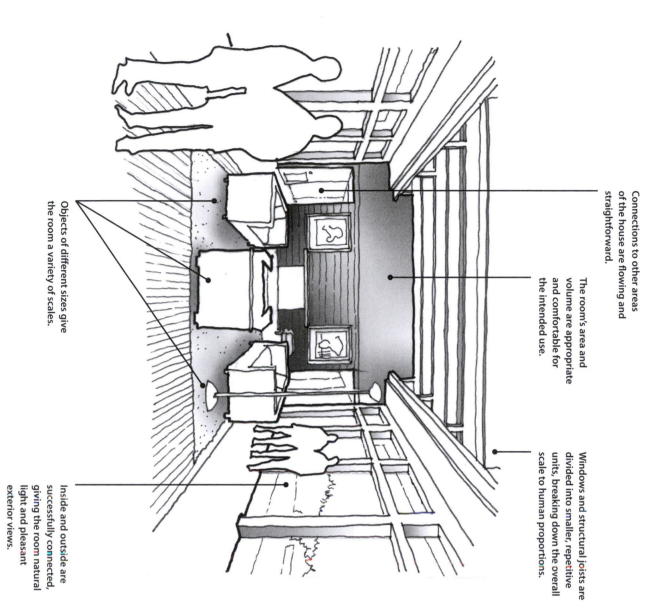

Connections to other areas of the house are flowing and straightforward.

The room's area and volume are appropriate and comfortable for the intended use.

Windows and structural joists are divided into smaller, repetitive units, breaking down the overall scale to human proportions.

Objects of different sizes give the room a variety of scales.

Inside and outside are successfully connected, giving the room natural light and pleasant exterior views.

Principles of Room Design

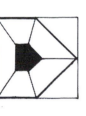

Envelope

The spatial envelope is functional and comfortable. It is the right size and has good shape and proportions.

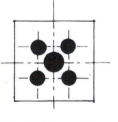

Contents

The furnishings, equipment, and accessories support the functions of the room. They are placed correctly and work well within the spatial envelope. They are well grounded and are grouped in legible configurations.

Connections

The room enjoys good connections to other interior spaces, to the exterior, and to special features within itself, such as focal elements. It receives natural light (except when meant to be dark) and offers good views to the outside.

Flow

The entry point to the room is logical, and contents are arranged in a way that makes movement within and through the space efficient and fluid.

Scales

Architectural and interior elements in the room are of various sizes, ranging from large to small. Large walls are subdivided into smaller units and articulated.

Shapes and Proportions

Once you know the approximate size a room needs to be, the next step is determining its shape and proportions in plan. The truth is that not many shapes and proportions will produce a good room. In fact, the great majority of simple rooms will have a rectangular shape or one close to it. Other common room shapes you'll encounter are the circle and the square. These, because of their geometric purity and symmetry, are often used when formal compositions are called for. In general, strive to create rooms that aren't overly long or narrow, or, as Jacobson, Silverstein, and Winslow stated, "rooms should be shaped more like a potato than a carrot—relatively compact and oblong, not long and skinny."[1] As a practice in their firm, these architects

sketch rooms as "fuzzy tuber-shaped blobs" early in the design process.

The famous sixteenth-century Italian architect Andrea Palladio proposed seven basic shapes and proportions for rooms, based on proportional studies. These are shown on the next page. You don't have to adhere strictly to these proportions, but do remember that if the length of a room exceeds its width, the proportion becomes uncomfortably narrow in relation to its length.

1. Max Jacobsen, Murray Silverstein, and Barbara Winslow, *Patterns of Home: The Ten Essentials of Enduring Design* (Newtown, CT: Taunton, 2002).

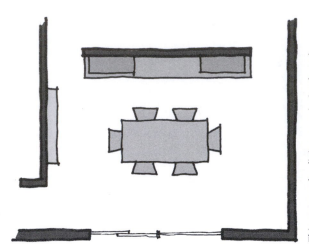

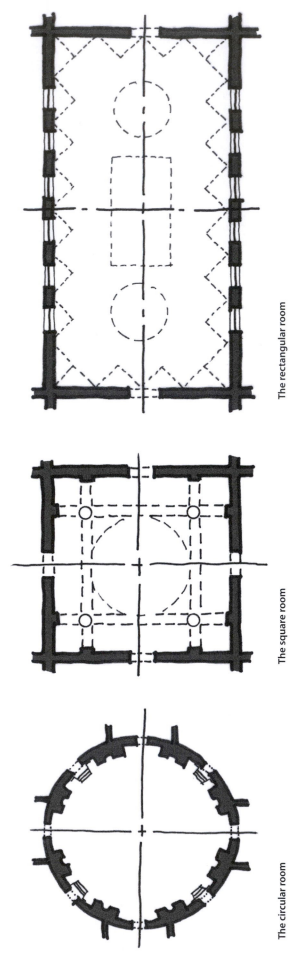

This rectangular dining room is simple and well proportioned. Its 21' × 28' (6.4 m × 8.5 m) dimensions have a 3:4 ratio or, put a different way, the length equals the width plus one third.

The rectangular room

The square room

The circular room

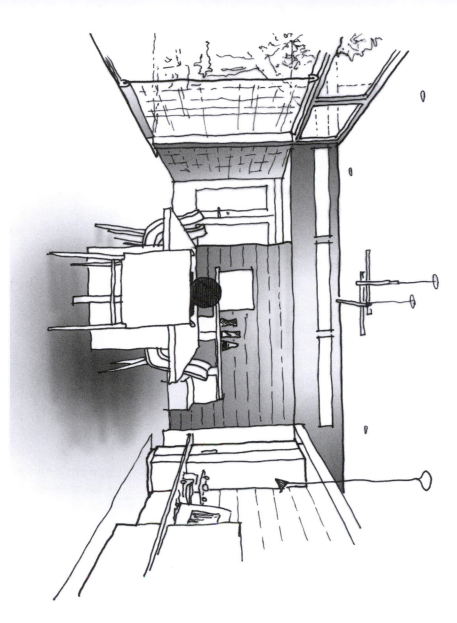

The Seven Proportions

Circular

Square
1:1

Diagonal of square
1:1.414

Square plus a third
3:4

Square plus a half
2:3

Square plus two thirds
3:5

Double square
1:2

Basic Plan Elements

Space planning interiors requires the availability of a certain area of space in a building. The area is subdivided through the use of walls, which also help create enclosed rooms, where necessary, for privacy or other needs. Openings in the walls connect spaces and allow people to move from one space to the next. These openings often have doors to create even more private conditions. In some cases, there are also windows, both as part of the base building itself and between interior spaces. Interior windows can be made of transparent or translucent materials, such as glass. Openings can also be completely open (punched holes between spaces). Many buildings also have columns, which become existing vertical elements to be addressed and incorporated into the design. Walls, doors, windows, and columns are the principal architectural elements used for space planning interiors. There are many variations of each. Some of the most common are shown here in diagrammatic form.

Walls

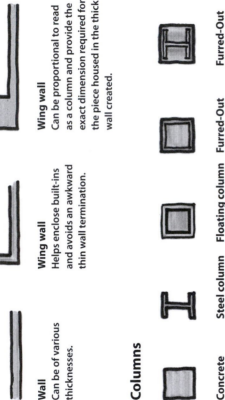

Wall
Can be of various thicknesses.

Wing wall
Helps enclose built-ins and avoids an awkward thin wall termination.

Wing wall
Can be proportional to read as a column and provide the exact dimension required for the piece housed in the thick wall created.

Niche
Requires a deeper wall and provides space for accents (artwork, flowers, and so on).

Shape
Can be achieved through understanding of how to manipulate wall thicknesses.

Columns

Concrete column
Found often; sometimes left exposed.

Steel column
Usually not left exposed because of the look of sprayed fireproofing.

Floating column
May sometimes be a fake column created to match an existing one.

Furred-Out column 1

Furred-Out column 2

Furred-Out column 3

Furred-Out column 4
Sometimes furred-out cavity is larger to house plumbing and so on.

Columns are usually covered with either drywall or other manufactured products for a more finished look. Many shapes are possible.

Attached column
Covered column may be connected with an adjacent wall.

Walls/Columns

Split protrusion
Creates a bump on both sides.

One-Side protrusion
Provides one smooth side.

Deep protrusion
Sometimes unavoidable; don't let it get too deep.

Corner protrusion
Houses a column cleanly.

Floating column
Sometimes unavoidable; often creates problems.

Windows

Window showing sill (shown schematically)

Simple interior window

Pass-Through window

Interior bay window or window wall
Sometimes a band of windows, other times a full-height storefront-type window.

Doors

Typical interior door
Can swing in or out of a room; most doors swing in, except when an outward swing is required by code.

Double doors
Used only for important gathering rooms or for rooms housing large groups.

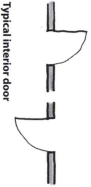

Corner door
Common and efficient.

Corner door
Careful: door should swing toward the sidewall, except in rooms where visual privacy is needed.

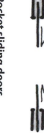

Recessed door pair
This and similar arrangements combine adjacent single doors into cohesive, larger elements.

Door in vestibule
Avoids the problem of doors swinging out into public corridors. (Clearances required by building codes will be addressed in Chapter 6.)

Single door on pivot
Sometimes swings in both directions.

Framed opening
Without doors is often the best solution.

Multiple pairs
Used occasionally to achieve wider openings between rooms to meet codes or for experiential reasons.

Pairs of doors
Sometimes required to permit egress in both directions.

Large doors on pivots
Sometimes used to create generous openings between spaces when held open.

Folding doors
Also commonly used for closets.

Pocket sliding door
Efficient and doesn't consume all the space required for a door swing.

Pocket sliding doors
Can also be double.

Double sliding doors
Common for closets.

Surface sliding doors
Sometimes detailed to achieve a particular desirable look.

Furniture Groups

The moveable contents of a room consist of furnishings, equipment, and accessories, such as artwork, decorative objects, and plants. You may think of a room as a stage set outfitted with furnishings and other, smaller props. Individual pieces of furniture are commonly combined to form cohesive groupings. These include living room seating areas, dining tables and chairs in a dining room, restaurant seating groups, and waiting rooms in various types of settings. You may have seen good and bad examples of the various furniture groups.

Space planning with furniture is tricky in the beginning. A couple of things must be achieved: First, a group (or groups) of furniture needs to be placed correctly within the room, both perceptually and functionally. Second, each furniture group itself has to be properly composed. Considerations include knowing the components of a particular furniture group, their typical sizes and shapes, the ways to arrange them, and the appropriate clearances between the pieces.

Shown here are typical arrangements of common furniture groups. These include living room seating-group arrangements, dining table arrangements, waiting area seating arrangements, restaurant seating arrangements, and conference room table arrangements. Some arrangements are fairly simple and rigid, such as those involving tables and chairs. Others offer more chances for variation. Yet, for all these groups, there are usually just a handful of configurations that work well. Although creativity has its merits, don't feel you have to constantly reinvent how things are done. There are not that many ways to arrange a table and a group of chairs for a meal, and that's fine.

Living Rooms

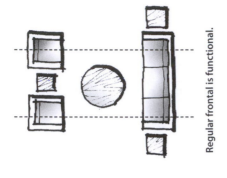

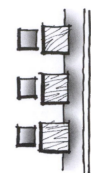

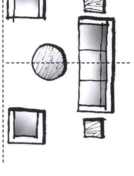

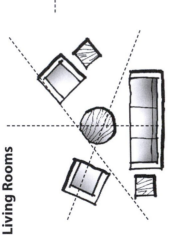

Regular frontal is functional.

Regular with two axes is formal.

Irregular arrangement is dynamic.

Conference Tables

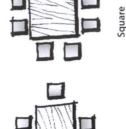

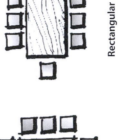

Square

Rectangular

Square

Round

Restaurant Tables

Two person banquettes and chairs are versatile.

Freestanding diagonal tables are dynamic.

Rectangular against wall are efficient.

Waiting Area Seating

Perpendicular

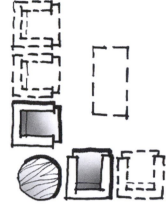

Parallel

Dining Tables

Rectangle

Large square

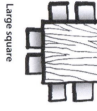

Small square

Small round

Booths are efficient and informal.

Four-person banquettes are efficient.

EXERCISE

Generate two seating groups for a hypothetical waiting room. Each group should consist of eight chairs. Use the furniture pieces shown below as reference for size. A 24" (61 cm) grid is provided for your convenience.

Grouping

Much of design involves organizing parts and pieces into cohesive and functional groups. Although we see instances of the single object by itself, such as a chair placed in a corner, it is more common to see multiple pieces arranged as a group. Group arrangements tend to be simple and straightforward; there is rarely a need to get too complicated.

Most groups consist of only a few parts. These groupings often repeat in the room, for example, a classroom with six tables, each accommodating five students. In a restaurant we may see several tables of four persons each. The majority of the furniture groups you are likely to encounter consist of pairs, trios, and groups of four. Look in any restaurant, hotel lobby, or corporate waiting area, and you will find mostly small groupings that repeat.

There are larger groups, of course. Most conference and dining tables allow for more than four people, perhaps seating as many as ten or twelve. Other examples may be seen in a hotel lobby or a waiting area in a doctor's office. There, you may encounter furniture arrangements of eight or more chairs planned as a group.

Become familiar with ways to assemble the common smaller groups. These are the groups you will use most of the time.

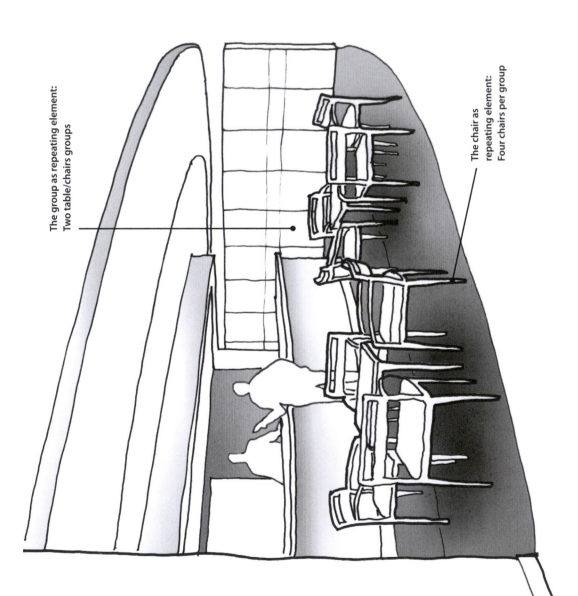

The group as repeating element:
Two table/chairs groups

**The chair as
repeating element:**
Four chairs per group

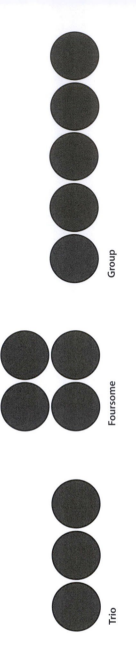

Single

Pair

Trio

Foursome

Group

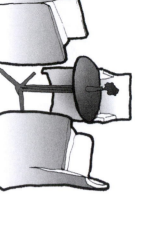

Although it is common to see chairs in groups, there are many instances of the single piece by itself.

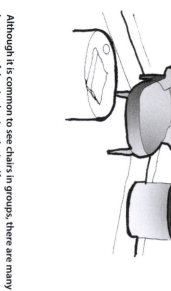

Threes in furniture tend to occur as closed groups rather than as side-by-side elements.

The pair is one of the most common groupings. Pairs of elements are often more satisfying than single ones.

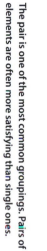

For gathering areas, such as in waiting rooms, the group of four chairs is one of the most common.

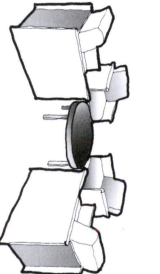

EXERCISE

In the space below generate three alternative seating groupings consisting of four chairs, and draw a plan view of each. One configuration is shown in perspective on this page. Try some different ones. Use the furniture sizes and the 24"(61 cm) grid provided below as reference.

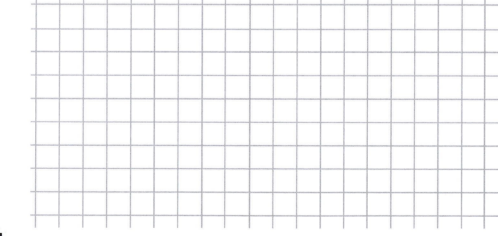

Zones and Regions

Rooms come in a variety of sizes and shapes. One of the challenges of interior planning is deciding where to place the various moveable components in the room. Luckily, there are not too many choices. If you consider the average undivided room of modest size, there are actually only four general regions where

you can place elements: the corners, the center, along the edges, or floating somewhere in the room. Using guidelines to define potential use zones in rooms can be helpful for medium- and large-size rooms. You can then place furnishings or other pieces in relation to them.

Pieces can be centered on, aligned with, or in between the guidelines. In general, guidelines are along the edges of the room, along the geometric center of the room, and, when space permits, somewhere in between, as shown in the examples.

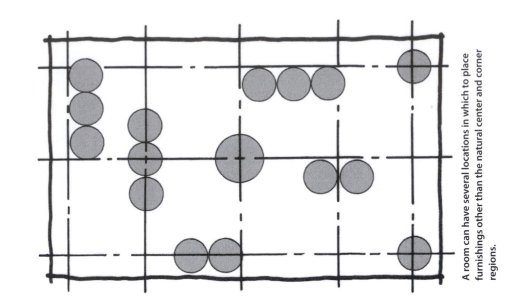

A room can have several locations in which to place furnishings other than the natural center and corner regions.

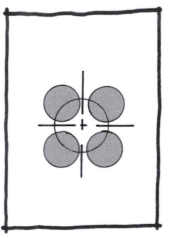

A central location is formal and dignified.

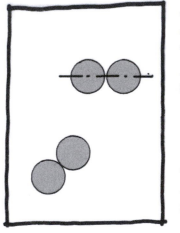

Achieving the proper sense of balance for floating elements and groups can be challenging and often relies on establishing effective relationships with other elements in the room.

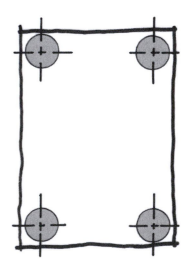

A corner location gives a sense of shelter and protection.

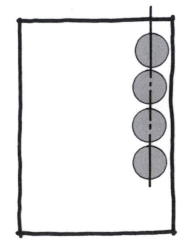

Edges serve as convenient backdrops along which to place furnishings.

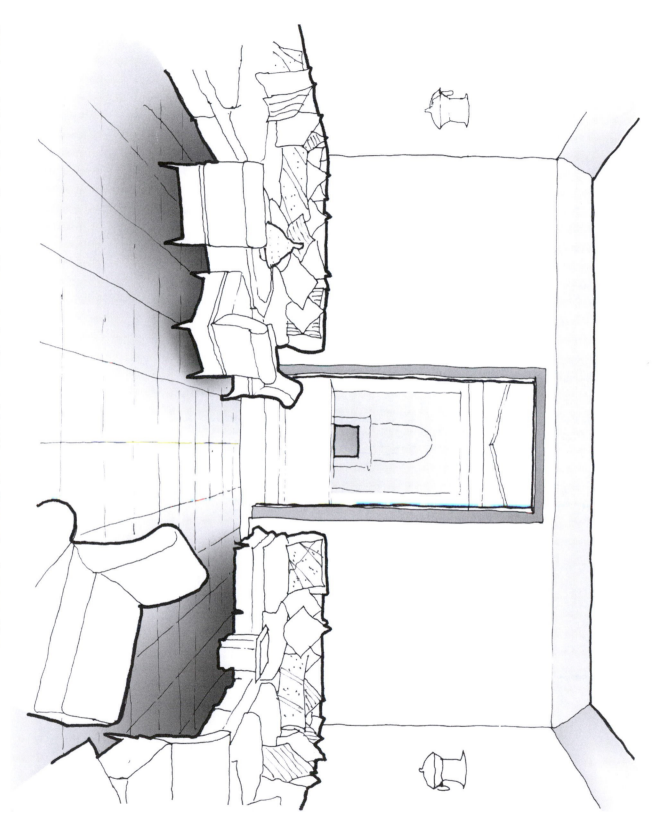

Corners have an intrinsic sheltering effect, and people have a natural tendency to push furnishings and objects, such as plants, toward them. This view of a four-corner furniture grouping strategy shows how even in tight spaces, the corner location gives each group a sense of place and autonomy.

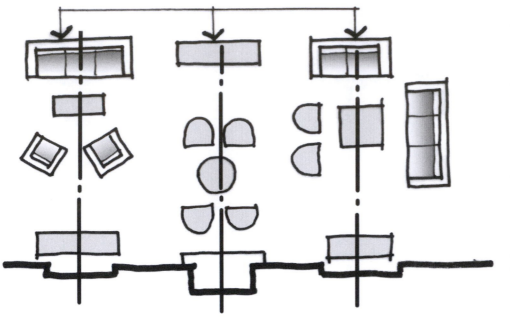

In one direction, each of the individual groups is centered with a wall element. In the other direction the organization is defined by the alignments along the outer edge.

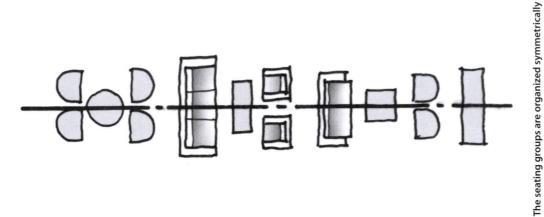

The seating groups are organized symmetrically along a common center line.

Centering is the alignment of the centers of various individual pieces or groupings. **Alignment** is the positioning of the edges of individual pieces or groupings along a common reference line. These two strategies can be used individually. They are also frequently used in combination.

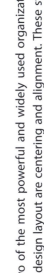

The wall, furniture fronts, and column are aligned, establishing a powerful imaginary line.

Centering and Alignment

Two of the most powerful and widely used organizational strategies in all aspects of design layout are centering and alignment. These strategies are used to organize everything from text on a printed page to furniture in a room. You will use them constantly.

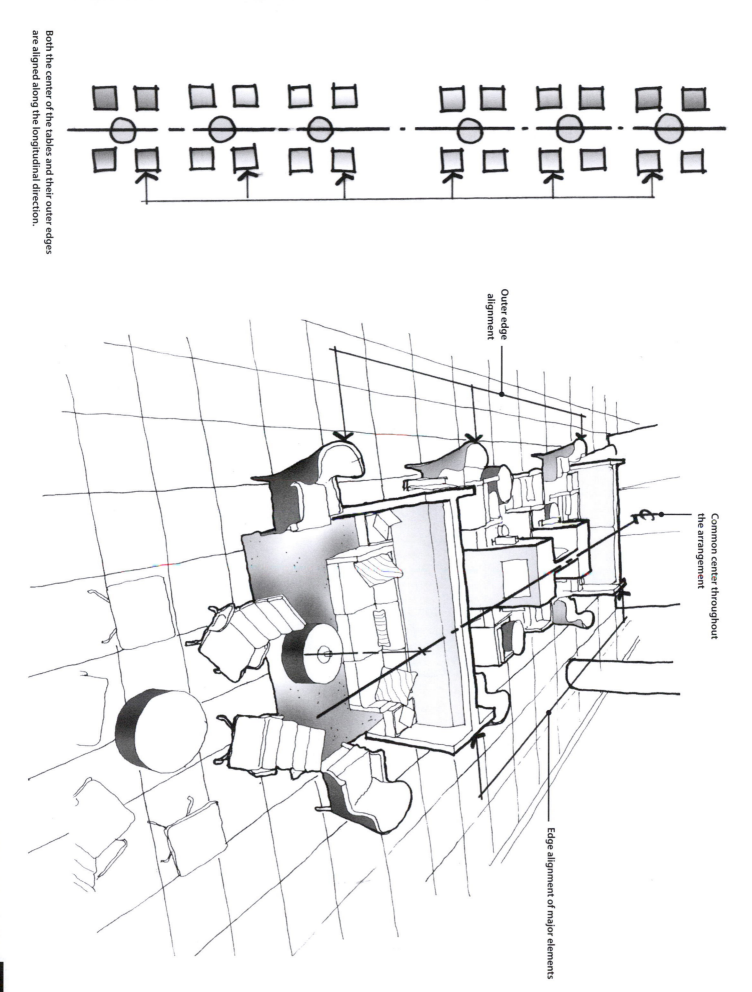

Both the center of the tables and their outer edges are aligned along the longitudinal direction.

Outer edge alignment

Common center throughout the arrangement

Edge alignment of major elements

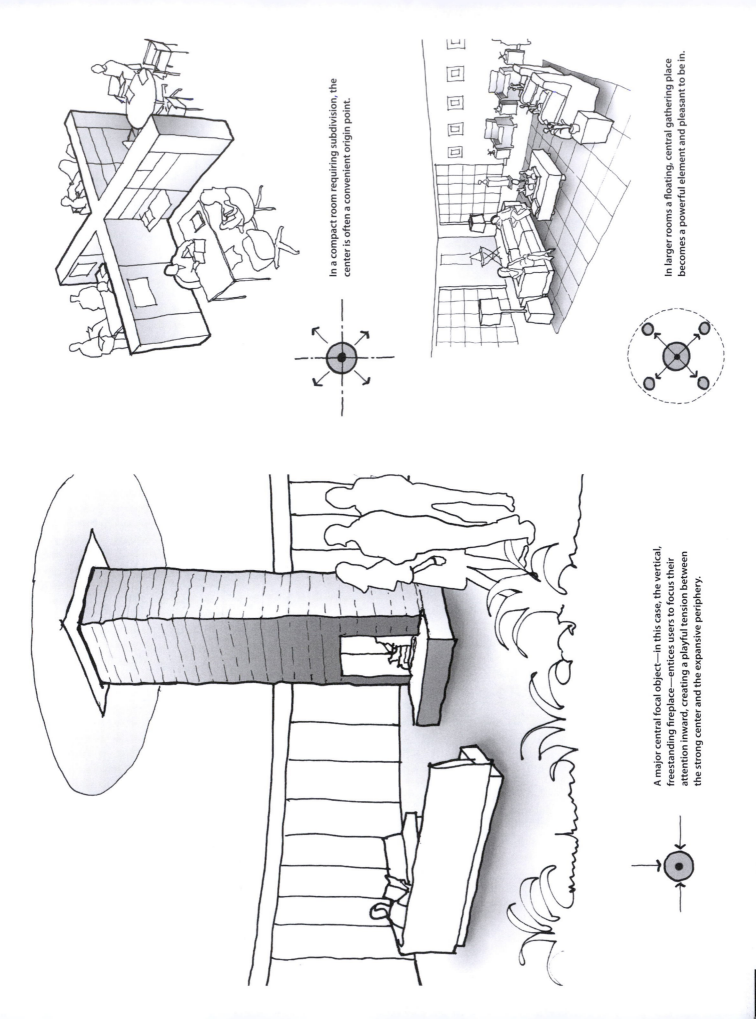

In a compact room requiring subdivision, the center is often a convenient origin point.

In larger rooms a floating, central gathering place becomes a powerful element and pleasant to be in.

A major central focal object—in this case, the vertical, freestanding fireplace—entices users to focus their attention inward, creating a playful tension between the strong center and the expansive periphery.

The Center

The central zone of a room is often its most powerful one. You can think of a room in terms of a perimeter zone, a central zone, and, sometimes, another zone in between. What should be at the center, and should what you place there be at precisely the geometric center of the room? Whatever goes at the center often is, but doesn't always need to be, at the exact center of the room. A dining table, for example, may be almost

centered, but placed slightly toward one of the two sidewalls to facilitate circulation on the other side.

The center can hold a gathering place, as in many living rooms (at home) and conference rooms (at work). The center can also be a spot for a focal element, such as a fountain, a large planter, a fireplace, or a point of origin from which elements such as partitions move

outward. In addition, the center can have a piece, such as a table or planter, that forces you to walk toward the outside of the room.

Not every room has something at the center. Sometimes, it is left empty for people to move through or gather at.

In some cases, a central element can serve as both a focal point and a gathering place.

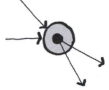

A centralized element, such as this dining table, is an obvious choice in regular rooms with pure geometric shapes, such as square, circular, and octagonal rooms. In this example, it is both a focal point and a gathering place.

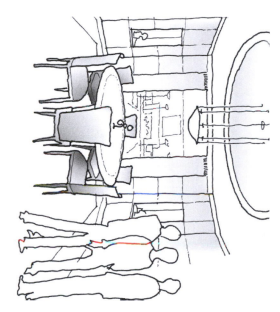

The central decorative table in this round circulation space forces people to walk in a concentric circular fashion around the table, thus enhancing the perception of the round room.

Grounding

When an object or group of objects, such as furniture, are perceived to have a home in a room, they can be said to be well grounded. Think of the picnic blanket and how it provides a territory that gives your group a very specific spot on which to settle for a couple of hours. It grounds you; that is, it provides you with a secure place in space. In a room, the perceived grounding quality is always due to the object's relationship to something else in the room. In some cases, the topological position of the object is enough; the corner table, the central fountain, and the row of planters along the sidewall all have the quality of being grounded.

However, it often takes more than the room's natural grounding spots to achieve, or reinforce, a sense of grounding. Sometimes, you need grounding elements. **Grounding elements** in a typical room can be existing, or they can be supplied by you, as the designer. If existing, such as a fireplace or a magnificent window, you react to what is given and place your objects accordingly. If nonexisting, you add them when and where needed. They work for you by providing a spot in which to place your objects.

Grounding elements in common rooms occur on the walls, on the floor, or overhead, at the ceiling. These define useful areas on which to position your elements, often using centering and alignment compositional strategies.

Fireplace as grounding element

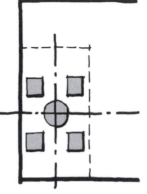
Centered flooring change as grounding element

Centered ceiling change as grounding element

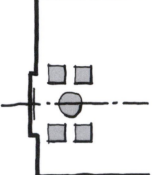
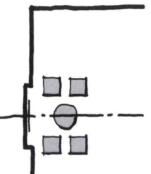
Recessed wall with artwork as grounding element

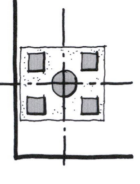
Floating flooring change as grounding element

Arbitrary ceiling change as grounding element

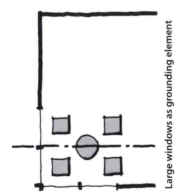
Large windows as grounding element

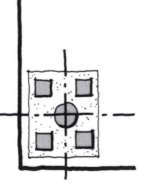
Flooring change at corner as grounding element

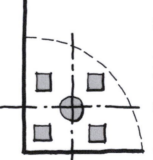
Corner ceiling height/material change as grounding element

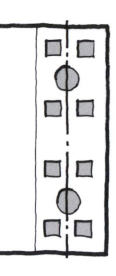

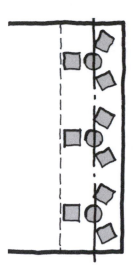

Furniture groups grounded in relation to the rhythm of the windows

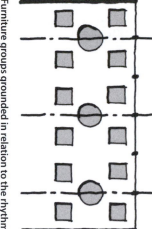

Furniture groups grounded in relation to the rhythm of the wall modulation

Furniture groups grounded by placement within a zone defined by flooring change

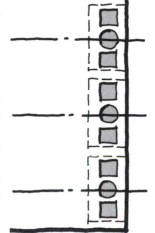

Furniture groups grounded by placement within a zone defined by ceiling change

Furniture groups grounded in relation to the three modules created by the flooring changes

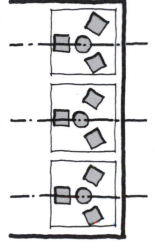

Furniture groups grounded in relation to the three modules defined by the ceiling changes

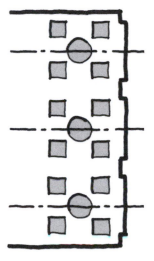

EXERCISE

Ground the furniture groups in the three spaces below by drawing in two grounding elements for each. Select a variety of wall, floor, and ceiling grounding elements. Use the size of the furniture as reference, and approximate the size and extent of the grounding elements.

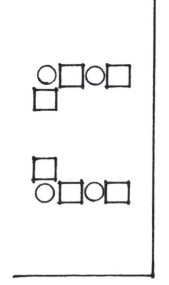

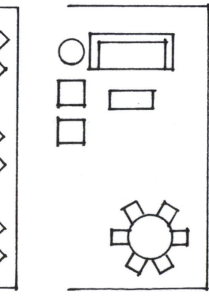

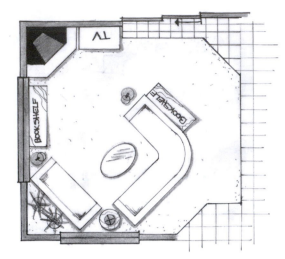

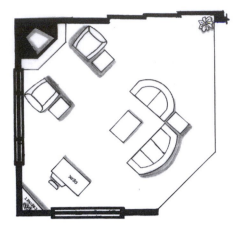

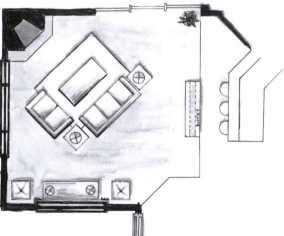

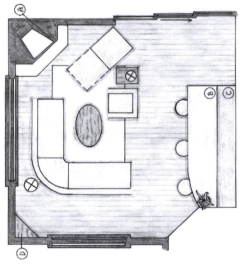

Approach 1: Full Attraction

Approach 2: Partial Attraction

Focal Element as Magnet

Certain design features become focal elements in space and attract our attention. Some, like a prominent piece of art or a nice view, provide a visual focus intended to stimulate and delight. Others, like a kiosk with information, attract and offer something different, in this case information. Still others, like a fountain or a fireplace, invite users to come close and gather around. Here I show several solutions to a small project for a room with a prominent fireplace at one corner. Such a prominent element usually has a strong influence over how you arrange the furnishings in the room. Let's look at various approaches to this design challenge.

The schemes that took approach 1 respond strongly to the magnetic force of the fireplace and arrange the main furnishings as a group in front of it. Things are positioned in relation to the fireplace as a dictator of form.

Approach 2 schemes also respond to the fireplace, but they do so from a distance, feeling that there is no need to get so close to enjoy the pleasant effects of this feature.

In approach 3, the furniture is not arranged in direct relation to the fireplace. They don't turn their backs at it, either. These designers seem to be saying, "Look, it's a small room; no matter where you are, you'll get to enjoy the effects of the fireplace. Therefore, let's not respond too literally to the magnetic pull of the fireplace and let's place the furniture where we really want it."

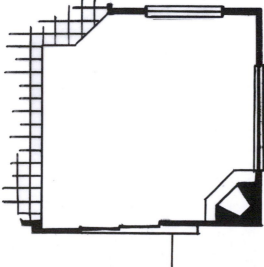

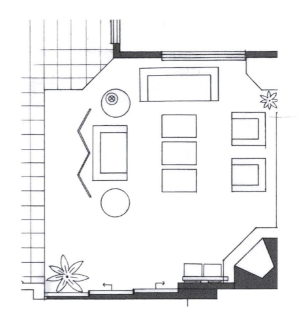

EXERCISE

Here is the same room with the same fireplace. Now it's your turn to come up with a scheme to furnish the room. Try something different. What will you do, respond literally to the fireplace? Or, perhaps respond more casually, as some of the other designers did? It is up to you.

Once you have finished, evaluate your two plans. Use the writing space given to describe your approach and briefly explain the benefits of your solutions.

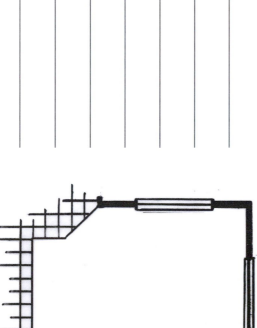

Windows

Windows are often inherited; they are there as part of the building. For projects in which the building is being designed simultaneously with the interiors, you may be in a position to influence the windows' location. Always consider the windows in a room before placing furniture and planning the orientation of the room's activities. Windows are generally good, providing natural light, warmth, and views. They can also be problematic: instead of good light, you may get unwanted glare; instead of warmth, too much heat; and instead of a good view, you may be afforded the view of a loud neighbor's window a few feet away.

Respond to windows on a case-by-case basis. Consider the room's functions and the attributes (both positive and negative) of the windows. Based on the particular realities of each case, you can then decide whether to face the window, turn your back to it, get close to it, or, in some cases, be merely indifferent to it.

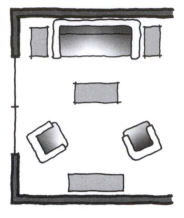

The neutral sideways arrangement of the living room furniture allows a convenient relationship with the window without forcing it.

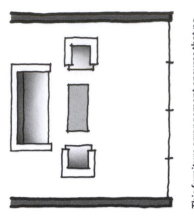

This furniture arrangement ensures that no one has his or her back against the window and that all users have direct access to the perimeter walls.

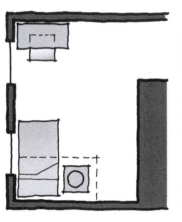

The placement of the bed and desk by the windows affords a direct relationship with the exterior.

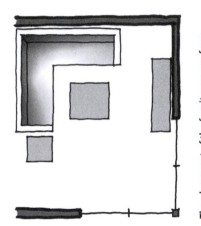

The placement of the furniture away from and diagonal to the window creates a strong face-to-face relationship between the users and the window.

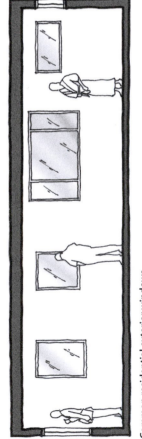

Common commercial exterior windows

Common residential exterior windows

EXERCISE

Locate the furniture below in the two partial rooms shown. Place the furniture based on desirable relationships to the windows. The furniture is to scale in relation to the rooms. You may turn the furniture as necessary to make it work in the rooms.

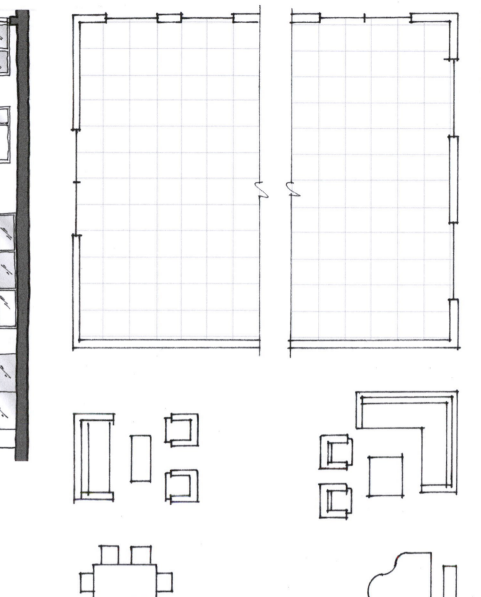

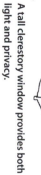

Common commercial interior windows

A tall clerestory window provides both light and privacy.

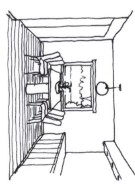

A central focal window anchors the table.

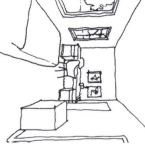

A distributed pair of windows reaches both sides of the room.

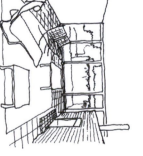

A full wall window opens up the room.

Circulation

One of the simplest principles of space planning, yet one that is often forgotten, is that people need adequate space for walking and getting around. A conference room, for example, requires space for the main table and the chairs around it and also space that allows people to enter the room comfortably and walk around the table. Such spaces are the alleys, streets, and boulevards of interiors. **Circulation** is the term commonly used to refer to these spaces. Projects need overall circulation routes that connect their various spaces and local circulation routes within individual rooms. Here we look at the latter. (Overall circulation will be addressed in Chapter 6.)

The circulation system for a room consists of the entry point, the main space in which to walk and get around, secondary spaces and clearances for reaching all zones in the room, and, sometimes, additional entry/exit points, as some rooms provide access to adjacent spaces beyond. Problems with circulation design include inadequate space, too much space, and various issues associated with the location and trajectory of the circulation route within the room.

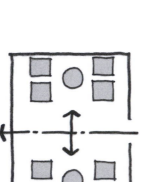

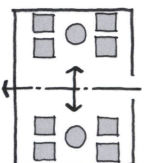

Central approach 1
Destination is on an axis with the entrance.

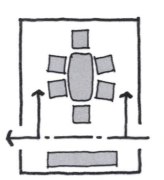

Central approach 2
Destinations are to either side of the entrance.

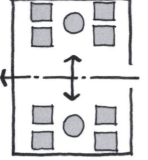

Central approach 3
Walk around the room to reach destination.

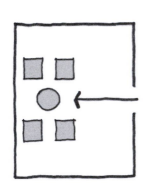

Lateral approach 1
Enter on the extreme left, and turn right, toward destination.

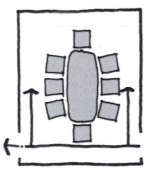

Lateral approach 2
Enter toward the left, and turn right, toward destination.

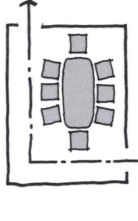

Lateral approach 3
Enter toward the left; destination is on either side.

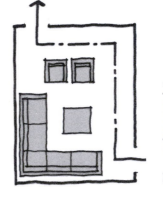

Diagonal approach 1
Careful: this arrangement pushes furniture toward the corner, and the circulation space is excessive.

Diagonal approach 2
Careful: this arrangement also pushes furniture to one corner, and the amount of circulation space is excessive.

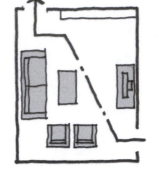

Diagonal approach 3
Careful: although tolerable, this arrangement can be disruptive to the people watching the TV.

The approach (entrance) to a room is either central or lateral, to one side. Which one is best for a particular situation varies from case to case. The main path of movement within the room can be straight ahead (usually best), straight but lateral (side to side), or some form of diagonal movement, whether diagonal or zigzagging (often problematic). The examples on the previous page show various possible combinations, some better than others.

Strive to produce circulation systems that are efficient, fluid, and discrete and that allow multiple furniture configuration options. These four principles are summarized at right. Once you become aware of them, they will make logical sense and guide your decision making related to circulation.

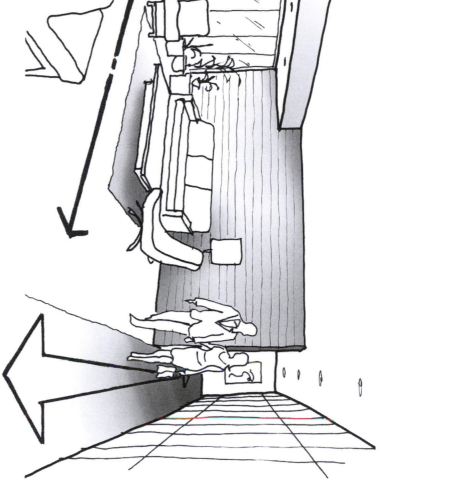

Efficiency

Strive for shorter routes that consume less circulation area in your room.

Efficient   Less efficient

Fluidity

Strive for smooth, flowing circulation routes with few twists, turns, and bumps.

Fluid   Less fluid

Discreteness

Avoid circulation routes that go through and interrupt otherwise cohesive furniture groups.

Discrete   Less discrete

Furnishability

Create circulation routes that make it possible to arrange furnishings many different ways.

Furnishable   Less furnishable

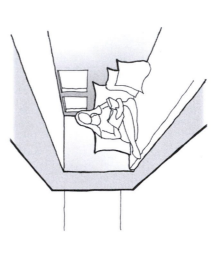

Frank Lloyd Wright's dining room for the Gerald B. Tonkens House features a thick wall that incorporates sideboards and cupboards.

Thick Walls

All walls and partitions have thicknesses; they are not the single lines that we sometimes draw diagrammatically. Walls occupy space and actually end up taking up a significant chunk of a project's total floor area. Many years ago, before the use of column and beam structural systems became prevalent, most interior walls in buildings were load-bearing walls and were often quite thick. We now tell students that, depending on the circumstances, non-load-bearing interior drywall partitions usually vary between roughly 4" and 6" (10 cm to 15 cm) and are pleased when students start drawing walls showing proper thicknesses. Suddenly, however, we see all interior walls becoming that thickness. This is generally good but quite limiting.

Now, let's explore the concept of "thick walls." Imagine you are designing an interior drywall partition, and you want to incorporate two niches for artwork flanking a gracious concave curve at the center. The partition separates two rooms. The niches and curved segment appear on one side only; the other room has a normal, straight-wall surface. Your solution might end up looking something like the drawing below.

But you might say: My instructor will tell me that I am being wasteful, with so much unused space devoted to the wall cavity. The reply you'll get from designers who use these techniques will be: It is okay to have deeper wall cavities, and the additional waste that comes with them, as long as you are doing so within reason and for the purpose of creating something good for the project.

Now, let's take the concept even further. Imagine that one or more of the walls in your room are not the usual thin walls (don't worry, the majority of your interior partitions will still be of this type) but are now allowed to be conceived as deep zones of 18" to 30" (46 cm to 76 cm) so that you can incorporate things like built-in bookshelves, files, and seating. Consequently, what used to be a thin partition now becomes a band of space. Say you are allowed to do this on one of your exterior walls, and you decide to incorporate a built-in window seat, like the one below. You have created another thick wall, one different from the first. This one is for people!

Congratulations, you have created a thick wall! Note that the wall had to get thicker than normal to allow for the niches and the curved recessed portion. Only the shallow central part of the wall might be close to the narrow dimension of common partitions.

Whether it's a thick wall to accommodate niches, recessed shapes, and storage or one used for seating and activity, these types of walls are used all the time. Make them part of your design vocabulary.

The living room in Frank Lloyd Wright's Bazett-Frank House features a long, thick wall with built-in seating and shelving. A dropped ceiling soffit further reinforces this perimeter zone.

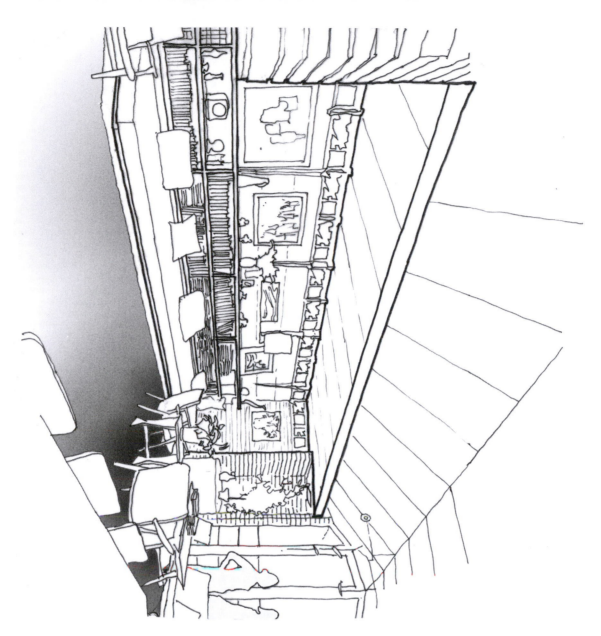

Imagine a modern builder were to build a room of roughly the same size and proportions as Robert Adams's library for Kenwood House. He or she would likely use the standard thin partitions found in most modern constructions and build something like this. If you need to incorporate books, you can go out and buy some bookshelves, this builder might say.

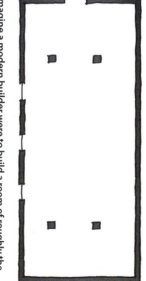

Examine this floor plan of the actual library designed by Adams. Note the thick walls. In general, walls were thicker then (1768), but note the ins and outs, the round shapes, the deep recesses at the windows, the play of surfaces around the central fireplace. Compare this with the solution using thin walls above. There is a lot more substance to this one.

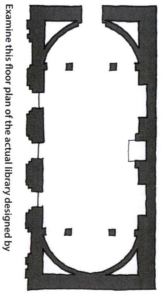

Let's have some fun now and add to the play of surfaces in the room. We've added a circular vestibule, niches, deeper recesses flanking the fireplace, corner pockets with insets for books, and even a very deep window at the far end of the longitudinal axis. This is the concept of thick walls applied.

Thick Walls: Practical Applications

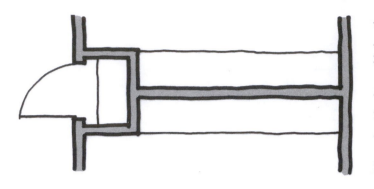

A linen closet has been added on the corridor side of this arrangement. The zones created in the rooms can have closets, casework, and shelving.

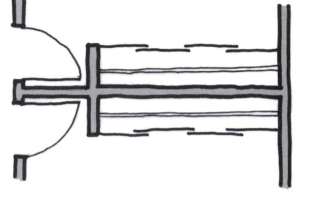

This typical back-to-back condition for bedrooms allows for back-to-back closets.

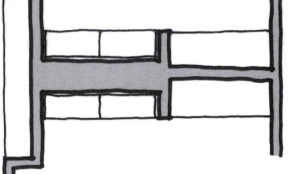

This wall accommodates files and a work center on either side plus space for files or storage on the corridor side.

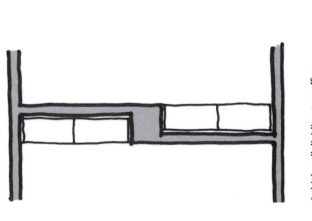

A thick wall dividing two offices provides space for lateral files in each office.

Although architects and interior designers have produced a number of magnificent examples of thick-wall applications over time, many of the uses of thick walls can be of a very straightforward and practical nature. Thick walls are used commonly to house file cabinets, counters, and storage units in offices as well as closets in residential bedrooms. Examine these simple examples. Note how walls are configured to accommodate pieces of exact dimensions. Also note how some examples have thick walls between sides and also between the rooms and the corridor space outside to house more files or a linen closet.

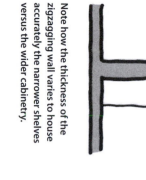

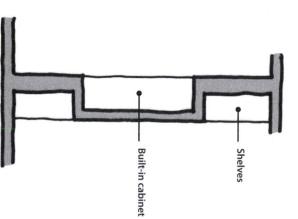

Built-in cabinet

Shelves

Note how the thickness of the zigzagging wall varies to house accurately the narrower shelves versus the wider cabinetry.

EXERCISE

Putting the concept of thick walls to work is not hard once you have a basic understanding of it. Here, you have an opportunity to practice with the exercises given. Have fun, and be creative.

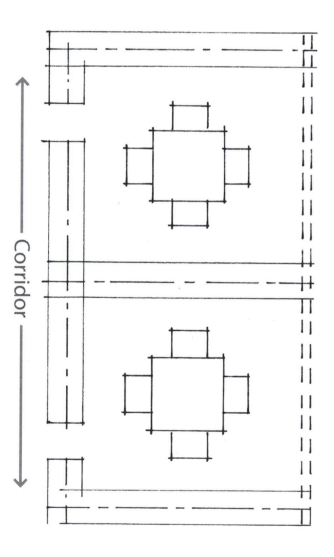

Corridor

For the two conference rooms above, add thick walls along the side and front walls shown as ─ · ─ · ─ to produce the following in each office:

1. Storage space (closet)
2. Counter space
3. Built-in bookshelves
4. Space for two lateral files

In addition, provide space for a bank of lateral files in a thick wall facing the corridor.

Note: A band of approximately 24" (61 cm) is shown for your reference in producing the thick walls.

Gathering Room Analysis

The four plans on this spread show different arrangements for the commons (social areas) in an assisted living facility for senior citizens. The basic geometry of the space was a given, as was the location of the formidable fireplace. Students were asked to provide multiple gathering zones, including spaces for conversation, a place to watch television, spaces for reading, and spaces to eat a snack or play cards. They also had to incorporate a piano as a musician comes in regularly to play the piano during the day and for special events.

Your task is to get inside each designer's mind and try to understand what the designers were thinking and why they placed the furnishings were they did. Pretend you have to sell the merits of the various designs. With that in mind, write below the various plans a list of features, benefits, and advantages their settings afford. This is similar to an annotated plan but will be done as a bulleted or numbered list.

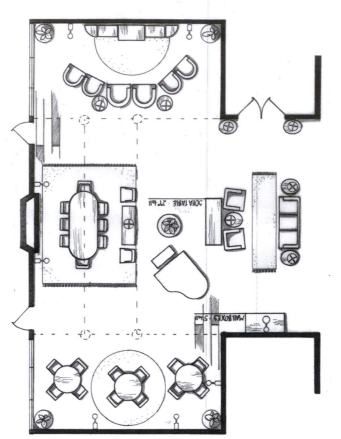

Scheme 2

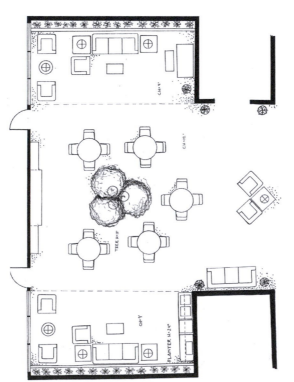

Scheme 1

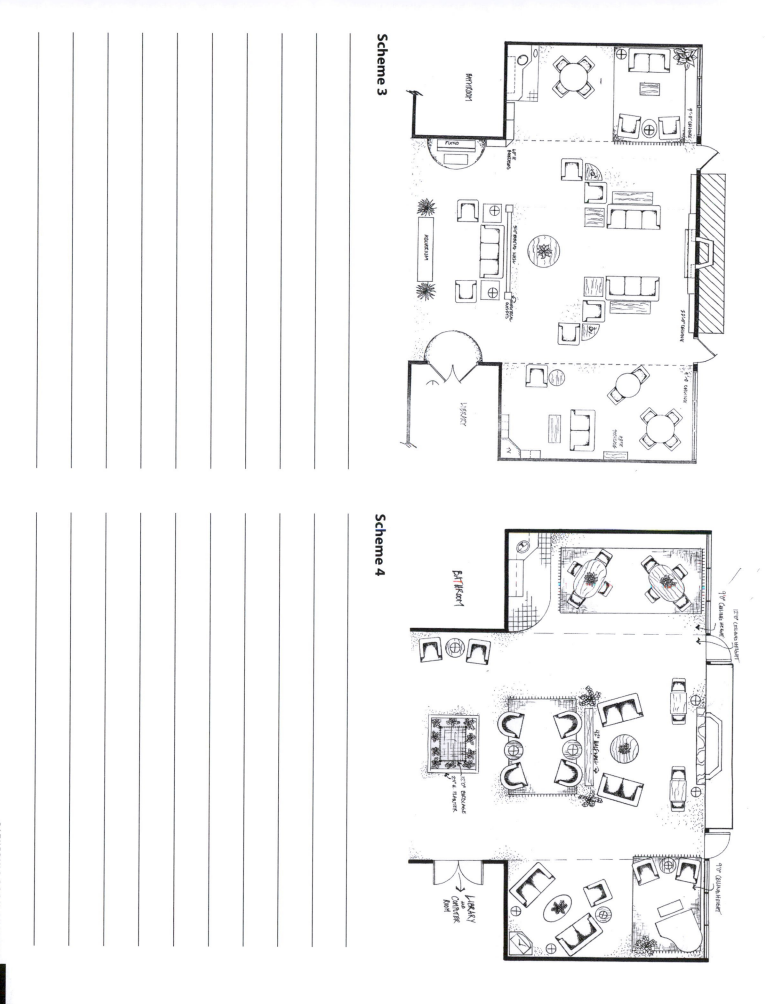

Scheme 3

Scheme 4

Hotel Lobby Critique

Here is a project for the design of a seating zone in a hotel lobby. It is a fairly large room with multiple potential zones. The main people traffic goes from right to left. Your task is to critique the four designs. You'll notice different organizational approaches.

The first scheme consists of three linear zones; two perimeter and one going down the center. The next two feature linear perimeter zones, but this time with a single focal element at the center, in one case a piano, in the other a fountain. The final scheme is quite different as it incorporates an organically shaped sculptural fountain in a looser, asymmetrical configuration.

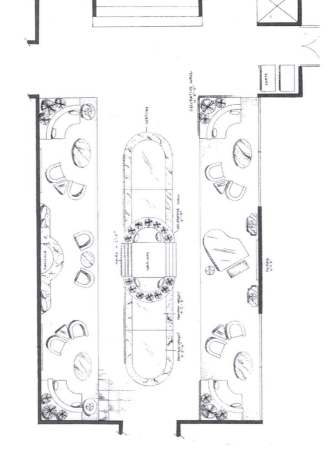

Scheme 1

Scheme 2

EXERCISE

Think about what makes a good hotel lobby where many different groups of people can gather. What qualities are needed for circulation along this high-traffic zone? What other desirable qualities can you think of? Comment on and critique each scheme in the space provided. If you had to select one of the schemes to pursue further, which one would it be? Why?

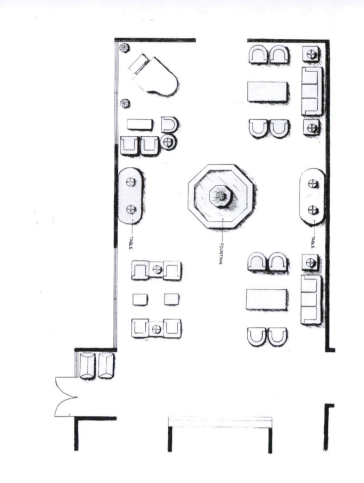

Scheme 3

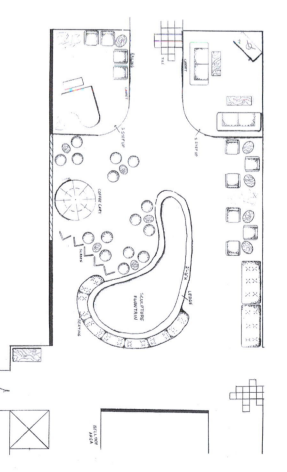

Scheme 4

5 Beyond the Room

Beyond the Room

Although the room may be the most basic container of interior environments, the majority of interior projects consist of a collection of rooms and other spaces. In this chapter, we look at groups of spaces and rooms. We examine contiguous spaces (sequences of spaces) and the many ways these can be joined and also separated. An important goal of this chapter is to show that there are many ways of using walls other than as the four sides of a room.

A key to the success of interior projects is the relationships between the various spaces in the project. There are many important questions to consider. What is the first space one sees? What is next to it? Can one see from one space to another? How are the spaces positioned? How are they separated? How do they attain a sense of being separate entities?

Look at the portion of Josef Hoffmann's Palais Stoclet on this page. One notes the group of public rooms joined by a generous common hall; can imagine the spaces animated by real people during an evening gathering; sees the guests arriving, being greeted at the entrance, moving to the hall to join other guests, and from there, proceeding to the music room, the sitting room, or the dining room. The project is from 1911, before floor plans really opened up. The spaces are well contained and autonomous.

Shift your attention now to the two partial floor plans on the following page. They are more contemporary floor plans. They are open and flowing. Although each function has its own dedicated space, these do not occur in dedicated rooms. One function flows into another. Living rooms are adjacent and connected visually to dining rooms. Kitchens have a strong definition and sense of territory, yet they are visually connected to the dining areas they serve. You may also note the distinction between main dwelling spaces such as living rooms and dining rooms, and auxiliary spaces, such as kitchens and bathrooms.

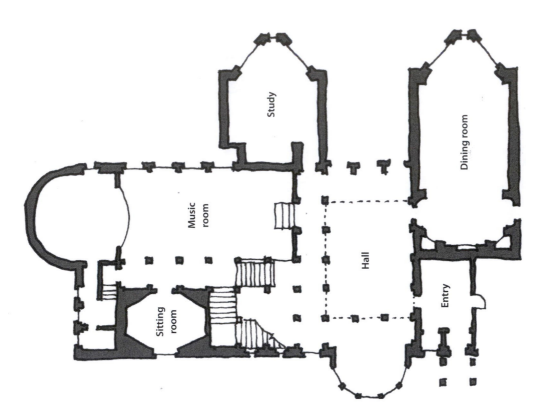

PALAIS STOCLET

Study

Music room

Sitting room

Hall

Dining room

Entry

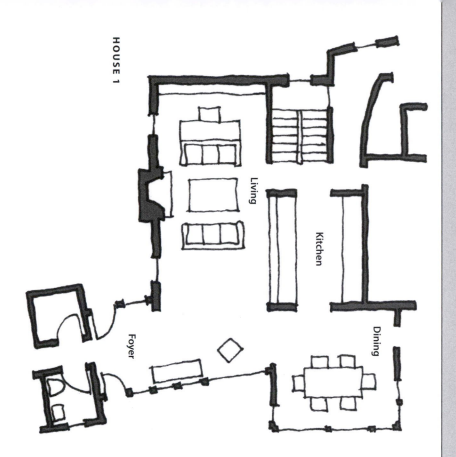

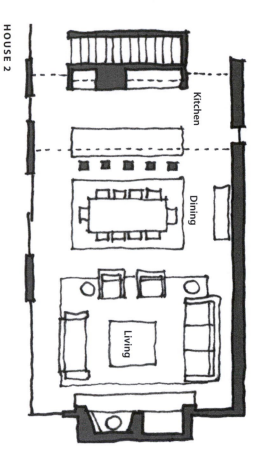

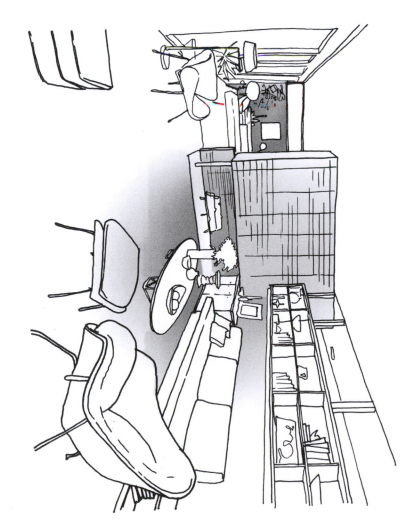

Living

Kitchen

Dining

Foyer

Kitchen

Dining

Living

Even public rooms need definition and some separation; however, they do not need to have four walls. The fireplace wall above provides strong spatial definition and a pleasant focal point for the living room area, while allowing for an open and inviting connection with the other areas beyond. The two spaces are two distinct areas but are not fully enclosed by four walls and a door.

Large Single Spaces

Some rooms are fairly large. They go beyond our normal conception of a room, and we come to think about them as spaces or areas, not rooms. These rooms often house one or more related functions and generally require multiple furniture groups, which must be organized into cohesive units. The example on this page shows a view of a hotel lobby/bar area. The area contains no hard separations, such as walls; instead, the furniture groups themselves define specific zones and territories.

You'll remember from the previous chapter that rooms have zones, such as perimeter and central zones. You might also remember that there is a need to allocate space for things (such as furnishings) and for walking (circulation). Note the perimeter and central bands in the hotel lobby example. Note also how similar furniture elements, such as the sitting areas with the tall dividers, near the middle, define specific zones when placed in groups, such as the pair here. The extra width provided around this zone for circulation gives even greater definition to the pair of seating groups. The bar areas, with their canopies, have prominence and read strongly. The balloon-like lighting fixtures provide a sense of rhythm and are coordinated with the groupings underneath. Even though the space is large and has many furniture pieces, everything seems to have its logical place, creating a sense of order. We might say that the various zones are autonomous, yet connected.

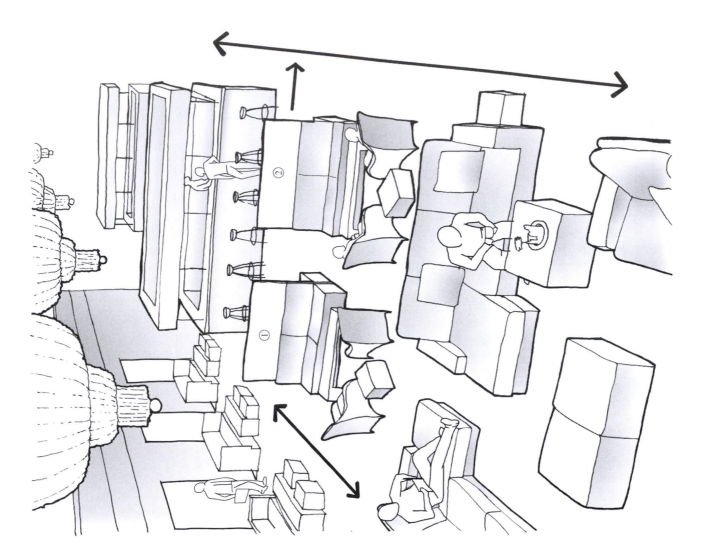

BERNS HOTEL

DEVI GARTH HOTEL

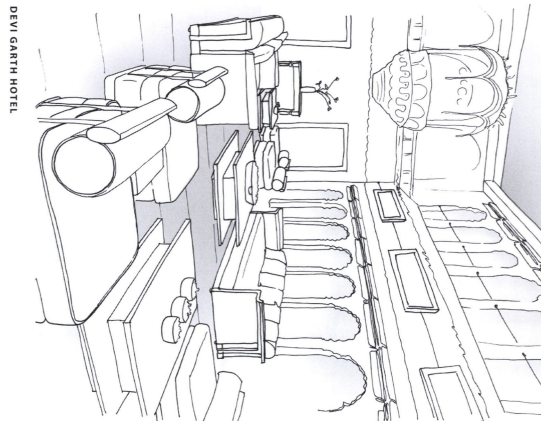

Above is a spacious sitting area with a rigid rhythm provided by the row of arched openings. The furniture is arranged in three groups. As in the previous example (of the hotel lobby/bar), multiple groups of users can occupy the space at the same time. The zones are connected, but each has a sense of spatial definition and territory.

SAARINEN HOUSE

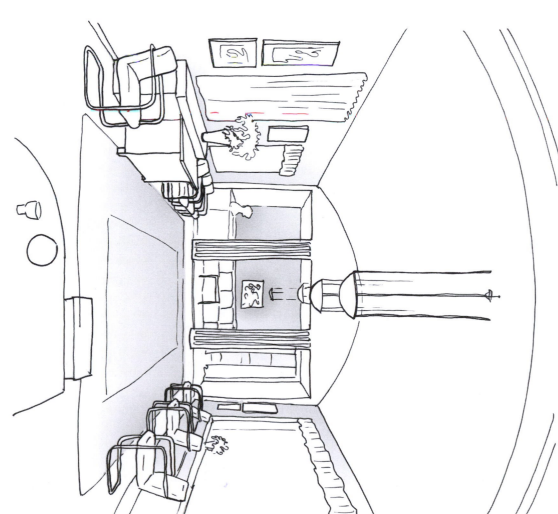

The living room above is not that large, yet it is spacious and comfortable. Note the furniture arrangement. Unlike the two previous examples, instead of being pulled together to form one or more tight groups, the pieces are pushed out toward the perimeter to form one single, large sitting arrangement. This type of arrangement is one of the options available. However, caution should be exercised, as there is a point at which the distance between opposite sides can be too great for comfortable conversation. In addition, in high-traffic areas the movement of people walking back and forth through the central circulation area could be disruptive.

Spatial Affinities

Certain kinds of spaces always seem to occur together. The kitchen and dining room are usually next to each other. The walk-in closet and master bathroom are always an integral part of the master bedroom suite. The reception area of an office facility tends to include the waiting area and is usually in close proximity to the conference room(s) used by visitors. These examples are instances of **spatial affinities**—related spaces that work well together as groups because of a strong functional relationship. These spaces are usually located adjacent to one another.

The placement of rooms and other spaces in any project is greatly affected by the functions that happen in them and by their relationship to other spaces. Some spaces need to be side by side to work well (e.g., the kitchen and dining room). Others require only a convenient short route (e.g., the bedroom and the bathroom down the hall). Still others ought to be far from each other (e.g., the rehearsal space for the house's drummer and the meditation room).

Many of the examples in this chapter are spaces that share spatial affinities. That's why the spaces occur together, as connected entities. Most are public areas in residential environments that work well as flowing units not requiring definite separation, as would be the case with bedrooms, for instance. These examples will help us focus on how to divide space and create separations while maintaining a sense of flow and connection.

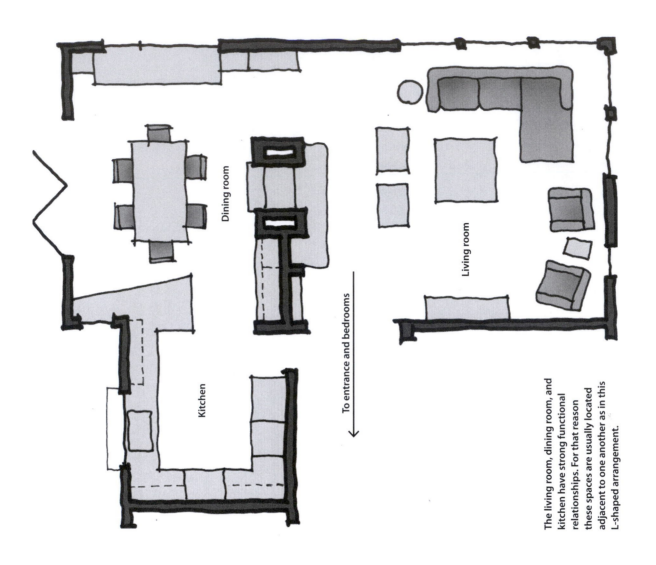

Dining room

Kitchen

To entrance and bedrooms

Living room

The living room, dining room, and kitchen have strong functional relationships. For that reason these spaces are usually located adjacent to one another as in this L-shaped arrangement.

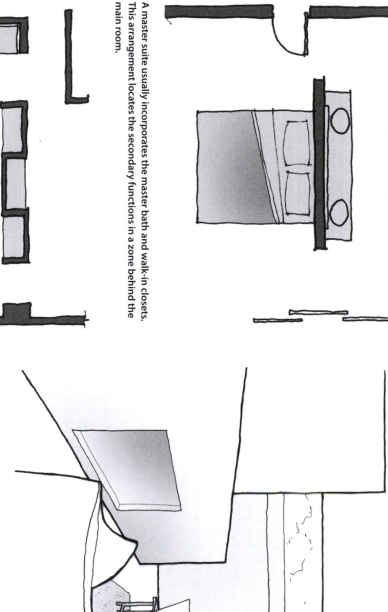

A master suite usually incorporates the master bath and walk-in closets. This arrangement locates the secondary functions in a zone behind the main room.

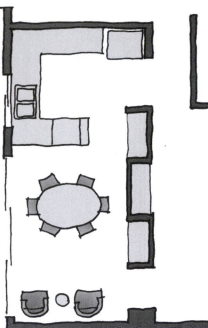

This partial view of an apartment shows the close proximity between the kitchen and the dining table, thus facilitating the transportation of dishes between the two areas.

LEE HOUSE

A common adjacency is the one between living room and dining area. These are often connected visually and functionally. Both occur within the public area of the house. This is usually where the family spends time together and where guests are received. There is also a natural flow from the living room to the dining table at dinnertime for many families. This, however, is an optional adjacency, not a required one. In fact, some families may insist on a more private dining room or on an arrangement that will allow a group (e.g., the children) to have dinner while another group (e.g., the parents and friends) converses privately in the living room.

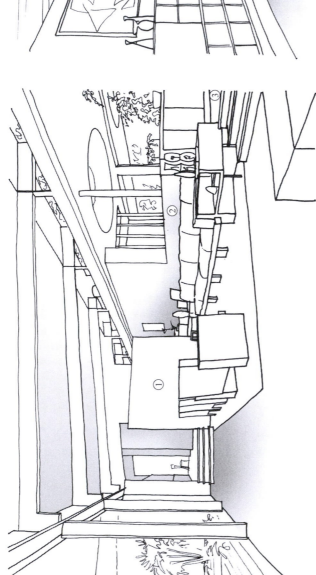

A. Partial-height walls and level changes

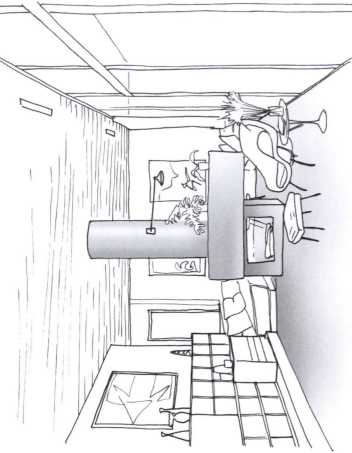

B. Floating architectural elements

Dividing Space

There are many ways of dividing and separating adjacent spaces beyond putting a full wall between them. Here are a few examples that provide separation while maintaining a sense of connection. Example A shows three ways to separate adjacent spaces. The first (1) is through the use of a tall, partial-height floating wall; the second (2) is by using the low (in this case, railing height) wall; and the third (3) is by having a level change between the two areas. Please note that even though it is common to have level changes requiring steps in residential projects, this practice should be avoided in most nonresidential projects because of the accessibility problems

they create. Example B illustrates the use of floating elements, such as furniture or architectural elements. In this instance, the floating, sculptural fireplace provides the separation between the two areas. Example C presents a short wall segment used in conjunction with low cabinetry to create effective separation/connection between kitchen, dining room, and living room. Example D shows a type of moveable partition (in this case, an accordion partition) that can be opened or closed as needed to afford different degrees of separation or connection between the three sleeping zones.

C. Wall segment and cabinetry

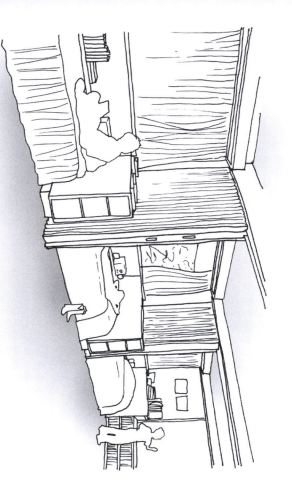

D. Moveable partitions

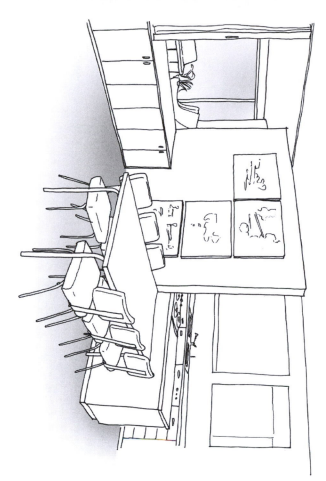

EXERCISE

For each of the three furniture groups shown below, design a dividing element along the dashed line to create a separation between the areas. The dividing element can be anything from a simple wall to a freestanding storage unit. The groups are living room and dining room in a residential setting (top), systems furniture cluster and adjacent meeting table in an office setting (center), and three informal work tables in an academic setting (bottom).

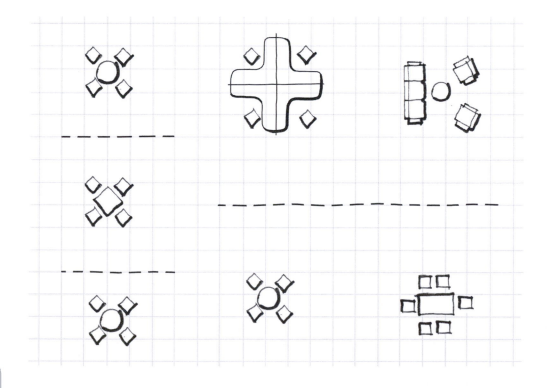

Dividing Space: Plan Views

The task of separating spaces while maintaining a sense of openness and connection is not that difficult once one becomes aware of the various strategies available to achieve it. Strategies usually require putting something partial between adjacent spaces, such as walls and screens. The size and extent of these pieces will differ. The goal is to provide enough separation without overdoing it. Specific requirements, of course, vary from case to case. In one instance, a minimal floating fireplace will work, whereas in another a longer, tall element, such as a solid wall, may be the right solution. Wall configurations for separating elements may be straight, straight with wing walls, or L-shaped. Elements with more mass include tall cabinets and various applications of "thick walls," often incorporating fireplaces in residential applications. These can become intricate configurations with storage, shelving, and similar devices, as shown in examples C and E on these pages. In some cases, actual floating rooms are used to subdivide space, as in example D.

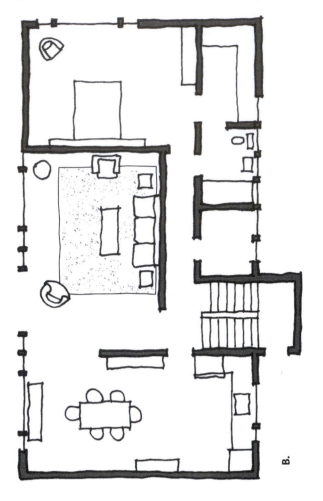

B.

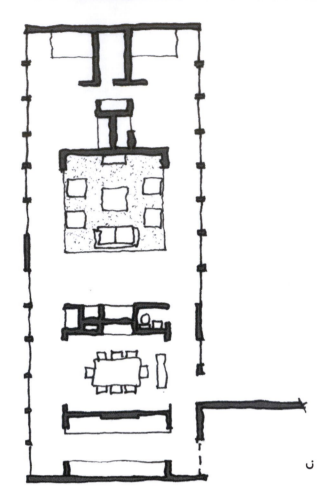

C.

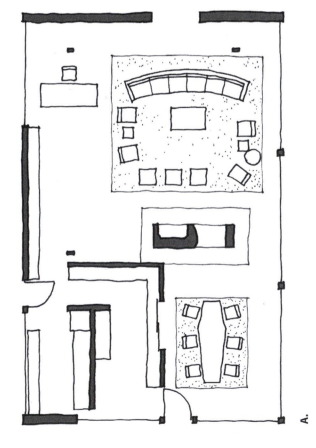

A.

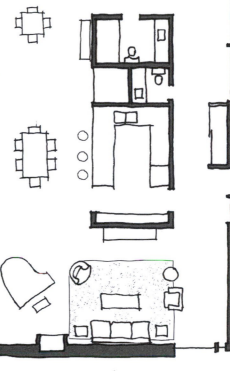

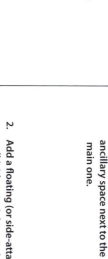

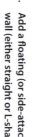

D.

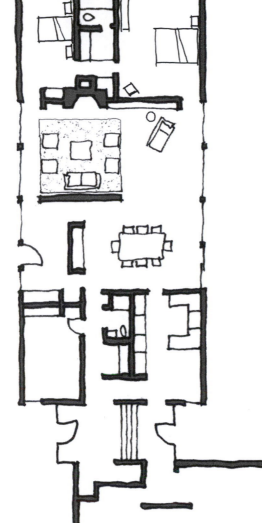

E.

Five Ways to Create Two Spaces

1. Protrude out, and create an ancillary space next to the main one.

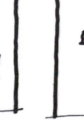
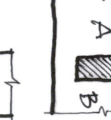

2. Add a floating (or side-attached) wall (either straight or L-shaped will work well).

3. Add a floating (or side-attached) mass. It may include cabinetry, shelving, or work counters, or a combination of these.

4. Add a floating (or side-attached) room or cluster of rooms.

5. Add a turn, such as an offset, to create two zones.

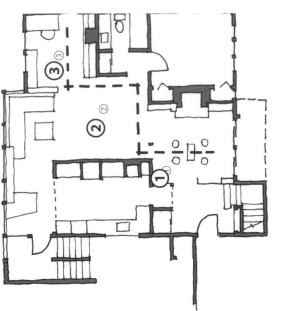

A. A freestanding central fireplace divides the main space into two subspaces.

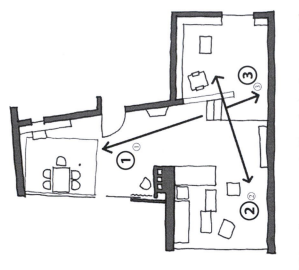

B. Triangular arrangement with wall extensions separate the three areas.

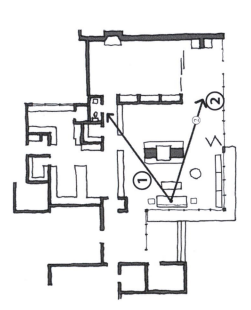

C. Two offsets define three sequential spaces.

Combining Spaces

One of the great pleasures one can experience in an interior environment is produced when conditions allow one to see parts of adjacent environments from one's vantage point. Such arrangement makes people feel connected and part of a greater whole. This connection obviously may not be desirable when high levels of privacy are required, but even in cases of moderate privacy needs, there can be a sense of enjoyment when one is able to see beyond, especially when looking out from a secure, protected environment. The three floor plan examples on this page show configurations that afford that ability to apprehend what we may call "the here and there." Example A features a main living space divided by a floating architectural element. Partial-height elements screen the main space from adjacent surrounding zones. Example B is arranged like a triangle, with a space in each of the three corners. Screening elements extend out slightly to give the living room and the study a bit more privacy, yet the minimal extent of screening allows for a sense of connection between the three spaces. Example C is a good example of using offset spatial sequences. The plan features two offsets, producing three sequential connected spaces, the living room, the central dining area, and the corner study.

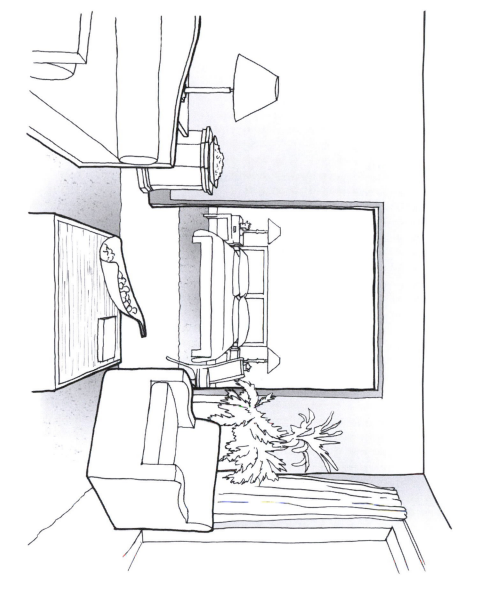

The axial view is formal and strong. The separating full wall between rooms has a wide central opening that frames the view of the centered bed beyond.

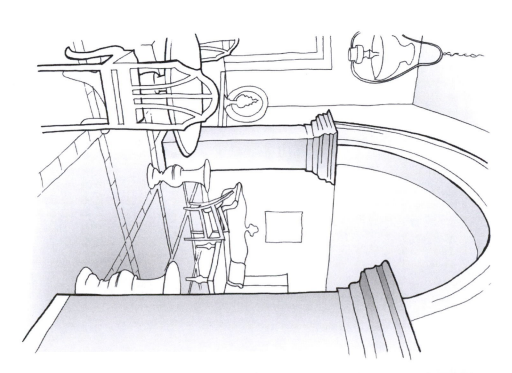

The lateral view is informal and appealing. In this case, the diagonal view framed by the tall archway gives a good angular glimpse of the seating area beyond.

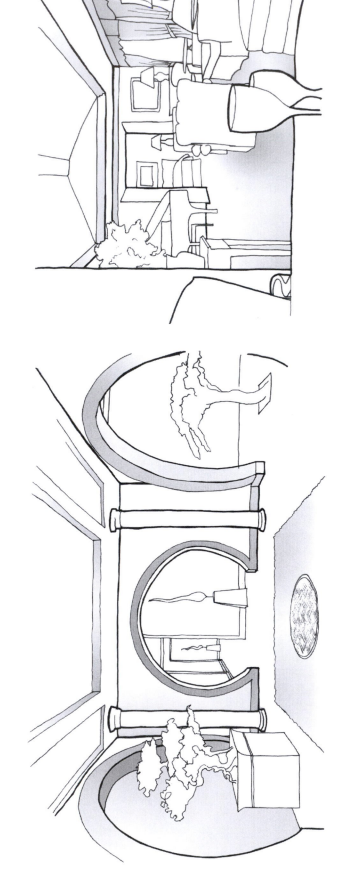

A. The offset corridor system and the sculptures beyond the great archway enhance the perception of spatial depth.

B. The wine glass, the chair, the piano, the bed, and the painting on the wall are perceived sequentially (from foreground to background) adding layers of depth and interest to the user's experience.

Layered Space

Certain experiences of the "here and there" are particularly pleasing and exciting. Some spatial arrangements are such that one can see not only the next space, but also the one beyond that and maybe even the one beyond that one, too. These arrangements help people see multiple layers of space at once, creating a true sense of spatial depth. Example A shows a view from a room into a staggered corridor that offers not one,

but two focal sculptural pieces of art, one beyond the central archway, the other one way in the back. The view in example B presents a long, multilayered room and then another room beyond that. One gets a real sense of foreground (here), middle ground (there), and background (farther there). The floor plan in example C shows a layered space in plan. Someone coming into the house, after taking a few steps, can see the

entry vestibule, the piano area, the living room with its fireplace divider, and the dining and kitchen areas beyond. In example D, the open shelving unit in the foreground provides a screened, filtered view of the spaces beyond. It is interesting how screened views and partial views can often contribute more to the positive experience than totally open views.

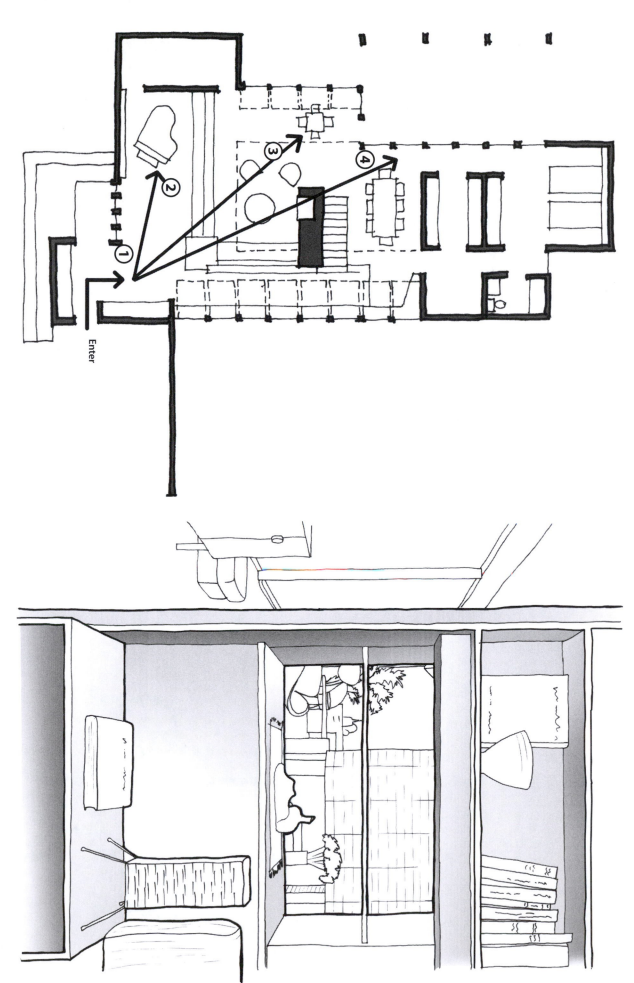

C. At least four spaces can be seen sequentially from the entry vestibule up front to the dining area in the back (and vice versa), giving this configuration a real sense of depth.

Enter

D. Screened partial views are often more intriguing and rewarding than open, panoramic views. The filtered view through the open shelving gives this visual experience a special interest.

KEDLESTON HALL

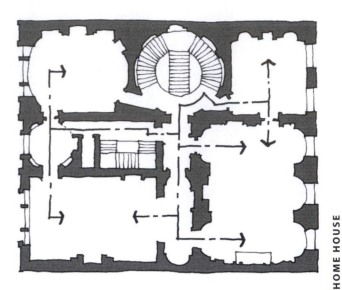

HOME HOUSE

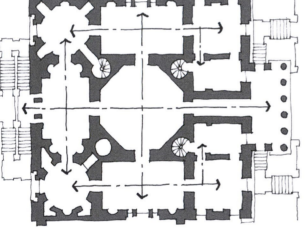

CHISWICK VILLA

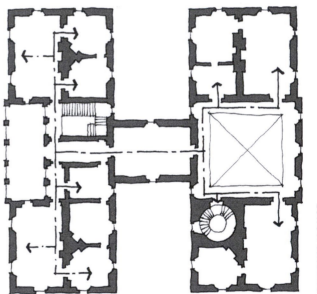

QUEEN'S HOUSE

Formal Sequences

The experiences offered by classical designs are different from those of modern designs. Classical designs tend to be formal and elegant. Although much of design done today favors open, less formal arrangements, designers have opportunities to use a more classical design vocabulary with certain projects. In classical design, strong emphasis is placed on the axis, and the experience is controlled and sequential. Random views are minimized in favor of well-planned views ahead and with each turn. Study the examples shown here carefully. Note the walls and how they are articulated. Note also the use of symmetry at both the overall level and the local level in the individual spaces.

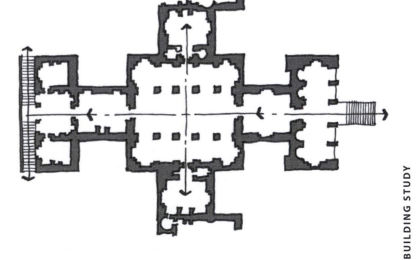

BUILDING STUDY

VILLA GALDES

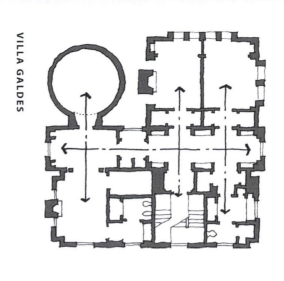

NAIMAN RESIDENCE

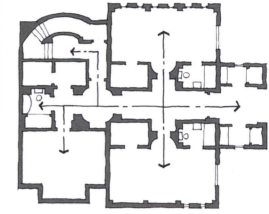

POOL ROOM, VILLA IN NEW JERSEY

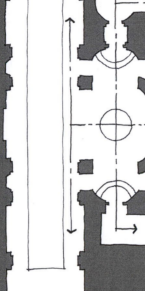

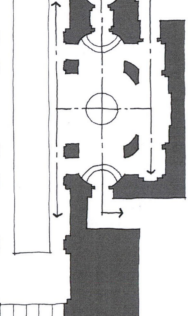

U.S. DEPARTMENT OF STATE

Formal, classical arrangements feature controlled circulation sequences with prominent axial qualities and well-planned focal points. These experiences are often multilayered as this view shows.

Informal Sequences

Informal sequences are open and free. Instead of strict axial views that look straight ahead, the user is offered unrestricted views in many directions. Arrangements are asymmetrical. Movement is also less restricted, more free. The same devices discussed under the topic of dividing space (see page 158) come into play here; floating elements, such as walls, are very common.

Example A has an axial circulation arrangement, but it is asymmetrical and pushed to one side. There is very little to block the views ahead. The partial wall by the steps and the steel column are just enough to provide a minimal sense of screening. The elevated section in the back provides a shift in the vertical dimension, and the person looking and walking from one end to another has to transition accordingly.

Examples B and C feature plans with open spatial sequences. Users move diagonally from front to back with ease and freedom. The exhibition hall in example D has an arrangement of floating, partial-height walls at right angles. The arrangement provides some structure to the experience of looking and moving about the space, but the experience is open, informal, and unrestricted.

There is no right or wrong about whether spatial sequences should be formal or informal. It is just a matter of fit. For many projects, one will make more sense than the other.

A. Living and dining room sequence

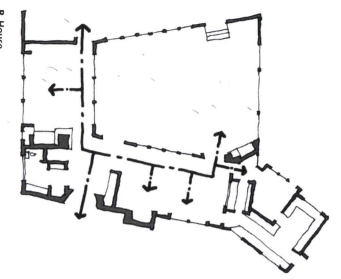

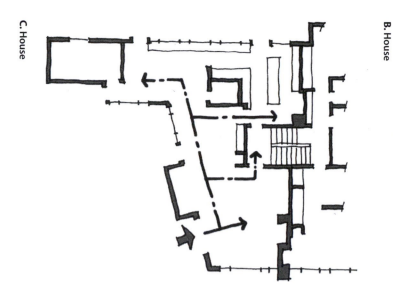

D. Exhibition hall

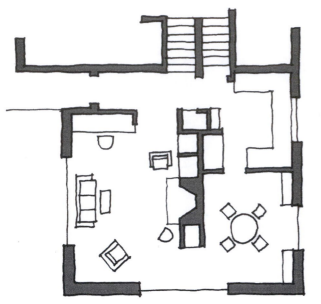

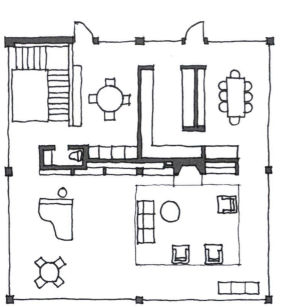

Floor plan A

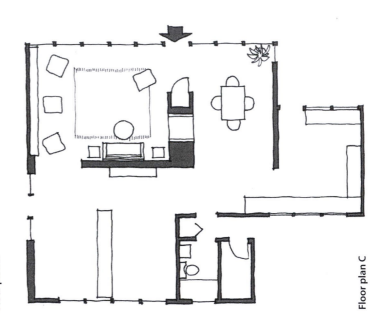

Floor plan B

Floor plan D

Floor plan C

Innovative Dividers

In the previous pages you saw examples of the kinds of elements used to divide spaces. One of these was the floating (or attached) wall. Another was the floating (or attached) element, such as cabinetry or a fireplace. Whereas some modern architecture pioneers, like Ludwig Mies van der Rohe, preferred the simple wall plane, others, such as Frank Lloyd Wright, favored more complex articulations of the floating element. It would often start with a fireplace. He would then add wall extensions and wing walls to the initial mass. Next, he would build in seating, cabinets, shelving, storage spaces. Eventually, the mass would end up looking like a spider or octopus, with all kinds of wings and projections.

Frequently, a single element alone can do the job of subdividing and defining space within the larger space. This is the case in Wright's Emil Bach House, in which a single floating element at the center addresses three different sides, integrating the fireplace and storage (example F). Study this element carefully, and get a sense of how it effectively acts as a divider, focal point, and storage space.

The other floor plan examples on these pages are just as fascinating, from a simple L-shaped divider (example C) to a long, T-shaped system that incorporates seating, cabinetry, a fireplace, and even a small bathroom (example A). Take some time to look at and understand the examples. Note how they all started with a single element (the fireplace) that evolved into efficient, complex systems addressing multiple sides and functions. Strive to understand how these elements work and what it takes to conceive and develop them. The exercise on the next page will give you a chance to create some of your own.

EXERCISE

Using the 3' × 3' (91 cm × 91 cm) grid as a guide, design three different innovative dividers inspired by the examples on these pages. Feel free to borrow ideas from the examples. Make sure your divider addresses at least two sides, maybe more. Try to combine multiple elements, such as a fireplace, extension walls, and storage. Have fun.

Floor plan E

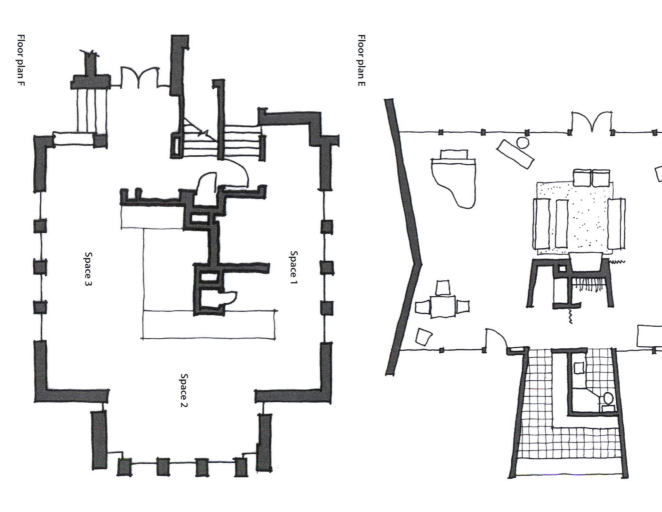

Space 1

Space 2

Floor plan F

Space 3

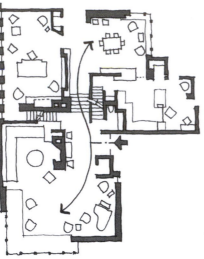

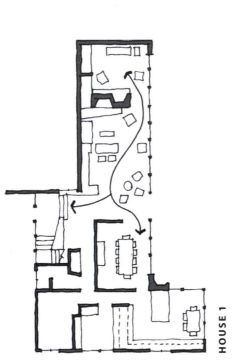

HOUSE 1

HOUSE 2

TUGENDHAT HOUSE

Flow in Spatial Sequences

Accommodating efficient and convenient circulation is necessary at all scales, from the single room to the entire project. Here, we focus on the idea of good flow between contiguous spaces. It is easy to make traffic paths that are bumpy and that lack flow. It is just as easy, however, to create good ones. All it takes is a commitment to keep circulation clear, simple, and efficient. Having fewer walls, fewer doors, and direct paths between spaces are all ways of creating flowing circulation routes.

You don't need all those factors, though. Sometimes you don't have one and compensate with another. For example, we saw with formal sequences how it was possible to create good circulation systems in projects with many walls and doors. This was achieved by using a simple and recognizable configuration of the path itself. The projects presented here lack the simple axial circulation systems of the classical examples. They make up for that by using open spaces that facilitate movement. Walls and doors are minimized in order to produce openness, which then allows for good flow.

Study the examples carefully. Some are simple, others, more complex. Yet, all are orchestrated in ways that facilitate flowing movement between the spaces.

A great room with a linear circulation system allows for flowing traffic between the kitchen and the living/dining areas.

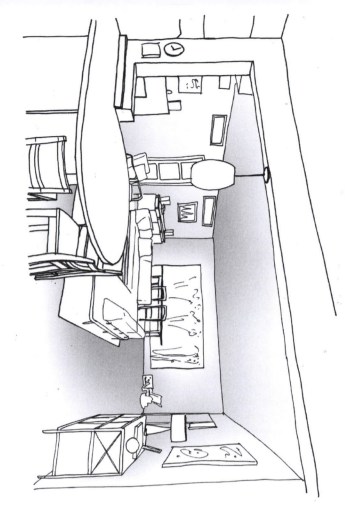

A hotel suite with a well placed door between rooms that connects the circulation routes provides good flow despite the many contents.

Think about where you place your rooms. The relationship of a given room or space to the circulation system is an important consideration that impacts the experience of the room. Spaces 1, 2, and 3 in the adjacent diagram are rooms right off the main circulation path. They are autonomous but easy to reach. Space 4 is peculiar. All back-and-forth traffic between the two sides of the system must go through this room. Space 6 is very different. One must go through another space (5) to find it. It is not the kind of room one accidentally bumps into. The location of space 7 is strategic. Its placement at the end of the main spine makes it more private, yet easy to find. Finally, the location of room 8 makes the room special. Its placement around the far corner and at the very end of the system makes it highly secluded and private.

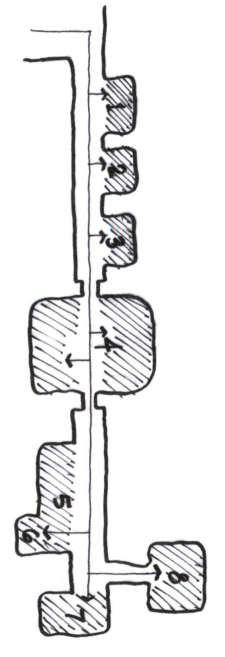

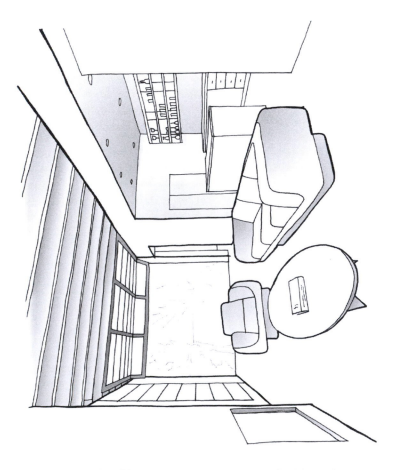

Grounding in Open Spaces

In Chapter 4 I introduced the notion of **grounding**, or **anchoring**, furnishings and other elements in relation to perimeter as well as internal grounding elements, which include wall segments, pockets, alcoves, corners, overhead ceiling elements, and flooring changes. In these cases, the grounding element defines a space in which, for example, a seating group can occur and not appear to be floating aimlessly. The seating group shown in perspective above is grounded in space by its relationship to the fireplace. The adjacent kitchen area is grounded within the carved space behind the seating group. The seating group and the kitchen are not drifting. They have a home.

As designers, we use both existing natural features and new ones created for grounding purposes. In fact, many of the dividers previously shown in this chapter also serve to ground surrounding furnishings and functions. The furniture plan on this spread shows examples of grounding strategies, both on the periphery and on the inside. Walls, rooms, columns, overhead features, and floor changes all serve the purpose.

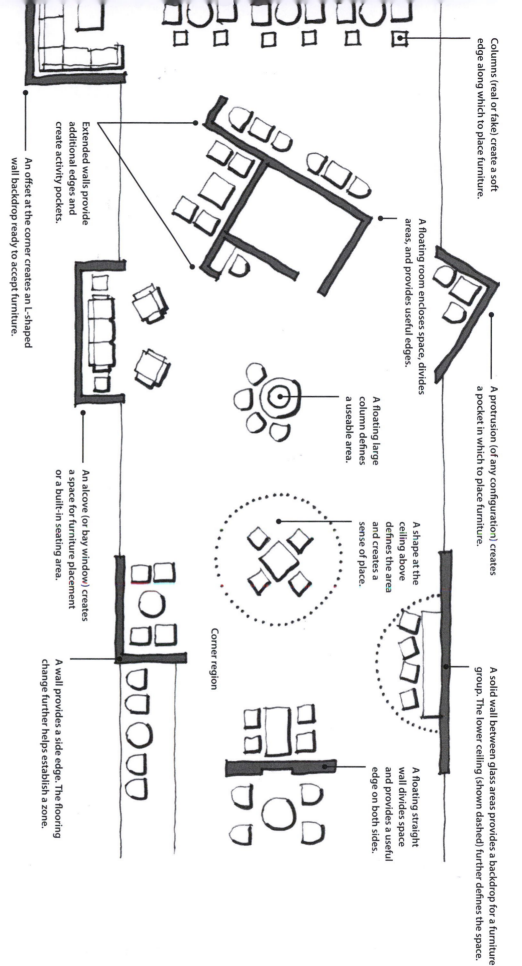

Columns (real or fake) create a soft edge along which to place furniture.

A protrusion (of any configuration) creates a pocket in which to place furniture.

A solid wall between glass areas provides a backdrop for a furniture group. The lower ceiling (shown dashed) further defines the space.

A floating room encloses space, divides areas, and provides useful edges.

A shape at the ceiling above defines the area and creates a sense of place.

A floating large column defines a useable area.

A floating straight wall divides space and provides a useful edge on both sides.

Extended walls provide additional edges and create activity pockets.

Corner region

A wall provides a side edge. The flooring change further helps establish a zone.

An offset at the corner creates an L-shaped wall backdrop ready to accept furniture.

An alcove (or bay window) creates a space for furniture placement or a built-in seating area.

EXERCISE 1

Using the 4'×4'(122 cm×122 cm) grid provided to the left, extend the room shown on this page. Create new grounding elements, and place furnishings by them. Use the plan shown both for ideas and as scale reference. You may use the same kinds of furniture groups on the exercise side. Good luck.

EXERCISE 2

As in the previous exercise, use the 4' × 4' (122 cm × 122 cm) grid provided to the left to extend the room shown on this page. Create new grounding elements, and place furnishings by them. Use the plan shown, both for ideas and as scale reference. You may use the same kinds of furniture groups on the exercise side. Try some new ideas and configurations this time. Have fun.

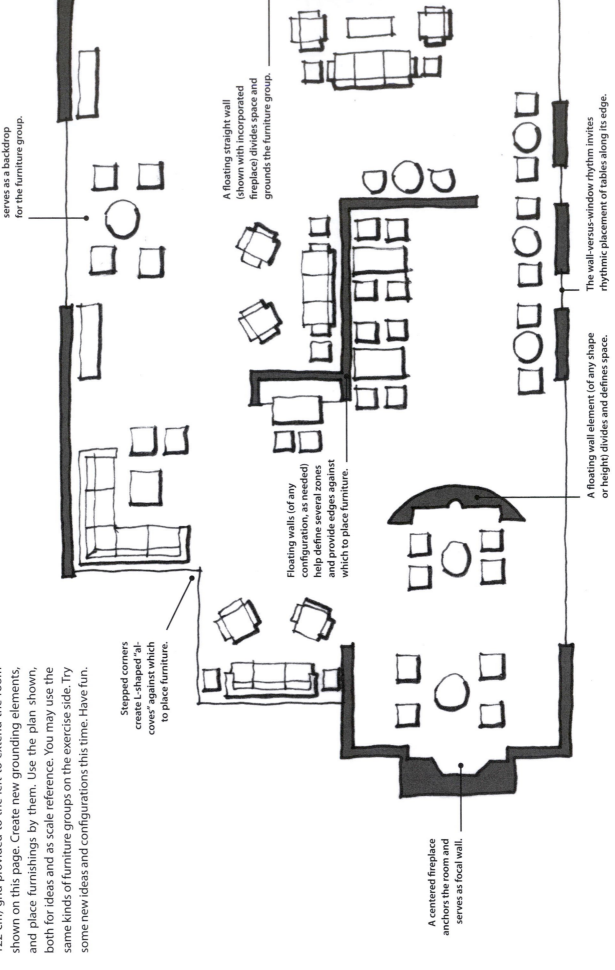

A wide linear window zone at the perimeter serves as a backdrop for the furniture group.

A floating straight wall (shown with incorporated fireplace) divides space and grounds the furniture group.

The wall-versus-window rhythm invites rhythmic placement of tables along its edge.

A floating wall element (of any shape or height) divides and defines space.

Floating walls (of any configuration, as needed) help define several zones and provide edges against which to place furniture.

Stepped corners create L-shaped "alcoves" against which to place furniture.

A centered fireplace anchors the room and serves as focal wall.

Thresholds and Prospect

The two concepts introduced in these pages influence spatial transitions and connections as well as the experience of walking around a project. They are not difficult concepts to grasp. Yet, many designers go about their daily design chores without paying much attention to them.

Threshold

You may have heard the term **threshold** used in reference to a door sill, such as the wood or metal sills found underneath the entrance doors to most houses and other buildings. That definition is correct and starts to point toward the larger meaning of the concept. A threshold is the point at which something new (in our case, a room or space) begins. It is also the line marking the boundary of an area. If you think back to the threshold under an entrance door, you realize that it is, in fact, the point at which the outside and the inside meet; it is a transition point, and by going through the door, we transition from one space to the next.

The idea of threshold is often used to articulate design transitions in projects. A threshold does not need to be a line on the floor at a doorway. A threshold can be deep and long. You can choose to make the transition between one space and the next a short corridor or "tunnel" or even a room between two spaces you want to join. Refer to Illustration A on this page for some ideas.

Although usually associated with transitions along circulation spaces, thresholds also occur at points where the connection between two spaces is visible. In other words, an interior window is as much a threshold as a doorway. Transparent glass partitions and other

screens that allow you to see from one space to the next are also threshold points. Illustration B shows some conceptual ideas of internal windows and similar thresholds that help connect one space with the next.

Prospect

The word **prospect** has several definitions. In architectural lingo, a prospect is a view or scene, usually seen ahead. Here, we are concerned with the way spaces and their features present themselves to us as we walk around an interior space, perhaps as we go down a

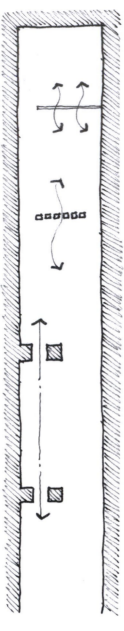

A. Thresholds

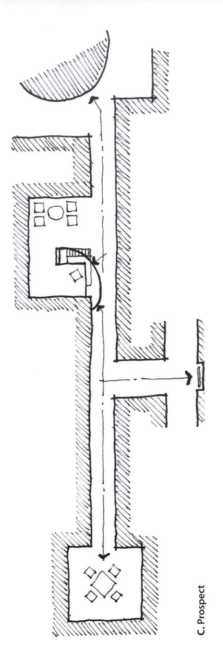

B. Windows and screens

C. Prospect

A window affords visual connection between rooms.

A threshold zone serves to connect two spaces. In this case, the threshold serves not only as a passageway but as bookshelves as well. The prospect ahead consists of a partial view of a seating area.

The underside of the stairway creates a threshold zone that connects the corridor with the space beyond. Here, the prospect is an axial symmetrical view of the fireplace and seating group ahead.

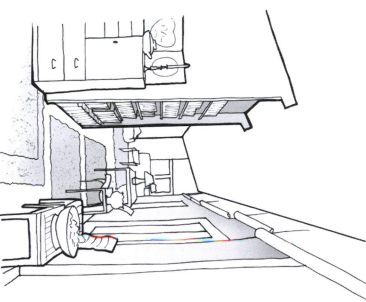
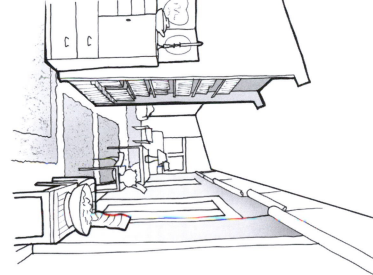

corridor. We may see a nicely framed interior vista at the end, with a piece of art or a seating group. This may be centered with the corridor. We may also see just a portion of the scene ahead, perhaps planned that way to make us curious and invite us to go further and explore.

The partial view may also be a way to provide a hint of a place we are trying to find, such as a reception area.

As you plan spatial sequences and circulation areas, always think about what is seen ahead or around the

turn. Is a focal point the thing to have? Do you want to present a nice, symmetrical framed view or just a portion of a furniture group to give users an indication of what lies ahead or to entice them to explore further? Illustration C shows some examples.

Joining Enclosed Rooms

So far we have been concerned with the division and connection of mostly open spaces. This emphasis has been intentional because orchestrating those kinds of sequences is harder than linking groups of rooms. Linking enclosed spaces as clusters, however, can be somewhat tricky for the novice designer, and many of the possibilities may go unexplored. Here, we look at a few ways of arranging enclosed spaces into clusters.

Before we get into clusters, let's take one last look at large single spaces and some of their subspaces. This will help us distinguish between minor secondary spaces along a main volume and major secondary additions that result in a compound shape. Look at the floor plan of the Basilica of Sant'Andrea by Leon Battista Alberti, on this page. Note the main nave space, with its many ancillary small chapels on either side. These are good examples of minor secondary spaces added along a main space. As we get to the transept and apse areas, toward the front of the church, we distinguish two fairly large spaces flanking the main nave and creating the Roman cross configuration. These are not the small side chapels along the nave; they are spaces of such size that they make the overall shape a compound shape in the form of a cross, or *T*.

The Walt Disney World Casting Center by Robert A. M. Stern (at right) serves as a good introduction to groups of enclosed spaces. Note three things: (1) there are many rooms of the same size; (2) rooms along the perimeter occur in rows, with occasional gaps between them; and (3) interior rooms are of various sizes and form a cluster with a clean, rectangular shape. These observations tell us a couple of things about interior enclosed spaces. First, there is a hierarchy of room importance and size; there are small rooms and large rooms, and both have to be accommodated. Second, groups of rooms tend to happen in rows (typically the case for perimeter rooms) or clusters (typically the case for interior rooms).

Study the diagrammatic examples on the following page. They show some common combinations of rooms.

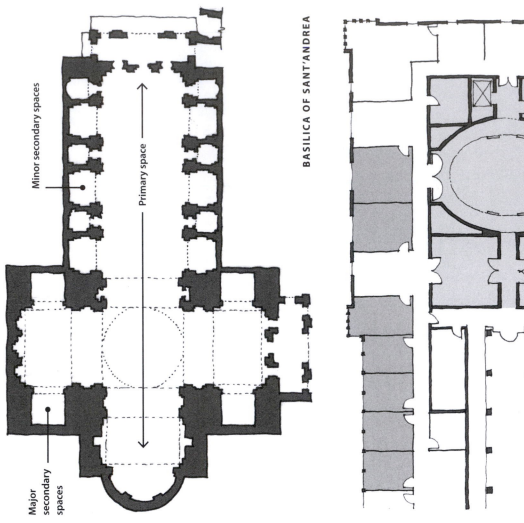

BASILICA OF SANT'ANDREA

Minor secondary spaces

Primary space

Major secondary spaces

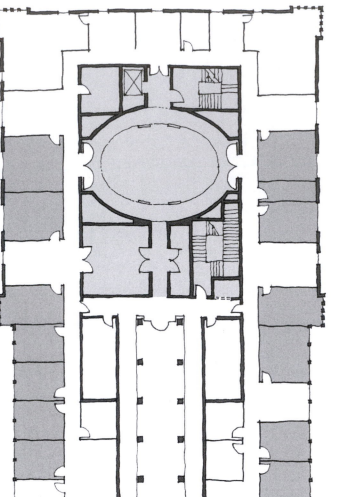

WALT DISNEY WORLD CASTING CENTER

Dividing Spaces

Rooms of Equal Size

Rooms of roughly equal size, such as offices, can be arranged in rows or as clusters, depending on conditions and location. Clusters simply require a back-to-back arrangement of rows to create a double-sided configuration. Location of doors requires careful consideration. Criteria include acoustic privacy, compositional arrangement of the doors (rhythm), and the occasional need for clean walls without doors.

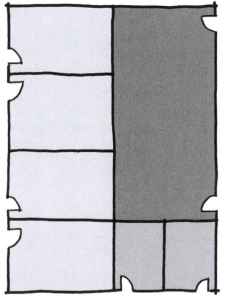

Rooms of Unequal Size

Most times, you will need to create clusters of rooms of different sizes plus storage areas, such as bands of files or closets. Above are two diagrammatic examples of such conditions. Note that usually the goal is to arrive at a good and regular overall shape. It doesn't always have to result in a neat rectangle, but it should almost always strive to be a clean, regular shape. In this case, too, it is important to give proper thought to the location of doors.

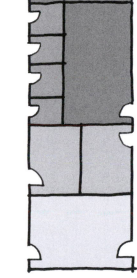

In the space provided, and using the grid as guide, distribute the spaces given below. Indicate door locations. Use almost all the shapes given, but leave a corner of the overall rectangle unused (as shown) to create a well-grounded seating area.

- Four spaces of 2 × 3 squares
- Two spaces of 4 × 5 squares
- Two spaces of 2 × 2 squares
- One space of 3 × 3 squares
- One space of 1 × 3 squares

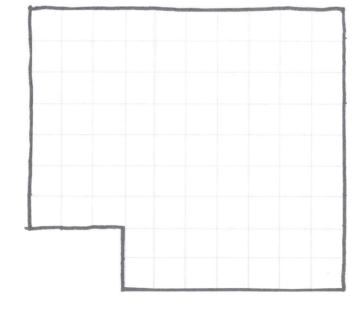

Executive Retreat Center

EXERCISE 1

Study the six schemes shown for the gathering spaces in an executive retreat center. They are all variations on the same theme with only subtle differences between one scheme and the next. In the space below, identify your favorite scheme and use bullets to explain why. Also identify your least favorite scheme and also explain why.

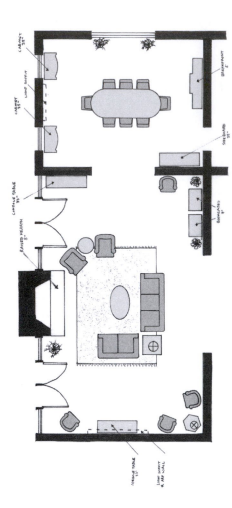

Scheme 1A

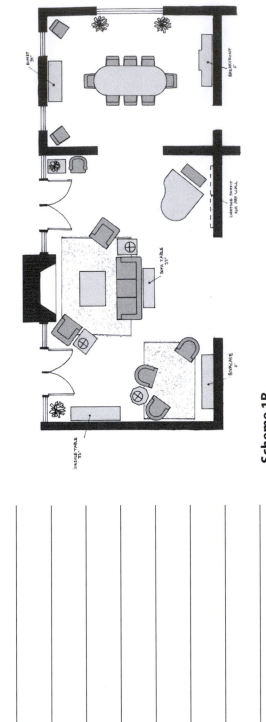

Scheme 1B

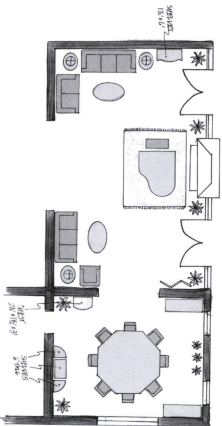

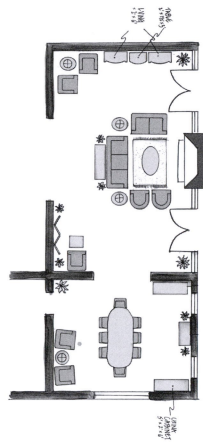

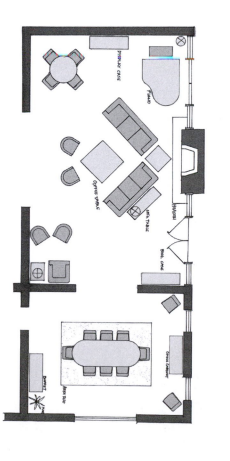

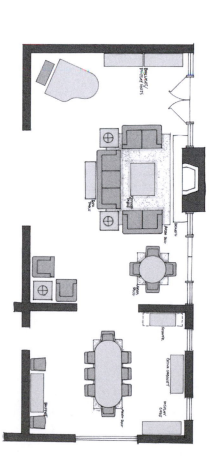

EXERCISE 2

Subdivide the spaces shown as described below. Assume the grid is 4′ × 4′ (122 cm × 122 cm).

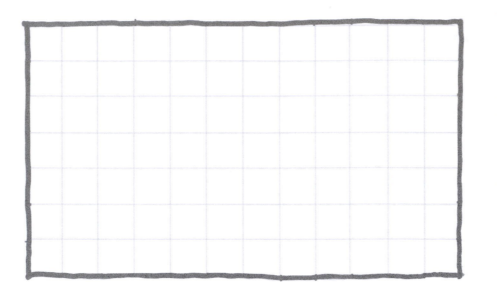

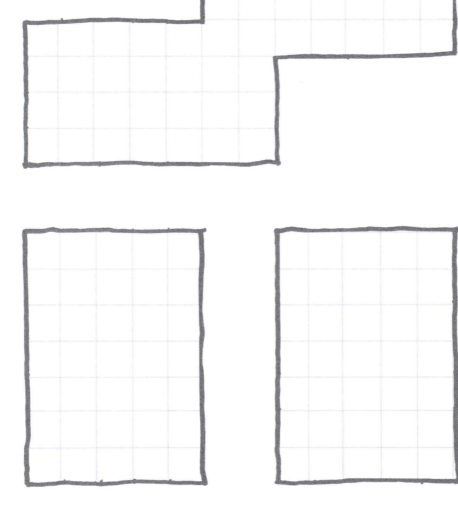

A. On one of the two rectangular areas, use one dividing element to create two sides. Make one side larger and primary and the other secondary. On the other rectangle, use one dividing element to create three zones: a primary zone and two secondary zones.

B. Within the offset configuration given, determine a space for a kitchen (approximately 6 to 8 squares in size). Use the walls of the kitchen, wall extensions, and one or two other dividers as needed to create spaces for a living room, a dining room, and a small study. Configure your solution to produce good continuity and flow.

C. Locate a room (approximately 12 squares) anywhere inside the large rectangle. Extend walls from this room as needed to incorporate a fireplace, shelving, and other storage areas. You need to end up with four well-defined areas of various sizes in addition to the original room. Good connections and flow are important for this solution, too.

EXERCISE 3

Assuming a 5' × 5' (152 cm × 152 cm) grid and the furniture types shown, space plan the space shown, of a hotel lobby, to accommodate as many seating areas as possible. Divide the space as needed with walls,

screens, and other elements. Use any combination of the furniture types given, in any configuration. Plan the circulation carefully, and show primary circulation with lines and arrows.

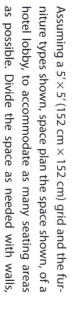

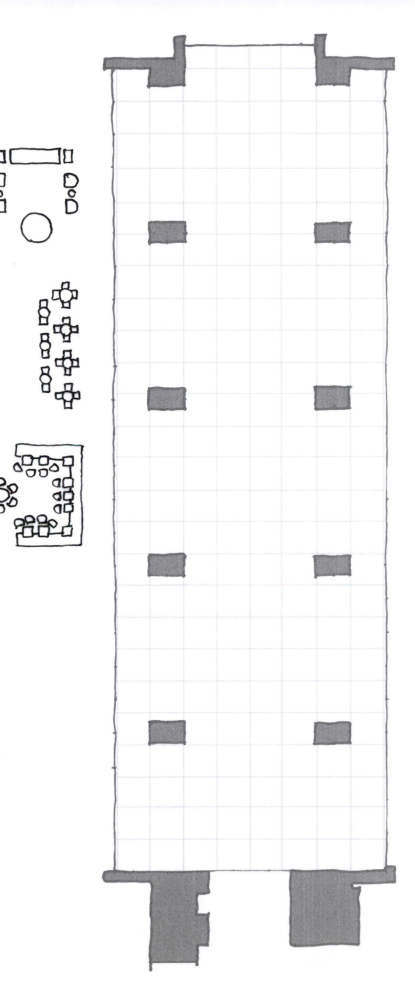

The Project

Projects can be judged a number of different ways. Four useful ways of looking at the space planning of full projects are suggested here. When you analyze a floor plan, you'll note a number of things. First, a plan is a collection of spaces (or "rooms") with particular physical characteristics. Some spaces are open and others are enclosed, some are large and some are small. Second, spaces can be assembled in different ways. Spaces can be autonomous, or they can flow into one another. They can occur toward the inside or around the perimeter. Third, it is possible to classify spaces based on the kind of function they perform. Some spaces are the main spaces, and others are supporting spaces. There are also service spaces, storage spaces, and circulation spaces, for getting around. Finally, spaces can be conceptualized in terms of the degree to which they are public or private. Some areas are clearly "front of the house" public zones, while others are private and off limits to visitors unless they have been given permission to enter. These principles are summarized at far right and are illustrated on the two floor plans shown on these pages.

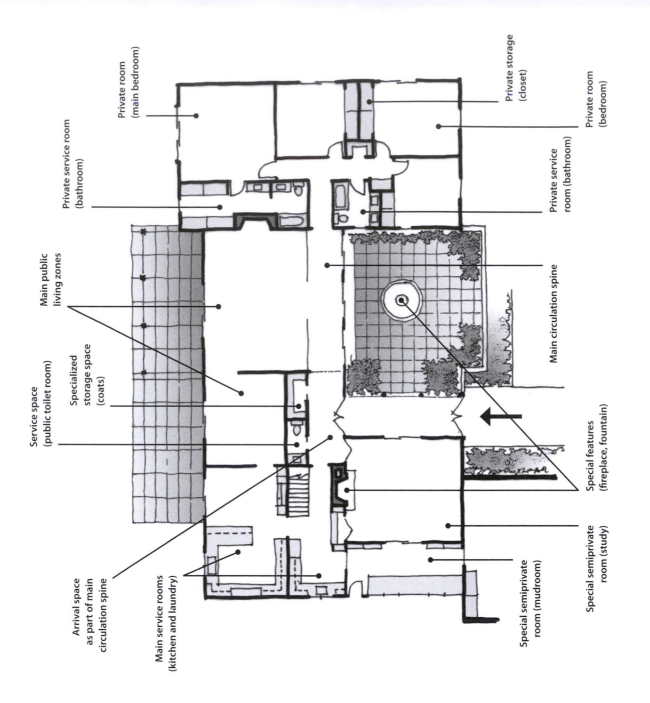

Private room (main bedroom)

Private service room (bathroom)

Main public living zones

Service space (public toilet room)

Specialized storage space (coats)

Arrival space as part of main circulation spine

Main service rooms (kitchen and laundry)

Special semiprivate room (mudroom)

Special semiprivate room (study)

Special features (fireplace, fountain)

Main circulation spine

Private service room (bathroom)

Private room (bedroom)

Private storage (closet)

Four Ways to Analyze Space Planning

Spaces may be analyzed according to the following considerations:

Spaces may be analyzed according to the following considerations:

1. Their physical characteristics
   - Open spaces
   - Enclosed spaces
   - Semienclosed spaces
   - Small spaces
   - Large spaces

2. The way they are combined and placed
   - Autonomous spaces
   - Connected spaces
   - Internal spaces
   - Perimeter spaces

3. The general function they perform
   - Main spaces
   - Supporting spaces
   - Service spaces
   - Storage spaces
   - Circulation spaces

4. Their degree of exposure
   - Public spaces
   - Semipublic spaces
   - Private spaces

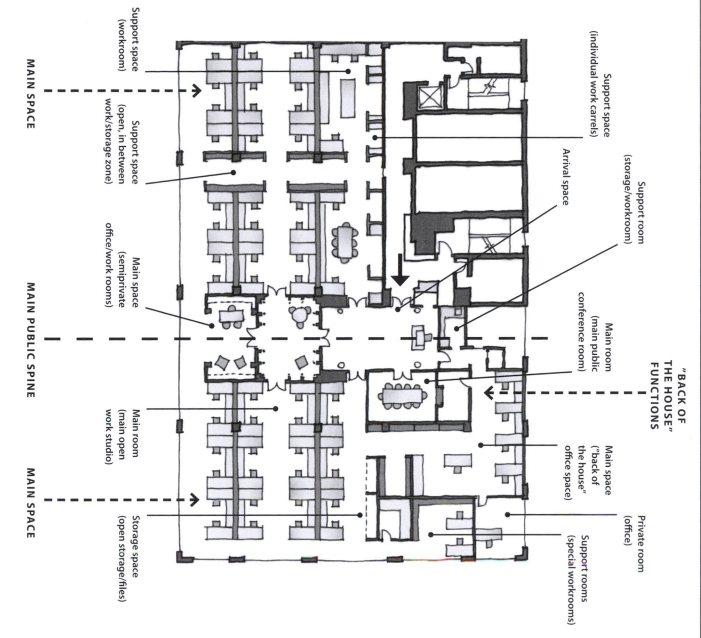

ARCHITECT'S OFFICE

MAIN SPACE

MAIN PUBLIC SPINE

MAIN SPACE

Support space (workroom)

Support space (open, in between work/storage zone)

Main space (semiprivate office/work rooms)

Main room (main open work studio)

Storage space (open storage/files)

Support room (storage/workroom)

Support space (individual work carrels)

Arrival space

Main room (main public conference room)

"BACK OF THE HOUSE" FUNCTIONS

Main space ("back of the house" office space)

Private room (office)

Support rooms (special workrooms)

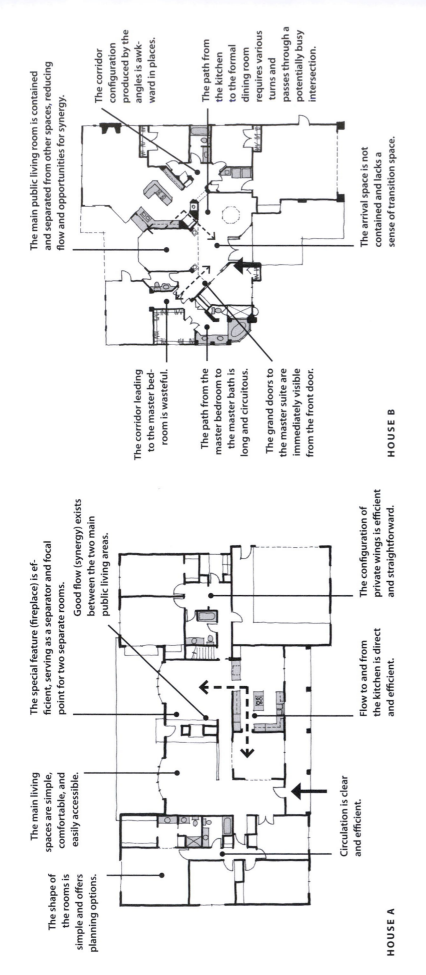

HOUSE B

The main public living room is contained and separated from other spaces, reducing flow and opportunities for synergy.

The corridor configuration produced by the angles is awkward in places.

The path from the kitchen to the formal dining room requires various turns and passes through a potentially busy intersection.

The corridor leading to the master bedroom is wasteful.

The path from the master bedroom to the master bath is long and circuitous.

The grand doors to the master suite are immediately visible from the front door.

The arrival space is not contained and lacks a sense of transition space.

HOUSE A

The shape of the rooms is simple and offers planning options.

The main living spaces are simple, comfortable, and easily accessible.

The special feature (fireplace) is efficient, serving as a separator and focal point for two separate rooms.

Good flow (synergy) exists between the two main public living areas.

Flow to and from the kitchen is direct and efficient.

The configuration of private wings is efficient and straightforward.

Circulation is clear and efficient.

Project Qualities

To design a successful project, you must pay careful attention to its basic functional and perceptual considerations. Two pairs of projects are presented here. The first is a pair of single-family residences. The plans are adaptations from standard house plan books. House A is simple, cohesive, practical, and efficient. The design is restrained and straightforward.

In House B, the designer is trying hard to create interest using a combination of orthogonal and angular geometries. Although that approach can be used successfully, it can produce a plan with too many twists and turns resulting from the combination of angular and orthogonal forms.

It is possible to produce successful designs that are intricate and complex, but they often take a lot more effort to resolve. For that reason, it is recommended that novice designers avoid unnecessary complexity.

The second pair of projects consists of two restaurants. Here, we compare their degree of practicality using functional criteria related to the entrance/waiting area, the bar area, and the traffic patterns to and from the kitchen by the waitstaff. Restaurant A seems to work better. The waiting area is clearly defined and comfortable, and the bar is conveniently located and presents itself as a clear destination. Moreover, the two separate ways to access the kitchen make it easier for waitstaff to

minimize conflicts with patrons' circulation. Restaurant B has a few problems. The dining tables by the waiting area are workable but increase traffic in an already busy location. Also, the placement of the bar in a separate space in the back makes it a somewhat hidden destination, clearly secondary. Finally, the single path from the kitchen to the dining areas produces some circulation conflicts between waitstaff and patrons.

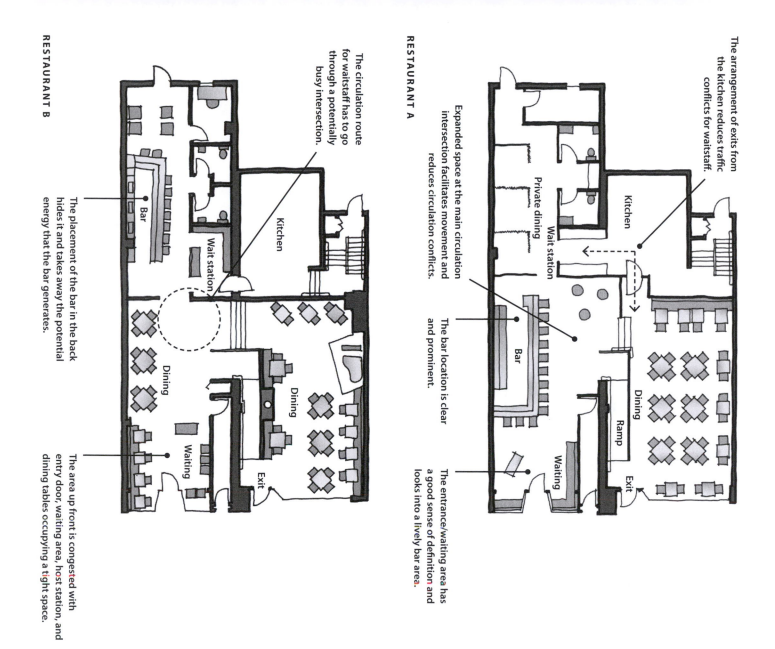

RESTAURANT A

The arrangement of exits from the kitchen reduces traffic conflicts for waitstaff.

Expanded space at the main circulation intersection facilitates movement and reduces circulation conflicts.

The bar location is clear and prominent.

The entrance/waiting area has a good sense of definition and looks into a lively bar area.

Private dining

Wait station

Kitchen

Bar

Dining

Ramp

Waiting

Exit

RESTAURANT B

The circulation route for waitstaff has to go through a potentially busy intersection.

The placement of the bar in the back hides it and takes away the potential energy that the bar generates.

The area up front is congested with entry door, waiting area, host station, and dining tables occupying a tight space.

Bar

Wait station

Kitchen

Dining

Dining

Waiting

Exit

Four Basic Qualities

Planning entire projects can be complex. It requires the synthesis of many requirements and circumstances into a cohesive whole. Chapter 3 addressed the process for space planning. Here, we focus on four basic qualities to strive for when beginning to plan interiors.

Simplicity

Strive for simplicity. It does not come easy and is sometimes consciously avoided by students in the interest of being expressive and creative. Take a complex project with many intricate requirements, and synthesize it into a well-organized, straightforward solution. Try to make your solution clear, not convoluted. Exercise restraint when making design decisions. Suppress the urge to force in foreign shapes and gestures for the sake of being creative.

Cohesion

Strive for a cohesive scheme, one that really "hangs together" and makes sense as a whole. Avoid excessive fragmentation. The basic organization of the project should be apparent and logical.

Practicality

Strive for planning solutions that afford convenience and comfort. Locate spaces appropriately. Plan your circulation system carefully to ensure good flow. Create a design that is conducive to the functions it houses, facilitating, not hindering, them.

Efficiency

Strive to avoid waste. Shorter routes are better than longer ones. While still aiming for comfort, avoid making spaces larger than they need to be. As much as possible, incorporate spaces and features that can perform more than one function (double duty). Try to do more with less.

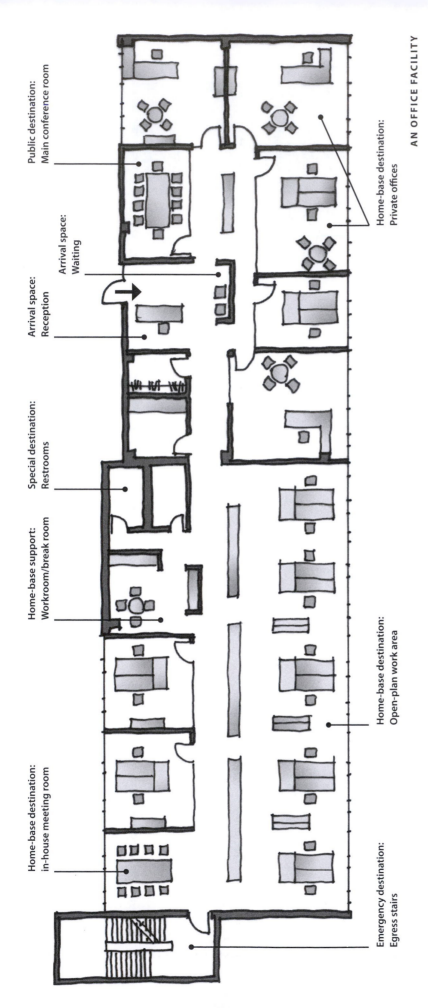

Public destination:
Main conference room

Arrival space:
Waiting

Arrival space:
Reception

Special destination:
Restrooms

Home-base support:
Workroom/break room

Home-base destination:
in-house meeting room

Home-base destination:
Private offices

Home-base destination:
Open-plan work area

Emergency destination:
Egress stairs

AN OFFICE FACILITY

Project Parts

Other than the house, apartment, or dormitory where we live, we go to places as visitors. The majority of interiors designers plan are places of temporary habitation. Of those spending time in these places, we can distinguish between what we might call locals and visitors. Locals are the people who spend time at a place regularly, usually working. Examples include the doctors, nurses, and assistants at a clinic; the employees of an office facility; and the clerks at a store. These people often have access to the entire facility, much like we have full access to our entire house. Visitors are those people who come to shop, dine, attend an appointment, or otherwise visit

briefly for some kind of exchange. They may come by regularly, or they may be one-time visitors.

An interior facility provides places for all these players to act out their roles. With that in mind, we now consider the typical events and destinations associated with most interior environments. All these require insightful planning in order to provide optimal experiences for both locals and visitors.

We start with the arrival and consider the experience of a visitor. There is usually a secured entry door and the

space into which one arrives. Pertinent questions to consider when designing include the following: Where is the main entrance? Is it easy to find? Once inside the door, is it easy to get oriented? What is the initial impression? Is the arrival space contained or open to other spaces? Frequently, the arrival space serves as an access control gate; in offices, clinics, and many restaurants someone will greet visitors, and they will often be asked to wait. What is the waiting experience like? Is the space comfortable or claustrophobic? Does the furniture arrangement facilitate being at ease among strangers? Are there views beyond the immediate waiting area? Are there views to the outside? Is there a focal point? Is the receptionist station and its surroundings pleasant for someone who has to sit there all day?

Then there are the various destinations. These usually constitute the majority of the space and house the main functions. If it's a clinic, the examination room is the main destination; if it's a shop, the retail space is the main destination; if it's a restaurant, the chosen table is the destination place for an hour or so. There are usually places for locals only and places where locals and visitors interact.

In a restaurant, the cook is in the kitchen. The waitstaff move back and forth between the kitchen and dining room. The patrons are limited to the dining room areas. In an office, each worker will have his or her own office or workstation. Visitors will usually be limited to the waiting area and one of the conference rooms.

Consider what happens in these and other places you are asked to design. Generally, there is a principal transaction. What is it, and where does it take place? Around a table in a conference room? At a dining table? While on the table in an examination room?

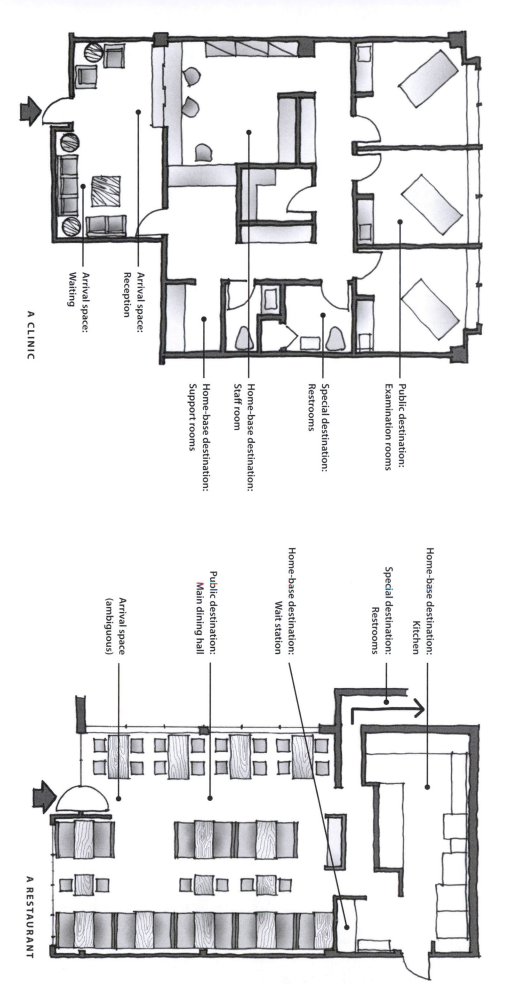

A CLINIC

Arrival space: Waiting

Arrival space: Reception

Special destination: Restrooms

Home-base destination: Staff room

Home-base destination: Support rooms

Public destination: Examination rooms

Home-base destination: Kitchen

Special destination: Restrooms

Home-base destination: Wait station

Public destination: Main dining hall

Arrival space (ambiguous)

A RESTAURANT

Over a transaction counter? Think, then, in terms of home-base spaces occupied by insiders and public places accessed by visitors. There will also be specialized auxiliary areas to assist both locals and visitors, such as workrooms, fitting rooms, and, in most cases, restroom facilities. Awareness of the events that take place in an environment for both locals and visitors, and of the types of spaces and features associated with each, will help you be a better designer. In these pages, I present three simple environments (an office, a clinic, and a restaurant) and point out some of the locations where events and transactions take place.

Open Space and Rooms

Space in interior environments is open or enclosed—or, quite often, a combination of open and enclosed spaces. Open space works well in most retail and restaurant environments, and in many office spaces. Open space allows greater flexibility, as the space may be reconfigured by moving nonpermanent furnishings and fixtures.

Enclosed spaces afford separation and privacy. Their walls help define the shape and character of the surrounding open spaces. Thus, space planning, to a great extent, consists of arranging rooms and open spaces. Add floating walls as an ingredient, and you have a simple but powerful kit of parts with which to shape space. Furniture, fixtures, and equipment add another layer of interior elements. Beyond that, there are still accessories, artwork, plants, and so on. We will concentrate on rooms and open spaces for now.

There are not that many ways to place rooms in space. Rooms can occur by themselves. They can also be joined to form rows or combined in regular or irregular configurations to form clusters. That's it. As for placement, rooms can be attached to the perimeter or floated somewhere in the middle. This results in eight generic possibilities for arranging rooms in space. They are summarized in the diagrams on this page.

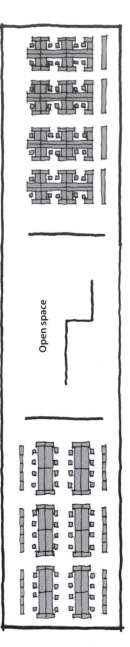

Open space

Open Space

Open space can be very comfortable and satisfying, in addition to being functional. It requires, however, the proper planning of the furniture and fixtures contained within it. Open space allows for a variety of densities, depending on needs. This example shows systems furniture and three floating walls that help subdivide the space and define areas.

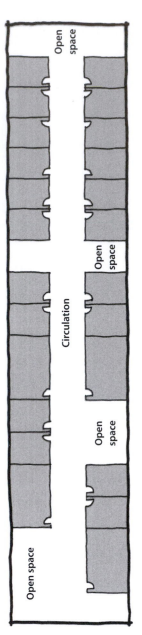

Open space

Circulation

Open space

Open space

Rooms and Open Space

Many projects consist of a combination of rooms, corridors, and open space. The number of rooms and their arrangement depend on the programmatic needs and contextual circumstances of the site. It is desirable, when possible, to create generous open pockets to permit deep light penetration and provide spatial relief.

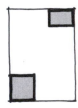

Rows at perimeter

Single room at center

Floating cluster

Floating cluster

Row at perimeter

Floating row

Single rooms at perimeter

Single floating rooms

Rooms: Placement and Arrangement

EXERCISE

Two generic templates are provided for your use. The grid is for reference; assume the first template uses a 20′ × 20′ grid and the second uses a 16′ × 16′ grid.

On the 20′ × 20′ template, draw rooms. Feel free to draw rows or clusters and to place them on the perimeter or floating inside, or both. Pay attention to the leftover open pockets you create, but it is up to you if you wish to end up with a few larger, open areas or perhaps with many smaller ones.

On the other, 16′ × 16′ template, draw a variety of furniture clusters for an office project. Clusters may be of between four and eight workstations and about 8′ × 8′ per individual workstation. Additionally, draw at least one floating wall in the space to divide or define space.

Repetitive Parts

Although the majority of projects have one-of-a-kind rooms, many also have units that repeat. Examination rooms in clinics, private offices and workstations in office facilities, retail fixtures in stores, and dining tables in restaurants are a few examples of rooms and elements that occur more than once. Repetitive parts can be handled in different ways. In some cases, you can establish similar modules that repeat as needed. The library shown on this page is a good example of this. The rhythm of stacks and tables is repeated to create eight equal modules. Variations of the module may be desirable when consistent repetition becomes too rigid. In those cases, strategies such as module rotation and dimensional variation can produce enough variety.

Repeating rooms can be arranged many different ways, depending on their number and the kind of project in which they occur. They may be arranged in clusters of two or three or many units that together form larger subgroups, or they may simply be arranged in long rows. The Swiss Pavilion and the Western Washington State College dormitory projects on the next page show two different approaches.

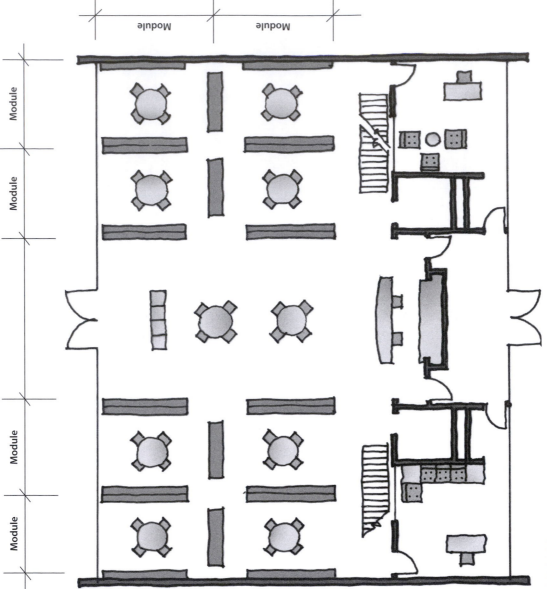

LIBRARY

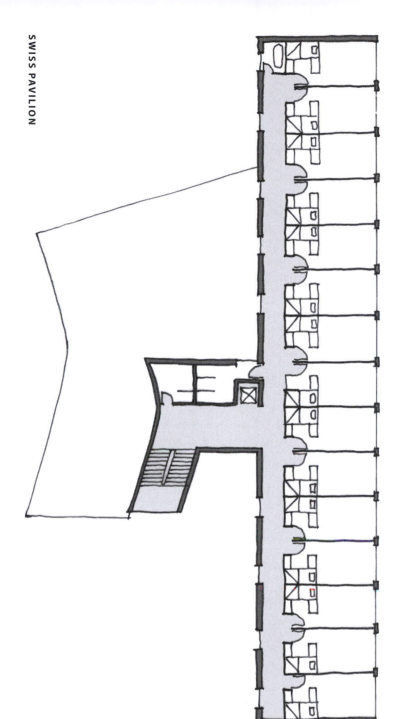

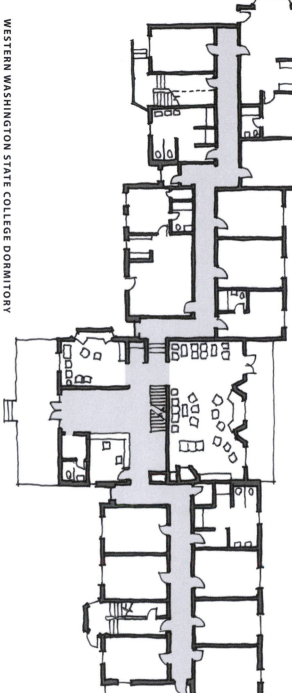

The Swiss Pavilion, in Paris (1930), is an example of the extreme and rigid repetition that is typical of buildings such as dormitories, apartment units, and hotels. In this example by Le Corbusier, there is no attempt to fight the necessary repetition required by the program. The more organic shape of the wing, housing the vertical circulation, the public restrooms, and the terrace, is a playful counterpoint to the rigidity of the row of repetitive units.

The college dormitory building presents a looser kind of repetition. The typical room unit is repetitive. Yet, the composition in this case varies the repetition, mixing the repetitive units with stairways, bathroom, lounges, and other unique, one-of-a-kind rooms to achieve a dynamic variety. As a result, the basic unit appears in single form, in pairs, and in rows of up to three, depending on the location. Note that of the three examples presented, this one has the most unique spaces mixed-in with the repetitive units.

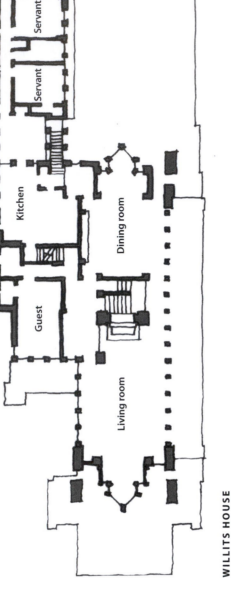

WILLITS HOUSE

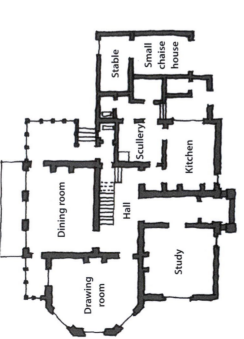

HOUSE IN MAIDSTONE, ENGLAND

Development of the Plan

Interior design work takes place in all kinds of buildings, old and new. A designer more or less inherits the attributes of the given building for a project. Planning a project within an old, traditional building requires a different approach from planning within a contemporary one. Much of design today uses the freer, more flowing way of designing developed in the twentieth century. Here, I briefly discuss the changes in buildings that resulted from structural design developments and spatial innovation by some of the pioneers of modern design.

Until the early years of the twentieth century, buildings required load-bearing walls for their support. For this

and other reasons, buildings consisted of clusters of enclosed rooms connected through narrow openings punched into the walls. The general effect was one of compartmentalization. The plan for a country house near Maidstone, England, is an example of such a plan (above).

It was Frank Lloyd Wright who first did away with the "box" in the early part of the twentieth century. Corners opened up, walls disappeared, dividers and partial walls were introduced, and a freer way of designing came about. Walls began to acquire new meaning; they were no longer uninterrupted enclosures placed

exactly at the boundary of each room and sealed at the corners. By moving and shortening walls, it was now possible to open up the interior space and make inside and outside continuous. The public zones of Wright's Willits House, shown on this page, provide a good example of this approach.

The German architect Ludwig Mies van der Rohe was another modern pioneer who contributed to the new, open way of designing buildings and their interior spaces. His German Pavilion, for the 1929 International Exposition, in Barcelona, remains one of the purest examples of free-flowing space unimpeded by

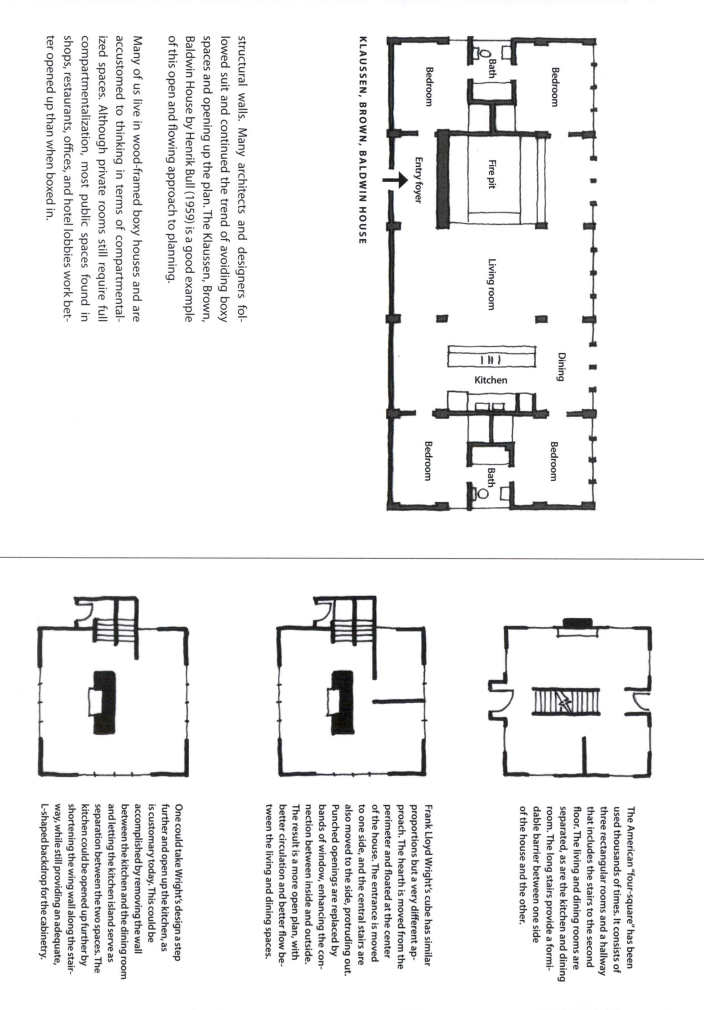

KLAUSSEN, BROWN, BALDWIN HOUSE

structural walls. Many architects and designers followed suit and continued the trend of avoiding boxy spaces and opening up the plan. The Klaussen, Brown, Baldwin House by Henrik Bull (1959) is a good example of this open and flowing approach to planning.

Many of us live in wood-framed boxy houses and are accustomed to thinking in terms of compartmentalized spaces. Although private rooms still require full compartmentalization, most public spaces found in shops, restaurants, offices, and hotel lobbies work better opened up than when boxed in.

The American "four-square" has been used thousands of times. It consists of three rectangular rooms and a hallway that includes the stairs to the second floor. The living and dining rooms are separated, as are the kitchen and dining room. The long stairs provide a formidable barrier between one side of the house and the other.

Frank Lloyd Wright's cube has similar proportions but a very different approach. The hearth is moved from the perimeter and floated at the center of the house. The entrance is moved to one side, and the central stairs are also moved to the side, protruding out. Punched openings are replaced by bands of window, enhancing the connection between inside and outside. The result is a more open plan, with better circulation and better flow between the living and dining spaces.

One could take Wright's design a step further and open up the kitchen. This could be accomplished by removing the wall between the kitchen and the dining room and letting the kitchen island serve as separation between the two spaces. The kitchen could be opened up further by shortening the wing wall along the stairway, while still providing an adequate, L-shaped backdrop for the cabinetry.

Base Building

Commercial facilities are normally housed in leased spaces. These are buildings built to contain those types of facilities, whether they are retail or office spaces. The specific conditions of the building housing the facility you are designing will dictate important planning decisions related to arrangement and spacing of parts.

The first condition to note is the distance from the core (or public corridor) to the perimeter, also known as the depth of the space. Your site may be shallow or, perhaps, deep. If you are designing an office facility that requires many private offices (both inside and along the perimeter), a deep plan will work better than a shallow one. As you can see from the sections on this page, a deep space of approximately 48' (14.63 m) will accommodate internal and perimeter offices plus open workstation and corridors in between.

The spacing of the vertical window mullions on the perimeter and the dimensions of the structural bay will also influence your planning. Window mullions at 4'-0" (122 cm) on center will suggest partitions at 12'-0" (3.65 m) on center for perimeter private offices. Likewise, the spacing between columns will greatly influence how you plan interior rooms and freestanding workstations.

Another important consideration is the specific condition along the perimeter, specifically, the extent of glass, the sill heights, and the window header heights. These will determine how you may handle the placement of furniture along the perimeter and how you work out the ceiling-to-perimeter-wall intersection.

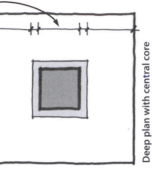

36'-62' (11–19 m)

Deep plan with central core

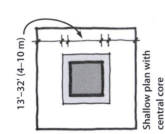

13'-32' (4–10 m)

Shallow plan with central core

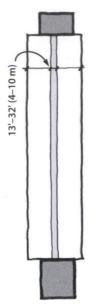

13'-32' (4–10 m)

Shallow plan with central corridor

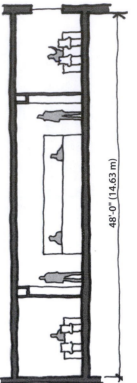

48'-0" (14.63 m)

Core-to-Perimeter section: Deep plan

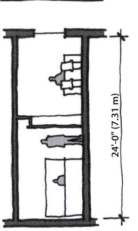

24'-0" (7.31 m)

Core-to-Perimeter section: Shallow plan

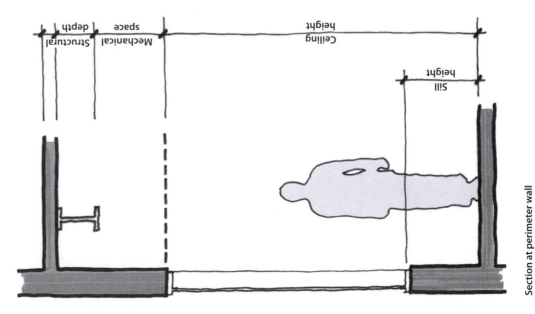

Structural depth

Mechanical space

Ceiling height

Sill height

Section at perimeter wall

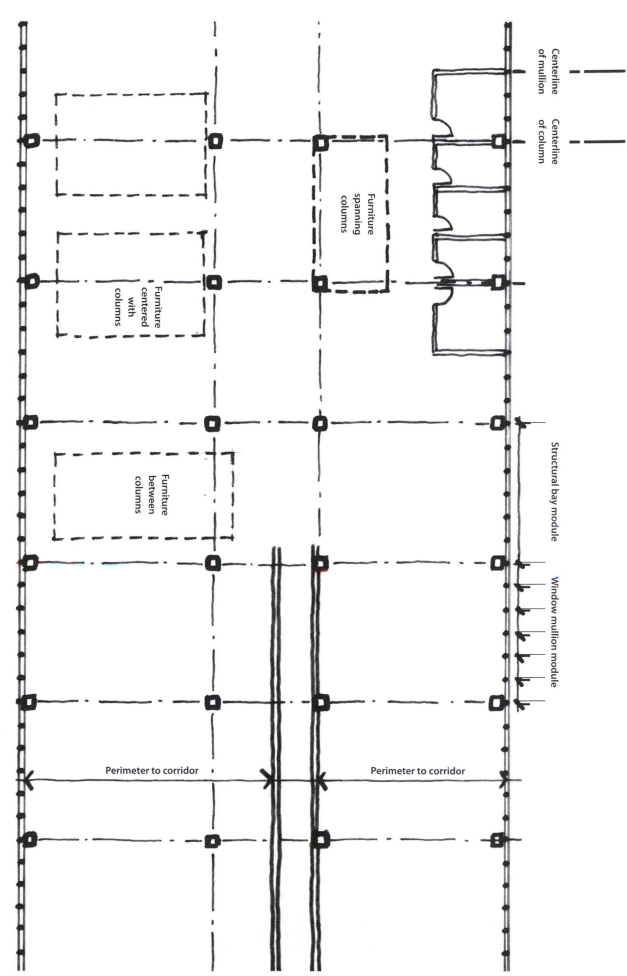

Centerline of mullion

Centerline of column

Furniture spanning columns

Furniture centered with columns

Furniture between columns

Structural bay module

Window mullion module

Perimeter to corridor

Perimeter to corridor

Above is a partial plan of a typical building shell. Note, in particular, the structural grid dictating the column spacing and the window mullion spacing on the perimeter. These two existing conditions will dictate how you space perimeter rooms (based on mullion locations), how you place interior walls in relation to columns, and how you place furniture groups in relation to columns.

Solids and Voids I

As discussed previously, projects consist primarily of some combination of enclosed rooms (solids) and open areas (voids) and the different ways of assembling them within a building shell. Now, we will put these ideas into practice through an exercise. First, look at what one student came up with when asked for four schemes for placing thirteen offices and one conference room in a space, while allowing for open space along the perimeter for open planning. Which schemes seem to produce the greatest clarity, cohesiveness, and quality of open areas? Are any of the schemes particularly successful or problematic?

Now, go ahead and do the exercise. The criteria will be a little bit different from those used in the original exercise.

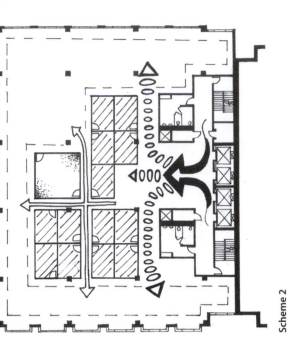

Scheme 2

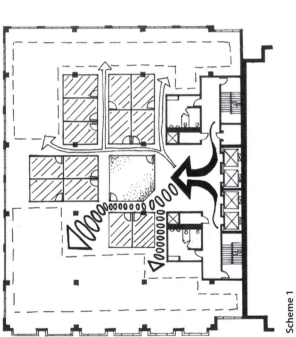

Scheme 1

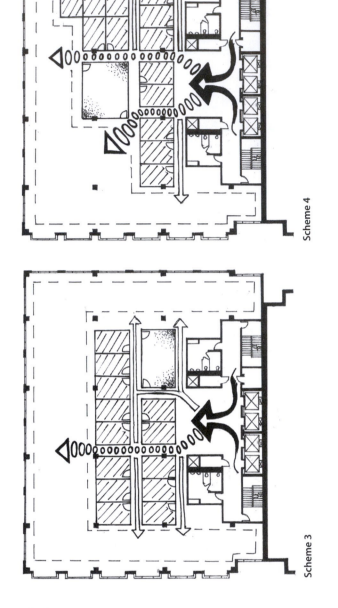

Scheme 4

Scheme 3

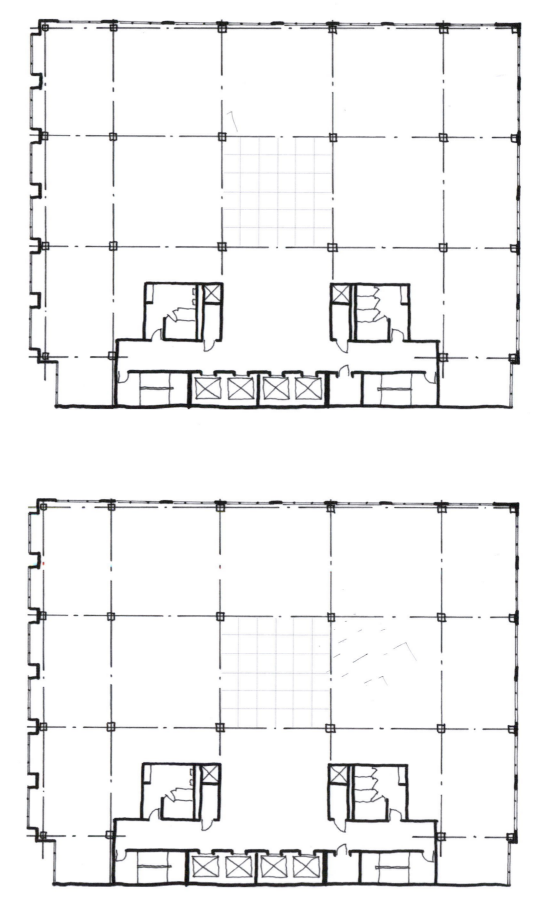

EXERCISE

You have been given the floor template for a corporate client. The company will occupy the entire floor, so the elevator doors are the front door. Your job is to study the template and come up with two alternative ways to locate eleven offices of approximately 150 square feet (13.85 sm) and one large conference room of approximately 350 square feet (27.70 sm). The grid shown at the center consists of 5' × 5' (152 cm × 152 cm) modules. You may use the perimeter for one of your two schemes, but you are only allowed to use one side, leaving the rest open to allow natural light in.

Avoid placing single offices by themselves. Arrange them in groups of at least two. Work lightly with pencil at first to explore alternatives. Once you decide what layouts to use, go ahead and draw them heavier with pencil or ink (freehand). Use the grid lines as guidelines so that your lines are nice and straight.

Make sure you leave good and useable open areas for future open planning with systems furniture. Finally, draw a big star or asterisk at the proposed main entrance to the space and nice lines and arrows indicating the main circulation routes.

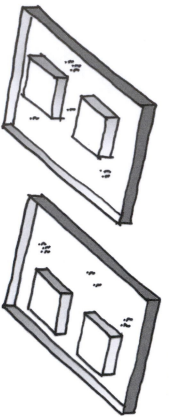

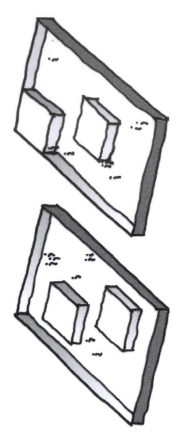

A pair of floating masses
These examples also show the difference between centered masses and masses moved toward the perimeter, producing a larger open space on the opposite side.

Two masses
The example on the left produces a greater number of smaller spaces and the example on the right produces fewer but larger open spaces. Depending on the project and its requirements for open zones, one of these would be more appropriate than the other.

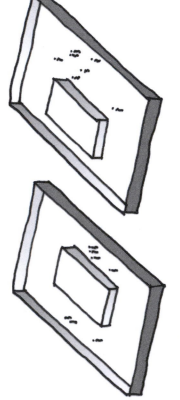

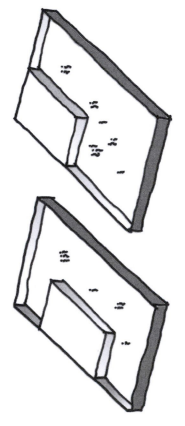

A single floating mass
Note the residual space difference between the example with the centered mass and the one with the floating mass moved toward the perimeter.

A single mass attached to perimeter
Note the different character of the open spaces produced in these two examples. The example on the left creates a major open area in front of the solid mass with two smaller secondary spaces. The example on the right produces a single large L-shaped space.

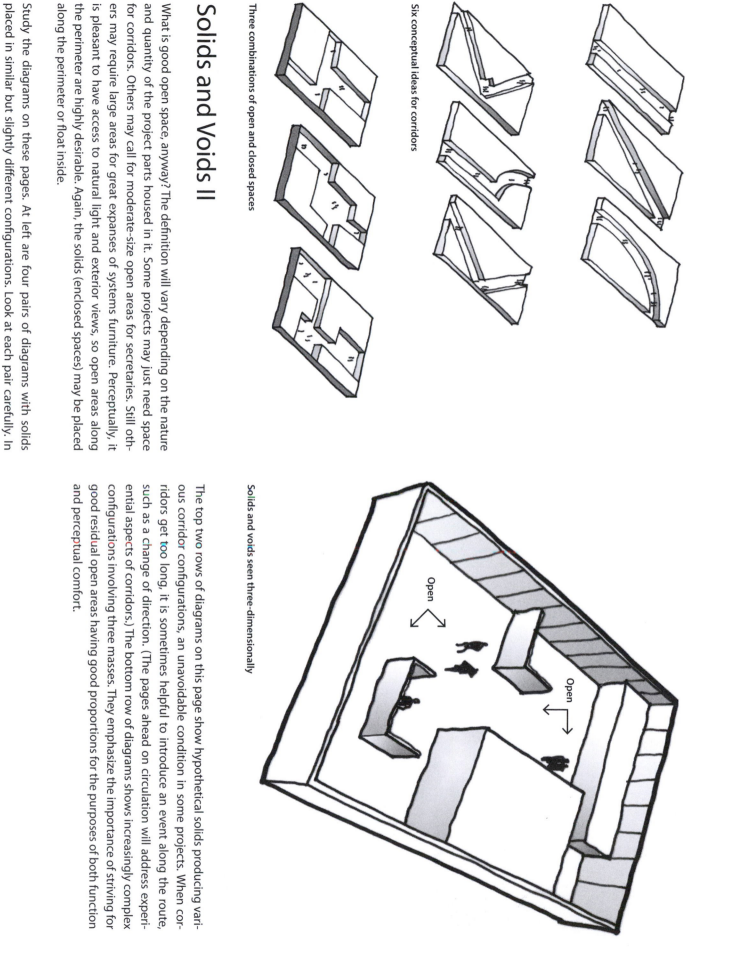

Six conceptual ideas for corridors

Three combinations of open and closed spaces

Solids and voids seen three-dimensionally

Solids and Voids II

What is good open space, anyway? The definition will vary depending on the nature and quantity of the project parts housed in it. Some projects may just need space for corridors. Others may call for moderate-size open areas for secretaries. Still others may require large areas for great expanses of systems furniture. Perceptually, it is pleasant to have access to natural light and exterior views, so open areas along the perimeter are highly desirable. Again, the solids (enclosed spaces) may be placed along the perimeter or float inside.

Study the diagrams on these pages. At left are four pairs of diagrams with solids placed in similar but slightly different configurations. Look at each pair carefully. In which circumstances would one be better than the other?

The top two rows of diagrams on this page show hypothetical solids producing various corridor configurations, an unavoidable condition in some projects. When corridors get too long, it is sometimes helpful to introduce an event along the route, such as a change of direction. (The pages ahead on circulation will address experiential aspects of corridors.) The bottom row of diagrams shows increasingly complex configurations involving three masses. They emphasize the importance of striving for good residual open areas having good proportions for the purposes of both function and perceptual comfort.

Growing the Core I

One of the keys to a clear project is to consolidate parts by combining them. Several rooms clustered together often produce a better solution than many isolated rooms scattered around. The scattered rooms increase the number of parts and produce fragmentation and confusion. When designing a space with existing enclosed spaces that produce mass, consider adding to the existing mass instead of producing new masses. Many projects include existing core elements housing egress stairways, elevator shafts, public restrooms, and various mechanical and electrical rooms. These are convenient masses to add on to.

The basic principle behind growing a core is simple: add rooms required by your project's program to the existing core mass. The example above illustrates how to execute the idea. A conference room is added behind the elevator core. The room aligns with the existing core mass on two sides and projects out away from the existing core as needed to achieve the required size. Rather than having two masses in space, both functions have been integrated into one.

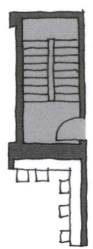

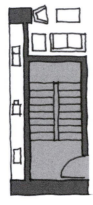

Two simple wall extensions on one side of the stairway produce a space for a work counter and a seating area.

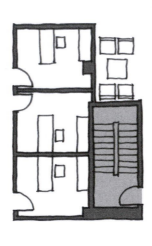

Three offices are placed back to back with the core. One of them protrudes out, creating a pocket for a seating area.

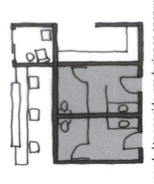

A lateral extension of one of the stairway walls creates an L-shaped, open work area.

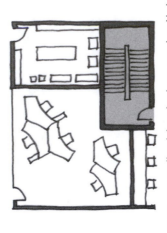

The core is expanded to one side, producing an open work room, a small telephone room, and a shallow work area.

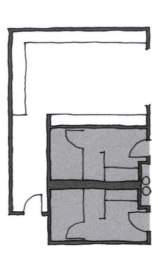

A large workroom is added to the side of the core. It is open on one side but has a door on the other side. The wall with the door is not brought up to the face of the core. Instead, it is intentionally kept back to create a vestibule in front of the entrance, which occurs on a high-traffic side of the facility.

Two rooms, one small and the other large, are placed behind the core. The larger extends beyond the core. One of its walls is intentionally offset (not aligned) from the face of the core in order to create a narrow space for a work counter.

Study the examples on the page. Then go ahead and try growing the cores given on the next page for practice. Add enclosed rooms, open rooms, cabinetry, or files. It is up to you. The added rooms and spaces need to occur on the sides and behind the core elements. Be careful not to add rooms up front that block access to the stairs, elevators, or restrooms.

The next few pages present examples of growing the core, in ascending order of complexity. We start with some simple ones on this page. Note that you can add not only rooms around the core, but also files, open work areas, seating areas, and so on. Also note that the practice of growing the core requires that the resulting shape be fairly simple and regular, although it doesn't always have to be a neat rectangle.

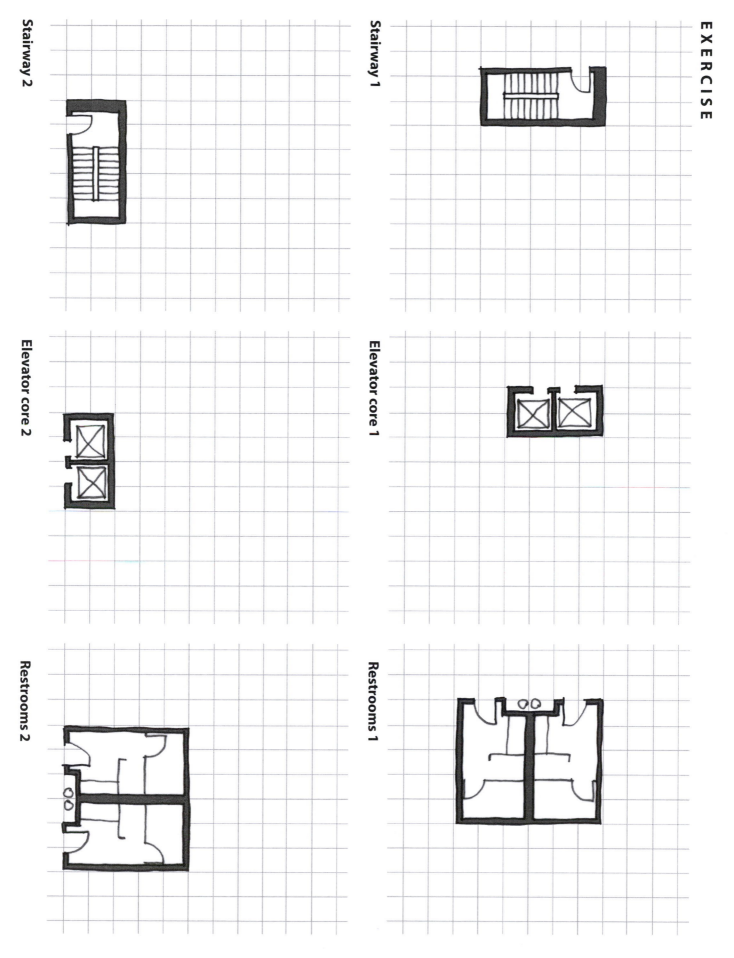

Stairway 1

Stairway 2

Elevator core 1

Elevator core 2

Restrooms 1

Restrooms 2

Growing the Core II

The examples shown here are based on the same basic principles of growing the core from the preceding pages; they are, however, more complex. Not only are rooms and spaces created around the immediate core, but also additional spaces are created between the core and other walls away from the core. In most of the examples, those walls are the building's outside wall, although the idea can work with any other adjacent wall.

Study the examples on these pages. Note how in some cases a new zone is created between the core and the adjacent wall and how in other cases there is an in-between wall creating two zones—one between it and the core and another between it and the adjacent wall.

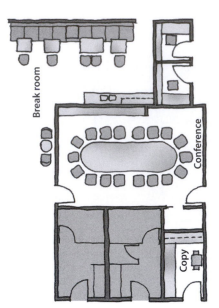

Lounge area

Copy/Work

Temporary work

A mass consisting of two small offices is added. It is pulled away from but aligns with the core. A workroom is created between the two. A work/lounge area is formed in the narrow zone between these masses and the upper perimeter wall. Additional pockets of space for work and seating are produced on the opposite side of these two masses.

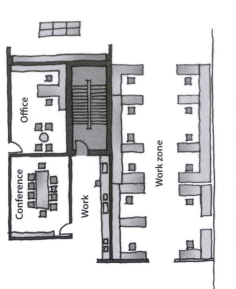

Break room

Conference

Copy

Various rooms are added below and behind the restroom core mass. The mass is grown further by adding additional rooms (two small study rooms) behind the conference room. These in turn, together with the adjacent floating wall, define a small area for a break room.

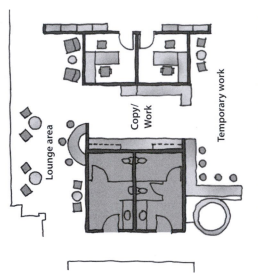

Study carrels

Work area

Informal work

A series of wall extensions originating from the restroom core wall create a series of spaces. In the zone closest to the core, an L-shaped counter is placed against the core, making a work area. The added wall extension continues on to form a series of study carrels. A small seating area, a narrow equipment area, and a work area with tables and counters are created on the other (outside) side of the added wall.

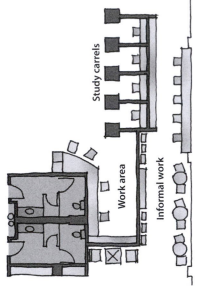

Conference

Office

Work

Work zone

Rooms are added above the stairway. The conference room projects forward. A wall extension across the conference room helps create an open work zone along the route to the stairway. Additional work areas are produced behind the stairway and between the stairway and the perimeter wall.

Rooms are added on both sides of the stairway. A zone for a reception area is created between the added conference room and an adjacent circular wall. Another work area is formed between the expanded core mass and the adjacent perimeter wall below.

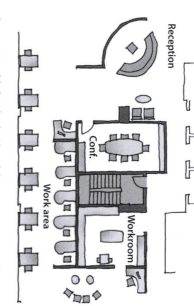

Reception

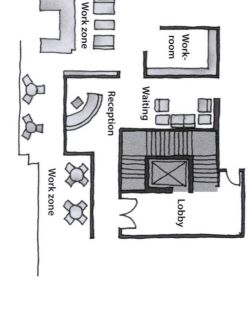

Conf.

Work area

Workroom

The core in this case includes the stairway; the central elevator; and the small, enclosed lobby space. By adding a short wall extension from the core; a floating but aligning workroom (left); and a floating, zigzagging wall (below), the designer defines space for a receptionist, a waiting area, and work areas consisting of tables and chairs next to the adjacent perimeter wall.

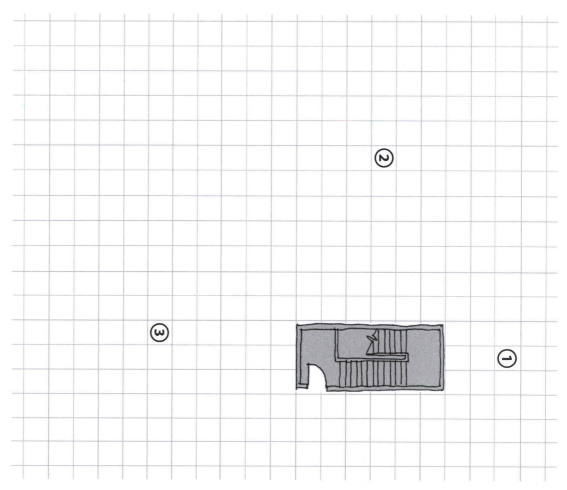

Work zone

Work-room

Waiting

Reception

Lobby

Work zone

EXERCISE

In the space provided, grow the stairway core, and try to achieve the following: On the narrow side (1), create a zone between the core and the adjacent wall similar to the ones shown as examples. On the wider side behind the core (2), introduce a wall element (attached or unattached) to create two zones, one adjacent to the core and the other adjacent to the perimeter wall. Add a room or open zone (at your discretion) on side 3. Again, use the examples as guides.

Growing the Core III

Here, I elaborate further on ways to grow the core to create hubs of rooms and open spaces around the original core elements. This time, we explore examples involving two core elements near each other. The principles are the same as before, but now we are bridging the two sides, integrating them and the added pieces into a functional whole.

The example below illustrates a simple application of this idea. You'll notice a stairway and an elevator shaft side by side but unattached. In this example, a room is created behind them, with the main entrance occurring between the two cores. A couple of small offices are added on one side to complete a simple overall rectangular shape.

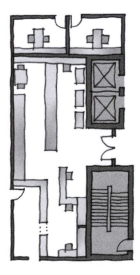

Once again, study the examples given. Essentially, they all bridge the two sides, put one or more functions between the two, and then establish a zone with other functions behind or beside them, or both. Then try the guided exercise provided.

This time, you will attempt a fairly complex exercise of bridging the two core elements given and creating surrounding rooms and areas around the cores. To help you concentrate on the composition itself, the exercise includes suggested locations for various types of activities, as if you had arrived at them after analyzing the programmatic requirements of a particular project.

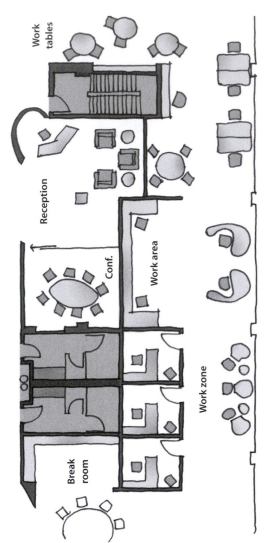

Break room

Reception

Conf.

Work area

Work zone

Work tables

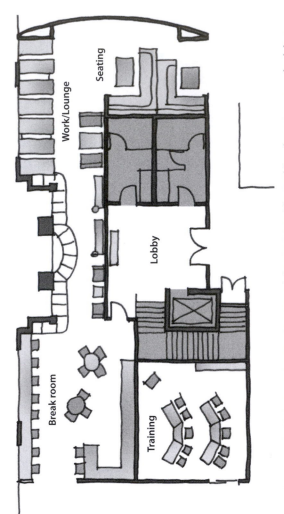

Seating

Work/Lounge

Lobby

Break room

Training

A reception desk/waiting area and a conference room are positioned between the stairway and the restrooms. Three private offices and an elongated work area are added behind the restroom core. These in turn help define a break room area adjacent to the restrooms, work zones along the perimeter wall and the reception area itself. Finally, the stairway core serves as backdrop to a few work tables and a work counter around it.

An arrival lobby is created between the stairs/elevator and the restrooms. The resulting shape serves as a backdrop for a training room on the left, a break room just above it, seating areas behind the restrooms, and a narrow zone with work/lounge areas between the core and the perimeter wall.

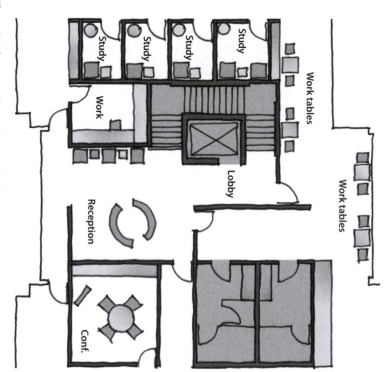

The stairs/elevator and a workroom added below the stairs help define a reception area. Four small study rooms are then added behind the new stairs/workroom mass. The upper wall of the new resulting mass serves as backdrop for a counter and a couple of small tables. This edge also helps define the overall zigzagging space above it. A wall is added to separate the restrooms from the arrival lobby, and a small conference room is added below the restrooms. This room helps square off the overall shape. An extended wall protruding from the small conference room serves to contain the reception area space.

EXERCISE

In the space at right, add a reception desk, a waiting area, one large conference room, three small study carrels, two private offices, files, a semienclosed but open work area, a work/lounge zone, and a break room. Locate everything approximately where suggested.

In the process of accommodating the above functions, integrate the two cores given, and create functional areas between, beside, and behind the cores. This is a good synthesis of many of the ideas learned about growing the core.

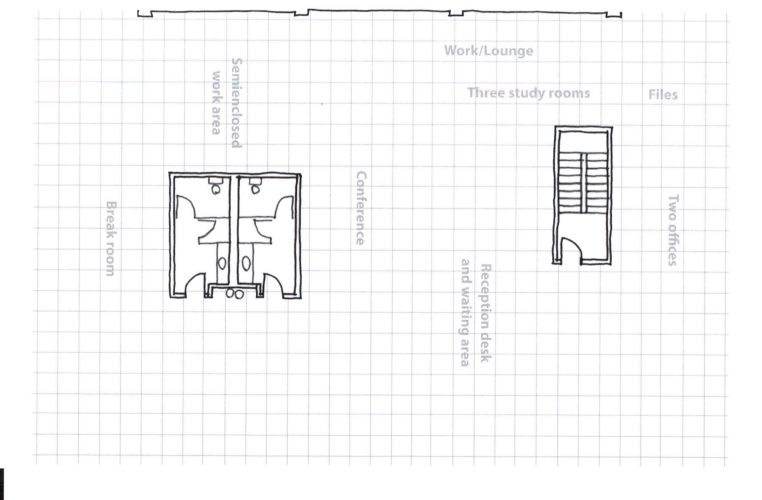

Work/Lounge

Three study rooms

Files

Semienclosed
work area

Conference

Two offices

Break room

Reception desk
and waiting area

Rooms and Machines I

The first building in which I was able to demonstrate the separation of servant spaces and the spaces that were served was the Trenton Bathhouse . . . [T]he hollow columns which I invented for it, which were containers, became the servant areas and all other spaces became open, served by these hollow columns . . . [T]hose constructions which serve were differently conceived than the structures of the rooms themselves, as though they were servants serving the spaces.[1]

Think of interior spaces and rooms in terms of main spaces in which to be, such as living rooms and bedrooms, and utilitarian spaces that house services such as kitchens and bathrooms. These two kinds of spaces occur in all kinds of projects and buildings, residential and nonresidential. Our goal here is to gain an understanding of the various ways the two can be arranged in relation to each other.

The American architect Louis Kahn spoke of the difference between what he called **servant spaces** and the spaces they serve. He cautioned that one must find ways to accommodate the serving areas of a space without destroying the main spaces they serve. Don't think of servant spaces as one problem and the **served spaces** as another problem; they work together.

Charles Moore, Gerald Allen, and Donlyn Lyndon referred to these spaces as **machines** (servant spaces) and **rooms** (areas served). Machines include not only actual machines (fixtures and appliances), such as refrigerators, toilets, and furnaces, but also the spaces that house them (machine domains). Also included in this category are other auxiliary spaces such as closets, stairs, and so on. Like Kahn, these architects warned that "machine" rooms exist to "serve" and that they work best when they are coordinated properly and do not infringe on the more general purpose of rooms.

Moore and his colleagues made a distinction as well between self-operating machines, such as furnaces, air conditioners, and water heaters, and their respective domains, and machines that require people to use them, such as those in bathrooms and kitchens.

They suggest that there are four ways to combine rooms and their supporting spaces.

1. Forming rooms around machines
2. Putting the machines inside the rooms
3. Putting the machines outside the rooms
4. Sandwiching the machines between the rooms

On the next page we examine three residential examples illustrating various approaches to planning main spaces and the auxiliary spaces that serve them.

1. Richard Saul Wurman, *What Will Be Has Always Been: The Words of Louis I. Kahn* (New York: Access Press, 1986).

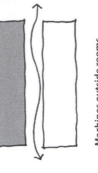

Machines outside rooms, across corridor

Machines outside rooms

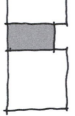

Machines between rooms

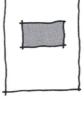

Machines inside room

Machines inside room

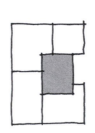

Rooms around machines

The food preparation domain occurs within the larger lateral wing of the house.

The island with the appliances floats in the middle, dividing kitchen from dining.

ADLER HOUSE

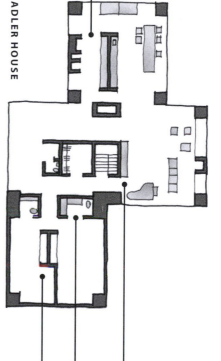

The central core housing stairs, coat/storage room, and powder room occurs within the main space of the house. The core's strategic location serves to separate the three main sections of the house.

The private restrooms are located inside the bedrooms they serve, at one end.

The closets are outside (but adjacent to) one of the rooms in one case and within the room in the other case.

FARNSWORTH HOUSE

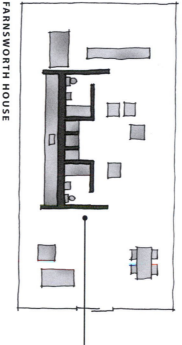

A single core element serves the entire house. It contains the bathrooms, storage, and the kitchen. The careful placement of this floating mass also serves to divide the open plan space into three distinct yet connected public areas plus the kitchen.

SCHWARTZ HOUSE

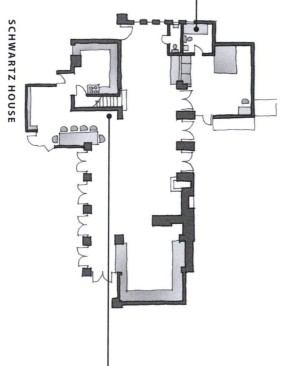

The private bathroom occurs within the bedroom it serves, but off to the side, minimally affecting the basic shape of the main room.

The powder room is within the main arrival space, at the corner.

The mass that houses the kitchen and stairs is at one corner of the main volume of space. This mass is not completely inside or outside the main space, but rather seems like an exterior mass that slightly interpenetrates the overall rectangular area.

Rooms and Machines II

For each of the examples, locate the service areas given within the given floor plan. The relative size of these areas is indicated. The size and shape of other living and sleeping spaces is up to you. Draw directly on the plans, working lightly with pencil until your ideas are firm. Once you have an arrangement you like, go over it, using heavier lines with either a pencil or a pen. Shapes can be rotated as needed.

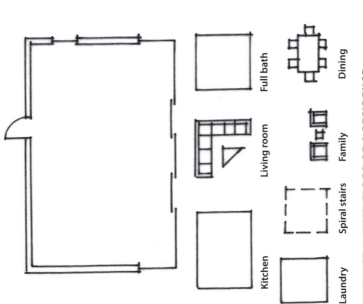

Kitchen   Spiral stairs   Family

Laundry   Living room   Dining

Full bath

EXERCISE 1: MAIN FLOOR OF A RESIDENCE

Accommodate the "machines" (bathroom, laundry, kitchen, stairs), and define the main living areas (living room, dining room, family area). Room footprints and main furnishings for the living areas are given.

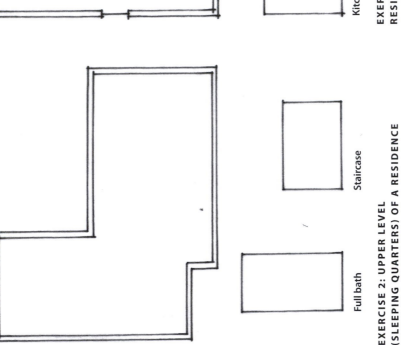

Full bath   Staircase

EXERCISE 2: UPPER LEVEL (SLEEPING QUARTERS) OF A RESIDENCE

Accommodate the bathroom, the staircase, two small bedrooms (both the same size), and a master bedroom.

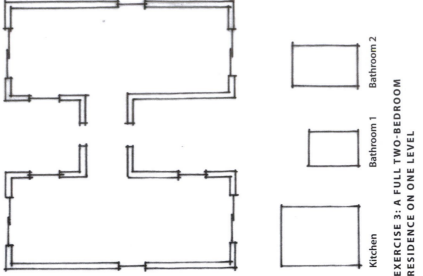

Kitchen   Bathroom 1   Bathroom 2

EXERCISE 3: A FULL TWO-BEDROOM RESIDENCE ON ONE LEVEL

Make one side the public side (living areas) and the other the private side (bedrooms). Accommodate the kitchen, a living room, and a dining room on the public side. Accommodate the two bathrooms and two roughly equal-size bedrooms on the private side.

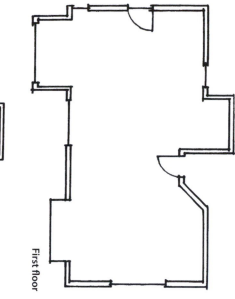

Second floor

First floor

EXERCISE 4: A TWO-STORY RESIDENCE

Accommodate the staircase, the kitchen, the powder room/mechanical, and the staircase. Define the living room and dining room areas. On the upper level, accommodate the stairs, the master bathroom, and two additional bedrooms.

Kitchen

Master bathroom

Stairs/Powder/Mechanical (same size)

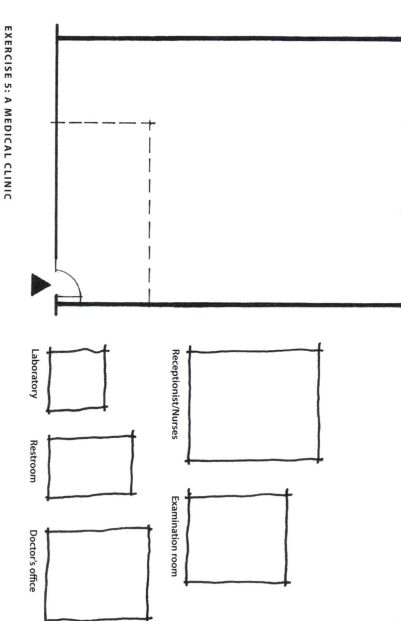

EXERCISE 5: A MEDICAL CLINIC

Accommodate the receptionist/nurse station room, a small laboratory, two restrooms, a doctor's private office, and three examination rooms. The location of the reception/waiting area is given.

Laboratory

Restroom

Doctor's office

Receptionist/Nurses

Examination room

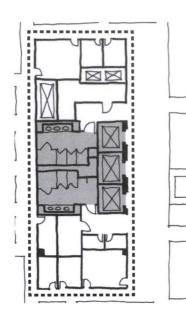

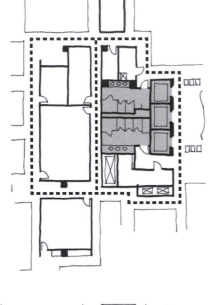

Scheme 1

Here is an example in which growing the core got out of hand, producing a very large and irregular mass that defines the project's main circulation system. Look at it, and note all the twists and turns needed to complete the loop. Go ahead and count the turns required; you'll be surprised how many there are. Not only is the journey a bumpy one, but also the mass is so large and irregular that it does not help as a point of reference when you are out in the open areas beyond trying to figure out your location. The great, irregular mass contributes to both bad circulation and disorientation.

Scheme 2

This scheme is in the same building. It is better than scheme 1. The mass of enclosed spaces is smaller and more regular. Count the turns; there are fewer. Look at the secondary cross-corridor between the core itself and the rooms above it. Would it be possible to eliminate it and move the doors to those rooms to the sides? How much convenience is that cross-corridor providing? Would it be too much trouble if the two masses were attached and one had to go around the resulting larger mass to get around?

Scheme 3

This third scheme for the same space is clearer, has better flow, and is more efficient than the other two. Where did all the rooms go? Some are there, but the designer of this scheme moved some of them elsewhere on the floor. The result is a clear, straightforward mass that improves circulation and the user's sense of orientation.

Circulation: Clarity, Flow, and Efficiency

A good circulation system is clear, flowing, and efficient. That means that users understand how it works, can form a mental picture of how to get around in it, and use it to enjoy flowing trips from one destination to another. Moreover, the route to get from one place to another is short and direct rather than long. It is that simple. Yet, many designers struggle with circulation, producing elaborate systems that are confusing, bumpy, and wasteful. Your goal is to design good, efficient routes for people to get around in. The more economical they are, the more space there will be for the other rooms and spaces needed.

The design process explained in Chapter 3 will help you address and resolve circulation systems early in the design process. You'll find that the sooner you have a circulation system, the faster the other parts of the project fall into place.

The examples shown here isolate a particular section of a project containing the main circulation loop. They illustrate good and not-so-good circulation solutions.

EXERCISE

The following page shows three partial plans with rooms and corridors. All the examples feature unnecessary (redundant) corridors. Designing too much circulation is one of the tendencies of inexperienced designers. Your job is to identify the problem and then come up with an alternate solution that fixes the problem. Work directly over the screened plans, and move parts and pieces as necessary to improve the circulation.

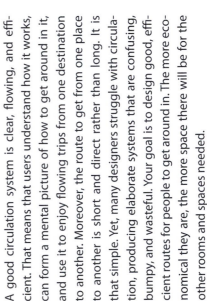

Problem 1: First try

Problem 1: Second try

Problem 2: First try

Problem 2: Second try

Problem 3: First try

Problem 3: Second try

Circulation: Schemes

Did you know? Prior to the seventeenth century, it was common practice to walk through rooms to get from one room to another. There were no real corridors. In the seventeenth century, designers of English country houses began to distinguish between private rooms and public corridors. This served to prevent occupied rooms from being disrupted by people passing through and also to provide privacy for both the owners and the servants. The parlor and dining room floors of Roger Pratt's Coleshill House (1650) are shown here to illustrate the concept of the full-length corridor separating circulation and rooms.

Circulation Space as Experiential Journey

The grand concourse of the Arthur M. Sackler Gallery and National Museum of African Art, in Washington, DC, was conceived as an experiential circulation spine full of events along the way. The concourse's experience, conceived by the architect Jean-Paul Carlhian, starts with a pause at street level and ends with a grand mural three levels below. The plan diagram below shows the various episodes (or events) along the way.

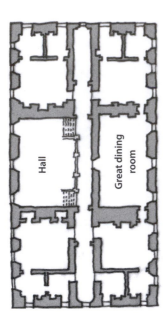

COLESHILL HOUSE

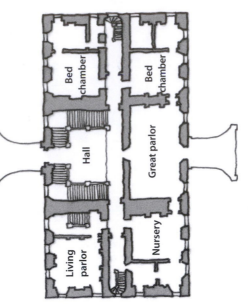

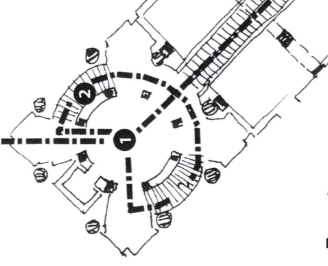

ARTHUR M. SACKLER GALLERY, NATIONAL MUSEUM OF AFRICAN ART

Events

1. Pause
2. Descent in the light
3. Descent into darkness
4. The rotunda
5. First surprise: The green room
6. Second surprise: The concourse, part I
7. Pause: The great crossing—discovery
8. Coda: The concourse, part 2
9. Final surprise: The mural

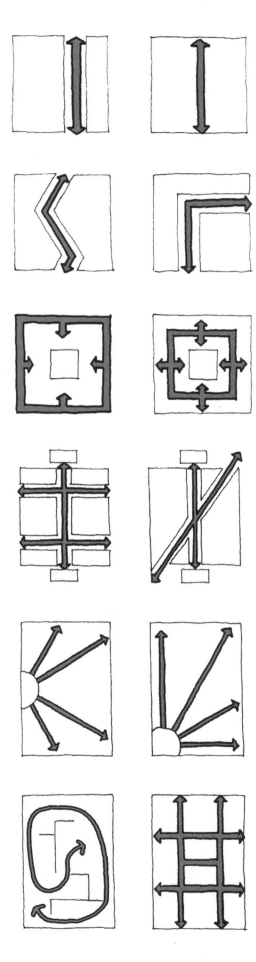

One of the best ways to arrive at clear and cohesive planning solutions is to have a clear circulation system. The circulation system is one of the principal determinants of interior schemes. Shown above are variations of some of the most common circulation systems: linear, loop, multiaxial, radial, grid, and free flowing. When you design, it is possible to start a design by devising the circulation system first and then filling in the rooms and other surrounding areas afterward.

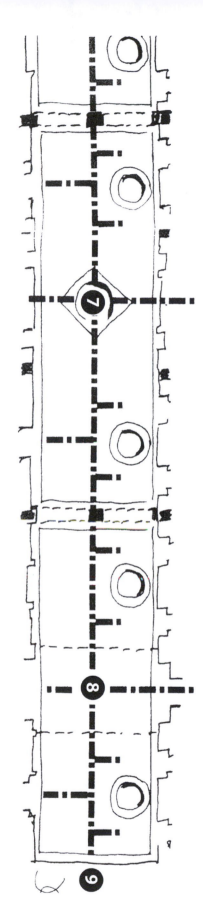

Circulation: Enrichment

Although circulation needs to be compact and efficient, it also needs to be pleasant. Projects are best experienced when moving through them, and this movement occurs within the circulation routes. Strive for efficient circulation routes, but strive also to create agreeable experiences along the way. Rely on focal points, expansion and contraction of space, views to both interior and exterior, playfulness, surprises, and similar strategies to make the journey memorable.

The views and diagrammatic journey on these pages show some examples of ways to make corridors come to life.

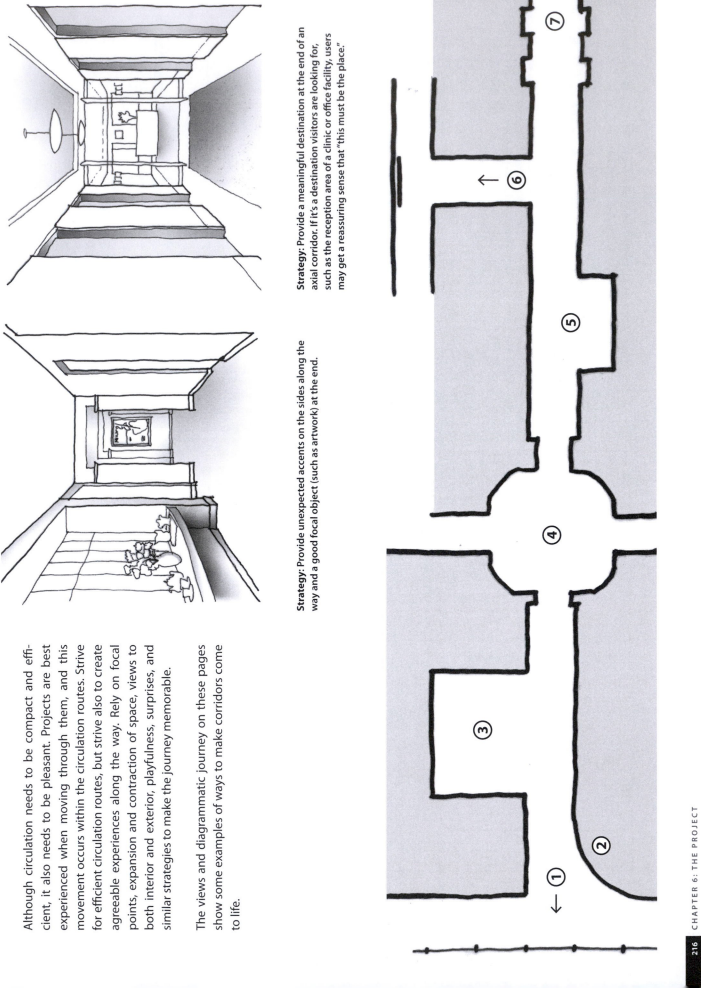

Strategy: Provide unexpected accents on the sides along the way and a good focal object (such as artwork) at the end.

Strategy: Provide a meaningful destination at the end of an axial corridor. If it's a destination visitors are looking for, such as the reception area of a clinic or office facility, users may get a reassuring sense that "this must be the place."

Eleven Ways to Enrich a Corridor

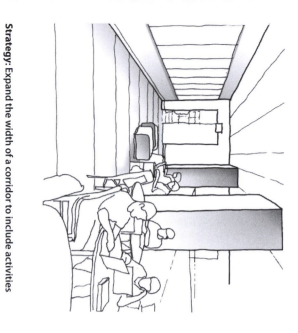

1. A panoramic (or Zen) view at the end
2. A sensual shape that guides movement
3. A vital space opening up to one side
4. An articulated main intersection
5. A cozy niche to step into
6. A side corridor with a pleasant focal point at the end
7. Rhythmic (or otherwise playful or interesting) articulation along a portion of the sidewalls
8. Playful articulation of room entrances or vestibules
9. An offset to provide relief from a long corridor
10. A lateral view along the way
11. A focal point at the end (artwork, niche, and so on)

Strategy: Have the corridor connect, in rhythmical fashion, to spaces along one side (or alternating from side to side), and put a meaningful destination at the end. That way, spaces will reveal themselves sequentially as users move forward.

Strategy: Expand the width of a corridor to include activities along one side. The corridor becomes both a circulation spine and a space to be in. This adds energy and vitality.

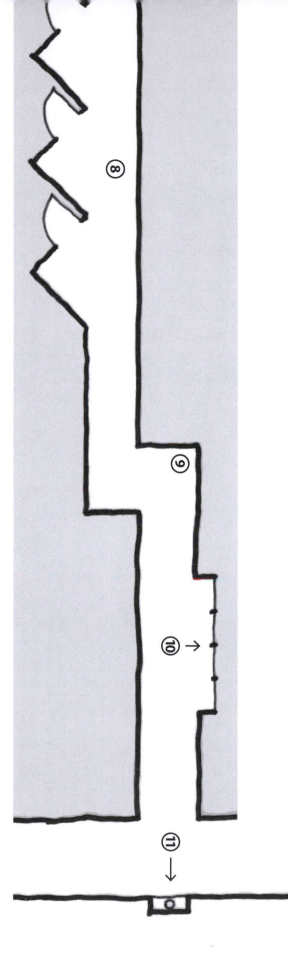

Annotated Plans

Thoughtful design solutions successfully address a large number of client needs and wants. Design decisions are made after carefully considering the problems they solve and the effects they produce. Consequently, developed designs embody a great number of "solved problems" that people familiar with the list of requirements can hopefully appreciate. A good design should be full of features and benefits for the users. It is hard to fully evaluate the merits of a design unless you have some awareness of the set of criteria given to the design team. A quick glance at the residential suite on this page does not begin to communicate the numerous conditions tackled and solved by the designer.

One tool used by designers to explicitly communicate the features and benefits of their designs is the annotated plan. These plans incorporate narratives that point out specific features of the design solution and the benefits they produce. Let's look at the design on these pages more closely. On this page is a project statement describing the client and some of the major goals the solution tried to address. Note that the goals are followed with specific objectives that suggest ways the goals may be tackled.

The client is an active couple in their early sixties. The husband is beginning to experience arthritis and wants to make sure the environment will be functional for him and his wife even as they grow older and their health continues to deteriorate. They want the space to be easily adaptable as they grow older. They also want some of the qualities we all want from our home environments, such as comfort, safety, and so on. On the next page is an annotated version of the space plan shown on this page. You begin to gain awareness of how the designer addressed some of the concerns about mobility, adaptability, comfort, and safety. Even if you don't agree that a particular feature produces the claimed effect, you can, at least, see how the designer attempted to deal with that particular issue. Take a moment to read through the annotations and you'll realize the many layers of intentional maneuvers by the designer.

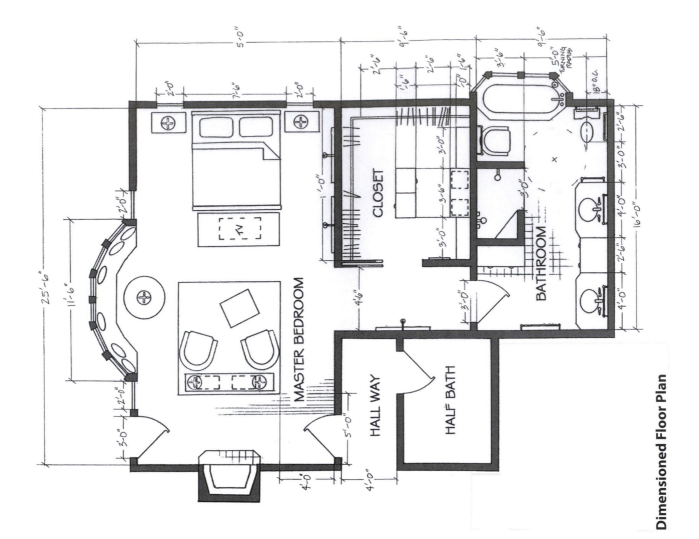

Dimensioned Floor Plan

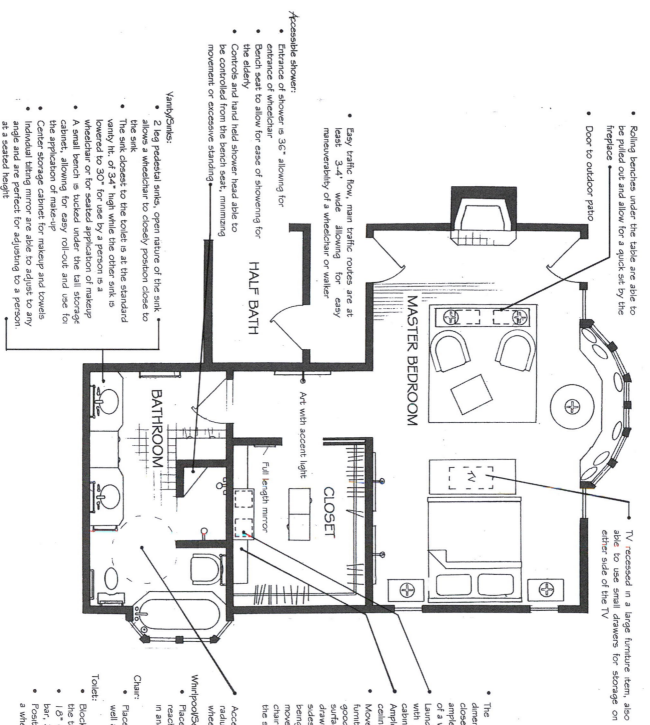

- Rolling benches under the table are able to be pulled out and allow for a quick sit by the fireplace

- Door to outdoor patio

Accessible shower:
- Entrance of shower is 36" allowing for entrance of wheelchair
- Bench seat to allow for ease of showering for the elderly
- Controls and hand held shower head able to be controlled from the bench seat, minimizing movement or excessive standing

- Easy traffic flow, main traffic routes are at least 3-4' wide allowing for easy maneuverability of a wheelchair or walker

HALF BATH

MASTER BEDROOM

Art with accent light

CLOSET

BATHROOM

Full length mirror

TV

Vanity/Sinks:
- 2 leg pedestal sinks, open nature of the sink allows a wheelchair to closely position close to the sink
- The sink closest to the toilet is at the standard vanity ht. of 34" high while the other sink is lowered to 30" for use by a person is a wheelchair or for seated application of makeup
- A small bench is tucked under the tall storage cabinet, allowing for easy roll-out and use for the application of make-up
- Center storage cabinet for makeup and towels
- Individual tilting mirror are able to adjust to any angle and are perfect for adjusting to a person at a seated height

- TV recessed in a large furniture item, also able to use small drawers for storage on either side of the TV

- The current dimensions of the closet allows for ample passageway of a walker
- Laundry bin storage with additional cabinet space above
- Ample floor to ceiling shoe storage
- Moveable drawer furniture provide a good folding top surface, access to drawers from both sides, in addition to being able to be moved if a wheel chair needs to use the space

- Accessible bathroom provides a 5' turning radius to allow for maneuverability of a wheelchair

Whirlpool/Soaking tub:
- Placement of faucet and knobs are easily reached, as well as allow for ease of movement in and out of the tub

Chair:
- Place to sit to help assist entrance into tub, as well as a place to set clothes

Toilet:
- Blocking along the South and East walls near the toilet for installation of grab bars
- 18" O.C. measurement from toilet to side grab bar, 33-36" Height A.F.F. of grab bar
- Position of toilet allows for ease of assess from a wheelchair from both front and side positions

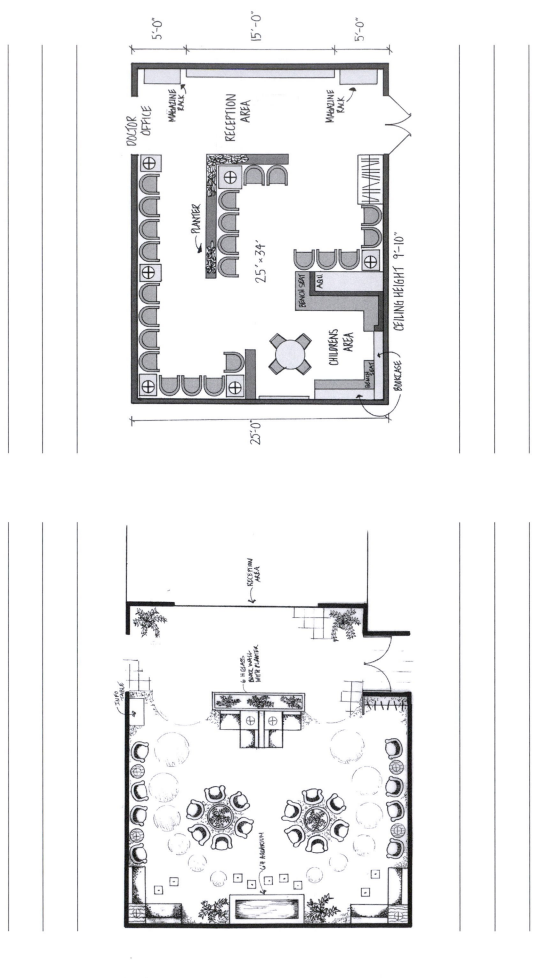

Explicit Intentions

EXERCISE

In the previous spread you saw an example of the use of annotations and how they communicate the way the designer tried to create conditions that produced a functional and comfortable environment for the intended use. Let's now get some practice in writing annotations.

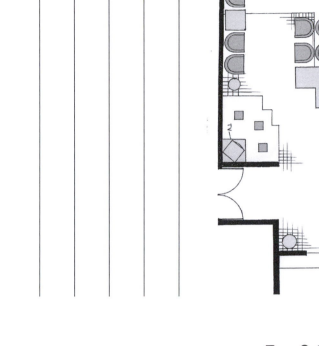

Shown here are three different solutions for the waiting area in a pediatrician's office. I'm sure you have been in these kinds of environments before and will probably have some opinions about desirable and undesirable attributes in them. The spaces feature a main entrance, a reception desk area, and access to the exam rooms toward the rear. The designers were given the task of creating multiple seating zones and options, a children's play area, a place for magazines, and a coat storage area.

Pretend that you have been hired to communicate all the good things about these solutions, their features, and their benefits. Think about what the designer was trying to accomplish. Look at the various seating areas and try to understand what they afford: perhaps a protected corner, or a way to avoid having to face everybody else in the room. Think about the children and the play area. What is good about its location and arrangement? Look at the previous example of annotations for the adaptable residential suite as an example. Go ahead and write at least five annotations per solution. Sell the design and its features.

Enjoy.

7 Residential Design

Residential Planning I

Of all the different project types designers work on, the residence is, perhaps, the most familiar to students. You are likely to have seen many houses and have spent considerable time in one or two. You probably have experienced dorm life and apartment living as well. That experience helps in understanding the dynamics of living in shared spaces. It is important to remember that although people have universal needs, when it comes to living, preferences and habits vary in meaningful ways from person to person and from family to family.

The design of a residential project starts, not surprisingly, with an assessment of the needs of the users and an understanding of their peculiar habits. What role does the TV play in the family's life? Do they cook a lot? Do they have people over for dinners and other social activities? Do they have young children to supervise? What are their hobbies? Do they listen to music? Are they avid readers, needing both a good reading space and room for their book collection? The answers to these and other similar questions will determine what furnishings and spaces need to be provided, how prominent each has to be, and how to best arrange them in relation to one another.

Below are some of the considerations when designing residential projects:

1. Dividing the residence into active and quiet spaces. Separating the bedrooms and other areas for quiet work or concentration from noisier living areas by placing neutral rooms, corridors, or other buffers in between.

2. Zoning functions carefully in relation to the surrounding context. Taking advantage of good views, natural light, and other site amenities while

avoiding, say, the noise from the street. Many living room areas are placed on the rear side of a property to take advantage of the increased level of privacy and access to private exterior areas.

3. Providing efficient and functionally sound **circulation systems.** Planning your spaces in a way that requires the shortest distance possible to move back and forth. In addition, planning your traffic patterns and door locations so as to avoid having users walk through, say, the living room in order to get to the bedrooms or the kitchen.

4. Arranging individual spaces and their elements to maximize **furnishability.** Arranging walls, doors, and windows in ways that will permit appropriate furniture placement, preferably allowing for multiple options.

5. Practicing economy by avoiding waste, sharing resources (e.g., walls, plumbing), and providing spaces that can work in more ways than one.

Depending on user preferences and existing conditions, the public areas of a residential project may be open and flowing or compartmentalized. In an openplan arrangement, the living and dining rooms may be combined as a single space, or they may occupy the two sides of an L configuration with little or no obstruction between the two. In some cases, there may be screening elements between the two, such as partial walls, fireplaces, or storage units. In a closed-plan configuration, the living and dining rooms would be separate spaces, possibly connected via archways or doors. Many houses built today actually have some of both, as they have a set of formal living and dining rooms that are separate from one another, plus an informal great room combining a family room, an informal dining space, and the kitchen in an open-plan arrangement.

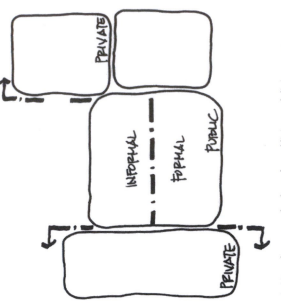

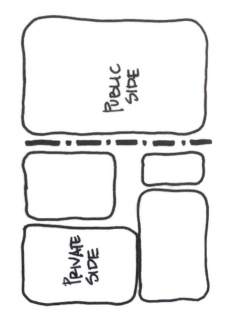

A. Many houses today have formal living and dining spaces used only for special occasions and informal spaces for the same functions that are used on a daily basis.

B. An essential goal of any residential project is the thoughtful separation of the public side (living and dining areas where one may entertain guests) and the private side (where bedrooms and other private functions are located).

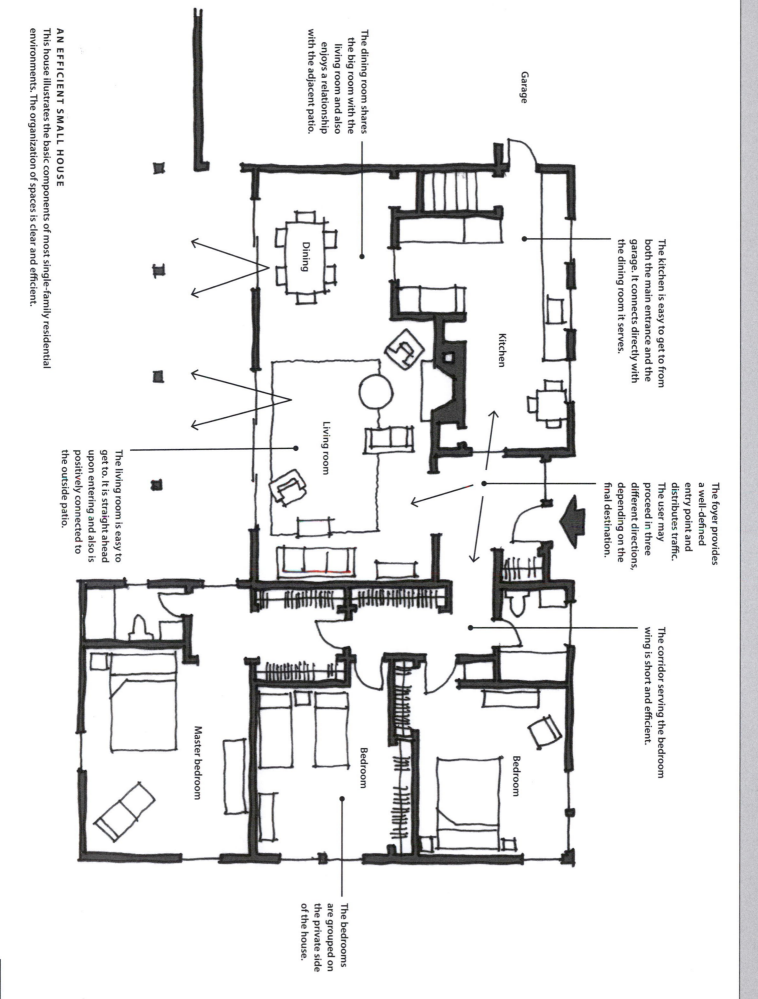

AN EFFICIENT SMALL HOUSE

This house illustrates the basic components of most single-family residential environments. The organization of spaces is clear and efficient.

Garage

The dining room shares the big room with the living room and also enjoys a relationship with the adjacent patio.

Dining

The kitchen is easy to get to from both the main entrance and the garage. It connects directly with the dining room it serves.

Kitchen

The foyer provides a well-defined entry point and distributes traffic. The user may proceed in three different directions, depending on the final destination.

Living room

The corridor serving the bedroom wing is short and efficient.

The living room is easy to get to. It is straight ahead upon entering and also is positively connected to the outside patio.

Master bedroom

Bedroom

Bedroom

The bedrooms are grouped on the private side of the house.

Residential Planning II

Once you know the list of requirements from the user, you can start determining furniture arrangements and room sizes. For some projects, you will have to plan the furniture arrangement within the existing spaces. For other projects, you will get to determine the size of the rooms or spaces and the appropriate level of enclosure for each. This chapter contains examples and dimensions to help you determine appropriate room sizes after allowing for proper furniture placements, clearances between elements, and required space for circulation.

The following rule of thumb area allocations may also help you in the early stages of residential planning. The areas indicated for each type of room range from small and economical to large.

Living rooms: 200 to 350 square feet
    (18.58 sm to 32.52 sm)
Dining rooms: 150 to 225 square feet
    (13.94 sm to 20.90 sm)
Kitchens: 120 to 200 square feet
    (11.15 sm to 18.58 sm)
Bedrooms: 120 to 300 square feet
    (11.15 sm to 27.87 sm)
Bathrooms: 40 to 120 square feet
    (3.72 sm to 11.15 sm)

Determining how to combine spaces requires some trial and error, and there are always multiple solutions that will work. Following the design process described in Chapter 3 can help you arrive at a number of good solutions for any project. With some experience, you will be able to gain speed and identify potential good solutions quicker.

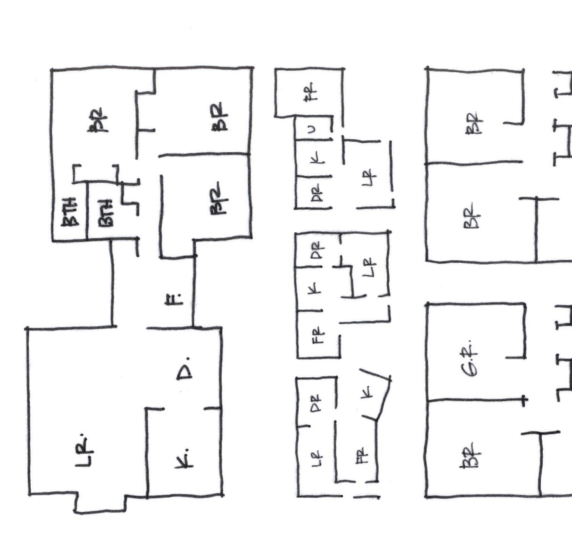

Blocking plans show the exploration in search of appropriate space relationships for a house project.

Efficiencies

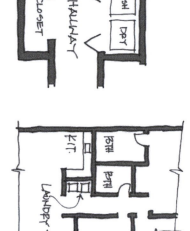

A particular goal you should strive for is economy. It can be manifested in different ways. The illustration labeled **"Efficiencies"** shows two examples of efficiency. The first one makes use of a closet on the upper floor of a small residence for the washer and dryer. By doing so, the client saved space (which she didn't have much of in this house). In addition, because of the closet's proximity to the bedrooms upstairs, the client saved countless trips up and down the stairs with clothes and linen. The other example shows a kitchen, a laundry closet, and two bathrooms in a back-to-back arrangement, thus concentrating the bulk of the plumbing for the small residence in one area and thereby saving considerable expense.

Economy can also be achieved by avoiding wasted space, such as unusable portions of rooms and unnecessarily long corridors. Some good and not-so-good examples of corridors are shown under "Efficient Corridors."

Shared plumbing

Inefficient

A.

B.

C.

More Efficient

Efficient Corridors

Try to minimize the length of corridors. As these examples show, there are always ways to combine rooms in ways that let you get to all the rooms with shorter corridors. On the left are examples of inefficient corridors. The better solution is to the right.

Entry Spaces

A good entrance greets, provides a functional transitional space, and distributes traffic in appropriate directions. It is undesirable to enter directly into the living room and have to walk through it to get to other areas of the house. A foyer space, even a small one, can do the job effectively.

The view upon entering a house is also something to be considered carefully. There are options. One option may be to walk in, face a wall or screen (with something interesting on it), and then turn one way to proceed in. Another may be to offer a partial glimpse of the main public areas ahead upon entering. This would draw people in, and guests could experience the unfolding view of the total living spaces as they moved in.

The entry space, or foyer, is also a space to transition from the outside to the inside. Providing a coat closet is common practice. In some homes there is also a place to take off and set one's shoes.

Finally, one of the main functions of a good foyer is to serve as a distribution point for traffic leading to the various zones of the house. One may walk straight ahead to get to the living spaces or turn to one side to go to the private bedrooms. Another scenario is to take a few steps forward and then encounter a cross corridor leading to the bedrooms on one side and, perhaps, the kitchen on the other. This page provides some anthropometric data for entry spaces and some examples of effective foyers.

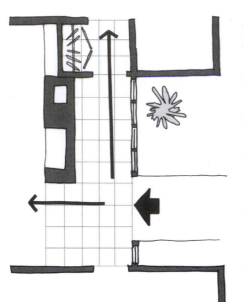

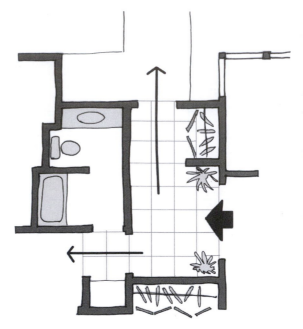

Foyer 1 consists of a short lateral corridor, with the coat closet slightly to one side. Upon entering, one may go in three different directions to various zones in the house.

Foyer 2 features a coat closet to one side immediately upon entering and a short corridor leading to a cross corridor, where one may take a left turn toward the private zones or a right turn toward the public zones of the house.

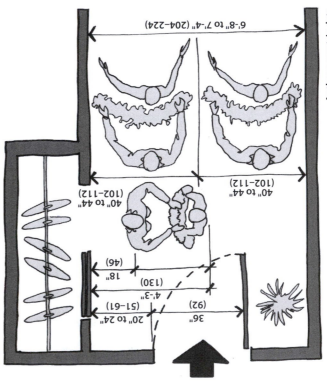

Anthropometric data

Entry Foyer Scenarios

A. Guest enters and sees a screen wall straight ahead and an opening to the right leading into the house.

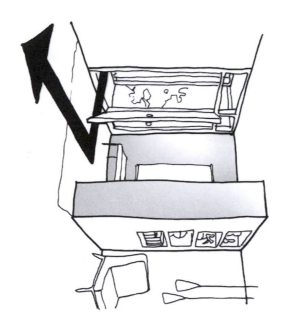

B. Guest enters into a cross corridor and faces a partial-height wall with storage. Guest may proceed left or right to the various zones of the house

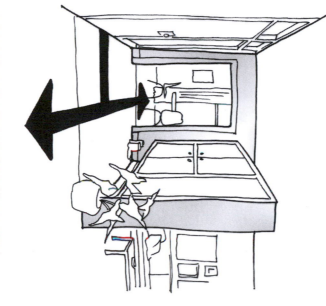

C. Guest enters into a corridor with a screening coat closet to the left. Guest may go straight, turn left, or turn right into the various parts of the house.

Living Rooms I

A good living room is comfortable, versatile, and pleasant overall. It serves as the heart of most homes, providing an environment in which family members can socialize with one another and with guests as well. Desirable attributes of a living room space include the following:

- Comfortable, well-grounded seating
- A focal point
- Visual connections to other interior spaces
- Views to the outside
- Natural lighting
- A good room-to-contents proportion
- An orderly, uncluttered appearance
- Good traffic patterns

The following pages include various examples showing common contents and arrangements.

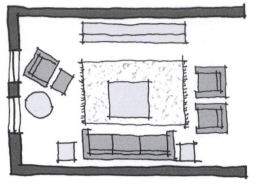

The room-to-contents proportion of a room is important. It needs to be harmonious. This also applies to the drawing process while designing. If you draw the furnishings at the wrong scale, you may end up with one of two unfortunate conditions shown above.

There is usually more than one room arrangement that will work. Shown above are four different furniture arrangements for the same modest-sized living room in an apartment. Which one would work best for you?

Four different arrangements for rooms of similar sizes and proportions

A.

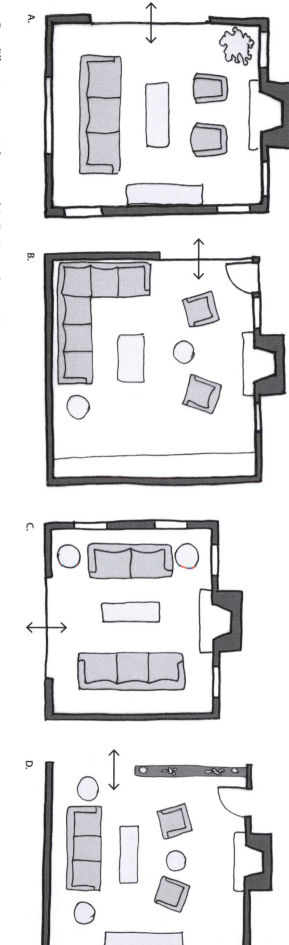

B.

C.

D.

Common living room furnishings and their approximate sizes

Sectional sofa

8'-0" (244)

8'-0" (244)

32" (82)

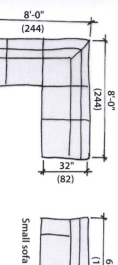

Small sofa

6'-6" (198)

32" (81)

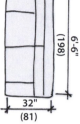

Full sofa

9'-0" (274)

32" (81)

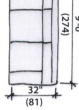

Loveseat

5'-0" (153)

32" (81)

Chairs

36" (92)

32" (81)

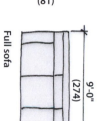

39" (99)

32" (81)

24" (61)

24" (61)

20" (51)

24" (61)

End and side tables

36" (92)

20" (51)

20" (51)

20" (51)

20" (51)

Coffee tables

36" (92)

24" (61)

36" (92)

36" (92)

36" (92)

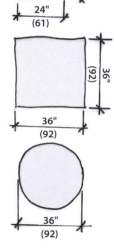

Living Rooms II

Two common living room design problems are fragmented seating groups and clutter. Plans A and B are examples of the first problem. The circled chairs in these two arrangements appear to have drifted away from the furniture groups they once belonged to. This tends to happen in tight spaces, where there may not be sufficient room to keep the entire group together. Plan A is particularly problematic, as the single chair by itself looks out of place. In plan B there are two drifting chairs, so there is a sense of triangulation with the main sofa that helps the scheme hang together a little better than in A. Still, the arrangement seems odd, plus one of the chairs is hampering the circulation route.

Plan C is an example of too much clutter around the room. There are too many objects around the periphery. Solutions to this problem include convincing the client to put some of the pieces elsewhere and grouping multiple contents into single elements that perform various functions, such as a long work wall with storage, display, and desk functions all in one.

Look at plan D. It performs better than the other three. The furniture group works as a unit with no drifting parts, and there is no clutter.

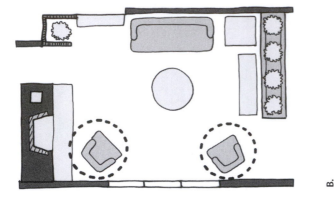

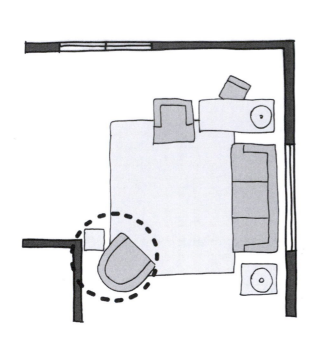

A.

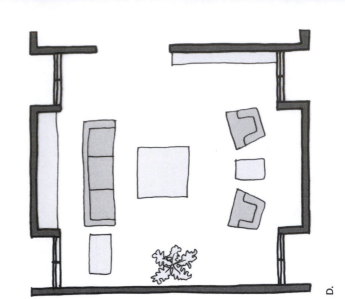

B.

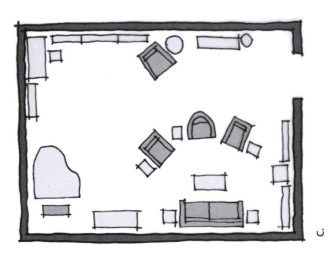

D.

C.

EXERCISE

Plan the living room space above, using all the furniture pieces shown. Anchoring the room is an existing fireplace wall, which includes a band of stone flooring from side to side. The opening next to the fireplace wall connects the living room with the adjacent dining room on the other side. The other opening connects the room to a hallway and the entrance. Use the 36" × 36" (91 cm × 91 cm) grid for scale reference.

Dining Rooms I

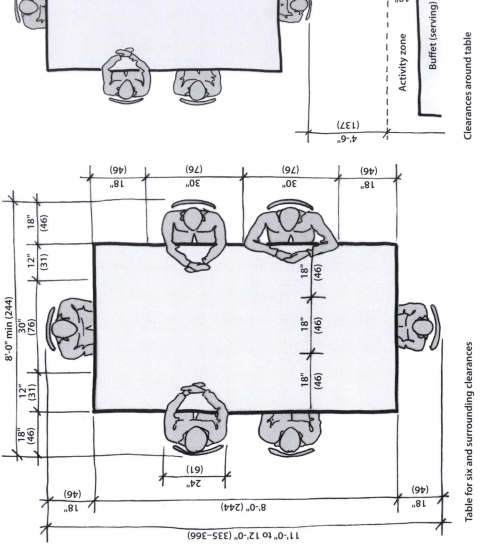

Table for six and surrounding clearances

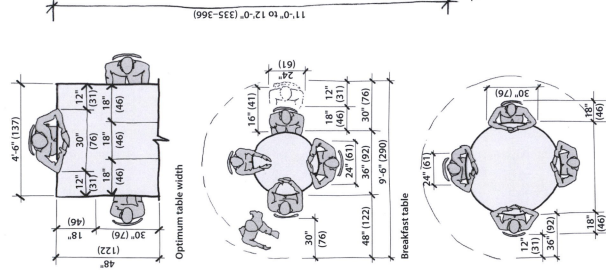

Clearances around table

Optimum table width

Breakfast table

Typical dining chairs and clearances

A. Open dining adjacent to living room

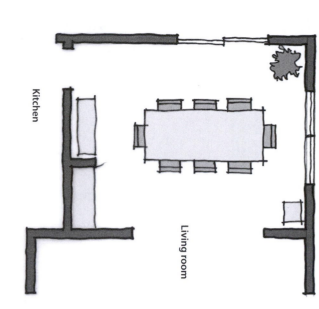

Living room

Kitchen

B. Open dining in own space around the corner from living room

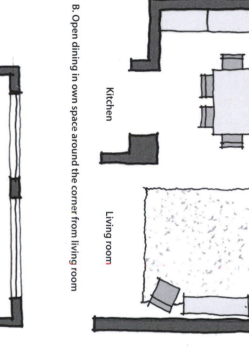

Kitchen

Living room

Dining Room Levels of Enclosure and Definition

C. Dining room with open archway to living room

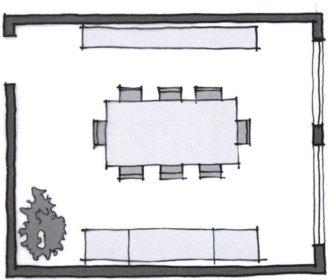

Kitchen

Living room

D. Fully enclosed dining room

EXERCISE

Based on the dimensions given on the preceding page, indicate optimal sizes for these tables in the space provided.

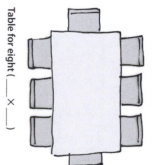

Table for eight (___ × ___)

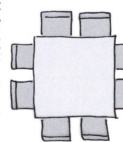

Table for eight (___ × ___)

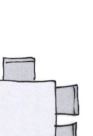

Table for four (___ × ___)

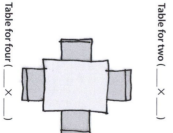

Table for two (___ × ___)

Dining Rooms II

The ways people dine in their homes vary according to lifestyle and occasion. Many modern homes and apartments have both a primary dining space and a secondary, less formal dining area by the kitchen. Primary dining spaces range from very formal rooms to informal, open dining areas. See page 233 for some examples. A couple or a small family may require a table for only four people, while larger families and families who entertain friends may need a table for six or eight people with an option to expand for special gatherings. Required room areas for the dining function may range from a modest 10' × 12' (3 m × 3.7 m) to a comfortable 14' × 18' (4.3 m × 5.5 m) or larger. Principal dining areas are typically separate from but adjacent to the kitchen space. They are often adjacent to the living room as well. This facilitates the flow of guests from the living room to the dining room during social gatherings.

Secondary dining spaces are informal and usually limited to family use. They are frequently referred to as the breakfast nook or breakfast room, even if they are also used for other meals. They are typically just off the main kitchen space and often take the form of alcoves or nooks. Stools on peninsula or land counters are also popular. Several examples of these secondary dining spaces are shown on this page with recommended dimensions.

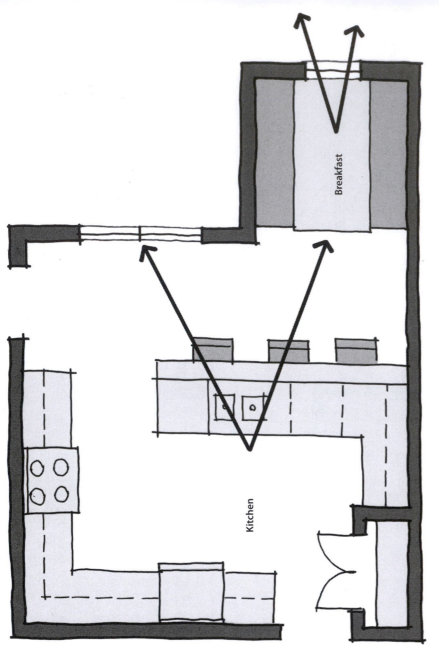

Kitchen

Breakfast

Breakfast nook with booth

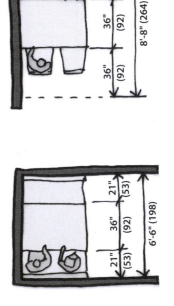

Dimensions for small tables at nook and corners

Exercises

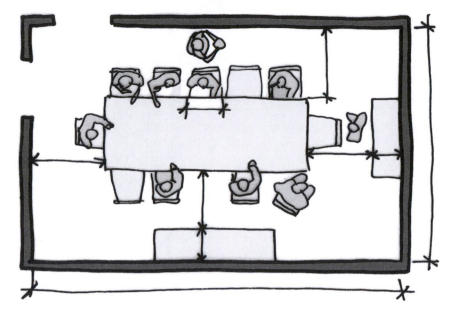

EXERCISE 1

Determine dimensions for the formal dining room shown based on the dimensions given on page 232. In addition to filling out the blank dimensions given on the plan, provide the following:

Room size: _____

Table size: _____

EXERCISE 2

The above plan shows a kitchen area with two adjacent spaces, one for the dining space and the other for the living room space. Draw an optimal-size dining table for six in the dining space. In addition, decide how to treat the dividing wall between the living room and dining table. Choose among the following options:

- Leave the dividing wall as is
- Extend the dividing wall further
- Add a segment of wall on the other side to create an archway

Use the 2'×2' (61 cm×61 cm) grid as a scale reference.

EXERCISE 3

Using the 2' × 2' (61 cm × 61 cm) grid shown, draw a dining room from scratch. Start with a table for eight (any configuration), and then add the necessary clearances around. Finally, decide how much enclosure you want to define/enclose the room, and draw the walls and openings.

Bedrooms I

Think of the bedrooms in your life. Think about how you have used them and what they have meant to you. For those fortunate enough to have their own bedroom, it represents their inner sanctum, their personal piece of real estate in the world. Bedrooms are more than private sleeping places; they are also the places where we get dressed, do homework, read, and dream. Still, bedrooms are mostly associated with sleeping, and their design and layout revolve around the bed or beds in them.

A typical bedroom includes a bed, one or more night stands, a closet, a dresser, and sometimes a desk-chair setup and additional seating. Space is provided on at least one side of the bed (both sides when it's a bed for two) for getting in and out.

Moreover, there is room at the foot of the bed for circulating, getting to the dresser or desk, and so on. All bedrooms should have at least one window. Bedrooms need not be large, although they can be, especially master bedrooms. Shown here are typical sizes for beds and the spaces around them. Also shown are bedroom configurations with different numbers and sizes of beds.

Perhaps the biggest decision in laying out bedrooms is where to put the bed. Any good bedroom will be planned in such a way as to provide more than one choice for bed location.

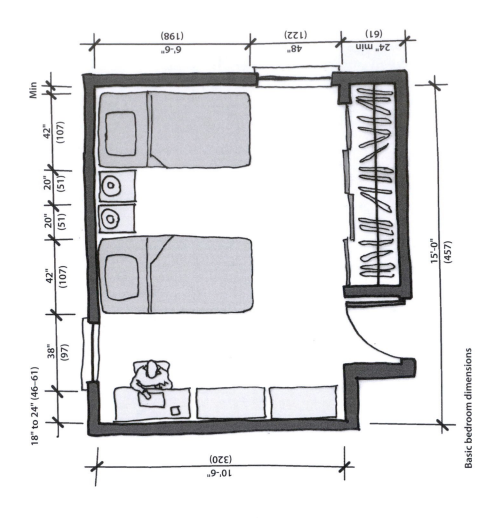

Basic bedroom dimensions

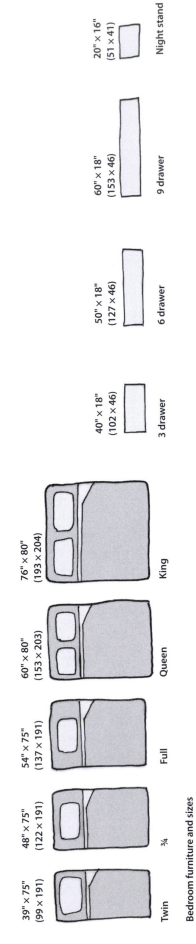

Bedroom furniture and sizes

A. Bedroom with queen bed

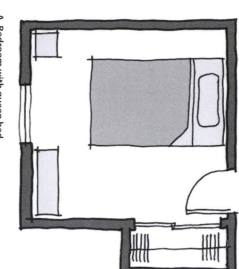

B. Same as A with alternate bed placement

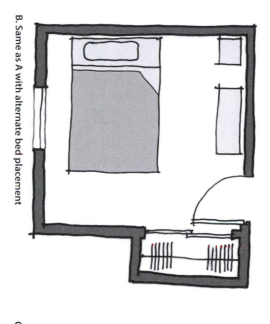

C. Bedroom with full-size bed

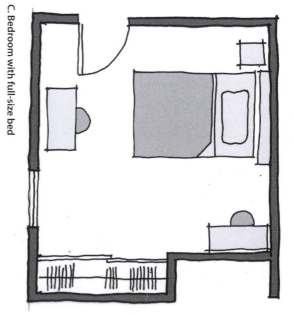

D. Small twin bed

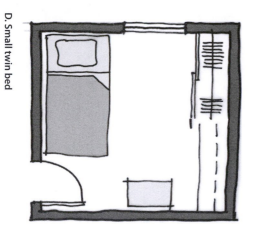

E. Bedroom with two twin beds

F. Bedroom with king-size bed

Bedroom Layouts

Bedrooms II: Master Suites

Master Suite with Closet by Entrance Door

This design is problematic for two reasons: the closet orientation is away from both the bathroom and dressing areas and the bed location in relation to the entrance corridor produces awkward circulation and vision lines upon entering. What improvements would you suggest?

Modest Master Suite with Small Bathroom

This design is highly effective despite its small size. The relationship between the entrance door and bed is much better than in the previous design. The dresser and closet arrangement is very efficient and well located in a private zone and close to the bathroom.

Master Suite with Queen Bed

This design is comfortable and effective. The circulation areas are wide enough to make it work as an accessible suite for wheelchair users. The second door, leading to a balcony, makes that corner of the room unusable. Otherwise, that would be a nice spot for a reading chair. The closet and bathroom arrangement works well, each in its own space and next to each other.

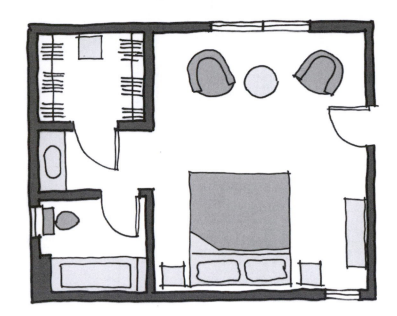

Modest-size Master Suite with Seating Area

This design is efficient and functional. It includes a seating area with two chairs. The only aspects that could be improved are the size (larger) and the location of the dresser (closer to closet and bathroom).

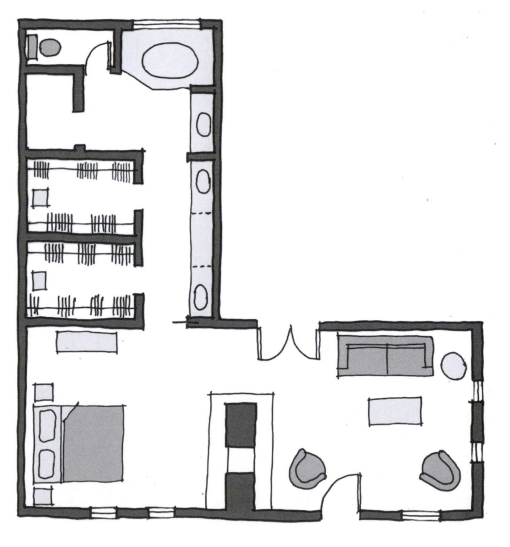

Deluxe Master Suite

This luxurious design features a separate seating room with access to a balcony and individual closets for him and her. It is much larger than the previous designs. The bathroom is divided into various zones, making it possible for multiple users to be in it simultaneously.

Bedroom Groups

Bedrooms are most often grouped within the private zone of a house or apartment. (The exception is contemporary homes, which sometimes separate the master suite from the other bedrooms.) One of the main objectives when designing the bedroom zone is to do so using the smallest amount of circulation space possible to get to the rooms. Another important objective is to give the best possible acoustic separation between rooms. To that end, closets and bathrooms are often sandwiched in between bedrooms to provide an acoustical buffer between them.

Several layouts of two- and three-bedroom clusters are shown here.

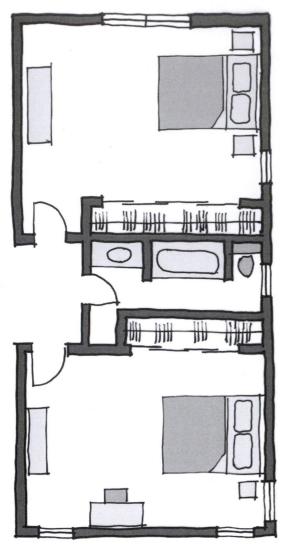

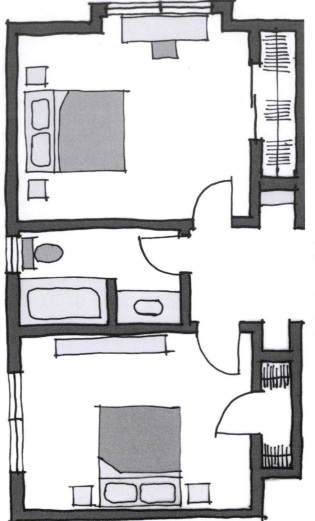

Examples of bathrooms and closets placed in between two bedrooms

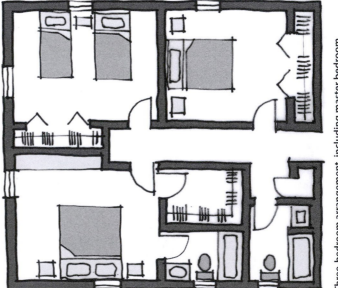

Three-bedroom arrangement, including master bedroom

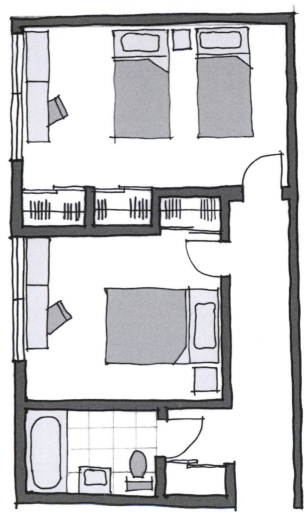

A. Two-bedroom cluster with long corridor to far bedroom

B. Efficient three-bedroom cluster with short corridor run

C. Two-bedroom cluster with bathroom at end

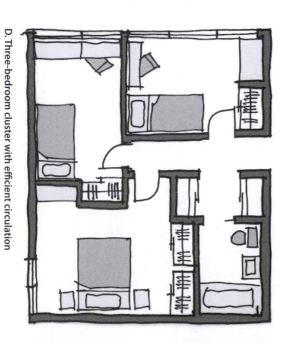

D. Three-bedroom cluster with efficient circulation

Bedroom Clusters

The arrangement of bedroom clusters entails the careful play between the bedrooms, closets, bathrooms, and the corridors that serve them. For any given bedroom zone various organizations are typically possible. Finding out which one meets the project requirements best requires a process of trial and error. Remember to plan the location of closets, windows, doors, and other elements within the bedrooms in a way that allows multiple options for the placement of the bed(s) in the rooms.

Kitchens I

For many families, the kitchen is the most important space in a house, both symbolically and functionally. Kitchen spaces have become increasingly sophisticated over the years, and their design has become so specialized that some designers do nothing but kitchen design work. Kitchen spaces range from the modest and functional to the large and extravagant.

Essentially, kitchens are places for the storage and preparation of food and the storage and cleaning of cooking equipment and dishware. Many users enjoy cooking and spend a considerable amount of time in kitchens multitasking while they prepare elaborate meals. In addition, kitchens are often used by two or more people simultaneously who share tasks and socialize. For these reasons, kitchens have to be places that promote productivity and efficient movement of people and things.

Most kitchen layouts are based on the concept of the **work triangle,** the idea that arrangements produce an efficient triangular relationship between elements with short travel distances that promote efficient movement. In kitchens the essential elements to consider are the stove/oven, the sink, and the refrigerator. The first four layouts on this page show different arrangements based on the work triangle idea.

Another important consideration for kitchen design is how a kitchen space relates to adjacent spaces and the exterior. Picture a couple in the kitchen preparing a meal on a nice sunny Sunday afternoon, while their young kids do their homework nearby in the living room. Outside, the birds are chirping away happily as they feed from the colorful birdhouse. If your design for their kitchen and surrounding areas is such that they can visually connect with the kids in the living room and also look out the window to enjoy the bird scene, you will have created a set of conditions that address important human needs beyond food preparation. For that reason, strive to design kitchen spaces that connect with their surroundings effectively. The synergies produced by such arrangements can be quite powerful. Three plans showing positive connections between kitchens and their surroundings are shown on the next page.

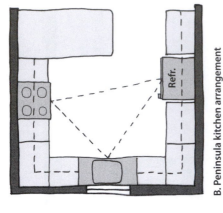
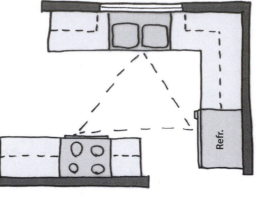

B. Peninsula kitchen arrangement

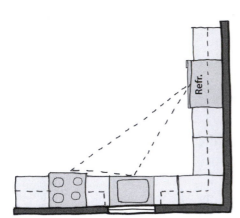

A. L-Shaped kitchen arrangement

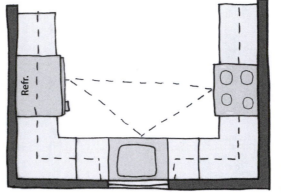

C. U-Shaped kitchen arrangement

D. Combination L-Shaped and single wall arrangement

E. One-Wall galley kitchen arrangement

Common Kitchen Arrangements

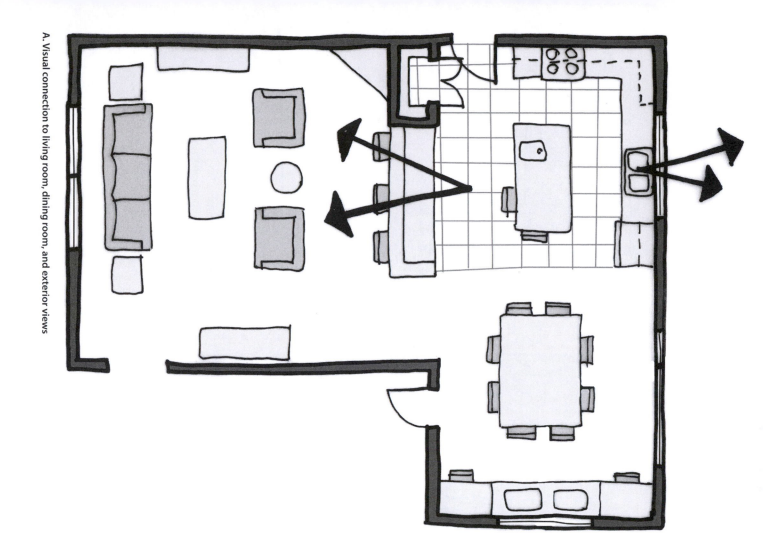

A. Visual connection to living room, dining room, and exterior views

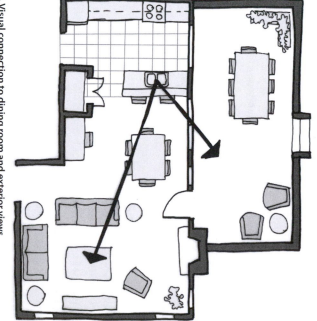

B. Visual connection to dining room and exterior views

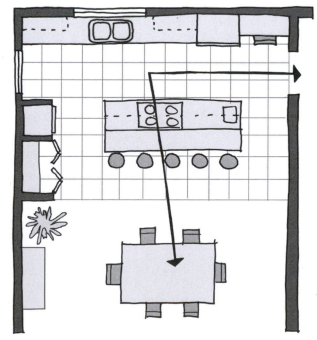

C. Visual connection to living and dining spaces

Kitchen Visual Connections

Kitchens II

Shown on this page are recommended dimensions and clearances for kitchens. The next page presents some of the considerations for designing adaptable kitchens. With the increased awareness of **universal design** principles, you will often be called on to design kitchen spaces that are accessible to the handicapped or that can be converted easily to become accessible in the future. The needs of wheelchair users have the greatest implications for planning purposes as they require special clearances. **Accessible kitchens** require proper dimensions for wheelchairs to get in and out, proper turning dimensions for maneuvering comfortably, and alternative designs to base cabinets in order to provide leg room for the wheelchair user. Once you know these things, it becomes relatively easy to design accessible (or adaptable) kitchen spaces, provided you have a room of adequate size.

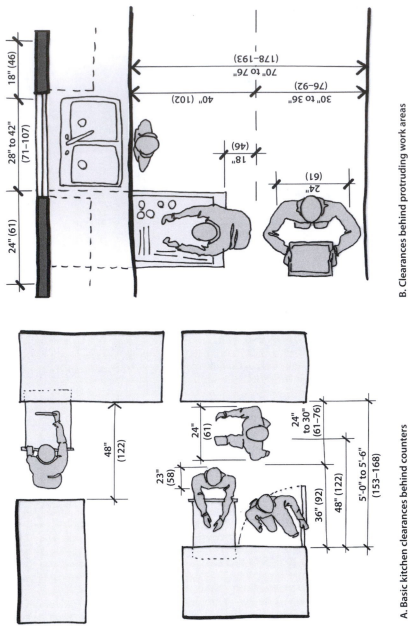

A. Basic kitchen clearances behind counters

B. Clearances behind protruding work areas

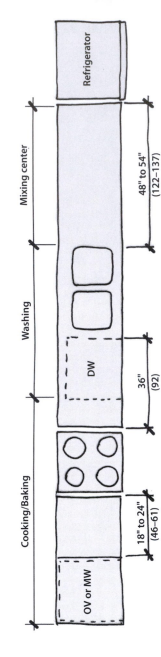

C. Basic counter work area spacing

Clearances in Kitchens

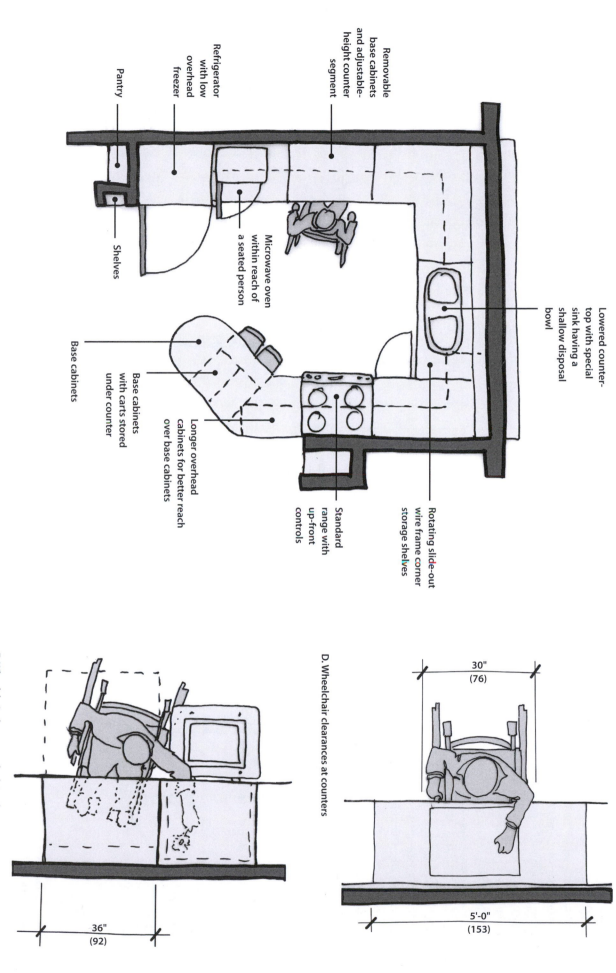

Removable base cabinets and adjustable-height counter segment

Pantry

Refrigerator with low overhead freezer

Shelves

Microwave oven within reach of a seated person

Base cabinets

Base cabinets with carts stored under counter

Longer overhead cabinets for better reach over base cabinets

Standard range with up-front controls

Rotating slide-out wire frame corner storage shelves

Lowered counter-top with special sink having a shallow disposal bowl

D. Wheelchair clearances at counters

30"
(76)

5'-0"
(153)

E. Wheelchair clearances for lateral access to counter

36"
(92)

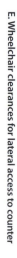

Bathrooms I

Designing bathrooms is usually an exercise in efficient functionality. Most bathrooms are modestly sized and house just the necessary fixtures. In some cases, however, they can be extravagant and include special features, such as saunas, Jacuzzis, and exercise areas. Here, we concentrate on basic, efficient bathroom design.

Powder rooms, or half-baths, are intended as conveniences for guests during short-term gatherings and visits and do not require a shower or bathtub. Powder rooms can be quite small and still do their job adequately. The traditional bathroom includes a bathtub or shower, a lavatory, and a toilet. These can be configured in many possible combinations, some as small as 5'-0" × 7'-6" (152 cm × 229 cm). Several common configurations are shown below. Note that the examples shown are of very efficient bathrooms with minimum clearances.

An important concept to stress for bathroom design is the idea of economy. Whenever possible, try to share resources such as the bathroom shown on the opposite page, serving two adjacent bedrooms. Another important application of economy is concerned with plumbing. Inside the wall cavity behind the lavatory, toilet, and bathtub are the plumbing pipes that supply clean water and return waste. Remember two basic things: First, in instances in which you are looking to add a new bathroom to an existing house, search for locations close to existing plumbing lines to reduce the length of new plumbing lines. Second, when planning multiple bathrooms and other spaces requiring plumbing, such as kitchens and utility/laundry rooms, try to locate them adjacent to one another so that the plumbing serving them can be combined and minimized. Below are examples of a typical set of back-to-back bathrooms and of a cluster of rooms with plumbing grouped together.

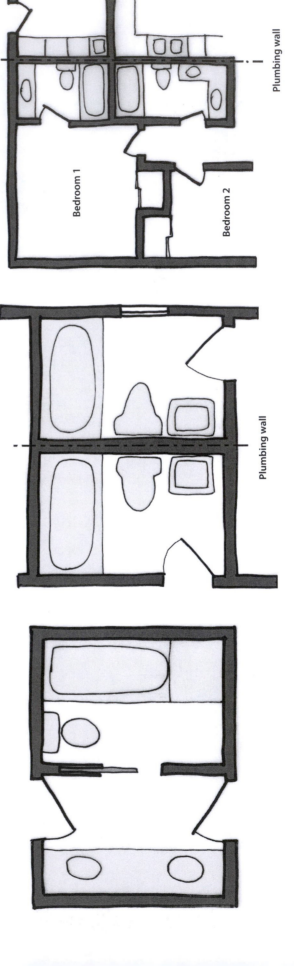

Plumbing wall

Bedroom 1

Bedroom 2

Plumbing wall

A single bathroom arranged to serve adjoining bedrooms shares a valuable resource and prevents duplication.

Efficient back-to-back bathroom arrangements such as this save considerable construction costs related to plumbing.

Maximum efficiency in a house is possible when several rooms with plumbing requirements are clustered in a group, thus sharing plumbing lines and saving money.

Seeking Efficiencies

Typical Bathroom Layouts

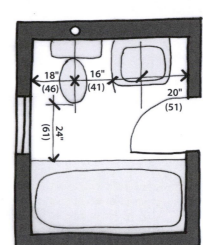

A. Approximately 5'-0" × 7'-0" (153 × 213)

18" (46) 16" (41) 20" (51) 24" (61)

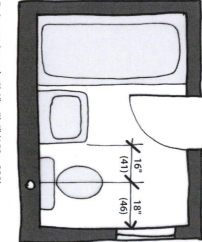

B. Approximately 5'-0" × 7'-6" (153 × 229)

16" (41) 18" (46)

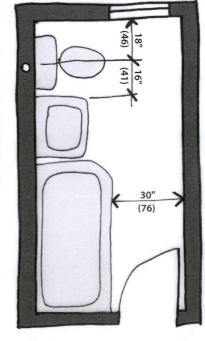

C. Approximately 5'-0" × 10'-0" (153 × 305)

18" (46) 16" (41) 30" (76)

D. Approximately 3'-4" × 6'-0" (102 × 183)

24" to 30" (61–76)

20" (51) both sides

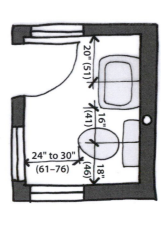

E. Approximately 4'-0" × 5'-6" (122 × 168)

20" (51) 16" (41) 18" (46) 24" to 30" (61–76)

F. Approximately 4'-0" × 4'-0" (122 × 122)

16" (41) 18" (46) 24" to 30" (61–76)

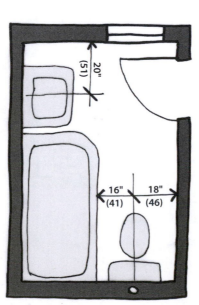

G. Approximately 5'-6" × 8'-6" (168 × 259)

20" (51) 16" (41) 18" (46)

Bathrooms II

Master suite bathrooms don't have to conform to the tight spatial efficiencies of other bathrooms in the house. They can be quite spacious and comfortable. The two examples on this page have two lavatories, a bathtub, and a separate shower. These are not unusual combinations for a master suite. One of them also has a bidet, a long-forgotten but still manufactured commodity.

As with kitchens, bathrooms are often designed for present or future accessibility. Requirements include proper turning and maneuvering dimensions for wheelchairs, wheelchair access under lavatories, and grab bars at toilets and bathtubs for transfer maneuvers. Curbless shower stalls are sometimes used to allow wheelchair-bound users to get inside with ease. Critical dimensions for accessibility to toilets, showers, and bathtubs are shown on the following page. (See also Chapter 2.)

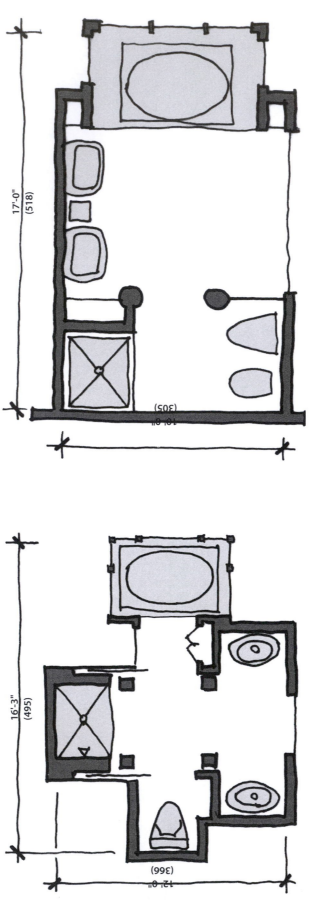

Two master suite bathroom units. Note the increased size, the use of two lavatories, and the provision of both a bathtub and a shower.

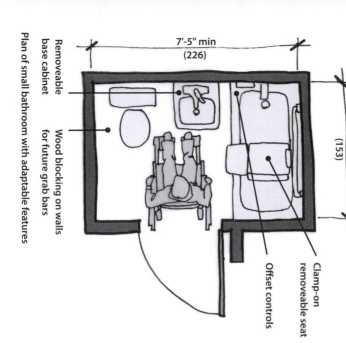

7'-5" min (226)

5'-0" min (153)

Removeable base cabinet

Wood blocking on walls for future grab bars

Offset controls

Clamp-on removeable seat

Plan of small bathroom with adaptable features

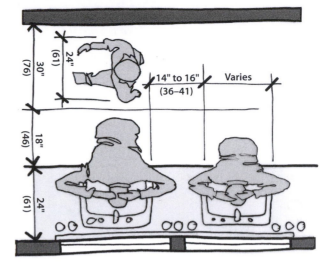

Clearances at lavatories in bathrooms used by multiple people

30" (76)

24" (61)

18" (46)

24" (61)

14" to 16" (36–41)

Varies

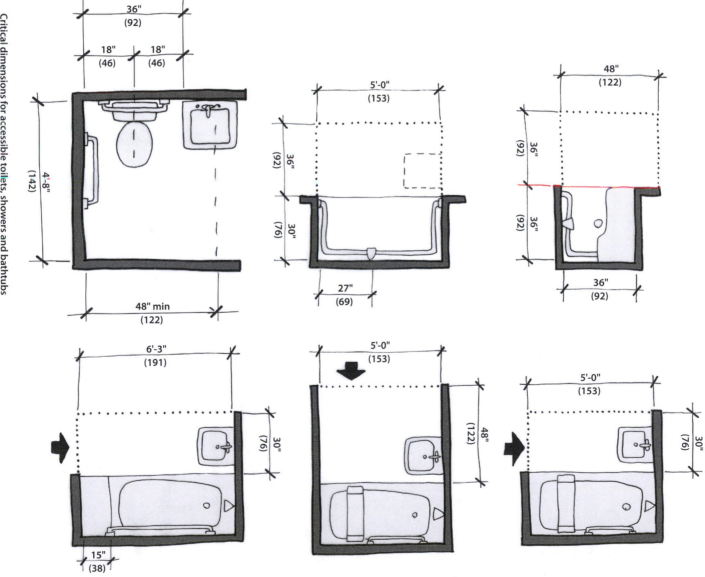

36" (92)

18" (46)

18" (46)

4'-8" (142)

48" min (122)

5'-0" (153)

36" (92)

30" (76)

27" (69)

48" (122)

36" (92)

36" (92)

36" (92)

6'-3" (191)

30" (76)

15" (38)

5'-0" (153)

48" (122)

5'-0" (153)

30" (76)

Critical dimensions for accessible toilets, showers and bathtubs

Storage

Ask any homeowner, and most will tell you that if they could have more of any one thing in the house, it would be storage. There never seems to be enough. People need places to put the many things they keep in the house, and it goes well beyond supplying closets in the bedrooms and cabinets in the kitchen and bathrooms, for those are only the start. Look at the house plan on this page showing the many storage spaces in a house, and you'll realize that there is a need for storage everywhere. With that in mind, seek ways to sneak in storage in as many nooks and crannies as possible.

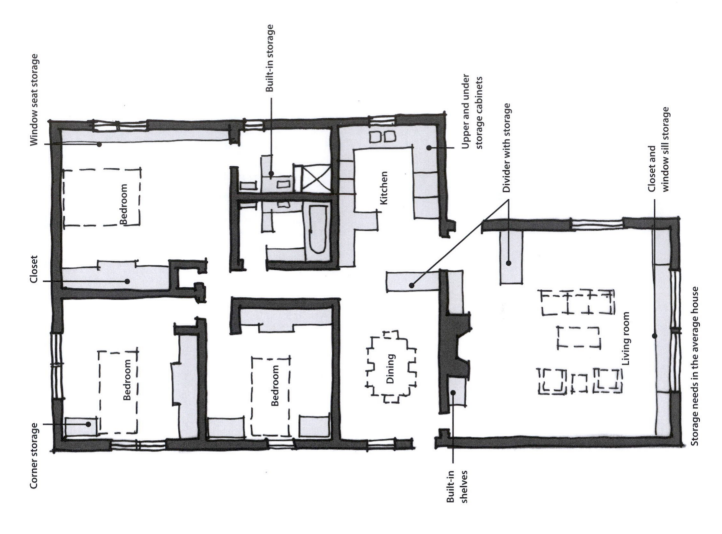

Storage needs in the average house

Window seat storage

Closet

Corner storage

Bedroom

Bedroom

Bedroom

Built-in storage

Kitchen

Dining

Upper and under storage cabinets

Divider with storage

Built-in shelves

Living room

Closet and window sill storage

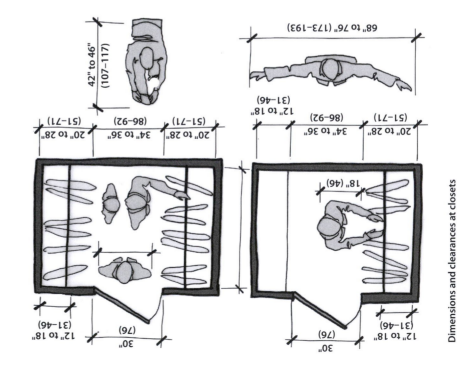

Dimensions and clearances at closets

42" to 46" (107–117)

20" to 28" (51–71)

34" to 36" (86–92)

20" to 28" (51–71)

12" to 18" (31–46)

30" (76)

68" to 76" (173–193)

12" to 18" (31–46)

34" to 36" (86–92)

20" to 28" (51–71)

18" (46)

12" to 18" (31–46)

30" (76)

Make a corridor a little deeper to sneak in a closet.

Bedroom

Closet

Bedroom

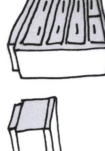
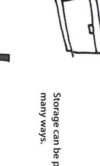

Storage can be provided in many ways.

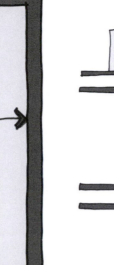

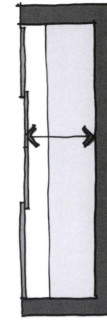

Avoid closets that take up a chunk of a room, leaving spaces of questionable functionality. Aim for the side-to-side and built-in arrangements instead.

Make closets deep enough to accommodate bulky items. 24" (61) is a good minimum depth dimension to use.

Combine closets with other functions, such as desks and shelves, for a complete side-to-side full-length arrangement.

Walk-in closet dimensions

24" (61)

24" (61)

5'-6" (168)

Varies

42" (107)

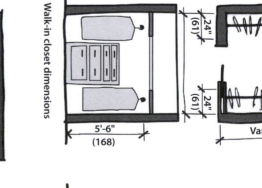
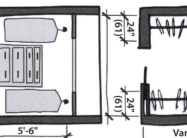
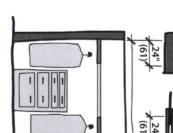
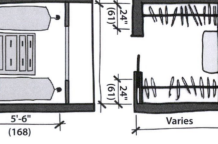
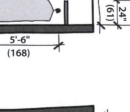

Flanking closets and work area

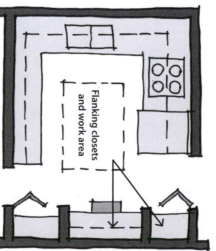

Built-in storage

Examples of extra storage in kitchens and bathrooms

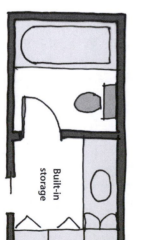
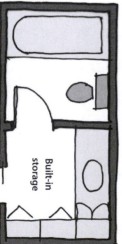

Apartments: Analysis

A good way to learn how to design efficient residential spaces is to study apartment plans, because they have to make the most of the space available and often do a great job of maximizing limited space. To help you look at these examples critically, I am going to ask you to conduct a quick analysis of the five designs shown. Following are the elements to be analyzed. Make your comments in the spaces provided.

Criteria for Analysis

1. Effectiveness of entrance
2. Means used to separate public from private zones
3. Overall success of the living/dining/kitchen arrangement
4. Handling of enclosed versus open spaces
5. Particularly innovative idea(s)

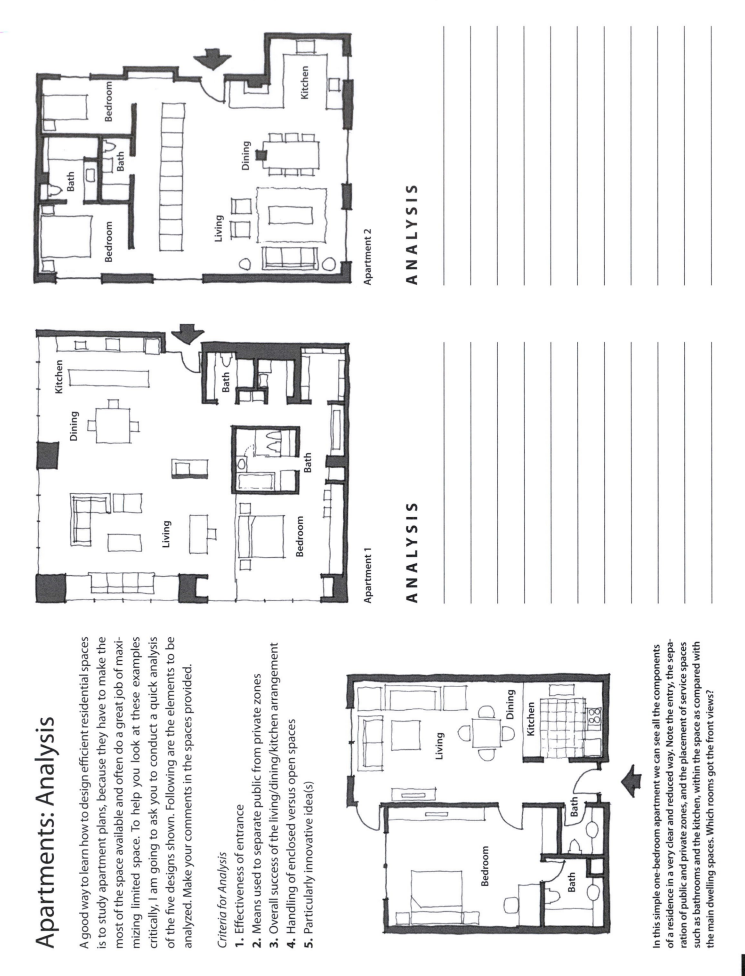

Apartment 2

A N A L Y S I S

Apartment 1

A N A L Y S I S

In this simple one-bedroom apartment we can see all the components of a residence in a very clear and reduced way. Note the entry, the separation of public and private zones, and the placement of service spaces such as bathrooms and the kitchen, within the space as compared with the main dwelling spaces. Which rooms got the front views?

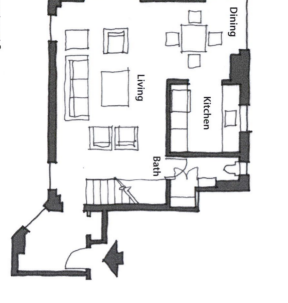

Apartment 3

ANALYSIS

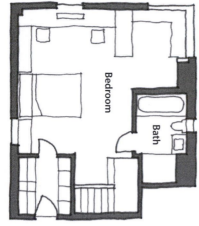

Apartment 4

ANALYSIS

Apartment 5

ANALYSIS

Small Homes: Analysis

Let's continue the analysis of small residential spaces. This time we look at small homes, and I will ask you to conduct a quick analysis of the four designs shown. You will analyze the same elements previously used for the apartments. Write your comments in the spaces provided.

Criteria for Analysis

1. Effectiveness of entrance
2. Means used to separate public from private zones
3. Overall success of the living/dining/kitchen arrangement
4. Analysis of handling of enclosed versus open spaces
5. Particularly innovative idea(s)

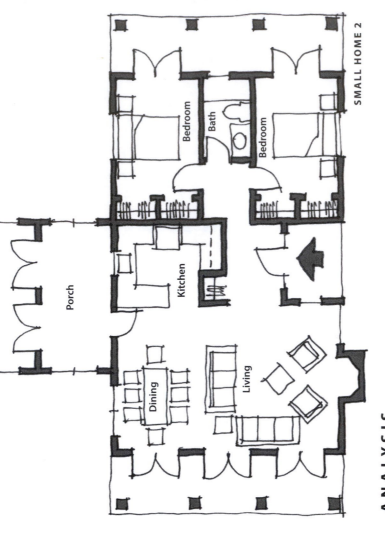

SMALL HOME 2

ANALYSIS

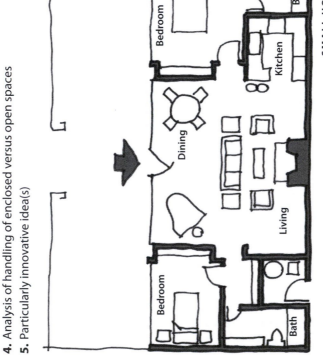

SMALL HOME 1

ANALYSIS

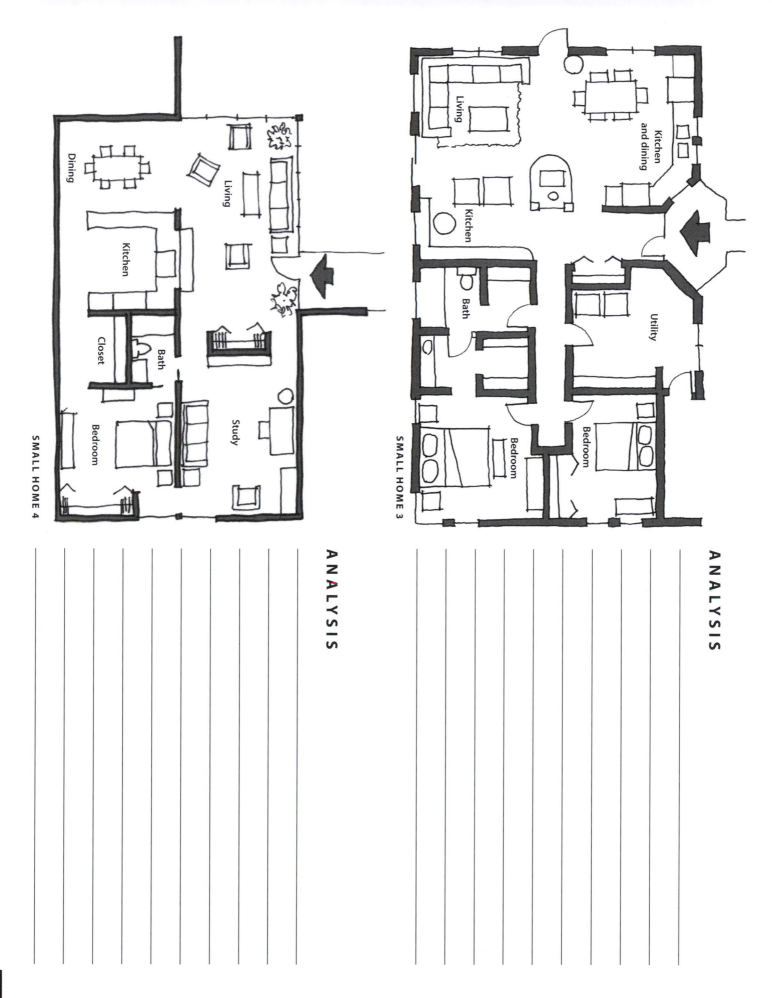

SMALL HOME 4

Dining

Living

Kitchen

Closet

Bath

Bedroom

Study

ANALYSIS

SMALL HOME 3

Living

Kitchen
and dining

Kitchen

Bath

Utility

Bedroom

Bedroom

ANALYSIS

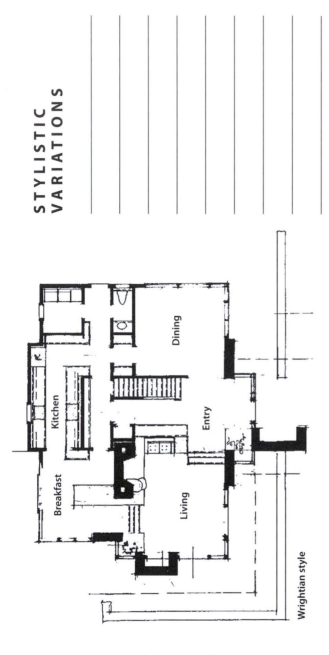

Wrightian style

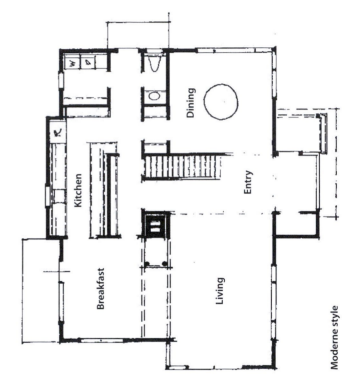

Moderne style

Style Influence

The way you approach and solve a design problem can be influenced by style. Different historical and stylistic styles have their own rules and tendencies. Here, I show you how different historical styles affect the planning of the public areas of a residence. Taken from John Milnes Baker's text *American House Styles: A Concise Guide*, I show his interpretation of the same living space designed for different historical styles. The basic space represents the first floor of a residence. It consists of the spaces listed below. It is also shown below in its basic form.

Basic Floor Plan:

- Entrance vestibule and corridor
- Stairs to second floor
- Dining room
- Living room with fireplace
- Breakfast room
- Kitchen
- Powder room
- Laundry room

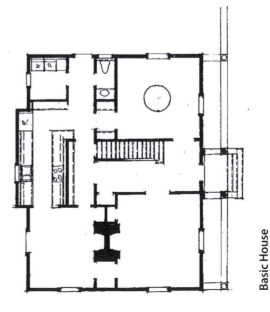

Basic House

Four Historical Styles

Look closely at the four examples, and note how they vary slightly from style to style. Some of the distinguishing characteristics of these four styles are given below. Next to each plan, note other stylistic variations and general observations.

Wrightian, 1940–1960
- Mitered glass at exterior corners
- Avoidance of contained spaces
- Cantilevered construction without corner posts
- Spatial freedom
- Strong asymmetrical geometry

Moderne, 1920–1940
- No ornament
- Plain surfaces
- Plateglass windows
- Use of glass block
- Streamlining
- Wraparound windows

Beaux Arts, 1890–1930
- Axial planning and composition
- Articulation of building masses
- Predilection for pictorial extravagance
- Ordered symmetry
- Classical forms

Queen Anne, 1880–1910
- Embellishments with knee braces, brackets, and spindles
- Open and flowing floor plans
- Use of double parlor doors
- Use of corner fireplaces
- Use of porches and verandas
- Incorporation of turrets, towers, and fanciful gazebos

Source: John Milnes Baker, *American House Styles: A Concise Guide* (New York: W.W. Norton, 1994).

STYLISTIC VARIATIONS

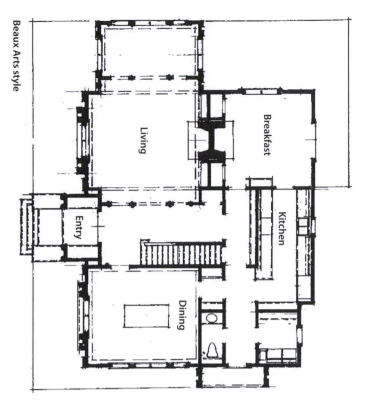

Beaux Arts style

STYLISTIC VARIATIONS

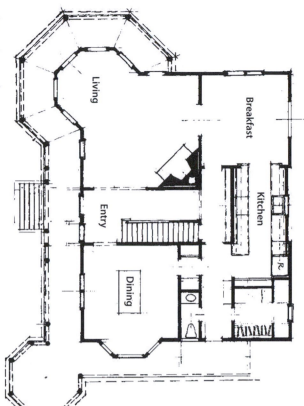

Queen Anne style

Bubbles to Block Plan to Loose Plan

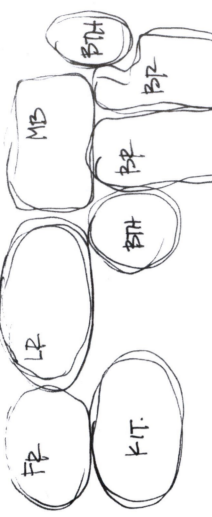

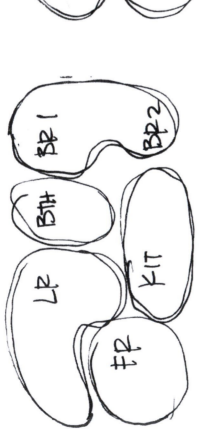

EXERCISE 1

Take the two adjacency bubble diagrams further, and convert each into a block plan configuration in the space provided. Use the 3' × 3' (92 cm × 92 cm) grid for scale reference. Good luck.

Convert the loose plans shown into more developed loose plans. Draw over the plans.
Two plans for each project are provided for your convenience.

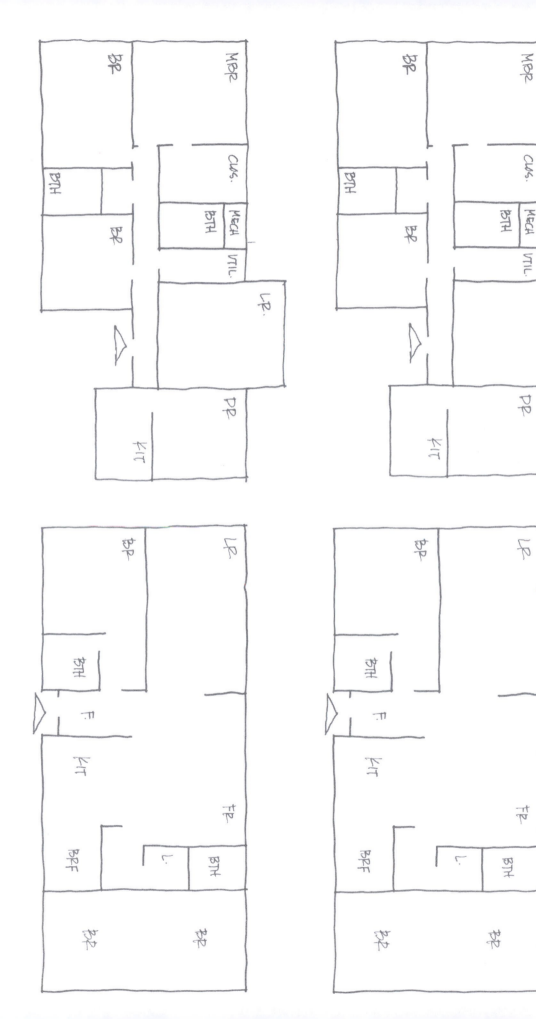

Block Plan Configurations

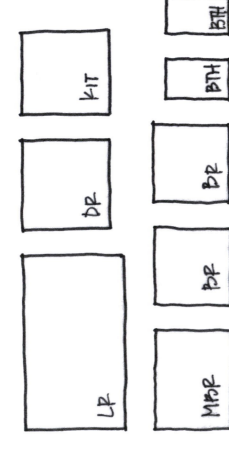

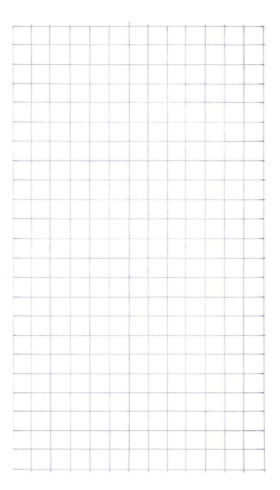

EXERCISE 1

Using the grids provided, assemble the blocks above, representing the various parts of a house, into three different workable arrangements. The spaces are a living room, a dining room, a kitchen, a master bedroom, two additional bedrooms, and two bathrooms.

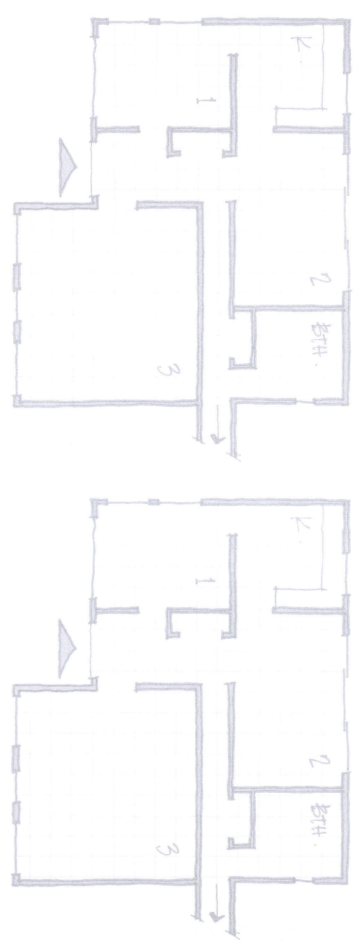

EXERCISE 2

Look at the two identical partial plans above. These represent the public zone of a house. Also shown, with an arrow, is a corridor that connects with the private half of the house. Only the entrance, the kitchen, and a bathroom are given. The other spaces (numbered) represent a living room, a dining room, and a family room, in no particular order. Your task is to come up with two different schemes that (1) determine what you want to use each of the numbered spaces for (living, dining, family) and (2) open the plan up. To open the place, you will need to remove some walls (assume all the walls are nonstructural). You may add as necessary elements commonly used to divide space, such as a fireplace. Draw furniture. Use the 2' × 2' (61 cm × 61 cm) grid for reference.

Plan Development

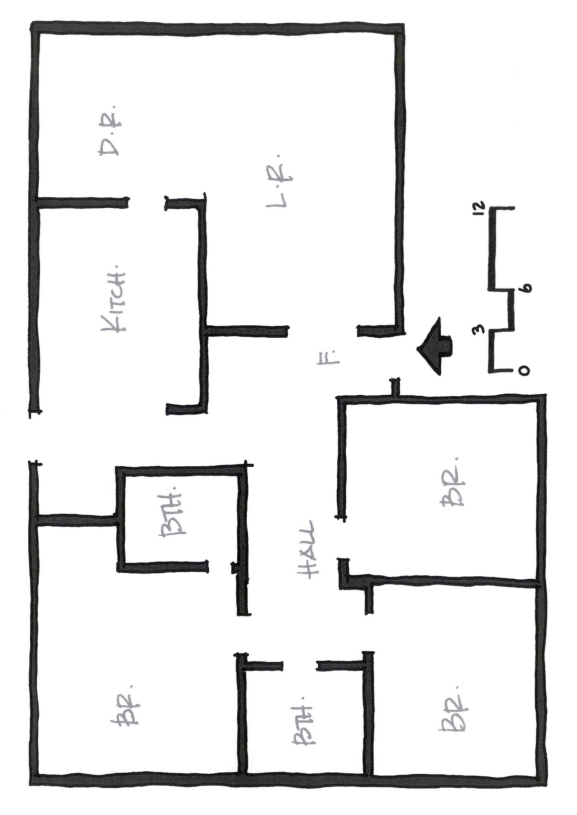

EXERCISE 1

Refine and further develop the plan above. In addition, add furniture and fixtures in the various spaces. No grid is included. This will be an exercise to test how well you can eyeball the approximate scale of a plan and draw furniture that is to scale.

EXERCISE 2

Furnish the bedroom above with the given scaled furniture. Use all the pieces. Use the 3′ × 3′ (92 cm × 92 cm) grid for reference.

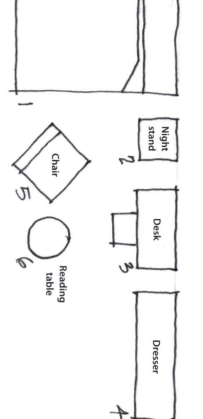

Night stand 2

Desk 3

Dresser 4

Chair 5

Reading table 6

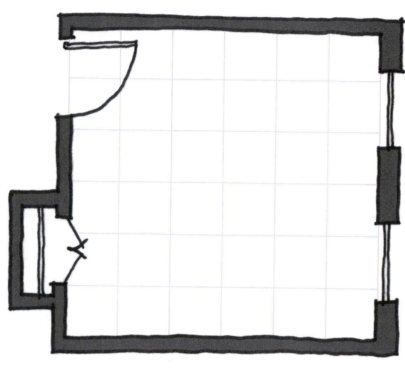

EXERCISE 3

Furnish the living room above with the given scaled furniture. Use all the pieces. Use the 3′ × 3′ (92 cm × 92 cm) grid for reference.

Table 1

2

Table 3

4

Coffee table 5

Chaise longue 6, 7

8

9

Lamp table 10

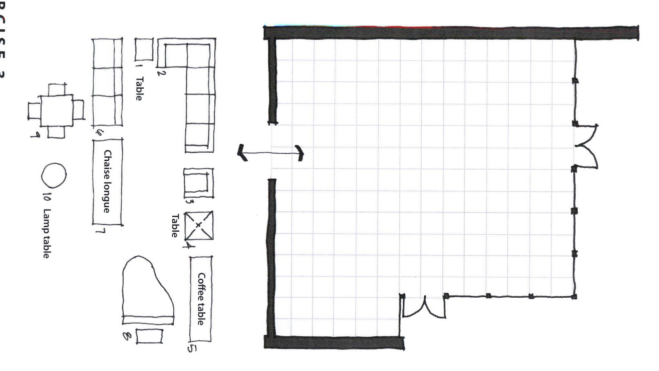

Furnishing Spaces

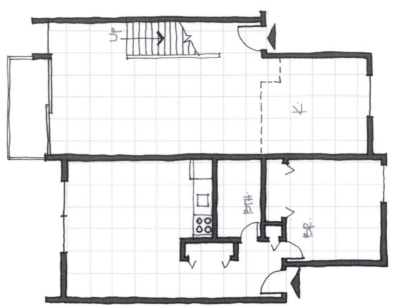

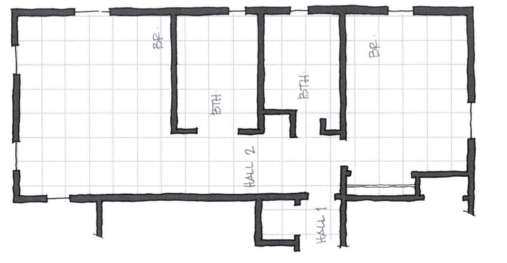

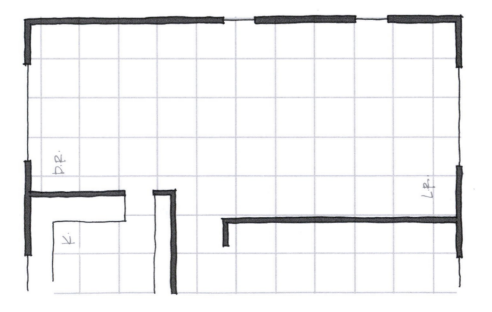

EXERCISE 1

Furnish the living and dining spaces shown. Use any furniture you want. Use the 3′ × 3′ (92 cm × 92 cm) grid for reference. Good luck.

EXERCISE 2

Furnish the bedroom and bathroom spaces shown. Use any furniture and fixtures you want. Use the 3′ × 3′ (92 cm × 92 cm) grid for reference. Enjoy.

EXERCISE 3

Furnish the two apartments shown. The one on the left is a complete one-bedroom apartment. The one on the right is the downstairs of a two-story apartment; it is where the living, kitchen, and dining spaces are located. Use any furniture you want. Use the 3′ × 3′ (92 cm × 92 cm) grid for reference. Good luck.

EXERCISE 4

Furnish the condominium shown. Spaces are labeled. You may add, remove, or use only part of the wall shown dashed (up to you). Use any furniture you want. Use the 3′ × 3′ (92 cm × 92 cm) grid for reference. Have fun.

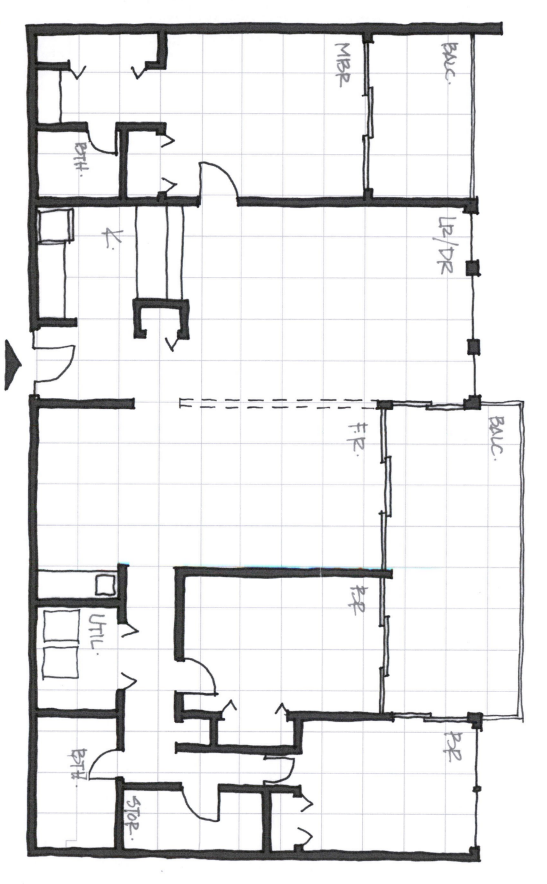

Efficiency Apartment

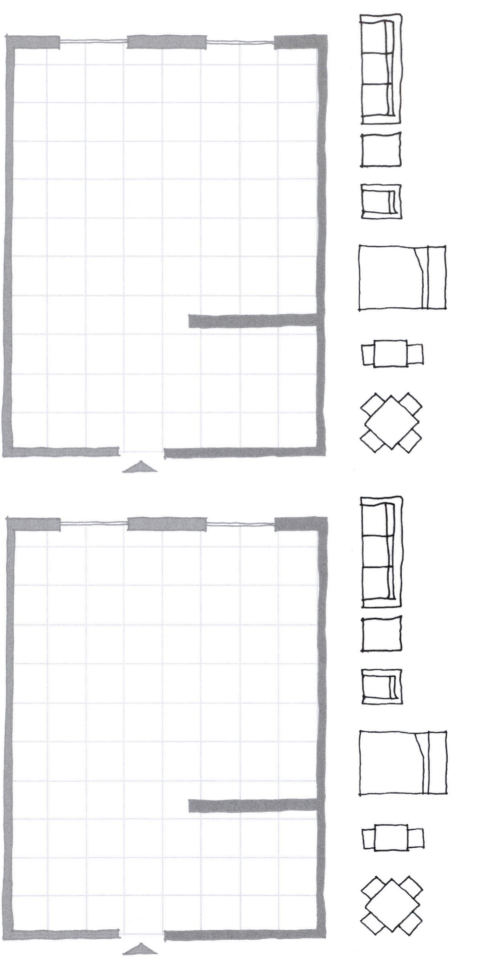

EXERCISE 1

Using the shell provided come up with two layouts for an efficiency apartment that includes sleeping, living, cooking, dining, studying, and bathroom functions. Add walls as necessary. The wall projecting into the space contains plumbing, so it is suggested that you place your spaces needing plumbing in that zone. Use any furniture you want. Use the 3′ × 3′ (92 cm × 92 cm) grid for reference. Good luck.

EXERCISE 2

As in the previous exercise, come up with two layouts for an efficiency apartment, using the shell provided. Include sleeping, living, cooking, dining, studying, and bathroom functions. Add walls as necessary. The walls on the bottom of the plan contain plumbing, so it is suggested that you place your spaces needing plumbing in that zone. Use any furniture you want. Use the 3′ × 3′ (92 cm × 92 cm) grid for reference. Have fun!

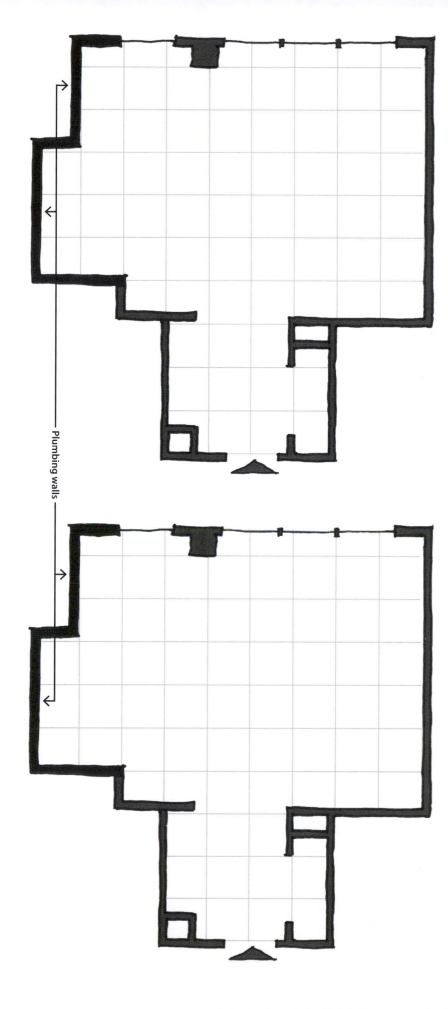

Plumbing walls

8 Nonresidential Design

Offices: Anatomy and Issues I

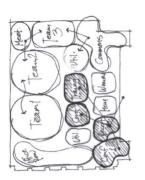
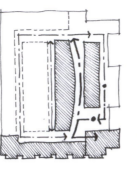
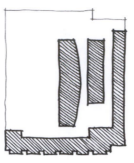
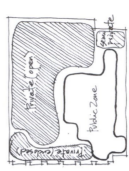
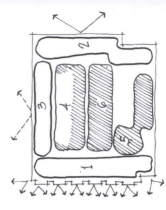

The diagrams shown illustrate five important considerations when designing office environments.

Allocation

How functions are accommodated efficiently in space

Circulation

How the corridors and aisles are organized into a clear, easy-to-understand movement system

Solids and Voids

How the enclosed spaces are arranged to produce masses and open spaces that are clear, cohesive, and comfortable

Public/Private

How space and functions are placed strategically to produce clear definition and the appropriate separation between public and private areas

Real Estate

How the relative worth of the different zones on the floor plate is perceived and functions placed accordingly

Office planning can be challenging for the young designer. Although most college-age students have repeatedly visited many other types of commercial projects, such as stores, restaurants, and hotels, few have visited very many corporate office environments. These projects can be complex, often having many parts and intricate relationships between them. With a little exposure and a few tips, you should be able to become a confident and competent office environment planner. Some of the issues to be aware of when designing office projects include the following:

Companies often lease office space. This is one of the major expenses of a company. For that reason, efficient space utilization is essential. Workers should be accommodated efficiently, yet comfortably.

Different companies and different units within the same company will often have different work styles. You have to understand the work styles you are designing for in order to provide suitable space-planning and furniture solutions.

Many companies still have formal hierarchical structures. This translates into decisions about who gets an office along the perimeter windows, who gets a large corner office, and so on. On the other hand, the hierarchies in many offices are being flattened, meaning fewer layers based on rank and fewer corner offices. In fact, many offices are moving toward having universal stations of uniform size for everybody, regardless of title and rank.

More and more, work groups are being organized based on team practices. This has implications that inform what kinds of workstations are used and how they are arranged.

Work environments are about work and productivity. Being able to concentrate and work efficiently is essential for workers.

A lot of what takes place in offices happens in group meetings. Designing good spaces for meeting, whether formal conference rooms or informal team areas, is important.

Companies work hard to project a favorable, professional image. For that reason, the public spaces seen by visitors often receive special treatment.

By law (and per code), office environments need to accommodate employees and visitors of all abilities. The environments need to be accessible to the entire cast of characters introduced in Chapter 2.

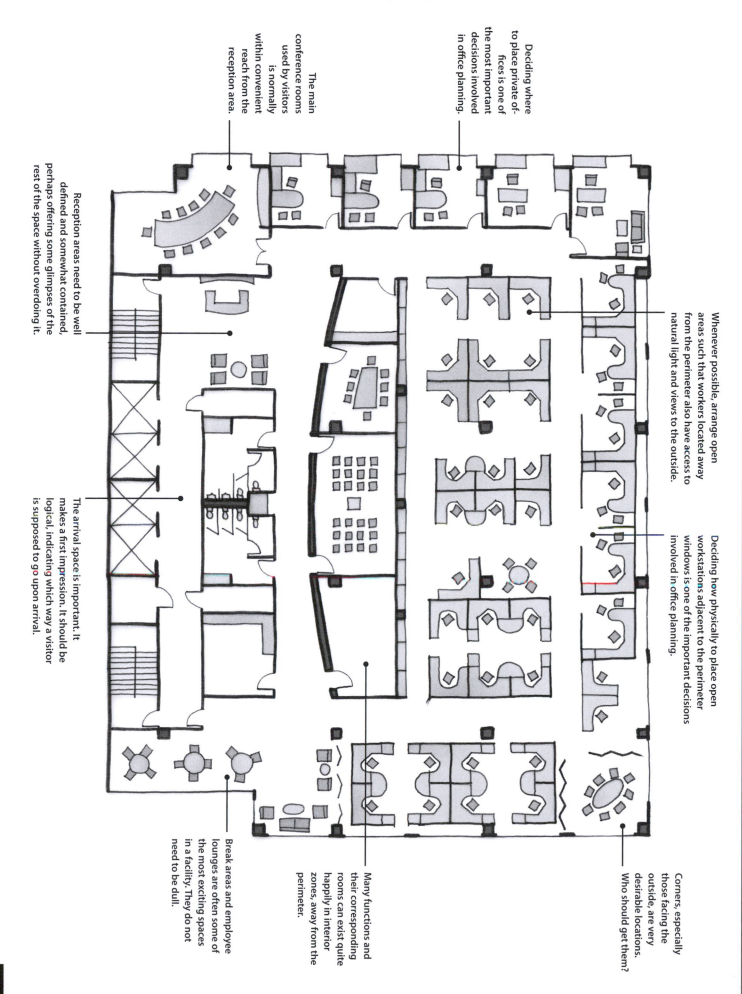

Deciding where to place private offices is one of the most important decisions involved in office planning.

The main conference rooms used by visitors is normally within convenient reach from the reception area.

Reception areas need to be well defined and somewhat contained, perhaps offering some glimpses of the rest of the space without overdoing it.

Whenever possible, arrange open areas such that workers located away from the perimeter also have access to natural light and views to the outside.

Deciding how physically to place open workstations adjacent to the perimeter windows is one of the important decisions involved in office planning.

Corners, especially those facing the outside, are very desirable locations. Who should get them?

The arrival space is important. It makes a first impression. It should be logical, indicating which way a visitor is supposed to go upon arrival.

Break areas and employee lounges are often some of the most exciting spaces in a facility. They do not need to be dull.

Many functions and their corresponding rooms can exist quite happily in interior zones, away from the perimeter.

Offices: Anatomy and Issues II

Students often try too hard to be creative when space planning an office facility, introducing all kinds of twists and angles that result in confusing, disjointed projects. As a rule, keep things simple, even when exploring dynamic geometries. Straightforwardness is our first rule for office planning. Others include the following:

- Combine and group similar parts and elements whenever possible. Attach workstations, and form groups that share panels (economy) and that produce cohesion, not fragmentation.

- Be sensitive to the privacy and acoustical needs of users in open areas. Utilize panel heights effectively to produce a healthy balance between communication needs and privacy/acoustical concerns.

- Be aware of the negative impact of excessive noise transmission between rooms. Plan your walls, partitions, and doors in ways that promote a comfortable acoustical environment.

- Seize every opportunity to bring in natural light, and allow it to penetrate into the space. Similarly, try to arrange spaces such that as many workers as possible have access to external views.

- When planning with furniture, orient it in ways that shelter the workers from people walking by or coming into an office. Don't expose people's backs to circulation areas.

- Office space is expensive. For this and other reasons, try to minimize the amount of space devoted to circulation. Devote most of your space to functional requirements other than circulation.

- Be careful when making decisions about where to place enclosed rooms. Whenever possible, place offices toward the interior of the space (you can give them glass fronts if you want), and open up the perimeter areas.

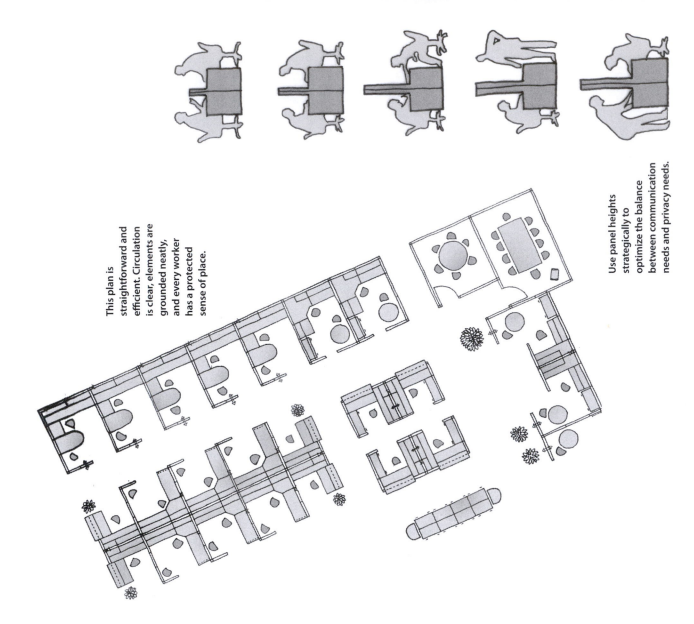

This plan is straightforward and efficient. Circulation is clear, elements are grounded neatly, and every worker has a protected sense of place.

Use panel heights strategically to optimize the balance between communication needs and privacy needs.

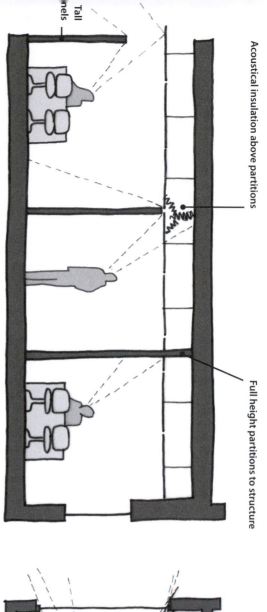

Acoustical insulation above partitions

Tall panels

Full height partitions to structure

Use planning practices that produce good acoustical environments.

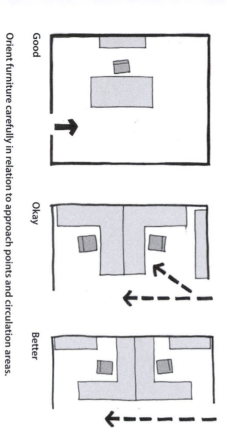

Good

Okay

Better

Orient furniture carefully in relation to approach points and circulation areas.

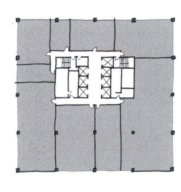

Minimize circulation.

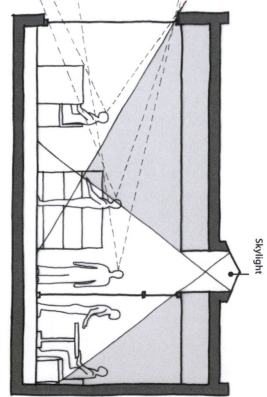

Skylight

Take advantage of the perimeter windows. Allow natural light to come in, while controlling unwanted glare.

Whenever possible, avoid devoting large portions of the perimeter window wall to private offices and other enclosed rooms. Also, some rooms, such as storage rooms, have no business being on the window wall. Some spaces belong on the perimeter; many don't.

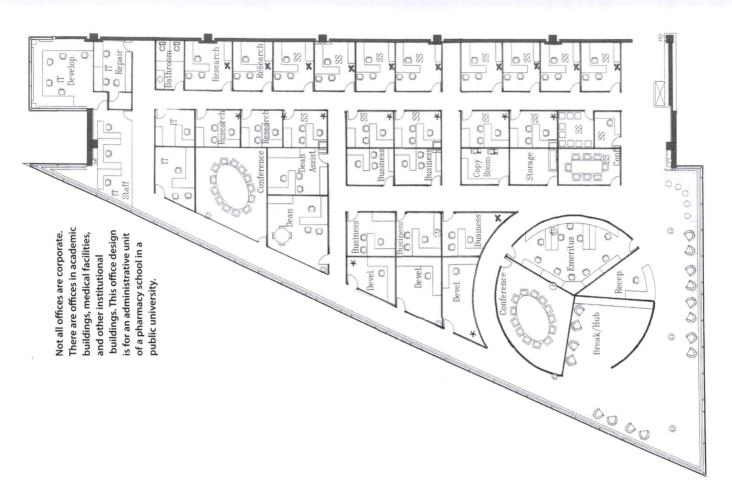

Not all offices are corporate. There are offices in academic buildings, medical facilities, and other institutional buildings. This office design is for an administrative unit of a pharmacy school in a public university.

Labels within plan: IT Develop., Repair, Bathroom, Research, Research, SS, SS, SS, SS, SS, SS, SS, SS, IT, Research, Research, SS, SS, SS, SS, SS, SS, SS, SS, Staff, IT, Conference, Dean Assist., Business, Business, Business, Business, Copy Room, Storage, SS, Conf., Dean, Business, Business, Business, Devel., Devel., Devel., Conference, Emeritus, Break/Hub, Recep., FEC

A professional business consulting firm with a strong sense of professionalism and a healthy balance between private (enclosed) and open office areas.

Office Types

There are many types of offices. The way an office is planned and designed overall varies widely, based on the type of firm and its work culture. The four offices shown here are diverse and illustrate this.

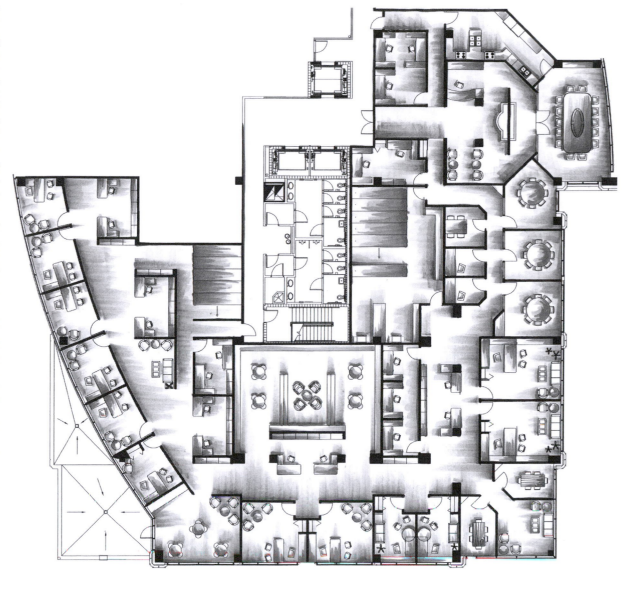

Some offices, such as law firms, tend to be hierarchical and fairly formal. In this kind of office, it is customary for attorneys to get offices along the perimeter windows. Partners' offices are larger, and senior partners' offices are the largest and usually located at the corners. Paralegals are mainly assigned internal rooms away from the perimeter.

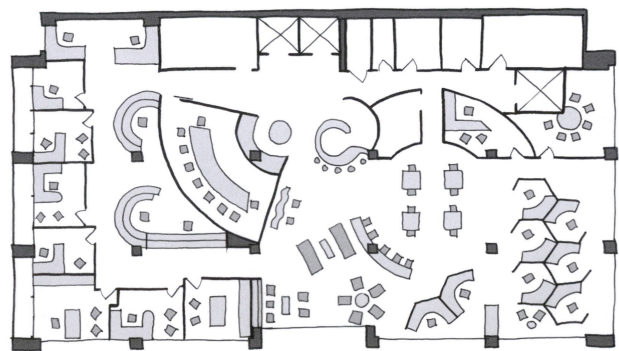

Some office environments are fun and creative. Advertising firms, such as this one, are notorious for being that way. Their projected image often conveys creativity.

Office Furnishings I

Give a start-up service business enterprise a long table, a few chairs, a file cabinet, and good internet connectivity, and it has all the furniture it needs to get started; things can be that simple. Yet, most office projects you are likely to get involved with, in school and in practice, have a much wider array of furnishings than that. Here, we look at some of the basic staples of office furnishings.

Most offices consist of a reception/waiting area; one or more meeting rooms; private offices; open offices; and special rooms, such as workrooms, copy rooms, and break rooms. Most of the work is done while sitting. Essentially, this translates into desks, tables, and chairs. To this we add file cabinets to store paper documents and other storage units and we have all the basics. This page illustrates these basics.

1. The conference table is available in many shapes and sizes. The size of the table will depend on how many people need to be accommodated. Later in this chapter I will give you some basic criteria that will help you determine the required table size for various groups.

2. Panel-mounted components, such as desks and overhead storage, are part of standardized furniture systems used mostly (but not exclusively) for open planning. Variations are plentiful and address just about every working condition conceivable. Systems enable efficient combinations of work surfaces, storage units, and screening devices for separation and privacy.

3. Storage units come in many sizes and styles, from the two-door metal cabinet available at your local office supply megastore to sophisticated and specialized units available through contract vendors.

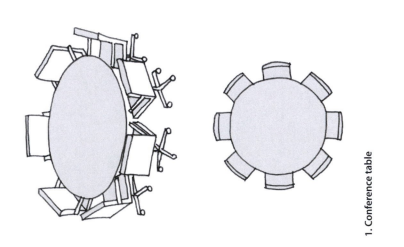

1. Conference table

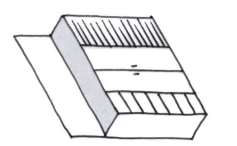

2. Systems furniture components

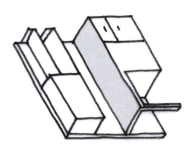

3. Storage cabinet

4. Cubicle or workstation

4. Another variation of a systems furniture workstation, the cubicle offers a compact but efficient work
surface, storage/file pedestals underneath the work
surface, and a partial-height panel that affords
some seating-height visual privacy.

5. The desk continues to be used widely today. The
example shown is an L-shaped freestanding configuration with a file cabinet underneath the work
surface.

6. The credenza is used in many private offices, usually behind the desk. It provides additional storage
and a work/holding surface.

7. Seating groups, such as the one shown, can be
found in reception areas and also, increasingly, in
other loungy parts of some offices.

8. The file cabinet is still a necessity. Despite well-
intended efforts to reduce paperwork, the reality
of most offices is one of a great many paper documents that need to be filed (and later retrieved) for
record-keeping purposes. Lateral files are particularly efficient and are used widely. They come in
various heights, depending on how many units are
stacked on top of each other (usually between two
and five).

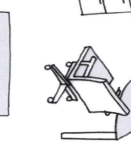

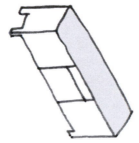

5. Desk

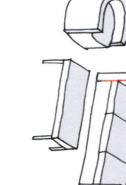

6. Credenza

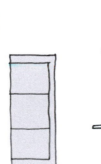

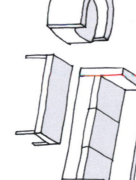
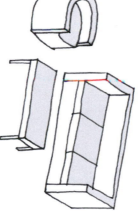

7. Seating group

8. Lateral file cabinet

Office Furnishings II

One of the great design inventions of the twentieth century is the **cubicle**, or office **workstation**. Although bad applications are easy to ridicule, good ones are just as easy to praise. They are efficient and versatile and respond well to the realities and needs of office environments. Planning with them requires some getting used to at first, but with a little patience even the novice designer can become a great systems furniture planner.

Unlike individual desks, **workstations** are meant to be joined and used in groups. That's when they yield the greatest economies of materials and space. They are available as a kit of parts and can be highly customized to meet any kind of work scenario imaginable. Based on factors such as workers' typical daily tasks, storage needs, and working styles, designers determine optimal workstation configurations for clients. It all starts with the individual workstation and then grows to the cluster and then the neighborhood. It is possible to have every single workstation customized to meet the specific requirements of each user, but it is more common to have just a few typical stations that are used throughout a project.

In the early days of open-office planning, it was customary to see mostly cubicles with high panels and workers working individually inside them. As work styles have become more collaborative, the use of low panels has become more prevalent in order to open up environments and promote communication among workers. The two drawings on this page of short rows of workstations illustrate examples with low panels between workers.

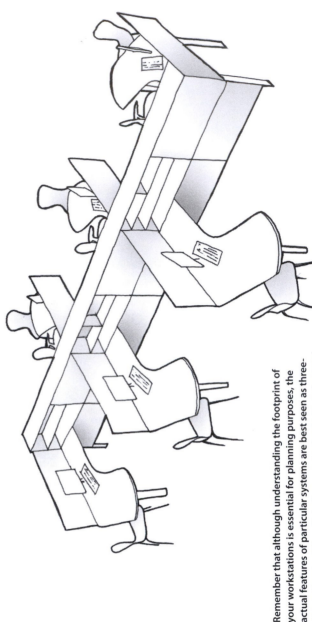

Remember that although understanding the footprint of your workstations is essential for planning purposes, the actual features of particular systems are best seen as three-dimensional entities. Only then can you begin to understand the particular work atmosphere you are creating.

This aerial view of an office environment shows a neatly organized open-office environment featuring single-row clusters of four workstations and back-to-back configurations consisting of eight total workstations. Each grouping is made up of 16 workers, resulting in very comfortable neighborhood sizes.

Office Furnishings III

Look at the various examples on these pages to see how workstations are combined in pairs and then larger groups of three, four, or more workers. Technically, you can group as many workstations as space will allow; however, for practical and perceptual reasons, you want to consider breaking up clusters once you get to approximately eight to ten workers. Groups of four to eight are very typical. The units can be designed to encourage interaction between adjacent workers by, for instance, using shared work/meeting surfaces between them or can go the other extreme and provide separation and privacy for workers needing to perform individual tasks requiring concentration. Different groups of workers within the same project often have different work styles and needs and require different configurations.

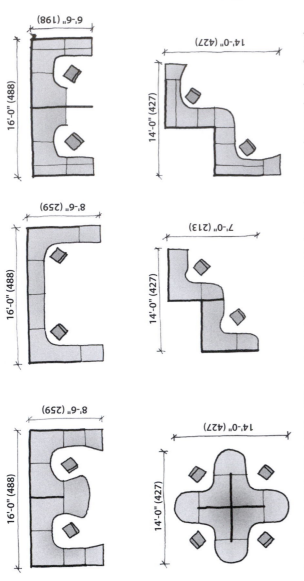

Start by becoming familiar with the different ways small groups of two to four workstations can be joined and configured.

Explore ways to create rows and clusters with the workstation system you are planning to use. You may want to look at different lines and models from different companies, although, when you are starting out, it is best to concentrate on a single line by a single manufacturer. Even then you will have more configuration choices than you can imagine.

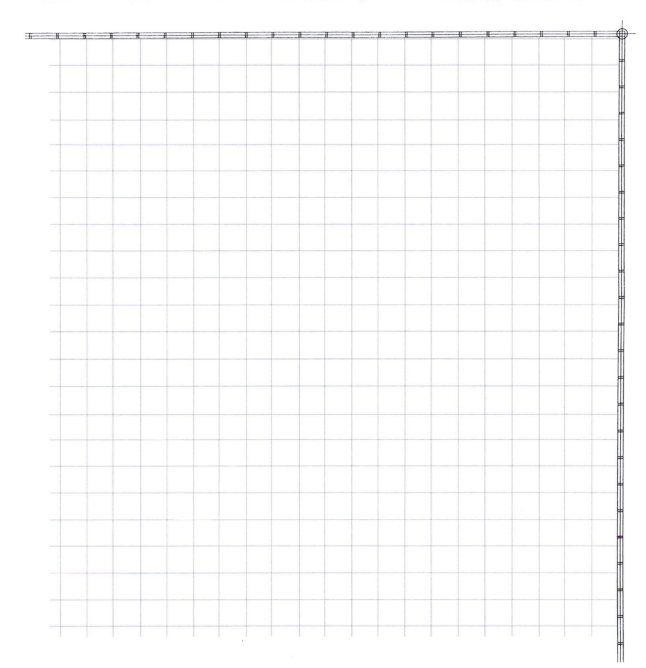

EXERCISE

In the space provided, plan a generic open-plan environment, using several of the workstation grouping examples shown at left. Be as efficient with space as possible. Use the 4'×4' (122 cm × 122 cm) grid as a scale reference.

Offices: Reception Area

An office reception area serves several important functions. It is a control point for visitors and an area where they are greeted and where they wait for the person or event they came for. It is also the place where first impressions are made. A reception area normally requires two zones, one for the reception desk and the receptionist and another for the seating area where visitors wait. The receptionist can be facing the incoming visitors or have a more discrete lateral relationship with the incoming people. The seating area can be placed several ways, but is often either across from or next to the receptionist. Unlike medical and dental offices, corporate reception areas offer just a few chairs. A group of four is common.

The following list gives a few basic considerations for good reception area design:

1. Contain the area with enough backdrops to achieve a sense of place (but don't fully enclose it).

2. Ground the receptionist and the seating area properly so that they are not floating.

3. Provide adequate clearances for smooth traffic around the reception desk.

4. Position the reception desk to ensure privacy from the sides and rear.

5. Provide proper clearances in the seating area.

6. Provide a place (usually on one wall) for the company's name.

7. Provide proper connections to the rest of the space, including the nearby conference rooms.

8. Control visual access to the rest of the space.

9. Place access corridors to the rest of the space carefully, following a sense of hierarchy between the public path to the conference rooms and other public areas, and secondary corridors for workers to get to their offices.

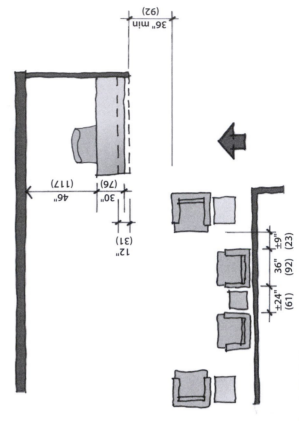

Typical dimensions at reception area

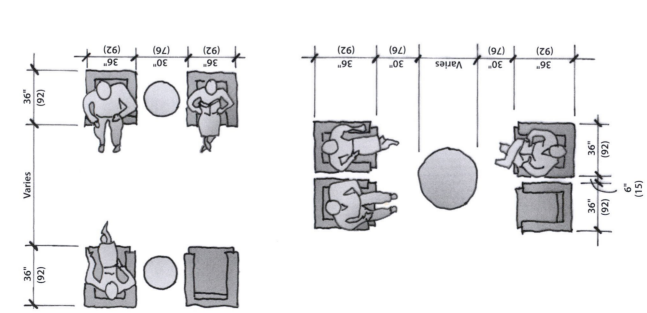

Typical dimensions for seating areas

EXERCISE

Prepare two quick designs for a corporate reception area. Provide a reception desk and seating for four. Two designs have been submitted (A and B), but the owner did not like either one. She disliked A because she felt the floating seating area disturbs the traffic flow right at the entry point. Furthermore, the corridor leading to the conference room does not follow the formal symmetry established by the classically shaped round arrival space. It is off axis and seems awkward. The owner also disliked option B. Although she was intrigued by the idea of moving the reception area slightly to one side, she felt the placement of the secondary corridor into the work areas was inappropriate as proposed. She also disliked the protruding column by the seating area.

The owner has asked that you provide two more options. Design them within the limits indicated. Use as much space as you need. You don't have to use it all. As part of the design, indicate which path leads to the conference room. Don't worry about what the surrounding rooms are. Provide containing walls as necessary to make your design work.

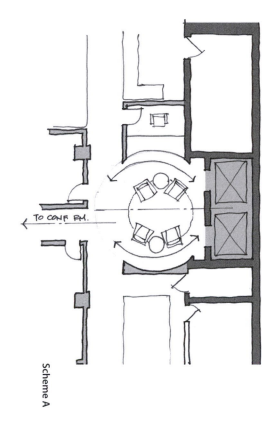

Scheme A

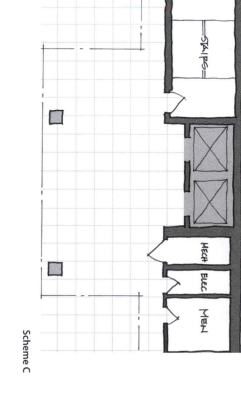

Scheme C

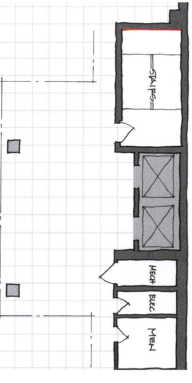

Scheme B

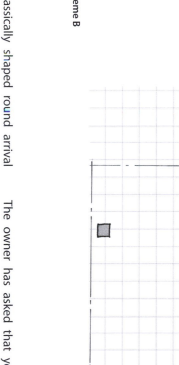

Scheme D

Offices: Open Areas

A particular corporation has offices around the world. They are each a little different. On this page we see partial views of the Montreal, London, Buenos Aires, and Hong Kong offices. Study the plans carefully. Consider the following:

How many different workstation types can you identify?

How many workstation types allow users to receive guests right at their space?

How many different team gathering areas can you identify?

How many instances feature adjacent informal areas for sitting?

How are rows of files used in space?

What are the relationships between the open-plan environments and the enclosed rooms?

How many instances feature enclosed meeting spaces nearby?

What are the relationships between workstations and columns out in the open?

What are the relationships between the walls of enclosed rooms and columns?

How would you describe the circulation spaces between workstations? Generous? Economic?

How many workers are there in the largest cluster of attached workstations?

How many workers are there in the smallest cluster of attached workstations?

Judging by the proportional size of the people shown, can you estimate the size of the various workstations?

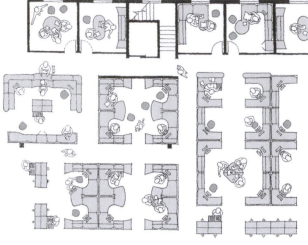

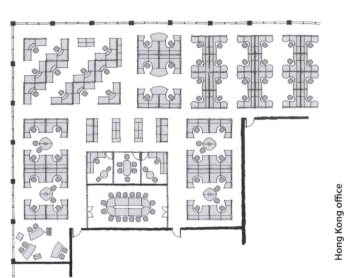

London office

Hong Kong office

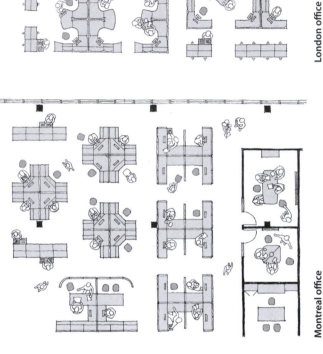

Montreal office

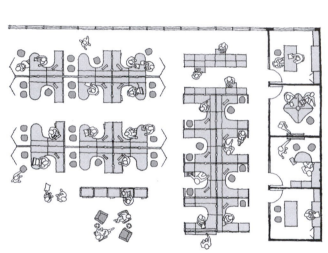

Buenos Aires office

Examine these four furniture arrangements. They are very typical configurations. Which ones would you say are sociopetal configurations? Which ones would you consider sociofugal configurations? (See Chapter 2, page 31, if you don't remember the meaning of these terms.)

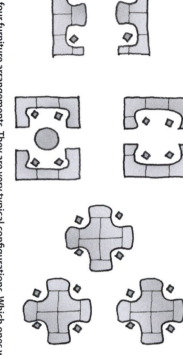

One thing we cannot tell from looking at floor plans is the height of the elements shown. This is an important consideration, as even among partial-height elements, the heights vary widely, producing different atmospheres and different degrees of connection/separation.

 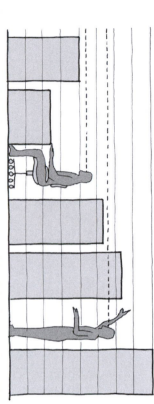

One tricky aspect of planning with systems furniture in the open is coordinating the modularity of the cluster units with the module of the structural columns. There are various ways of relating to columns and most entail "missing the column," that is, avoiding having columns fall in the middle of, say, someone's workstation. This seems obvious, but it is sometimes easier said than done. The example above shows three examples of workstation-to-column relationships. Note that many times you try to miss the column but want to be right next to it, as electrical wiring and data cables are often fed to the workstations from the ceiling plenum above, via the column cavity.

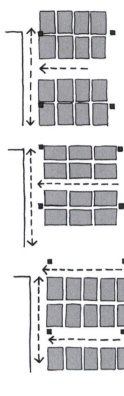 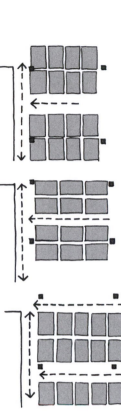

EXERCISE

The column grid above shows an open space with structural columns on a 30' × 30' (9.14 m × 9.14 m) grid. Using workstations with side dimensions of 6'-0" (183 cm) or 8'-0" (244 cm) (any combination), come up with as many arrangements as possible that work well with the columns. Use aisles of 36" (92 cm) or 4'-0" (122 cm) or some-thing in between (if you must). You may show the workstation units as blocks, as in the example on this page. The planning grid shown is 24" × 24" (61 cm × 61 cm).

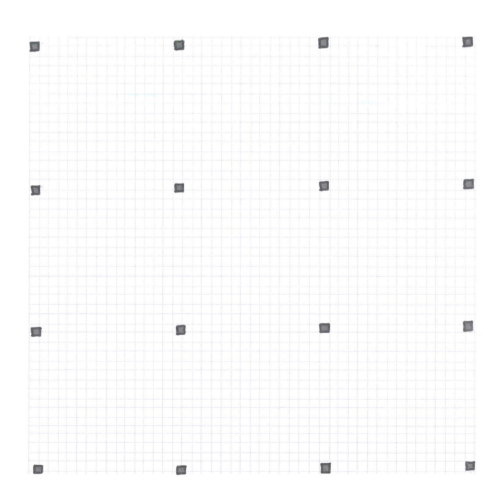

Offices: Private Offices

Private offices provide the user with an enclosed personal room in which to work and meet others. They can be shared, although usually they have a single occupant. Offices vary widely in size. At its smallest, all an office needs is space for a modest-size desk and a chair and maneuvering space to get around. Executive offices, on the other hand, can be three or four times the size of a small office and include multiple meeting spaces within the same room.

Who really needs an office? And, to what extent should a company house its workers in private offices? High-ranking managers and executives have traditionally been assigned private office spaces, but that trend is changing in some companies. Other workers get private offices, too. The determination is made based on how much privacy an individual needs and office culture. Typically, offices are assigned to workers needing considerable levels of privacy because of the sensitive nature of their meetings and phone conversations and to workers who perform tasks requiring high levels of concentration. Generally, these are decisions made by the client, not the designer. Most times, designers are just told what to provide.

What goes in an office? Typically, workers get a certain number of work surfaces (e.g., desks, credenzas), storage/filing space (e.g., file cabinets, pencil drawers, overhead bins), and some way of accommodating visitors (e.g., guest chairs, small meeting tables). Office furniture manufacturers today have many product offerings that go beyond the old desk-and-credenza arrangement, such as highly efficient work walls running along one side of the room. This page and the next show examples of various private office configurations as well as anthropometric data that will help you determine practical configuration and sizes.

When laying out private offices, pay attention to the following criteria:

- Relation of user/desk to the front door
- Relation of main work surface to the walls and power/data outlet locations
- Appropriate clearances for circulation
- How the office sidewalls meet the perimeter window walls
- How the building's window mullion module affects office wall locations
- The materials used for the front wall of the office (solid, glass, partial glass)
- Whether meetings with visitors will be around the desk or at a remote table
- Maintaining proper wheelchair accessibility clearances around doors

G.

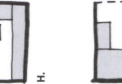
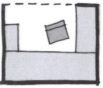

H.

I.

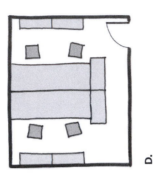

D.

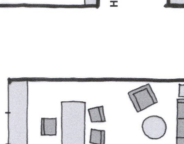

E.

F.

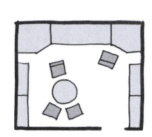

A.

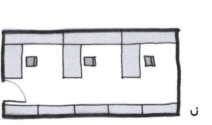

B.

C.

N.

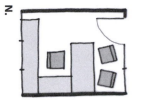

M.

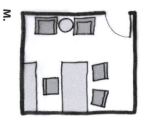

L.

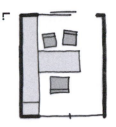

K.

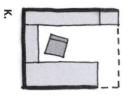

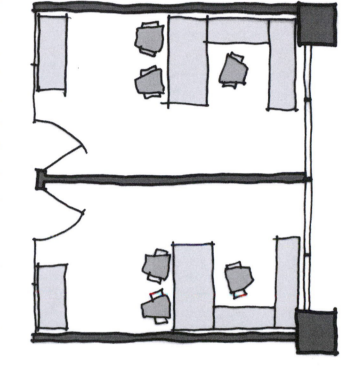

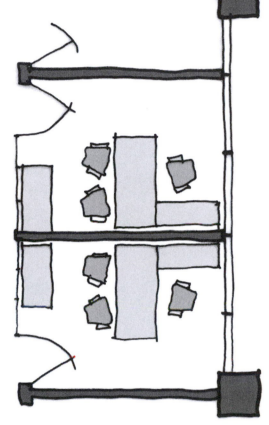

Possible width dimensions for offices along the perimeter of a commercial building are affected by the spacing of vertical mullions on the perimeter window wall and the spacing of columns and other solid wall elements along the perimeter. With few exceptions, drywall partitions need to connect to a window mullion or a solid element as these two examples illustrate.

Desk Measurements and Clearances

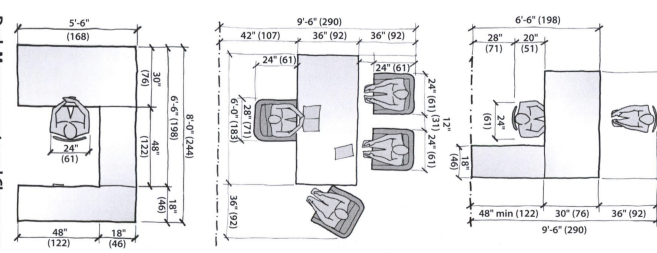

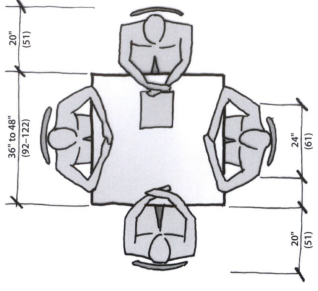

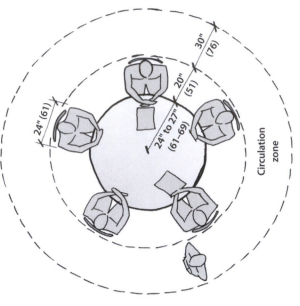

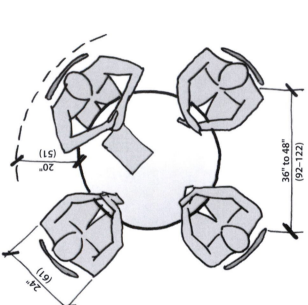

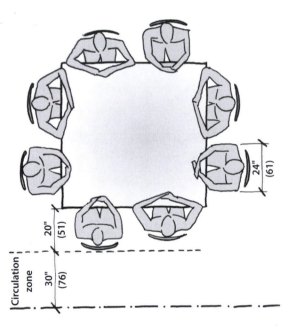

Anthropometric data for conference tables

Offices: Conference Rooms

The conference room is as basic in office environments as the desk. Office workers need to meet among themselves as well as with outside clients and consultants to talk about projects and initiatives, give presentations, handle problems, make decisions, and so on. There is usually a need for conference rooms of various sizes to accommodate different meeting sizes. Some rooms may be devoted to client meetings; these will tend to be close to the main entrance and reception areas. Other rooms may be for internal meetings and may be in the more private regions of the office. Still other meeting rooms may be for training sessions and will require appropriate seating configurations for that purpose. Note that we are talking here about private, enclosed rooms and not about more informal meeting areas out in the open.

Examine the various examples of meeting rooms at far right. There are rooms for four people, rooms for eight people, rooms for twelve people, and so on. Note the configurations used, the sizes and shapes of the tables, and the space surrounding the table and chairs. Note also that many include built-in or floating casework or furniture on which to put beverages, handouts, and other objects. In some instances these occur in recessed niches especially designed for that purpose. In addition, look at the different seating configurations in the three training rooms. Which is the most appropriate? The answer lies in the kind of training offered in those rooms. If it varies, then it makes sense to use modular tables that can be configured in multiple arrangements.

The anthropometric diagrams on this page show recommended dimensions and clearances at and around tables. You may use this information to determine conference table and room sizes.

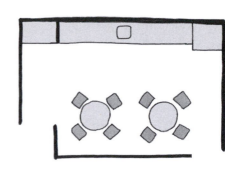

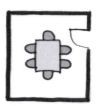

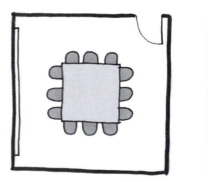

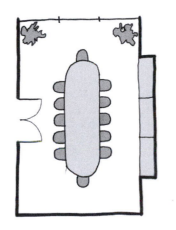
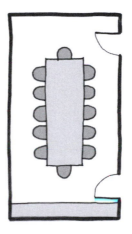

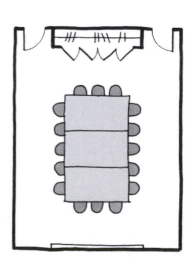

Office Analysis

An effective way to increase your understanding of space planning is by critically analyzing your projects as well as those of your peers. Especially effective is the practice of analyzing multiple solutions to the same design problem. By assessing the relative success of specific design decisions, you can increase your awareness of multiple problem-solving options (there is always more than one way to solve a problem) and also remind yourself that design is full of trade-offs.

Here, I suggest ten elements to analyze in the floor plans for a modest-size consulting firm. I perform the analysis of the first project to show you how the thinking goes. Space is provided for you to analyze the other two planning solutions for the same project.

Criteria for Analysis

1. Treatment of the arrival space (main entrance) and the reception space
2. Placement of the main conference rooms
3. Strategy to accommodate enclosed private offices
4. Distribution and character of the main open areas
5. Shape of the principal open spaces
6. Location of file cabinets
7. Disposition of secondary and informal conference rooms
8. Location and treatment of the main break room
9. Accommodation of support spaces (mail/copy/supplies)
10. Utilization of residual spaces

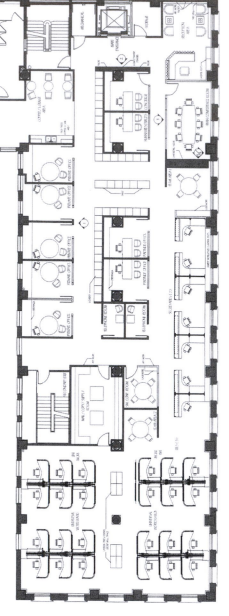

Office plan 1

OFFICE PLAN 1 ANALYSIS
(numbers correspond to analysis criteria numbers)

1. Focal wall upon entrance. Reception visible to the left, by the windows facing the front of the building.
2. Located immediately next to the reception area on main side, facing the street (best views).
3. Some (not all) offices on perimeter, on the back side. Some are floating inside. These have glass fronts.
4. Main open area is at the end of the space and has exterior exposure on three sides. Secondary narrow open zone along front windows, allowing light to penetrate space.
5. There are three discernible open areas (other than rooms and corridors); the two mentioned above (under number 4) and the break room area (and adjacent areas by the restrooms).
6. Majority of files centralized up front. They occur along the corridors and within a designated space that is fairly centrally located.
7. There are three secondary conference rooms: two team meeting spaces and a small conference room. They are spread out and deeper into the space (rather than up front). Team areas are not fully enclosed, open on one side.
8. The break room area is ingeniously combined with the residual space in front of the restrooms for a synergetic, expanded feel.
9. There is one principal mail/copy/supplies room, toward the back. The rear stair core is expanded to include this and another two rooms, creating a protruding mass that provides separation between the main front zone and the rear, open-plan area.
10. There is one small, unexplored residual area just outside the door to the rear stairway. The shallow open area outside the restrooms had potential but was underdeveloped.

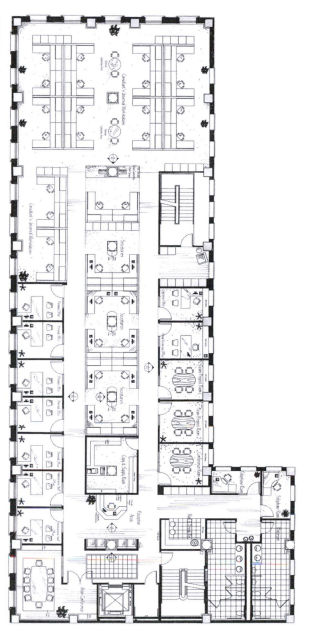

ANALYSIS

ANALYSIS

Design Office Critique

Shown here are three solutions to the design of a small office for a design firm. In each case you see an initial organizational diagram, an early loose plan, and a subsequent iteration of the first plan. Study the progression from diagram to loose plan to the next plan. The success of any space plan rests on a handful of criteria. These are some of the questions you need to ask to evaluate a plan, even a small one such as this:

For each space: Is that a good location for that function? Does it make sense where it is?

Is that a good sequence from front to back, from public to private?

Are things that should be close to each other positioned accordingly?

Is the general form good? Are the resulting shapes of rooms and open areas good?

Were good decisions made concerning the use of natural light coming from the one side with windows?

Do all spaces seem perceptually comfortable?

Think of these questions and evaluate the project. Additionally comment on the qualities and relative success of the individual parts of the project listed below:

The reception area

The conference room

The office of the principals of the firm

The open studio area

The project room/pin-up room/lounge

Good luck.

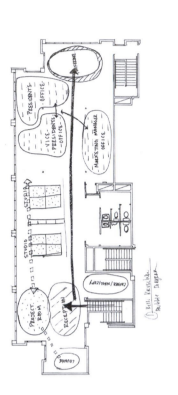

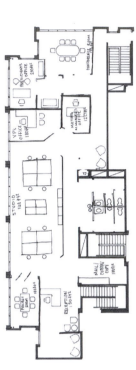

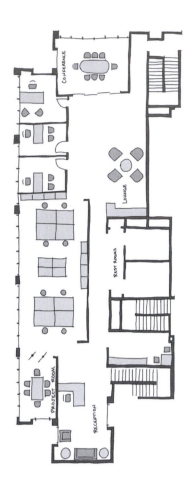

DESIGN SOLUTION 1

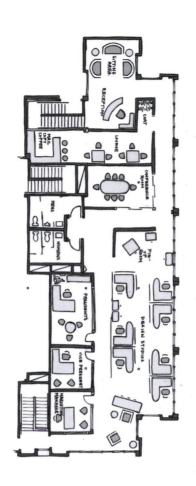
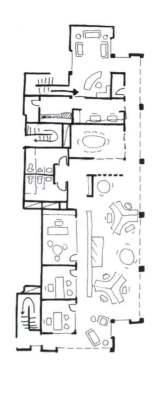
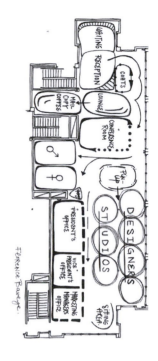
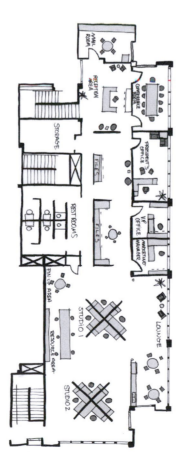
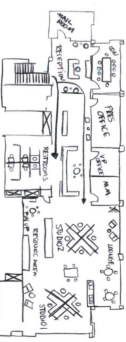
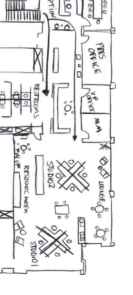
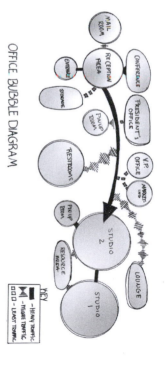

OFFICE BUBBLE DIAGRAM

Offices: Process

Chapter 3 was devoted to design process and illustrated design steps from programming to final plan. Emphasis was placed on the use of diagrams of various types to allocate space and the process of translating those into rooms and open areas. Here, I expand on that conversation and show additional examples of design process activities.

Example A shows explorations performed by a student for an intermediate/advanced office project. The task was to gain an understanding of the organizational structure for each of the client's units. Using the Competing Values Framework used by Haworth and client interviews, students determined each unit's organizational structure and translated that knowledge into specific products and arrangements that would work best for each group.

Example B illustrates the process of self-editing. After an intermediate presentation halfway through the design stage, the student diagrammed over the presented plan to try to understand the features and problems of the design solution she was conceiving.

The drawings in example C offer a partial block plan for a large office project and then the final developed plan. Note how the form of major areas and important intersections was developed and articulated into neat rotundas and formal, classical squares. Note, too, the extensive development around the boardroom and surrounding rooms.

Example D shows the process of moving into greater detail at a local level as the designer starts to zoom in and develop specific rooms, such as the main conference room and the reception area, in greater detail.

SKETCHES/APPLICATION
ORGANIZATIONAL CULTURE: COLLABORATE (CLAN)

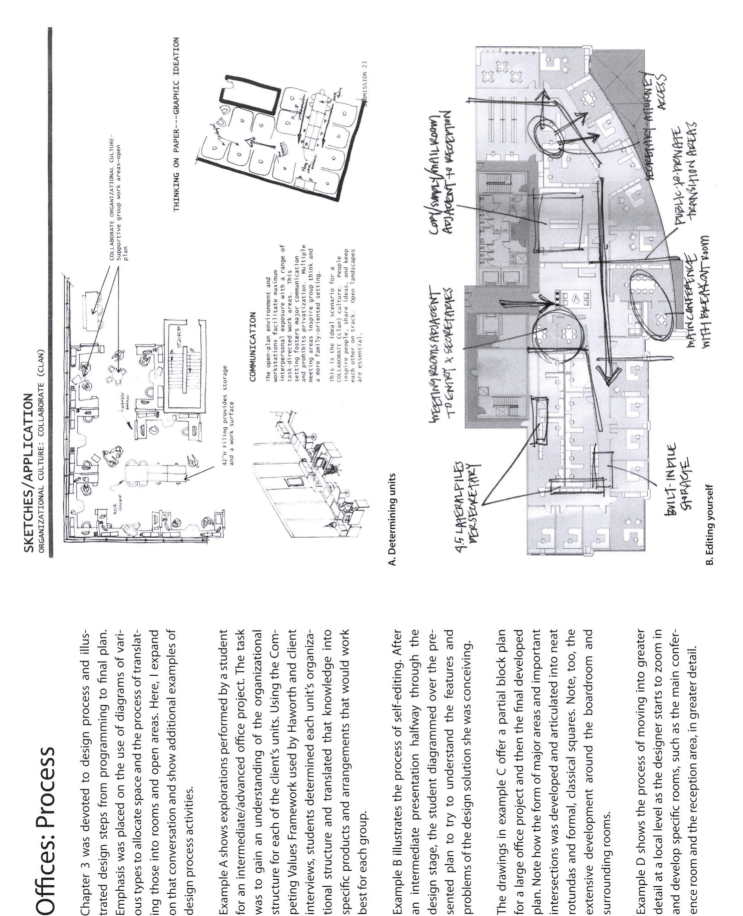

COLLABORATE ORGANIZATIONAL CULTURE-
Supportive group work areas–open
plan

THINKING ON PAPER—GRAPHIC IDEATION

42"h filing provides storage
and a work surface

COMMUNICATION

The open-plan environment and workstations facilitate maximum interpersonal exposure with a range of task-directed work areas. This setting fosters major communication and prohibits privatization. Multiple meeting areas inspire group think and a more family-oriented setting.

This is the ideal scenario for a COLLABORATE (clan) culture. People inspire people, share ideas, and keep each other on track. Open landscapes are essential.

A. Determining units

B. Editing yourself

Block plan

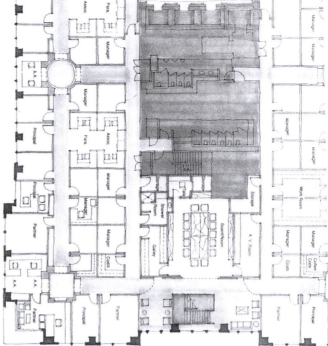

Refined plan

D. Zooming in

Enlarged plan

Overall plan

Enlarged plan

Office Layouts

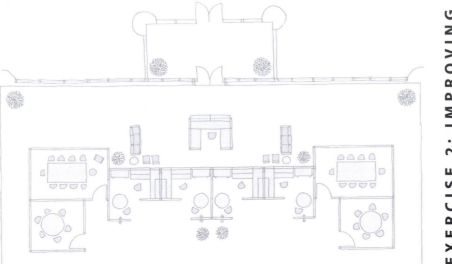

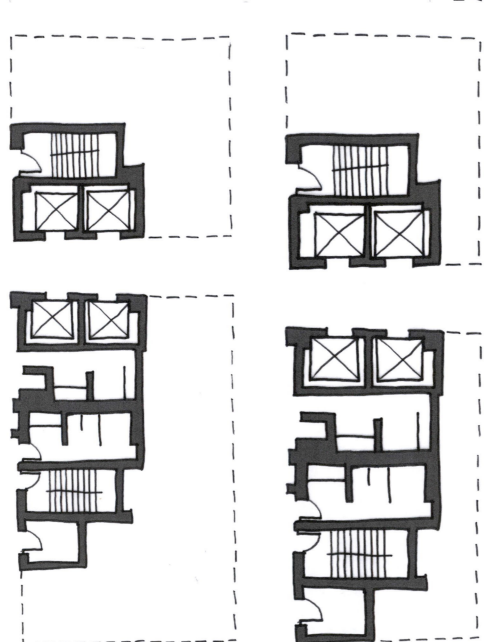

EXERCISE 1: GROW THE CORE

Grow the two cores above up to the dashed lines shown. You'll notice that one plan has a larger expansion zone than the other. For that plan, add rooms, such as workrooms, conference rooms, offices, or a combination of these (you decide) to complete the shape. You may want to practice wall articulation between rooms by doing thick walls with built-ins and other features. For the other plan you will need to use some shallower functions, such as storage spaces, pockets of space (for various functions, e.g., informal small meetings), private telephone calling rooms, and so on.

EXERCISE 2: IMPROVING AN ENTRANCE AREA

Look at the plan shown for the front of an office facility. During a design presentation, the client complained that there seemed to be too much wasted space (although he does want some sense of spaciousness). He also disliked that visitors have to go all the way around (and walk through some private work zones) to get to the conference rooms. Try to come up with a solution that solves the two problems.

EXERCISE 3: BUBBLES TO LOOSE PLAN

Translate the adjacency bubble diagram shown into a loose plan inside the space given for this generic office. Office 1 and office 2 are general open office areas housing several employees in open-plan environments. The bookkeeping area also houses several employees in an open-plan environment. Only the bookkeeping area as a whole and the small human resources office need to be enclosed. Go from bubbles to a loose plan. Start by lightly superimposing the bubbles on the plan, and then begin figuring out the walls and other dividing elements. Enjoy.

Note: The W. C. (water closets) are not needed since there are restrooms (R. R.) elsewhere on the floor.

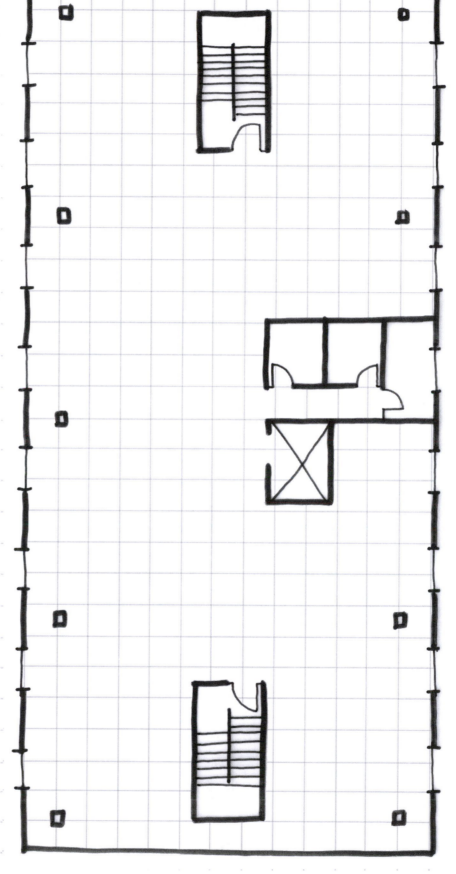

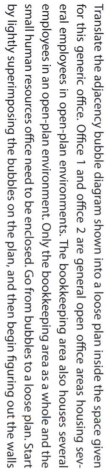

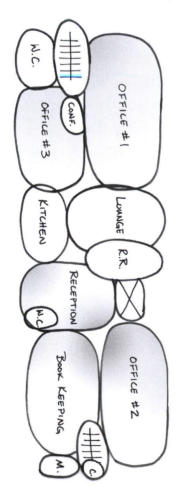

Retail: Anatomy and Issues

Retail design is one of the most exciting interior design sectors. In retail projects the merchandise, the spatial envelope, graphics, and signage create a unique and strategic mix based on a branding concept. The basic goal is the strategic accommodation of these elements to promote sales. A good store design attracts potential shoppers and induces them to buy.

Although the design of the store on its own cannot be fully responsible for the financial success of the store, it is one of the key ingredients. The successful store provides an environment where merchandise is presented effectively and persuasively. Shoppers should feel comfortable in the space and receptive to buying the merchandise.

The physical shell provided for a store is often a simple rectangular space with the long direction going from front to back. The short dimension is usually the frontage of the store, its face to the outside world. It is generally about a third to a fourth of the space's depth. The space in the store is allocated to the merchandise displays, service areas, or circulation zones. The display spaces of a store are normally not compartmentalized with walls. Open space is preferable to maximize visual exposure and to facilitate orientation.

Stores lure people in by providing open, transparent conditions that allow passersby to see inside. Views that provide visual access deep into the store and toward key focal areas, together with strategic displays near the entrance, also serve to draw shoppers.

Products sold in the store are staple items, convenience items, or impulse items. Staple items are the principal items sold by a particular kind of store, like shirts and pants in a men's apparel store. These are the items most shoppers come to buy. A common merchandising strategy is to situate the staple items deep in the store to expose shoppers to other merchandise while getting there. Convenience items, such as socks and underwear in the apparel store, are secondary. Impulse items are miscellaneous items, such as accessories, that are normally located close to the cash register to entice lined-up shoppers while they prepare to pay.

Products are most often displayed in groups and arranged by type, color, or size. Mass displays make the organization of products intuitive and easier to understand. They also serve to provide visual order, such as when rows or clusters of same-color shirts are combined to produce harmonious visual fields of merchandise. Products may also be combined with other products to form a cohesive functional whole. For instance, plates, napkins, and silverware may be grouped as a unit to convey entire table place settings and help customers visualize how they appear in a group.

Service areas are usually in the back. They provide storage space, employee restrooms, a shipping and receiving area, access to a service alley, and sometimes a small office. Cash wrap stations are placed within the retail space and can be accommodated toward the front, middle, or back, depending on the store and its specific circumstances. In all cases they need to be convenient and should have sufficient space around them to allow smooth circulation.

Shoe store perspective

Retail Store Considerations

Movement: Two of the most important goals of retail environments are to attract shoppers inside and make it easy for them to move throughout the store. Strategically located focal points attract potential buyers and entice them to move toward the back of the store. A transition zone inside the entrance allows shoppers to scrutinize the store before committing to proceed all the way in.

Merchandise: The front-to-back placement of merchandise within a department or throughout the entire store is strategically executed. Featured presentations are close to the main aisles and highly visible. Secondary locations are often between featured items. Focal locations are distributed throughout the store, anchoring their respective zones. High-demand items are often placed in the back regions of the store to serve as magnets.

Display: Store merchandise and display fixtures are moved around frequently. Some fixtures need to be moveable. Perimeter zones are often fixed although many display systems can accommodate different types of attachments (i.e. hooks, shelves, and hangers), and allow merchandise changes. The specific displays on fixed focal points throughout the store also change as needed.

Service: Stock rooms, employee restrooms, manager offices, and shipping/receiving functions occur in the back of the store as not to take up valuable front space. Service spaces within the sales space are usually limited to the cash wrap. These are strategically located to offer convenience and security.

Miscellaneous: The effective handling of building elements such as columns and the provision of proper clearances are important design considerations. Display islands or vertical displays are often built around columns and pilasters. Clearances around display areas need to be such that passersby can walk by stationary fellow shoppers in the process of inspecting merchandise.

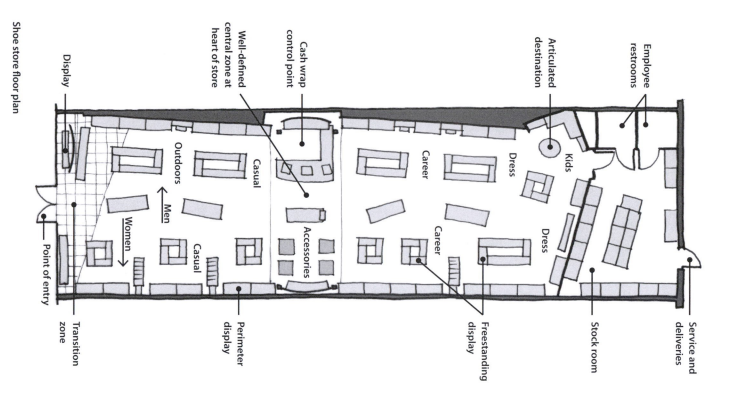

Employee restrooms

Service and deliveries

Articulated destination

Kids

Dress

Career

Dress

Career

Stock room

Cash wrap control point

Well-defined central zone at heart of store

Freestanding display

Accessories

Outdoors

Casual

Casual

Men

Women

Display

Perimeter display

Transition zone

Point of entry

Shoe store floor plan

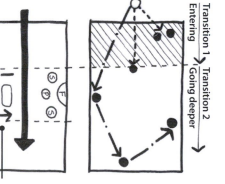

Transition 1 Entering | Transition 2 Going deeper

Front | Middle | Back

P - Primary
S - Secondary
F - Focal feature

Easy access to and retreat from all departments and zones

Focal display

Permanent display

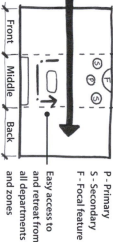

Flexible storefront

Flexible display

Office

Stock room

Cash wrap and service

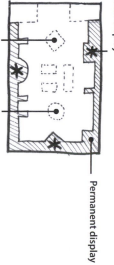

Restroom

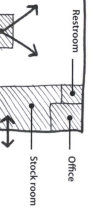

Displays around columns and architectural elements

Clearance for browsers and customers passing by

Sufficient clearance around cash wrap

Retail: Store Types

There are many kinds of retail stores. Most are merchandise driven, whereas others sell services. Types of merchandise include fashion and apparel, household goods, jewelry, books, toys, food, liquor, gifts, greeting cards, and home electronics. Service retail includes travel agencies, financial service companies, and even the post office.

Retail stores also vary by design approach. Specialty boutiques tend to be minimalistic and abstract, whereas convenience stores are more straightforward and dense. The common denominator is that these stores always represent an environment that has been designed to bring the merchandise, the buyers, and the sellers together in effective ways.

Shown here are six diverse stores to give you an idea of what they look like in plan view. They range from a convenience store to a bookstore.

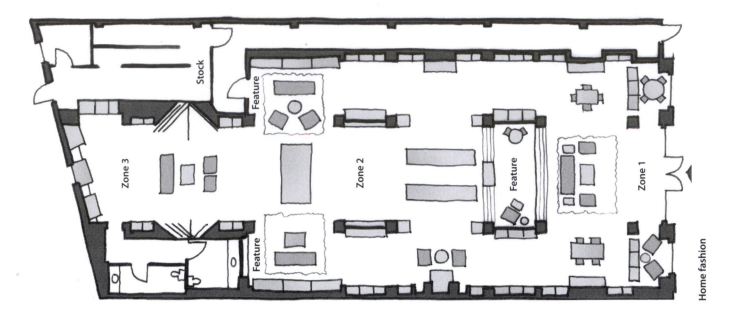

Home fashion

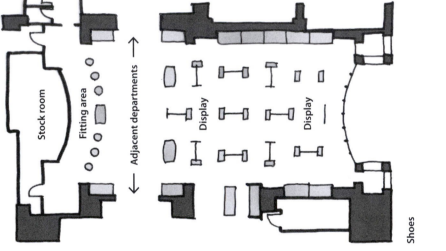

Shoes

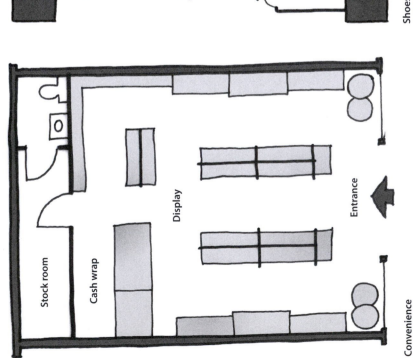

Convenience

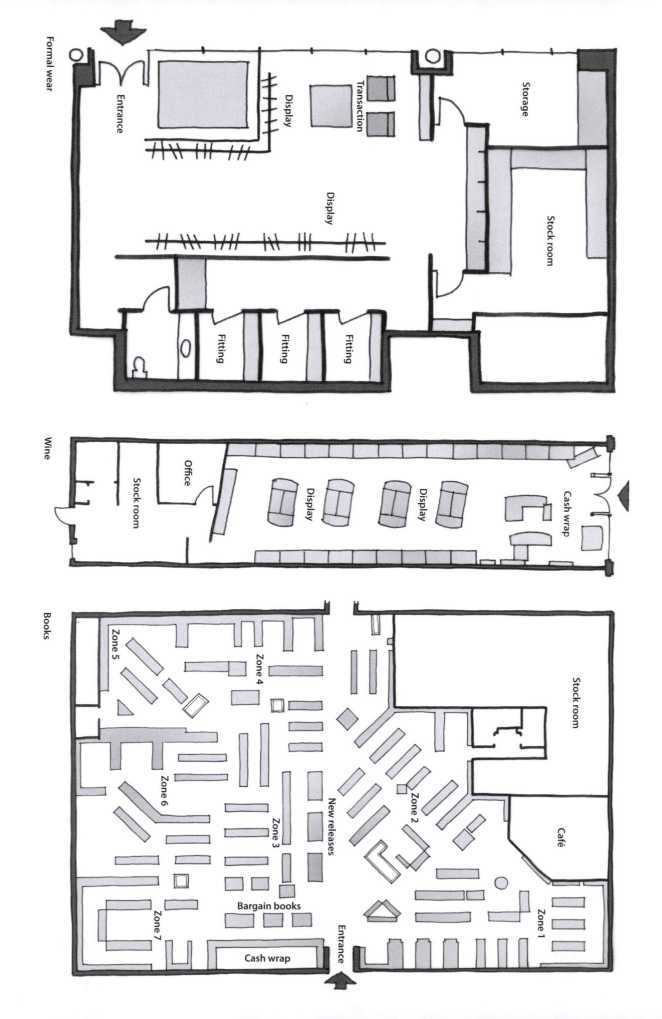

Formal wear

Entrance

Display

Transaction

Display

Storage

Stock room

Fitting

Fitting

Fitting

Wine

Office

Stock room

Display

Display

Cash wrap

Books

Zone 5

Zone 4

Zone 6

Zone 3

Zone 2

New releases

Zone 7

Bargain books

Cash wrap

Entrance

Stock room

Café

Zone 1

Retail: Circulation

For a customer, walking through a store should be a rich and rewarding visual experience. Circulation needs to be fluid and relatively simple so shoppers are not required to expend much mental energy on it. Shoppers should not have to think about the route but rather be led through it. Their attention and energy should be focused on the merchandise.

Movement through the store should offer some variety and follow a strategic and logical sequence. Normally, this sequence will be in confluence with the visual merchandising strategy, and, in general, will aim to move the shopper through the entire store.

Observe shoppers in a busy store one day. You'll realize that customers rarely move in a straight line in the store. Instead they bounce back and forth between sequential points in the store. For that reason, many store designers avoid defining a rigid circulation track and chose fluid circulation schemes that more easily allow the back-and-forth bouncing between locations. Circulation routes should be comfortable and allow enough space for shoppers to pass one another, or bypass customers who might be examining the merchandise. They are also the routes to be used for egress in case of emergency. However, avoid circulation schemes that are too open.

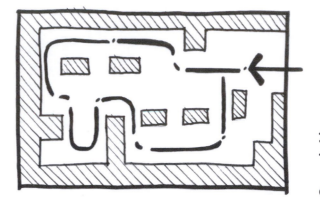

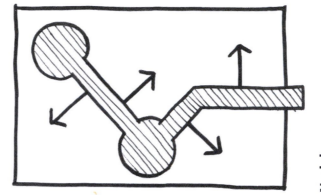

Organic Linear

The circulation pattern in this type of scheme is derived from the available walking space defined by the location of the display fixtures and islands. In the case of the linear organic arrangement, the movement is primarily front to back and side to side. It is freer than a simple loop scheme.

Nodal

A nodal scheme is possible with a linear or loop circulation configuration. Here it is shown with a multidirectional linear path. The main feature of this approach is the presence of one or more nodal areas where an event takes place. The event may be around a focal display or at a juncture where the space expands to accommodate the event area.

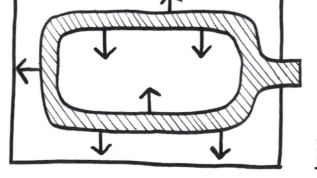

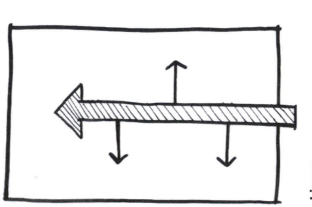

Loop

For stores with a central display zone and perimeter zones, a loop circulation scheme is convenient and effective. While walking along the loop customers have access to both the perimeter zone and the central islands.

Linear

A front-to-back central spine may be used for narrow stores. It may be an uninterrupted path or may include a central island that customers walk around. The linear approach is clear and efficient.

When laying out the circulation scheme for a store, remember to coordinate routes and display elements to provide adequate sightlines to the various focal points in the store. Also, avoid creating zones that are too deep between the circulation spine and the end wall as many shoppers will not explore zones that do not provide clear and easy ways to exit.

Circulation schemes for stores include front-to-back approaches, angular side-to-side arrangements, loop or racetrack configurations, or freer, meandering paths. The diagrams on these pages show some variations.

Diagonal

The movement pattern in a diagonal circulation scheme progresses from front to back but not in a direct linear fashion. In this case, movement occurs diagonally, at certain angles (e.g. 45 degrees), as dictated by the angles produced by the arrangement of display fixtures and perimeter elements.

Organic Free

Movement in this scheme takes place in a highly organic fashion and is determined by the location of perimeter and floating fixtures. In this case, the arrangement of the display fixtures is organic and free, resulting in a more meandering movement.

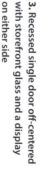

Storefronts

1. Storefront glass and a display along one side with recessed double doors at one end

2. Recessed doors at center with storefront glass and a display on either end

3. Recessed single door off-centered with storefront glass and a display on either side

4. Overhead coiling door with freestanding display fixtures; no doors and no storefront glass

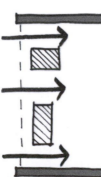

5. Angled storefront glass with a display on either side and double doors centered

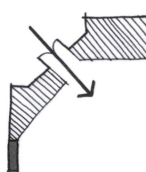

Retail Anthropometrics

Dimensions and clearances vary widely, depending on the store. Some stores have fewer displays and more generous space for walking around. Other stores are packed densely, with tighter circulation spaces. Density is, in fact, one of the most important considerations in retail. The representative situations shown here will give you some ideas of recommended clearances and dimensions for retail.

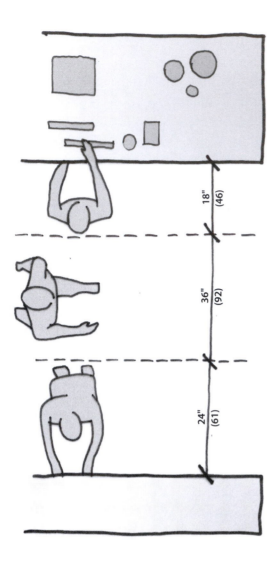

24" (61)   36" (92)   18" (46)

Clearances and walkway dimensions between counters

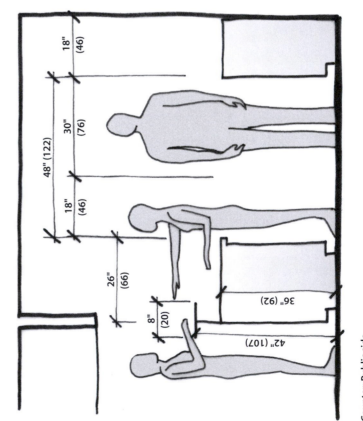

18" min (46)   30" min (76)   18" min (46)   5'-6" min (168)

5'-8" (173) (top shelf)

Perimeter and freestanding displays

18" (46)   30" (76)   18" (46)   48" (122)

26" (66)   8" (20)   36" (92)   42" (107)

Counter: Public side

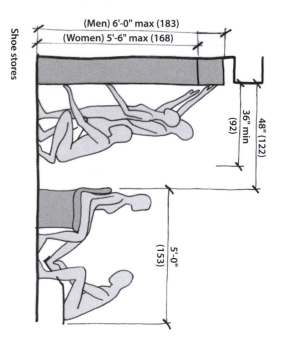

Shoe stores

(Men) 6'-0" max (183)
(Women) 5'-6" max (168)

48" min (122)
36" (92)

5'-0" (153)

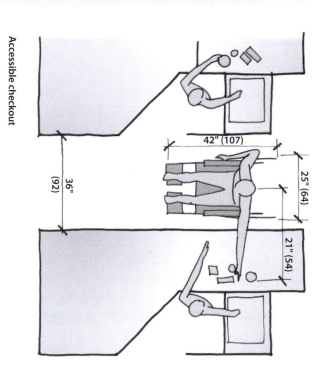

Accessible checkout

42" (107)

36" (92)

25" (64)

21" (54)

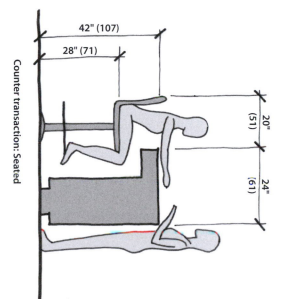

Counter transaction: Seated

42" (107)

28" (71)

20" (51)

24" (61)

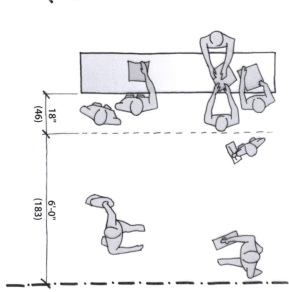

Changing room

36" min (92)

24" (61)

42" (107)

5'-0" (153)

18" (46)

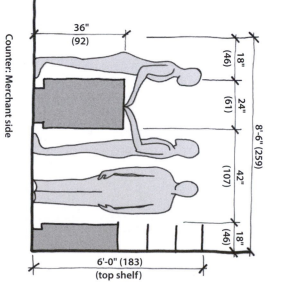

Counter: Merchant side

36" (92)

18" (46)

24" (61)

8'-6" (259)

42" (107)

18" (46)

6'-0" (183)
(top shelf)

Entrance spaces at cash wrap

18" (46)

6'-0" (183)

Retail: Fixtures

In retail the fixture is the furniture. Unlike other settings, in retail you want the fixtures to do their work and disappear, to become just background for the merchandise in the foreground. Fixtures are available through specialized manufacturers. They are also frequently custom designed. It varies widely. A few examples are shown here.

Most merchandise is meant to be seen frontally and is therefore displayed vertically, hence, the importance of the frontal elevation. Note, too, the important role the perimeter display wall has and the many variations possible.

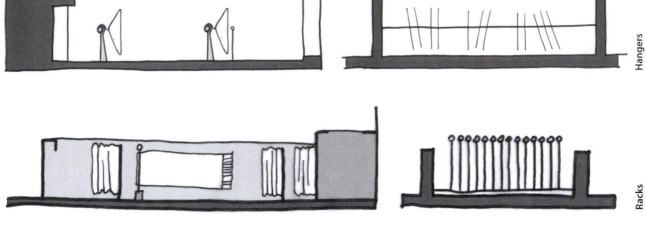

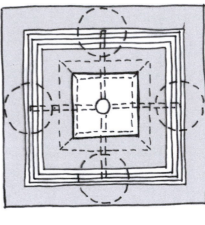

Hangers

Racks

Perimeter displays

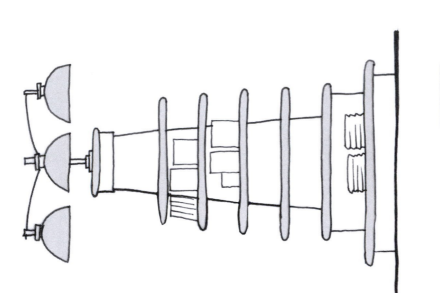

Freestanding column with stepping shelves

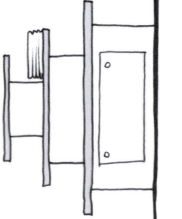

Stepping display at wall

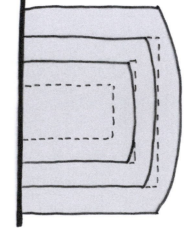

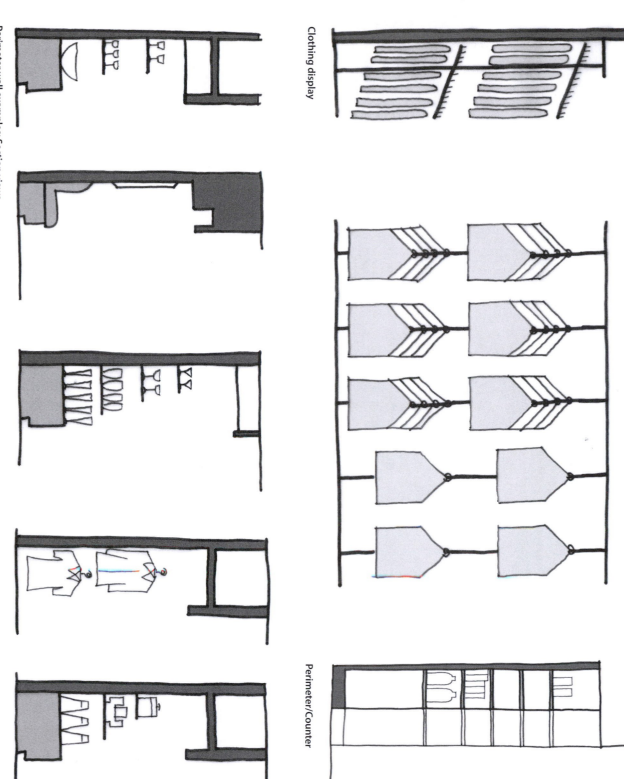

Clothing display

Perimeter/Counter

Retail Examples I

Retail design is creative. It is a total experience involving the three dimensions of space plus a fourth dimension (movement). Although I emphasize the importance of conceiving the store as a volumetric container, the plan can serve as an important generator and organizer. In these examples the plan diagrams show, the plan diagrams convey a strong sense of purpose and organization. The hierarchical structure of the various plans comes through. The circular specialty display nodes in the semicircles scheme help highlight special merchandise items and attract customers. In the snake scheme the flowing, snakelike circulation arrangement leading to the focal point at the end wall defines the scheme. The trinode scheme relies on three major nodes where special displays feature select merchandise. Finally, the X-factor scheme is anchored by a dominant X-shaped structure at the heart of the store.

The thing these four schemes have in common is the use of powerful ideas (e.g., shapes, circulation, strategic location, sequence) that give the stores a strong sense of hierarchy. While the main features of the schemes attract attention, the other, more ordinary components are accommodated throughout the rest of the stores. These, of course, hold the bulk of the merchandise and are very important, too.

Perspective

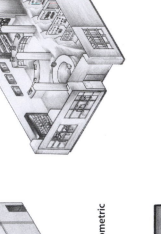

Axonometric

Scheme plan/Diagram

Snake

Perspective

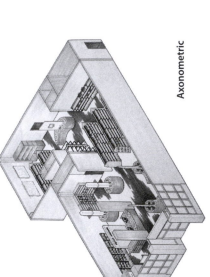

Axonometric

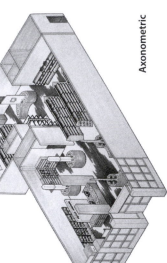

Scheme plan/Diagram

Semicircles

Trinode

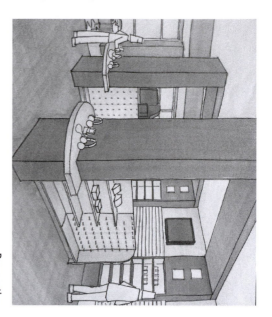

Perspective

Perspective

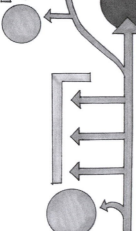

Scheme plan/Diagram

X-Factor

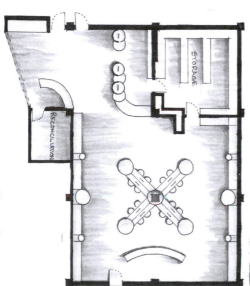

Scheme plan/Diagram

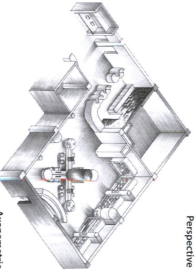

Axonometric

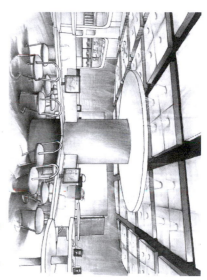

Perspective

Fixtures in Plan

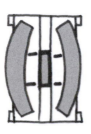
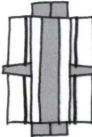
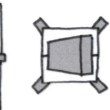
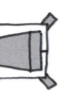

Plan view symbols for fixtures vary and are not always standard. Shown here are customized plan symbols for fixtures used by a computer/software retailer.

Retail Examples II

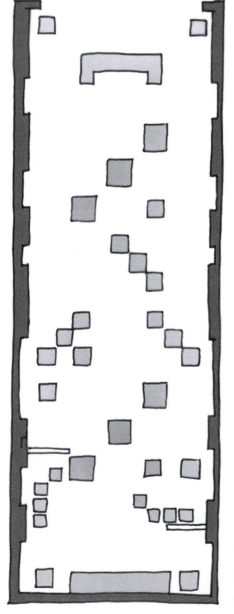

Plan/Diagram

Perspective

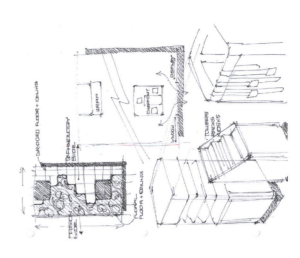

Design development sketches

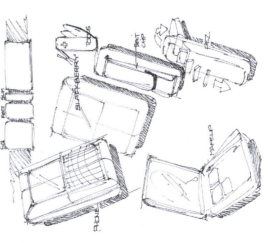

Technology Gadget Store

This is a good example of how it is sometimes impossible to know what is going on in a store from a plan view. It is not until one sees some of the other drawings that one begins to understand what kind of display (stacked cubes and freestanding pedestals) the square shapes represent. Note that, unlike the examples on the previous page, there are no clear dominant locations in this design, as seen on plan. The hierarchical treatment in this case is fairly even. This is also a good example of the use of design development sketches (beyond bubbles and diagrams) to help visualize space and its contents.

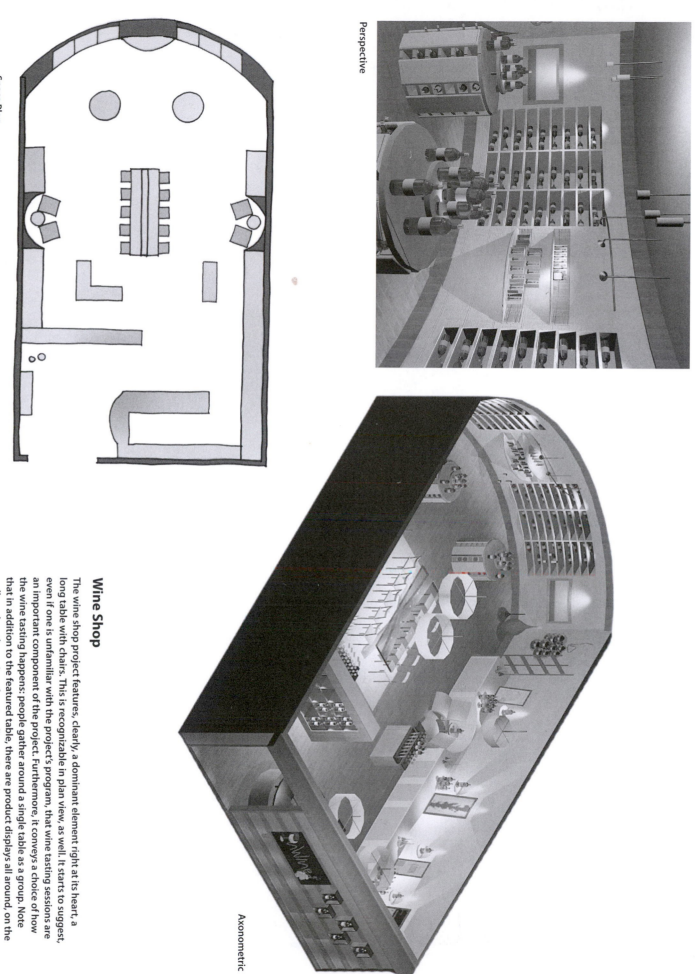

Perspective

Space Plan

Axonometric

Wine Shop

The wine shop project features, clearly, a dominant element right at its heart, a long table with chairs. This is recognizable in plan view, as well. It starts to suggest, even if one is unfamiliar with the project's program, that wine tasting sessions are an important component of the project. Furthermore, it conveys a choice of how the wine tasting happens: people gather around a single table as a group. Note that in addition to the featured table, there are product displays all around, on the walls and on the various freestanding pedestals surrounding the main table.

Gourmet Food and Wine Shop

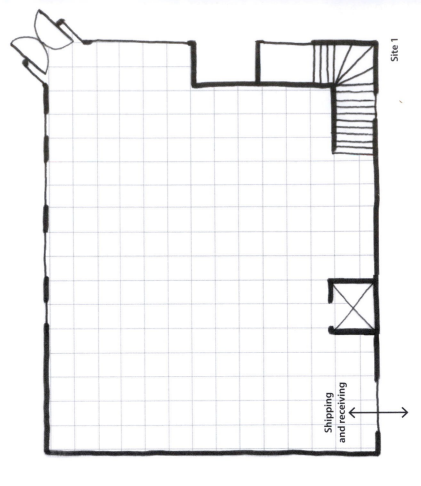

Site 1

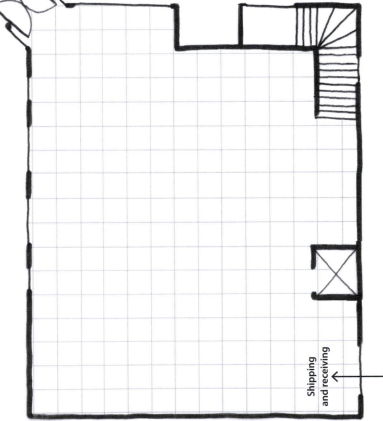

Shipping
and receiving

E X E R C I S E

Gourmet Food and Wine Shop

The store features and sells fine wines, local artisan food items, and gourmet food products and accessories from around the world. It caters to the local gourmet food connoisseur as well as to tourists.

Problem Statement

Develop a schematic plan in each of the two sites being considered by the owners. Two plans are given for each site, one for diagramming and the other for refinement.

Merchandise categories include local and international wine, handcrafted beer, other local beverages, artisan cheeses, crackers, breads, cookies, cakes, sauces, condiments, T-shirts, sweatshirts, golf shirts, golf jackets, aprons, oven mitts, small kitchen appliances, kitchen utensils, cookbooks, cookbook magazines, posters, puzzles, cookware, ceramic tableware, glassware, barware, flatware, barbeque items, bakeware, serving dishes, and outdoor patio furniture.

Provide the following:

1. Public bathrooms for men and women
2. Employee break area (adjacent to the shipping and receiving area)
3. Shipping and receiving area—minimum square footage: 400
4. Office (adjacent to the shipping and receiving area)
5. Cash wrap area(s)
6. Small food and beverage tasting area
7. Merchandise

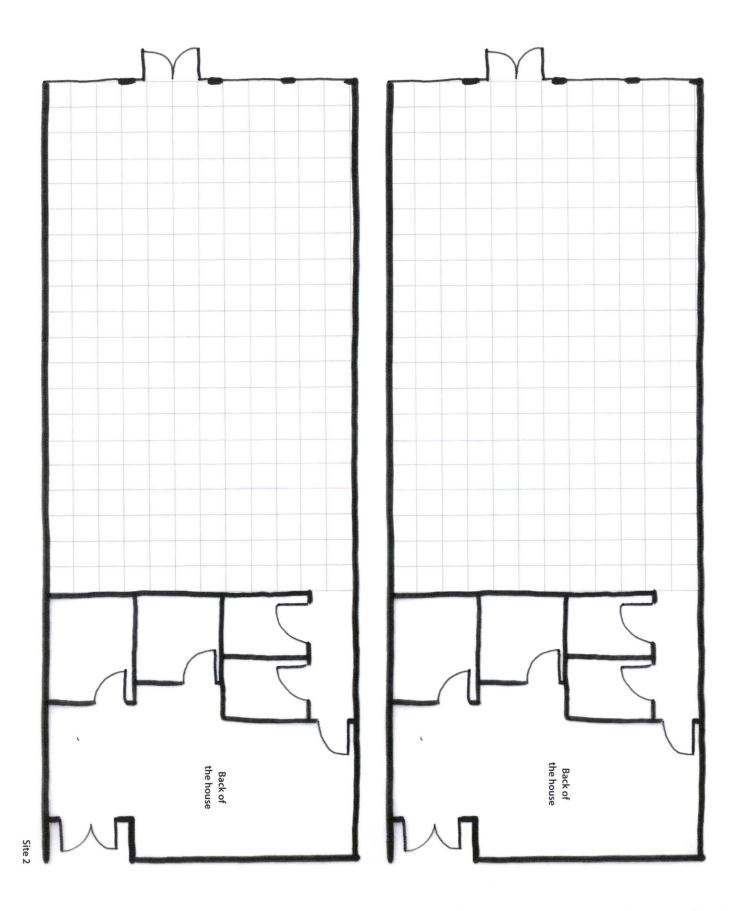

Back of
the house

Back of
the house

Restaurants: Anatomy and Issues

The two basic components of a restaurant are a kitchen, where the food is prepared, and a dining room, where the food is served. In addition to the two essential settings, restaurants also include a bar area and restrooms (required by code) in the public area and often a small office and an employee area in the private back area. At a more detailed level, the front of the house (or public area) usually has a host station up front, with a waiting area, and one or more waiter service stations somewhere in the facility. The most characteristic thing we see in the public side of restaurants is people eating at tables. The table, and its many variations, is then one of the basic elements to be understood by designers.

Seeing a restaurant operation from a **back-of-the-house** perspective is a fascinating experience. There is the frequent arrival of raw ingredients; the storage of food; its preparation on demand; busy waitstaff running back and forth, bringing in new orders and taking out completed meals, while being careful not to run into patrons crossing just outside the kitchen door on their way to the restroom. The bartender at the bar is also busy preparing drinks for patrons at the bar and customers already seated at tables. Up front, the hostess greets incoming customers and escorts them to their assigned tables.

The following are some of the questions to be addressed before space planning a restaurant facility:

- What is the desired seating capacity?
- Will there be a single large dining hall or multiple smaller areas?
- Will there be a bar? If so, for how many people? Where should it go?
- Will the kitchen be full service? How large should it be?
- Where will deliveries come in?
- How will food be ordered? Will waiters take orders at tables?
- Are there any special considerations regarding how the food will be served, such as in a Japanese sushi bar or a Spanish tapas bar?
- What should the turnover time be? Fast, as in a fast-food restaurant, or more leisurely?

Not all restaurants are alike, and understanding the specific requirements to be addressed in their design is necessary in order to be on target with the design strategy.

Here are five important design considerations:

1. Good flow
2. Kitchen (size and location)
3. Kitchen–dining relationship
4. Volume of business
5. Speed of service

Dining area

Bar area

Design for a Full-Service Restaurant in a Medium-Size City in the United States

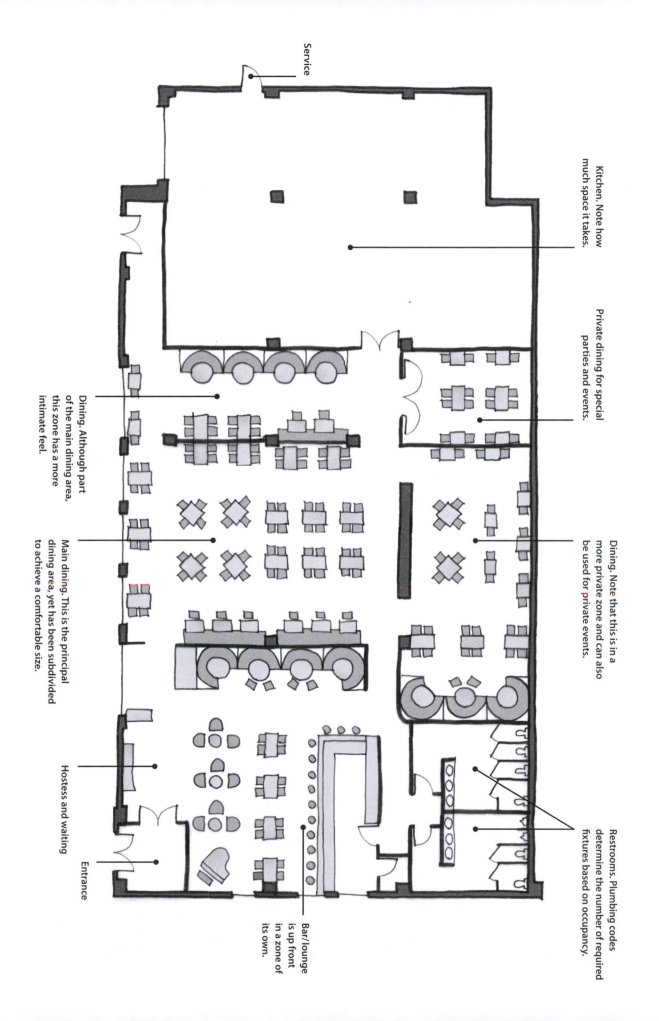

Service

Kitchen. Note how much space it takes.

Private dining for special parties and events.

Dining. Although part of the main dining area, this zone has a more intimate feel.

Dining. Note that this is in a more private zone and can also be used for private events.

Main dining. This is the principal dining area, yet has been subdivided to achieve a comfortable size.

Hostess and waiting

Entrance

Bar/lounge is up front in a zone of its own.

Restrooms. Plumbing codes determine the number of required fixtures based on occupancy.

Restaurant Types

Restaurants can be classified many different ways. Several categories are presented here.

General Restaurant Categories
Freestanding versus inside existing complex
Independent versus chain
Eat-in versus takeout
Theme versus no theme
Ethnic versus nonethnic

Categories by Service Type
Fast food
Coffee shop
Family restaurant
Corporate cafeteria

Categories by Service Systems
A la carte
Tableside
Fast food
Banquet
Family style
Buffet
Takeout
Delivery
Cafeteria

Restaurant Concepts' Inspiration
A certain theme
A certain time frame, such as a historic period
An idea, image, architectural style (nontheme)
A market segment style
A food idea or type of cuisine
A design idea

CONSIDERATIONS

Speed of Service
Fast food: 15 to 20 minutes
Cafeteria: 15 to 30 minutes
Family restaurant: 1 hour
Gourmet experience: Up to 4 hours

Per-Customer Check Average
Economical
Moderate
Pricy

General Ambiance
Stimulating versus relaxing
Joyful versus serious

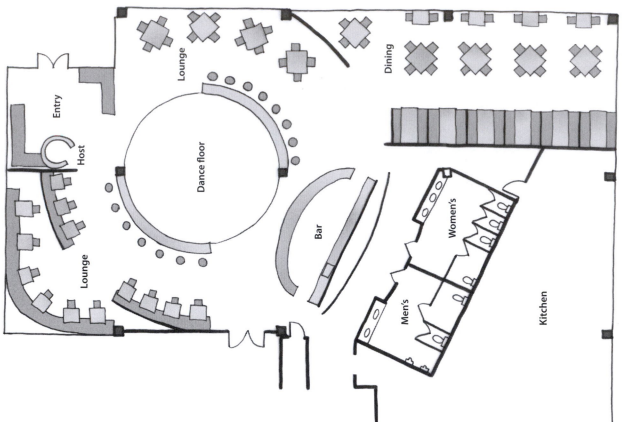

Design of a trendy urban restaurant featuring new cuisine and dancing after hours

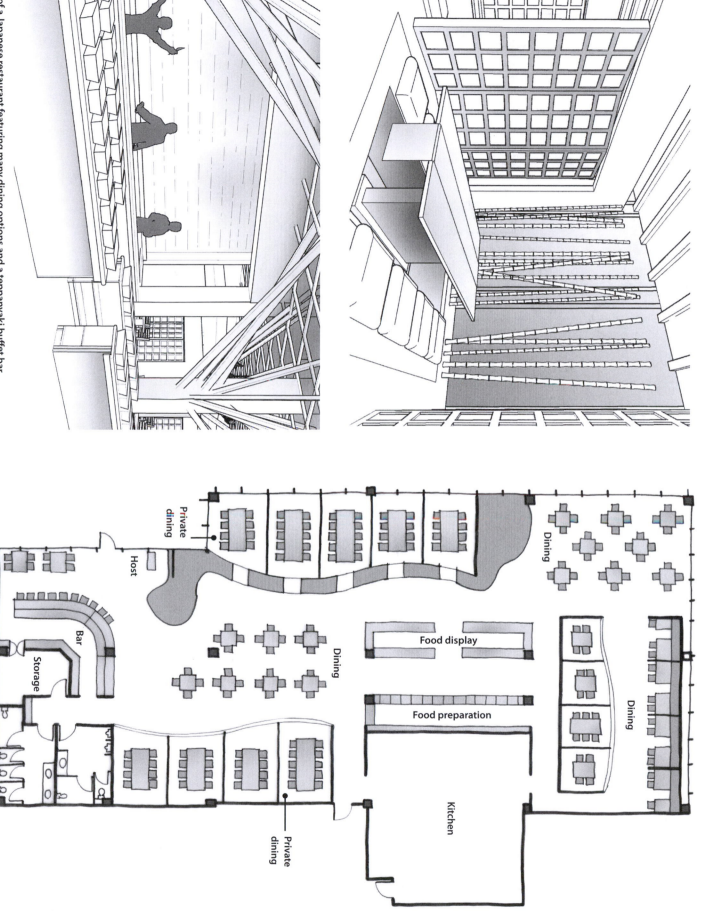

Design of a Japanese restaurant featuring many dining options and a teppanyaki buffet bar

Private dining

Host

Bar

Storage

Dining

Dining

Food display

Food preparation

Dining

Kitchen

Private dining

Restaurants: Furnishings

The principal pieces of furniture in a restaurant are the table and chairs and their variations, such as the banquette and the booth. There are many layout possibilities using one or more of these. Four-person tables are used frequently. They are versatile and can be joined together to accommodate larger groups. Some two-person tables are also good to have so that parties of two can be seated efficiently and without waste. Tables at banquette seating areas can also be moved and combined for groups of various sizes. (Booths are fixed, however.)

How large is a table? How much space does it consume? And how much space is needed to circulate around the tables? Interestingly, not all two-person or four-person tables are the same size; they are available in various sizes, from the economic to the very comfortable.

The tables at right show a range of sizes for common restaurant tables and minimum clearances between them.

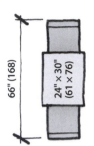

24" × 30" (61 × 76)
66" (168)

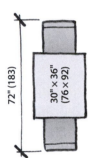

24" × 30" (61 × 76)
60" (153)

24" × 24" (61 × 61)

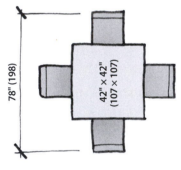

30" × 36" (76 × 92)
72" (183)

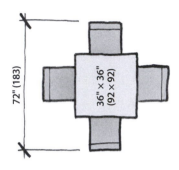

30" × 30" (76 × 76)
66" (168)

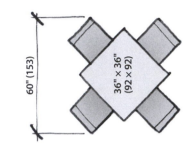

36" × 36" (92 × 92)
72" (183)

42" × 42" (107 × 107)
78" (198)

30" × 30" (76 × 76)
54" (137)

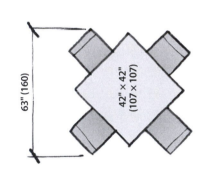

36" × 36" (92 × 92)
60" (153)

42" × 42" (107 × 107)
63" (160)

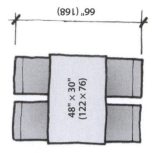

48" × 30" (122 × 76)
66" (168)

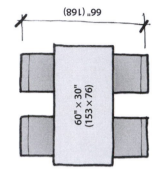

60" × 30" (153 × 76)
66" (168)

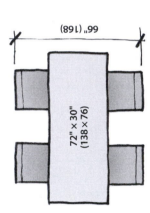

72" × 30" (138 × 76)
66" (168)

Table Arrangements

Good circulation flow is crucial in restaurants. It is desirable, for instance, to separate patrons and service staff circulation routes as much as possible. Desirable clearances between tables and circulation space widths are always a question mark. The answers will vary, as some restaurants have high-density dining areas, and others don't. In either case, the following recommended spacings should give you some useful information to start with.

Clearances at tables and circulation

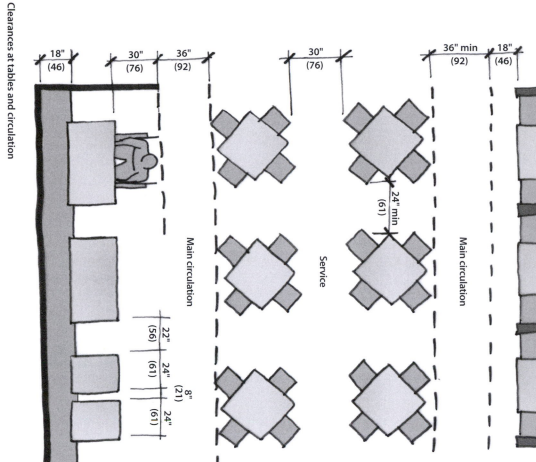

Table Sizes

Note that the spacing between these tables is very generous. Many restaurants have much closer spacing, resulting in higher table densities.

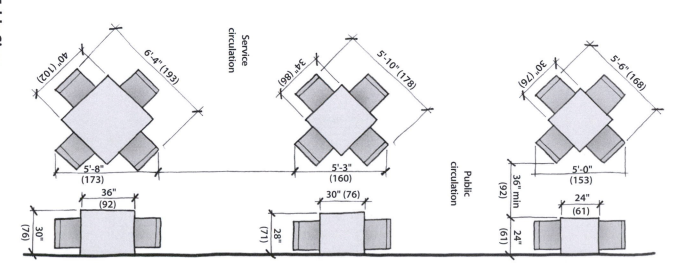

Restaurants: Dining Areas

Table layout combinations vary widely in restaurants. The goal is usually to maximize seating capacity. Similar to optimizing workstation capacity in office projects, the process consists of identifying the critical overall dimensions of the spaces in question and then determining, through math and also trial and error, which combinations and configurations yield the best results. Going to smaller tables will, in some cases, give you just the extra bit of space needed to add one more row of tables. In other cases, the critical width dimension may be such that there is no way to add a row, in which case, you could use larger tables or leave more space in between, or both.

Study the five layouts shown here. They use square, rectangular, and round tables. Some also feature banquettes and booths. In some cases, the square (or round) tables for four are laid out straight. In other cases, they are positioned diagonally. You'll find that there are always periphery zones and central rows or zones.

Using a combination of table sizes and shapes as well as banquettes and booths, one can arrive at many different layouts. The examples illustrate some of the possibilities.

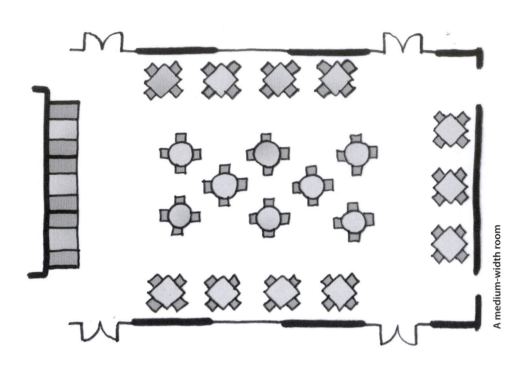

A medium-width room

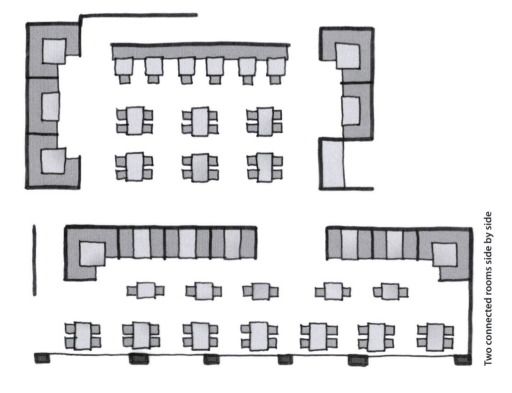

Two connected rooms side by side

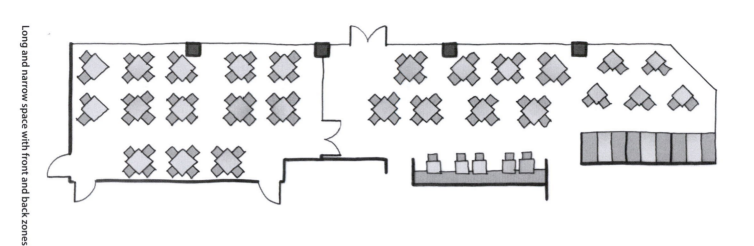

Long and narrow space with front and back zones

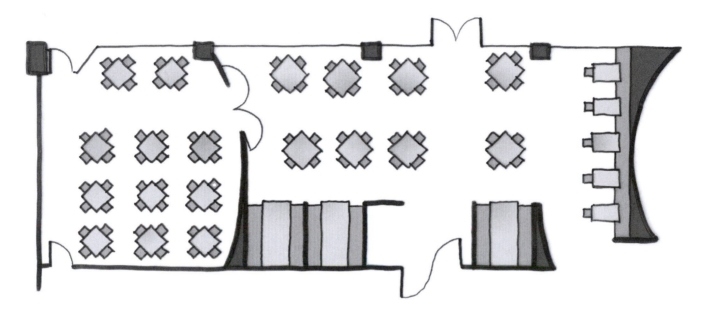

A front-and-back arrangement

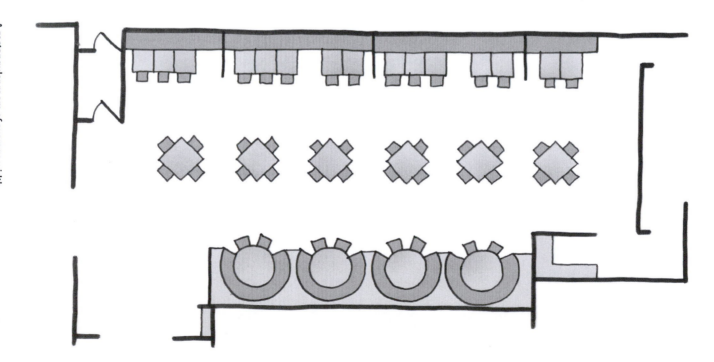

A rectangular room of average width

Restaurants: The Bar

Visit a typical restaurant in most cities and you'll notice that it has a bar. In many cultures, going out to eat with friends includes drinks or "spirits." Some time ago, restaurant owners realized that for the average group of diners, the beverage tab amounts to about a third of the total bill, not an insignificant amount. No wonder there are bars in restaurants. They are profitable.

Patrons can consume drinks while they wait for a table, or they can go into the restaurant just for a drink. Even after patrons are seated at their table, they often order something to drink. At that point, the waiter usually takes care of getting and serving the drink.

The illustrations on this page show recommended dimensions at bars and examples of some common bar layouts. These are shown as a point of reference, but keep in mind that the configuration of bars is often customized to suit specific site conditions and design ideas.

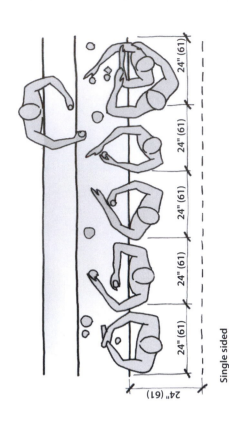

Single sided

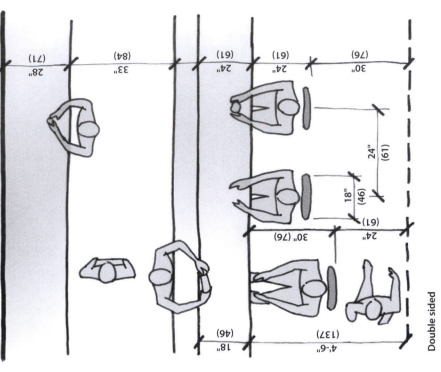

Double sided

Dimensions at bars

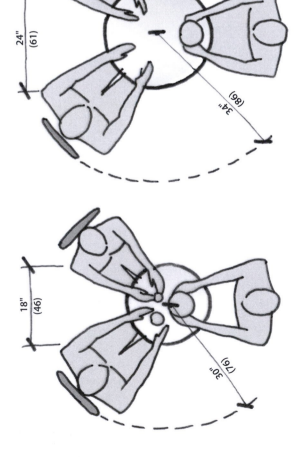

Bar tables

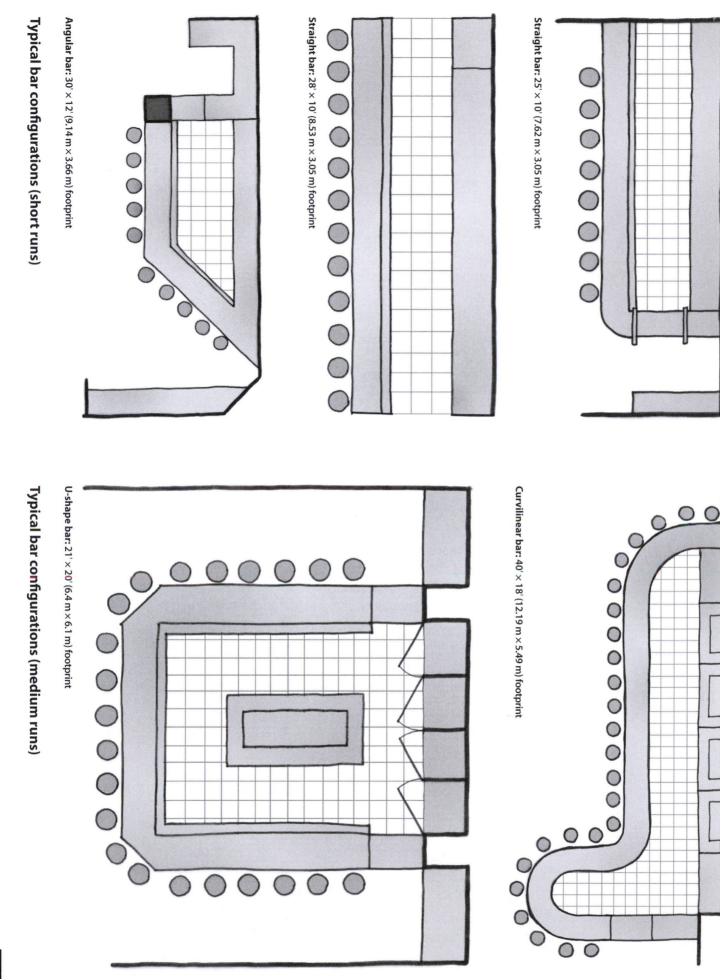

Straight bar: 28' × 10' (8.53 m × 3.05 m) footprint

Angular bar: 30' × 12' (9.14 m × 3.66 m) footprint

Typical bar configurations (short runs)

Curvilinear bar: 40' × 18' (12.19 m × 5.49 m) footprint

U-shape bar: 21' × 20' (6.4 m × 6.1 m) footprint

Typical bar configurations (medium runs)

Restaurant Examples: Four Small Bistros

The following examples illustrate four different solutions to the design of a small restaurant. The solutions had to provide space for a large dining room with a minimum seating capacity of forty, a small bar and lounge area, an ADA accessible restroom, and a front entry with a host station and a wait station. Approximately 30 to 40 percent of the total space had to be allocated to the kitchen.

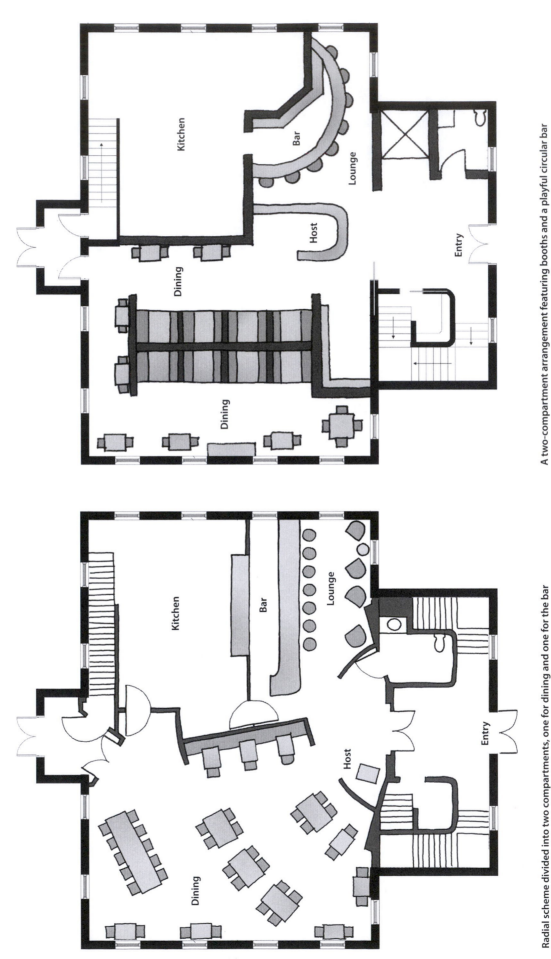

A two-compartment arrangement featuring booths and a playful circular bar

Radial scheme divided into two compartments, one for dining and one for the bar

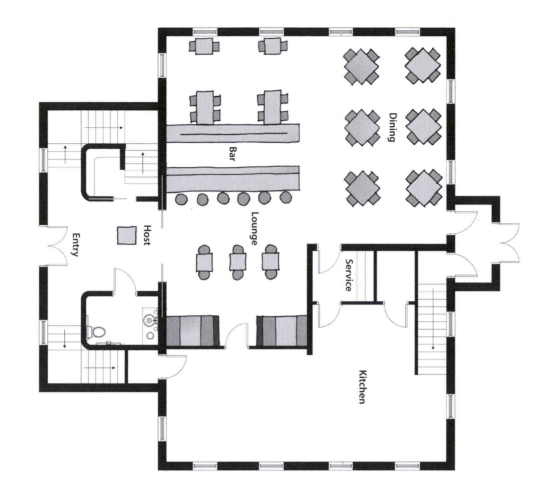

A one-room L-shaped scheme with the bar at the point

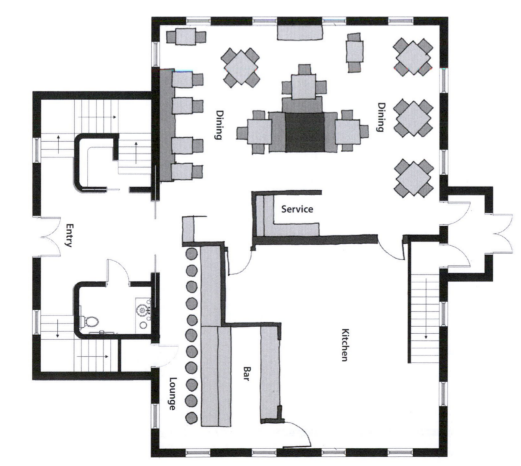

A two-compartment scheme featuring a central object in the dining area and a narrow longitudinal bar zone

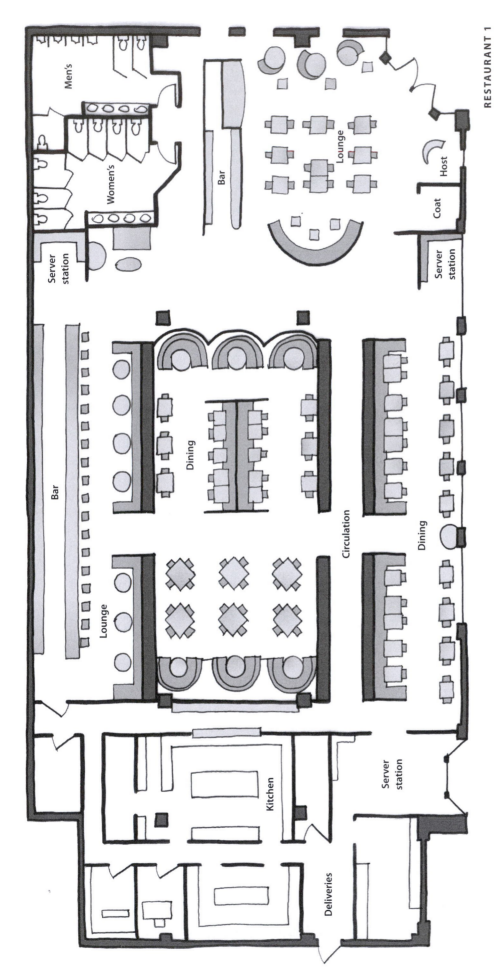

Restaurant Analysis

Perform an analysis of the following elements for the two restaurants on these pages:

Criteria for Analysis

ANALYSIS

1. Effectiveness of the entrance/waiting area
2. Overall success of the bar/lounge design
3. Appropriateness of the size and definition of dining area units
4. Handling of the circulation and flow

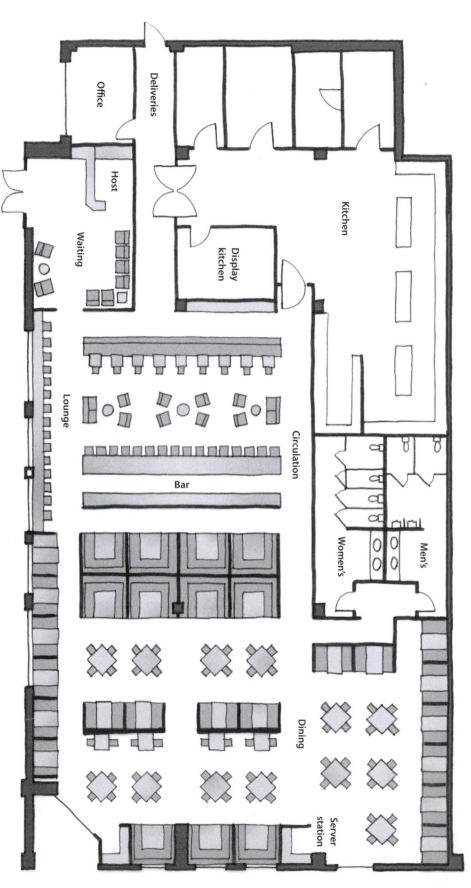

RESTAURANT 2

Restaurant Layouts

EXERCISE 1

Using any combination from the tables shown, produce a layout that maximizes the capacity of the space available. Use the 4′×4′ (122 cm × 122 cm) grid for scale reference.

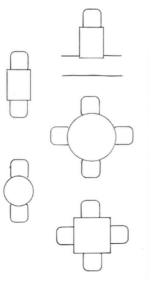

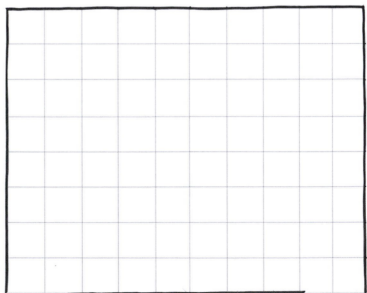

EXERCISE 2

Take a shot at planning your version of the bistro project shown earlier in this chapter. The solution must provide space for a large dining room that seats forty, a bar and lounge area that seats from eight to twelve, an ADA accessible restroom, a front entry, a host station, and a wait station. Allot between 30 and 40 percent of the total space to the kitchen. You may use freestanding tables and chairs, as well as booths. Provide a welcoming entrance to the restaurant with a host stand and coat storage space. Assume that the waiting area will be in the bar. Finally, include a single-person ADA accessible bathroom.

Determine the location and configuration of the kitchen. It should be roughly a fourth to a third of the total space. It may be rectangular or L-shaped. Then produce a layout that maximizes seating capacity. It should include a small bar for about eight people. The remaining space should be devoted to regular seating, using either tables or banquettes. Remember to leave access to the rear egress door. Use the 4′×4′ (122 cm × 122 cm) grid for scale reference. Good luck.

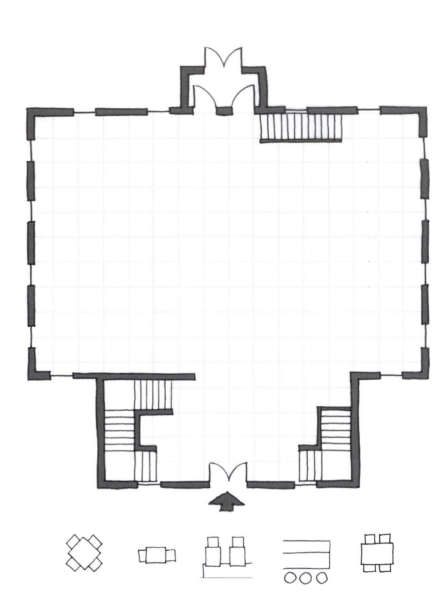

Using the 3' × 3' (92 cm × 92 cm) grid for scale reference, prepare a layout for a small restaurant in an urban setting. There is a full glass wall and a central door (main entrance) up front, leading to the sidewalk. A door at the rear leads to a second exit. This rear door is also used as a service door for food deliveries. Shown are two existing restrooms that must remain and the location of an existing hood, thus suggesting where the kitchen (or part of the kitchen) may go. Allot between 30 and 40 percent of the total space to the kitchen. Maximize the seating capacity.

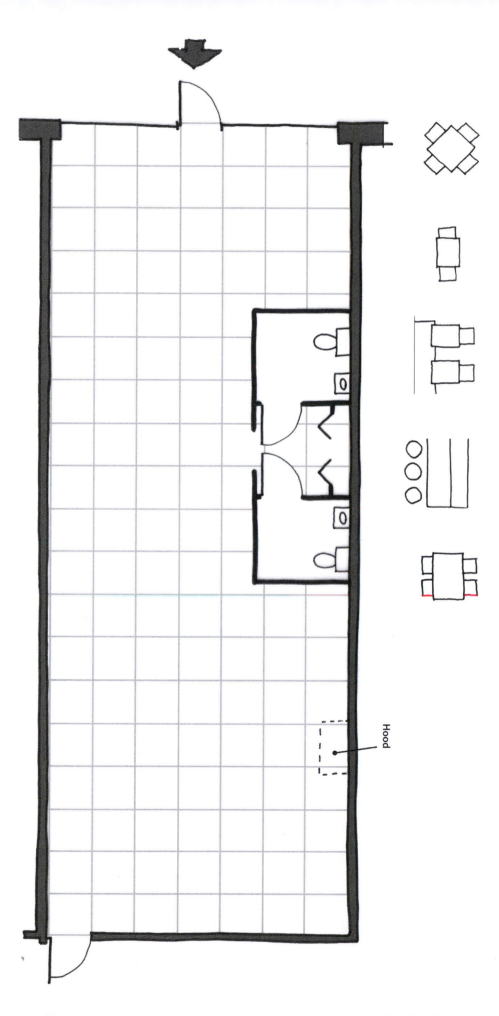

Hood

Basic Metric Conversion Table

Distances

ENGLISH	METRIC
1 inch	2.54 centimeters
1 foot	0.3048 meter / 30.48 centimeters
1 yard	0.9144 meter

METRIC	ENGLISH
1 centimeter	0.3937 inch
1 meter	3.280 feet

General formula for converting:

Number of Units × Conversion Number = New Number of Units

TO CONVERT INCHES TO CENTIMETERS:
[number of inches] × 2.54 = [number of centimeters]

TO CONVERT CENTIMETERS TO INCHES:
[number of centimeters] × 0.3937 = [number of inches]

TO CONVERT FEET TO METERS:
[number of feet] × 0.3048 = [number of meters]

TO CONVERT METERS TO FEET:
[number of meters] × 3.280 = [number of feet]

TO CONVERT YARDS TO METERS:
[number of yards] × 0.9144 = [number of meters]

Art/Design Credits

193. Western Washington State Bassetti and Morse, College Dormitory
194. Willits House Frank Lloyd Wright
195. Klaussen, Brown, Baldwin House Henrik Bull
198. Drawings Krista Bollig
209. Adler House Louis I. Kahn
209. Farnsworth House Ludwig Mies van der Rohe
209. Schwartz House Frank Lloyd Wright
214. Coleshill House Roger Pratt
214. Arthur M. Sackler Gallery, Jean-Paul Carlhian, National Museum of African Art
218/219. unknown
220/221. Carrie Bruenig, Jenn Henrich, Jenny Schulkin

CHAPTER 7

226. Lower left Panero
232. All Panero
234. Lower plans DeChiara
244. Top left Panero
244. Center on the right Panero
244. Bottom DeChiara
245. Left plan DeChiara
245. Top right DeChiara
245. Bottom right DeChiara
246. All DeChiara

247. All DeChiara
248. Both DeChiara
249. Top left DeChiara
249. Bottom left DeChiara
249. Six plans on right ADAAG
250. Two plans on left DeChiara

CHAPTER 8

269. Plan Anh Nguyen
272. Left Kylie Engle
272. Right Chelsea Wolfenberg, Genell Walcott
273. Left Julie Foote
273. Right Jessica Hagen
280. Top/bottom left DeChiara
285. Three on right Panero
286. From top left, clockwise Panero
288. Plan Stephanie Blair
289. Top plan Rebecca Wydra
289. Bottom plan Rachel Ouimette
290/291. Kelli Kruschke, Florence Baveye, Sara Catania
292. Top Anna Gimmer
292. Bottom Leah Nichols
293. Right side Skye Beach
302. Clockwise from top Panero
303. Clockwise from upper left Panero

304. From left to right column Broudy
306. Left column Erin Meyers, Cassie Anderson
306. Right column Sarah Jensen, Jovita Williamson
307. Left column Clara Neale, Syazwani Abdkadir
307. Center column Julie Foote, Theresa Brennan, Miranda Mandole
308. All Dave Richter-O'Connell
309. All Annie Rummelhoff
312. All Lindsay Preboske
313. Plan Lindsay Preboske
314. Plan Karen O'Brien
315. All Julie Foote
316. Top 3 rows DeChiara
316. Bottom row DeChiara
320. Two on the left Panero
320. Top right Panero
320. Bottom right Panero
321. Clockwise from top left DeChiara
322. Left plan Kenneth Casper
322. Right plan Amy Huebner
323. Left plan Emily Stepien
323. Right plan Shannon Stuntebeck
324. Plan Tobin Morrison
325. Plan Stephanie Lauer

Glossary

A

Accessible doors: doors that permit passage to people of all abilities, including wheelchair-bound users.

Accessible kitchens: kitchens that are useable by people of all abilities, including the wheelchair-bound and others.

ADA requirements: guidelines set to comply with the Americans with Disabilities Act.

Adjacency bubble diagrams: diagrams that show the topological relationship of spaces using simple shapes such as bubbles to represent the various spaces.

Adjacency diagram: a type of relationship diagram that depicts the parts of a project and indicates the necessary adjacencies (proximity or distance) between the parts.

Adjacency matrix diagram: a table chart used by designers to determine and record the desired proximity among project parts to one another.

Alignment: the arrangement of objects or groups of objects (such as walls or furnishings) such that their edges on one or both sides are aligned.

Anthropometrics: measurements of the human body used to determine design standards in relation to range of motion.

Assembly occupancies: high-density spaces where there is a need to evacuate large numbers of people in case of emergency, such as theaters.

Attributes: subjective qualities resulting from a design, such as spaciousness and coziness.

B

Back of the house: those areas of a facility devoted to service, like a kitchen in a restaurant.

Block plan: a schematic type of floor plan that shows the rooms or spaces as simple blocks, often including designations for circulation.

Brief (see also **programming**)**:** refers to the document that describes the goals and requirements of a project.

Bubble diagrams: diagrams that show the topological relationship of spaces using simple shapes such as bubbles to represent the various spaces.

Building codes: codes that exist to protect the health, safety, and welfare of the public.

Business occupancies: occupancies used for business purposes, such as office spaces.

C

Centering: the arrangement of objects or groups of objects (such as walls or furnishings) such that their centers are aligned.

Circulation: the name given to those spaces of a project devoted to moving from place to place, such as corridors and aisles.

Circulation systems: systems of movement in a building, such as aisles and corridors.

Cohesion: the quality produced when elements work well together as a cohesive and complementary composition.

Common path of travel: the distance occupants have to travel when exiting before they reach a point where they have a choice of two separate directions in which to go.

Connections: the relationships, both visual and physical, between adjacent spaces and also between a space and the exterior.

Contents: the furnishings, equipment, and accessories within a space.

Cross-section: a two-dimensional architectural drawing that cuts through the building and shows the resulting view looking in.

Cubicle (see also **workstation**)**:** a common name for a small furniture workstation in office facilities.

D

Dead-end corridor: a corridor that dead-ends and does not lead to an exit. When these become too long, they become a hazard, so their length is limited by the codes.

Desires: in programming these are the variable, subjective requirements of a project.

Design process: the process of engaging with design problems using a systematic and sequential approach typical of design disciplines that aims to solve problems hierarchically, where the main decisions are solved first and the smaller, more detailed ones are solved once the main ones are in place.

E

Efficiency: the quality produced when a design achieves more with less.

Egress corridor: a corridor used for egress. Part of an egress route.

Egress doors: doors that are part of the egress system and must comply with the requirements of the code.

Egress route: a route, such as a corridor system, that leads to an exit, such as a corridor system, that leads to an exit.

Egress system: a complete system that allows users to evacuate a building safely, consisting of rooms, exit access corridors, enclosed exit stairways, exit discharge doors, and a safe public way.

Enrichment needs: the needs for knowledge, creativity, and aesthetic experience.

Envelope: the total volume of a space is often referred to as its envelope.

Exit doors: doors that lead to an exit, such as a protected corridor, a protected stairway, or the exterior.

F

Fixed architectural elements: fixed elements of the base building such as columns, beams, and mechanical rooms.

Flow: refers to the relative ease with which one can move within a space.

Furnishability: the property of rooms to provide multiple options to the arrangement of furniture.

Furnishings: moveable interior elements such as furniture and equipment.

G

Grounding: the act of defining the location of an object or group of objects such as furniture groups so they are strongly connected to more permanent elements and don't appear to be floating.

Grounding elements: elements that help ground parts that otherwise seem to be drifting or floating, such as a fountain around which or a fireplace along which one can put seating groups.

I

Individual needs: the needs of humans as single individuals.

Interior architectural elements: building elements that are part of the interior nonpermanent construction, such as non-load-bearing partitions and interior doors.

International Building Code (IBC): codes used throughout the United States as the main source in matters of building code compliance.

M

Machines: in this context, the term is one coined by the architect Louis Kahn, referring to the utilitarian spaces in a building that house the required services such as toilet rooms, electrical closets, and stairs.

Mercantile occupancies: occupancies dedicated to merchandising, such as retail stores.

Multitenant corridors: public corridors in a building serving more than one tenant.

Multitenant floors: floors in a building that serve more than one tenant, such as a floor in a medical building housing many individual suites for various clinics.

N

Needs: in programming, these are the hard, tangible requirements of a project.

Noise: unwelcome sounds, often (but not always) loud.

Number of exits: requirements set by the codes determining the minimum number of doors required for egress from a space or floor based on the size of the space and the type of occupancy it is.

P

Parti diagram: a minimalist diagram that tries to capture the basic essence of an organizational scheme.

Personal space: the space surrounding our individual body and designating the area that is off limits to all except, sometimes, our loved ones.

Perspective drawing: a drawing that shows a pictorial, three-dimensional representation of an environment or object.

Physical factors: the relationships between the physical characteristics of people and the environment.

Physiological factors: the interaction of our biological conditions with the physical environment.

Privacy: one's ability to control environmental conditions so as to regulate the back-and-forth exposure to visual, auditory, and olfactory stimuli.

Private office: a workspace within an enclosed room.

Programming (see also brief)**:** refers to the document that describes the goals and requirements of a project.

Properties: concrete, observable characteristics of a design, such as straight, curvilinear, and tall.

Prospect: a view or scene ahead arranged strategically, usually to pull people toward it.

Proxemics: the study of the distances between people as they interact.

Psychological factors: these encompass human aspects related to behavior patterns and social needs.

R

Relationship diagrams: diagrammatic sketches that show relationships between the different parts of a project.

Room adjacencies: the desired functional proximity between rooms, as determined by location and the nature of their dividing walls and access points.

S

Scales: refers to the relative size of architectural and other nonfixed elements within a space, ranging from large pieces to small ones.

Section diagram: diagrammatic sketches that show relationships in section view. These are helpful to study elevation changes of floors and ceiling elements.

Self-expression needs: the needs for self-assertion, achievement, esteem, and power.

Servant spaces (see also machines)**:** the utilitarian spaces in a building that house the required services such as toilet rooms, electrical closets, and stairs.

Served spaces: in the context of servant and served spaces, these are the principal spaces in a facility where the main public rituals take place. These are usually "served" by adjacent "servant spaces" such as kitchens, storage areas, and so on.

Simplicity: the quality produced when a design avoids excessive components and utilizes a straightforward solution.

Social needs: needs for social interaction, group affiliation, companionship, and love.

Sociofugal arrangements: arrangements, such as back-to-back seating, that allow proximity while discouraging interaction.

Sociopetal arrangements: arrangements, such as facing chairs, that promote face-to-face contact.

Sorting qualities: the criteria used to determine the location of spaces in a project based on common criteria used to group them together. Examples include rooms needing access to the sunny side of a building or to the service alley in the back.

Space data sheets: pages in a program (or brief) that provide a summary of the requirements of individual spaces and rooms.

Space plan: a type of floor-plan drawing that shows the distribution of interior elements such as partitions, doors, and furnishings.

Spatial affinities: the property of groups of spaces having a strong need to be close to one another for functional or other reasons.

Stabilizing needs: the need to be free from fear, anxiety, and danger.

T

Territoriality: the space to which a person or group lays claim.

Thick walls: walls given an extra thickness dimension in order to accommodate built-in elements such as storage or seating.

Threshold: the in-between space between two areas. It can be as minimal as just a line defined by different finishes on the floor. It can also be a band or transitional small space, or even a deeper tunnel connecting two rooms.

U

Universal design: design principles that make environments, products, and communications user-friendly to people of all abilities.

User occupancies: classifications set by the building codes based on use and degree of fire hazard.

W

Work triangle: a concept promoting a triangular placement of the cooking range, the washing sink, and the refrigerator in a kitchen to foster convenience and productivity.

Workstation: a work space consisting of furniture elements and furniture panels in the open, as opposed to a private office in a room.

Index